NEW YORK
EXPOSED

NEW YORK EXPOSED

The Gilded Age
Police Scandal
That Launched the
Progressive Era

DANIEL CZITROM

OXFORD
UNIVERSITY PRESS

OXFORD

UNIVERSITY PRESS

Oxford University Press is a department of the University of Oxford.
It furthers the University's objective of excellence in research, scholarship,
and education by publishing worldwide. Oxford is a registered trademark of
Oxford University Press in the UK and certain other countries.

Published in the United States of America by Oxford University Press
198 Madison Avenue, New York, NY 10016, United States of America.

Library of Congress Cataloging-in-Publication Data
Names: Czitrom, Daniel J., 1951- author.
Title: New York exposed : the gilded age police scandal that launched the
progressive era / Daniel Czitrom.
Description: Oxford ; New York : Oxford University Press, 2016. | Includes
bibliographical references and index.
Identifiers: LCCN 2015036293 | ISBN 9780199837007
Subjects: LCSH: Parkhurst, C. H. (Charles Henry), 1842-1933. | Police
corruption—New York (State)—New York—History—19th century. | Vice
control—New York (State)—New York—History—19th century. | Political
corruption—New York (State)—New York—History—19th century. |
Progressivism (United States politics)—History—19th century. | New York
(N.Y.)—History—1865-1898.
Classification: LCC HV8148.N5 C95 2016 | DDC 364.1/32309747109034—dc23
LC record available at http://lccn.loc.gov/2015036293

Printed by Sheridan Books, Inc., USA

1 3 5 7 9 8 6 4 2

Printed in the United States of America
on acid-free paper

For Meryl, who lived it with me.
For my brothers, Ralph and Michael, always there for me.
And in memory of my parents, Louis Czitrom and Betty Barsky Czitrom,
the greatest New Yorkers I ever knew.

CONTENTS

. . . .

PREFACE

. . . .

Standing before the clutch of reporters gathered outside his home on East
Thirty-Fifth Street on March 1, 1892, the Reverend Doctor Charles H.
Parkhurst was clearly incensed. He was also rendered silent, a new state of
affairs for the minister. Two weeks earlier he had delivered the most politically explosive sermon in New York history, denouncing the men who
ran the city—the whole bunch of them—as "a lying, perjured, rum
soaked, and libidinous lot." Parkhurst's most controversial charge targeted District Attorney DeLancey Nicoll and a police captain for failing
to prosecute the notorious Billy McGlory, who ran a brothel in the guise
of a hotel on East Fourteenth Street. McGlory, the only criminal actually
named in the sermon, embodied politically protected vice.

An equally enraged DA Nicoll had denounced Parkhurst's charges as
intemperate ravings, and he threatened a libel suit unless the minister
either substantiated or withdrew them. There was no middle ground. On
February 23, Nicoll brought Parkhurst before the grand jury, where the
minister was asked to give any specific evidence he had about criminal
acts or the district attorney's negligence in prosecuting Billy McGlory. He
could offer none.

The grand jury presentment found the minister's charges so sweeping
and general that "no cognizance could be taken of them." On the specific
issue of the DA's allegedly lenient treatment of McGlory, the grand jury
vindicated Nicoll and found that Parkhurst had no evidence upon which

to base them except newspaper reports that had no basis in facts. Judge Randolph Martine, who had heard the presentment read in the court of general sessions, agreed with the jurors and denounced Parkhurst. The minister had gotten his comeuppance. If he could not prove his charges, as the *Sun* put it, "let him be indicted, tried, and punished himself as a wicked, malicious, reckless, and criminal slanderer."

Confronted with this as he stood outside his home, Parkhurst, isolated and now himself under withering attack, faced a moment of truth. He was angered and embarrassed by this stinging rebuke, and he was unprepared for the scorn heaped upon him from so many sides. He did not want to back down from his claims that police and city officials routinely colluded with criminals. Indeed he hoped to create a Christian revival in New York centered upon exposing such connivance. Yet he would have to figure out a way to gather empirical proof for his charges, to acquaint himself personally with the city's underworld. Parkhurst resolved to get it. Unsure of his next move, he offered a terse "no comment" to reporters eager for his reaction to the grand jury's censure.

He did not stay silent for long. No grand jury's verdict would stop Parkhurst, for he was a man on a crusade. Two years later, that crusade forced the first sensational political investigation of the modern era and kick-started the Progressive movement. Established by the New York State Senate, the Lexow Committee (named for its chairman, State Senator Clarence Lexow) collected testimony from nearly 700 witnesses, representing all walks of New York life. It revealed—with shocking and unprecedented specificity—how the police force managed New York's lucrative vice economy. A veritable parade of brothel keepers, prostitutes, counterfeiters, and burglars told how regular payments to police captains were just another cost of doing business. More respectable entrepreneurs described the payoffs required to run a steamship line or put up a new building. Bruised and bandaged victims of police brutality crowded into the hearing room to tell their stories, while stone-faced policemen denied it all.

By November 1894, the stream of Lexow revelations had lit up New York, turning popular opinion against the Tammany Hall Democrats who ran the city, propelling reform candidate William Strong into the mayor's office. As the hearings built to a climax in late December, they brought extraordinary revelations from police officials about the payoffs needed to gain promotion and the fortunes they accumulated. In early

1895, as the committee adjourned to write its official report, the prospects for reforming the police department and cleaning up city politics never looked better. Dr. Parkhurst emerged as the undisputed leader of the "Goo-Goos," municipal reformers who believed that only nonpartisan "good government" could save America's cities. In the space of the two and a half years between Parkhurst's humiliation and the Lexow revelations, New York had been transformed, and the inner workings of New York politics and government were laid bare in unparalleled detail. The effort to root out crooked cops and dishonest politicians morphed into something much more profound: a public reckoning, messy and contentious, over what New York—and the American city—had become since the Civil War.

New York Exposed offers the story of Parkhurst's crusade and the ensuing Lexow investigation. At the heart of it is a central question: How did the excesses of Gilded Age New York give birth to a powerful national movement for urban reform? The book argues that Progressivism, the movement that remade American politics and society in the first two decades of the twentieth century, flowered in the political soil first plowed by Parkhurst and the Lexow revelations. Attacking political corruption, gathering facts to make an empirical case against injustice, mobilizing citizens on a nonpartisan basis to fight for reform, exploiting press coverage to arouse the public conscience, bringing more businesslike methods to governing—all these would become hallmarks of the Progressive Era reformers who believed that a new sense of civic democracy was necessary to bring about social justice.

Yet Parkhurst's campaign and the Lexow exposures also revealed the limits and contradictions that would vex Progressive reform, especially as it wrestled with the overwhelming challenges of American city life. Hundreds of thousands of working-class New Yorkers, especially those of non-Protestant immigrant stock, saw Parkhurst's crusade as blind to the realities and rituals of their everyday lives. "Reform" too often meant a repressive moralism that depended upon undemocratic surveillance and a policing of personal behavior.

New York in the 1890s offered harbingers of the coming century's newly urbanized America: a swelling population of Catholic and Jewish immigrants from Southern and Eastern Europe, a deeply partisan political culture based on the idea of politics as a business, a more organized and aggressive labor movement, a large class of wage-earning poor buffeted by the economic insecurities of urban capitalism, a huge tenement population packed into some of the most overcrowded districts in the world, a more sensational mass media competing every day for the latest revelation of corruption. No wonder that so much of the urge to "reform" American cities was often indistinguishable from the tides of anti-urban prejudice that had long surged through the nation's political and cultural life.

Over the last third of the nineteenth century, New York had established itself as the nation's largest metropolis, its financial and corporate center, the engine driving commercial culture, and the entry point for a new mass immigration that would reshape America. And because it was the largest city in the largest state, New York also stood at the center of national politics. Its vote had enormous strategic importance in Gilded Age America, reversing the old adage: In New York City, all politics was national. If, as Parkhurst had claimed in the first use of the term, the city government itself was a form of "organized crime," what did that portend for American politics and culture on the cusp of a new century? New York's population had more than doubled in the previous twenty-five years, producing levels of overcrowding and threats to public health that Americans had previously associated only with the slums of London or Calcutta. Record numbers of immigrants from Eastern and Southern Europe remade whole neighborhoods, occupations, indeed the character of New York itself. A militant labor movement, much of it energized by radicals of various stripes, faced violent opposition from a business community that had come to rely upon city police to do Capital's dirty work.

By 1890 three decades of unprecedented immigration had fundamentally transformed the city's ethnic and religious makeup. Some 275,000 New Yorkers were born in Ireland, and more than 600,000 people were of Irish extraction. Another 210,000 were born in Germany. These earlier migrants, who had fled the Great Hunger in Ireland and the political strife of the German states, were joined after 1880 by a rush of "new immigrants" from eastern and southern Europe, including more than 170,000 Jews and almost as many Italians. The new federal immigration center on Ellis Island opened in 1892, processing nearly 450,000 emigrants annually, more than double the annual figure arriving in the city twenty years earlier.

The economic depression that began during the winter of 1893–94, the worst in American history to that point, revealed unimagined depths of human misery and the elemental struggle for survival faced by hundreds of thousands of poor and working-class New Yorkers. Even before the depression hit, a large fraction of New Yorkers found themselves trapped in structural poverty. Between 1882 and 1890 some 135,000 families were registered as asking for or receiving charity—nearly half a million people, roughly one-third of the city, forced to beg for food or other help. That deep insecurity, a fundamental fact of urban life before the modern safety net stitched together from unemployment insurance, Social Security, Medicare, and welfare, forced many thousands to exchange their votes in return for services from (mostly Democratic) machine politicians.

Yet New York's outsized influence did not translate into national acceptance. Parkhurst's movement and the Lexow investigation both bared and intensified the deep currents of anti-urbanism flowing through American life, obstructing the nation's ability to create coherent and compassionate policies for improving the quality of urban life. Dislike of big cities and the people who inhabit them was never as clear as during the "dark year" of 1975—more than three-quarters of a century after Lexow—when New York faced the threat of municipal bankruptcy. The national response to the city's fiscal crisis underlined the tangled and messy relationship between Gotham and America. Representatives of the political and financial elite—the mayor, the governor, major banks, big Wall Street firms—made repeated journeys to Washington, pleading, cajoling, insisting on the need for federal loan guarantees and other aid. Millions who worked for the city, attended the free City University, used the public library system, rode mass transit daily, visited city museums, parks, and zoos, or sent their children to public schools, worried that the essence of New York life—particularly its robust public sector—was now imperiled. Didn't the nation understand that no other city in the U.S. had provided such a range of free services, had welcomed so many immigrants, schooling and housing them for a better life, while also providing welfare for millions of migrants from the South, Puerto Rico, and the Caribbean?

They understood too well. President Gerald Ford argued that New York City's problems were confined to New York and its default would only hurt the city. New York's bankruptcy might be a tragedy, but it was not a national one. Opponents of federal aid to the city, including Republicans and Democrats from all over the country, drew on a deep history of anti–New York and anti-urban prejudices to make their case. The president's press secretary described the city as "a wayward daughter hooked on heroin." Was Treasury Secretary William Simon only joking when he announced, "We're going to sell New York to the Shah of Iran. It's a hell of an investment." A Florida Republican said simply, "We should build a wall around New York and let it collapse." An Iowa Democrat declared, "New York City is incomprehensible.... Congressmen regard New York as a place where you'll pay for your sin and get rolled before you get it. In Des Moines, if you pay for your sin, you'll get it." Future vice president Joseph Biden found the Senate a place where "cities are viewed as the seed of corruption and duplicity, and New York is the biggest city."

Even advocates of federal aid found themselves invoking some of the oldest stereotypes. Sociologist Herbert Gans noted that New York was "America's principal poorhouse, innovator, dissident, creditor, playboy, and stripper, and the rest of the country is reluctant to admit to itself that it uses or needs these things." After months of wrangling, tense negotiations, and complicated deal-making in New York and Washington, the Ford administration finally agreed to $2.3 billion in short term federal loans and the state-created Municipal Assistance Corporation (MAC) essentially took over responsibility for the city's fiscal affairs. The catastrophe of bankruptcy had been avoided.

The 9/11 terrorist attacks on the World Trade Center brought the city back into the national fold. The assault on New York was an assault on America, and city cops, firemen, EMTs, doctors, nurses, and construction workers bore the brunt with their heroic sacrifices and by simply doing their difficult jobs. Compared to 1975, the twenty-first-century city is more defined by its expanding financial sector than by organized labor, by skyrocketing real estate values than by rent control, and by digitized media and a high end service sector than by street culture or individual neighborhoods. Yet as the 9/11 crisis revealed, it still relied upon skilled blue-collar workers, municipal employees, and an immigrant working class that represented the same percentage of city population—roughly 40 percent—as it had in 1900.

In fact, New York City history has always been American history, regardless of the pendulum swings of public opinion: from the settling of New Amsterdam as a distant outpost of the Dutch empire to the English takeover and the ordeal of the American Revolution; the building of the Erie Canal and the nineteenth-century rush of commercial development; the city's emergence as the center of capital markets; its federal designation as the main port of entry for immigrants; as the creative engine for the nation's commercial culture—publishing, theater, music, sports; and, between the Civil War and World War II, as the most hotly contested prize in American electoral politics. Yet so much of this history has been overwhelmed, even erased, by the distorted imagery and cartoon-like rendering of New York's past. Parkhurst's crusade and the Lexow investigation it spawned grappled with issues and problems deeply resonant with our own era: political and business corruption, the persistence of widespread urban poverty and growing inequality, unchecked police brutality, vote fraud and vote suppression, the tenacity of the two-party system, the place of commercial sex in urban life, an expanding mass media that reshaped politics and amplified the city's national influence, the volatile relations between evangelicals and political parties, and the nation's profound fear and distrust of New York City.

It all began with an infuriated minister, a migrant from the small towns of New England, undaunted by a grand jury presentment and intent upon shaking up the city and the nation.

NEW YORK
EXPOSED

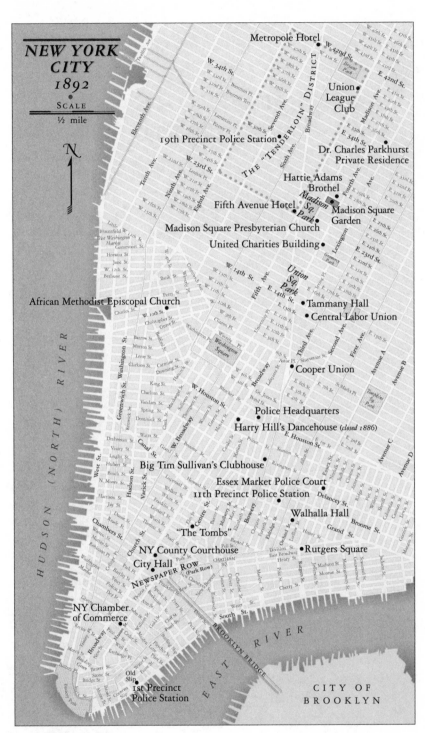

NEW YORK CITY 1892

SCALE
½ mile

N

W. 46th St. E. 46th St.
W. 45th St. E. 45th St.
W. 44th St. E. 44th St.
W. 43rd St. E. 43rd St.
Metropole Hotel ● W. 42nd St. Bryant Park
W. 41st St. E. 42nd St.
W. 40th St.
W. 39th St.
W. 38th St.
W. 34th St. W. 37th St. Union ● E. 41st St.
W. 33rd St. Bowman Pl. W. 36th St. League E. 41st St.
W. 32nd St. Bowman Terr. W. 35th St. Club E. 40th St.
W. 31st St. E. 39th St.
W. 30th St. Seventh Ave. E. 38th St.
W. 29th St. E. 37th St.
W. 28th St. Laramie Pl. W. 33rd St. Dr. Charles Parkhurst E. 36th St.
19th Precinct Police Station ● W. 27th St. Pitney Pl. E. 34th St. Private Residence
W. 26th St. Hattie Adams E. 33rd St.
W. 25th St. Brothel E. 32nd St.
W. 23rd St. W. 24th St. E. 31st St.
W. 22nd St. Madison E. 30th St.
W. 21st St. Fifth Avenue Hotel ● Sq. ● Madison Square E. 29th St.
W. 20th St. Park Garden E. 28th St.
W. 19th St. Madison Square Presbyterian Church ● E. 27th St.
W. 18th St. United Charities Building ● E. 26th St.
W. 16th St. W. 17th St. Greenwich Park E. 25th St.
W. 15th St. E. 24th St.
E. 23rd St.

THE "TENDERLOIN" DISTRICT

Little Bloomfield St.
West Washington Market
Gansevoort St.
Horatio St.
Jane St.
W. 12th St.
Bethune St.

W. 13th St. E. 21st St.
W. 12th St. Union E. 20th St.
W. 11th St. Sq. E. 19th St.
Bank St. W. 10th St. Park E. 18th St.
Perry St. W. 14th St. E. 17th St.
Charles St. E. 16th St.
African Methodist Episcopal Church ● W. 10th St. E. 14th St. ● Tammany Hall
Christopher St. ● Central Labor Union
Barrow St. Grove St.
Morton St. Waverly Pl.
Leroy St. Washington Sq.
Clarkson St. Washington Square
Carmine St. Cooper Union ●
Downing St.
King St. Broadway
Charlton St. W. Houston St.
Vandam St. Gt. Jones St.
Spring St. Police Headquarters ●
Dominick St. Harry Hill's Dancehouse (closed 1886) ●
Watts St. E. Houston St.
Big Tim Sullivan's Clubhouse ●
Canal St. Essex Market Police Court ●
11th Precinct Police Station ●
Walhalla Hall ●
Broome St.
"The Tombs" Grand St.
NY County Courthouse ● Rutgers Square ●
City Hall ●
NEWSPAPER ROW (Park Row)

NY Chamber of Commerce ●

1st Precinct Police Station

HUDSON (NORTH) RIVER

EAST RIVER

BROOKLYN BRIDGE

CITY OF BROOKLYN

Map by Adrian Kitzinger

1
....

PARKHURST'S CHALLENGE

On a blustery and cold February morning, the minister walked briskly across the ten blocks from his house on East Thirty-Fifth Street to the Madison Square Presbyterian Church, where he would give his Sunday sermon. All 1,200 seats in the Gothic brownstone church on Madison Avenue and Twenty-Fourth Street were filled with parishioners, including many of New York City's commercial and political elite. The Reverend Doctor Charles H. Parkhurst's anger had been swelling for years, and on February 14, 1892, he served up the most explosive sermon in New York City's history.

The fifty-year-old Parkhurst presented a commanding-looking figure in the pulpit in his black ministerial robes: though medium height and slender, he had bushy eyebrows and high forehead, a mass of long black hair falling to his collar. A sallow face, eyeglasses, and graying whiskers reinforced his solemnity. A scholar but not a pedant, a devout but un-sanctimonious man, he was a skilled teacher, with no interest in theolog-ical disputes or sectarian wrangles. Parkhurst was above all a passionate moralist. As usual, he read his carefully written out homily deliberately and calmly, hardly ever looking up from the manuscript. He had no use for oratorical tricks and his voice was thin and unimpressive. Yet Parkhurst spoke with a quiet fury that kept audiences on the edge of their pews.

He chose as his text, "Ye are the salt of the earth" (Matthew 5:13), from Christ's statement of fundamentals in the Sermon on the Mount. The problem of the day, Parkhurst noted in a theme he invoked repeatedly, was that contemporary Christianity had proven unable to redeem modern urban life. The "municipal life of our city is thoroughly rotten," but to-day's Christianity "lacks distinct purpose, and it lacks virility." It appeared helpless against "the polluted harpies that, under the pretence of governing this city, are feeding day and night on its quivering vitals. They are a lying, perjured, rum-soaked, and libidinous lot." He meant his appeal to "quicken our Christian sense of the obligatory relation in which we stand toward the official and administrative criminality that is filthifying our entire municipal life, making New York a very hotbed of knavery, debauchery, and bestiality." Every brothel, gambling hall, and unlicensed saloon, Parkhurst claimed, "has an immunity secured to it by a scale of police taxation that is as carefully graded and thoroughly systematized as any that obtains in the assessment of personal property or real estate." Only by stating these facts out loud, Parkhurst argued, could they "let in a great lot of light into the subterranean mysteries of this rum-besotted and Tammany debauched town."

In one of his most controversial charges, Parkhurst accused the "guile-less" and "callow" district attorney, DeLancey Nicoll, of failing to indict "Billy" McGlory for running a brothel in the guise of a concert saloon on Fourteenth Street. Mention of McGlory, the only criminal he named, served as shorthand for the worst kinds of moral degradation. McGlory had become famous in the 1880s as the flamboyant and politically con-nected proprietor of Armory Hall on Hester Street, a regular attraction for out-of-town slumming parties and famous as a combination dance hall, house of prostitution, and gathering spot for homosexuals. "The most effective allies which McGlory had in the prosecution of his vile trade," Parkhurst claimed, "were the district attorney and the captain of the pre-cinct."[1]

Parkhurst's sermon started a crusade that, two years later, launched the first major political investigation of the modern era and did nothing less than kick-start the Progressive movement. Established by the New York State Senate, the Lexow Committee (named for its chairman, State Senator Clarence Lexow) heard testimony from a parade of nearly 700 witnesses, representing all walks of New York life. It revealed the fundamental truth behind Parkhurst's charges: that the police force itself managed New York's lucrative vice economy. Parkhurst's campaign resonated nationally, stitching together so many of the threads that created the fabric of Progressive Era reform: attacking political corruption, mobilizing citizens on a nonpartisan basis, gathering facts and figures to make an empirical case against injustice, calling for more scientific methods to be brought to governing, exploiting the press to arouse the public conscience. And it also revealed the limits and contradictions that would vex Progressive reform, especially as it wrestled with the overwhelming challenges of American city life.

But in the winter of 1892, before the term Progressive had achieved much traction, Parkhurst's fiery sermon appeared more a quixotic outburst from a publicity-conscious minister than the start of a civic movement. City officials immediately hit back. District Attorney DeLancey Nicoll called Parkhurst's charges "the coarsest and most outrageously false statements I have ever seen in print." He defended his efforts to prosecute McGlory (who in fact had gone to jail in January) and insisted that he continued gathering evidence about the city's "more notorious places." Mayor Hugh J. Grant, elected on the Tammany Hall ticket in 1888, merely smiled and told reporters who asked him about the accusations against the police that he had no comment. Police superintendent William Murray chose to ignore the sermon, explaining, "If one took cognizance the result would only be renewed attacks." But public works commissioner Thomas F. Gilroy, a Tammany stalwart who would succeed Grant as the next mayor, attacked Parkhurst for "his intemperate ravings." John Voorhis, a member of the four-man Board of Police Commissioners of the City of New York, thought Parkhurst vulgar, libelous, and plain wrong about the city's condition. Compared with any other city, Voorhis boasted, New York had less wickedness and crime than in years past; he claimed there were "fewer disorderly characters upon our streets now than there were ten, fifteen, or twenty years ago."[2]

The city's newspapers in those days regularly reported on Sunday sermons in prominent churches, and reactions to Parkhurst's diatribe broke along predictably partisan lines. The stolidly Republican *NY Tribune* described it as "the most scathing denunciation of [city government] ever hurled from a platform," and praised Parkhurst for "allowing no euphemism to cloak the names and character of the city officials and their relations to the criminal classes." The Democratic but anti-Tammany *NY World* acknowledged that there was much to criticize in the city's government, "but nothing to excuse so violent an outburst of vituperation as that which Mr. Parkhurst preached for a sermon yesterday." The *NY Sun*, strongest supporter of the Democrats among the city's major papers, provided both the most detailed account of the sermon and acidic criticism, calling on Parkhurst to offer specific facts and proof of his charges, else prove himself a "a slanderous pulpit blatherskite" who should feel the full force of the law.[3]

Parkhurst's anger was deeply personal. There were heavily patronized brothels within a stone's throw of his church, and he occasionally found himself solicited by the highly visible streetwalkers around Madison Square Park. Conversations with his young male parishioners, as well as doctors and lawyers, revealed that venereal disease, alcoholism, and degenerate gambling were much more widespread than commonly thought. His explicit treatment of this subject went far beyond the norm for the day, and he pulled no punches in blaming Tammany. "Every effort to make men respectable, honest, temperate and sexually clean," he declared in his controversial sermon, "is a direct blow between the eyes of the mayor and his whole gang of drunken and lecherous subordinates." The atmosphere they had created was so poisonous, so corrosive that "there is not a young man so noble, nor a young girl so pure, as not to be in a degree infected by the fetid contamination."[4]

Parkhurst's neighborhood—and indeed the entire city—had seen enormous changes since he had arrived twelve years earlier from rural Lenox, Massachusetts, to take the Madison Square pulpit. New York in 1880 stood on the cusp of the last great rush of nineteenth-century development. Even with a population of 1.2 million, the city still had the feel of a sprawling frontier town. With a half million New Yorkers packed tightly into the oldest part of the city below Fourteenth Street, and the rest living "uptown" north to Fifty-Ninth Street, the pressure to expand had never been greater. Manhattan's street grid system, established in 1811, was about two-thirds completed as far north as Ninety-Sixth Street. But most of the blocks thus formed remained empty, save for scattered shanty towns, market gardens, pre–Civil War country homes, and inns serving travelers. The end of the business depression that lingered long after the Panic of 1873, combined with rapid development of new transportation and communication technologies, brought a spurt of growth. The extension of steam-powered elevated railroads along Ninth and Sixth Avenues on the West Side, and Third Avenue on the East Side, spurred rapid settlement in upper Manhattan. The ten-mile trip from Chatham Square to Harlem could now be made in forty minutes, half the time it took in a horse-drawn streetcar. Electric lights replaced gas lamps in Madison Square Park in 1880, and quickly spread to major thoroughfares such as Broadway and Fifth Avenue. That same year the Edison Electric Illuminating Company began wiring homes and businesses in the neighborhood just south of City Hall. By 1885 more than 250,000 electric lights were in use around the city. New York's first telephone directory had appeared in 1879, with 252 subscribers; by the early 1880s that number exceeded 20,000.[5]

Parkhurst's church stood on the eastern boundary of the "Tenderloin," bounded roughly by Twenty-Third and Forty-Second Streets and Fifth and Eighth Avenues and notorious around the city and nation as New York's preeminent vice district. In fact the Tenderloin was much more than that. In the pre–Civil War era, real estate developers made the area into a fashionable suburb, where wealthier New Yorkers enjoyed life in elegant brownstones far away from the crowds and commercial bustle of downtown. After the war the neighborhood's character changed dramatically, as major commercial institutions—theaters, hotels, and department stores—moved north of Fourteenth Street, driving away many residents and catering increasingly to visiting businessmen, out-of-town shoppers, and patrons of the city's nightlife. Madison Square Garden (then its original location on Madison Square Park), opened in 1879 as the largest indoor entertainment space in the nation, just two blocks from Parkhurst's church. Along with the circus, flower shows, bicycle races, and aquatic exhibitions, the Garden had quickly become the center for the quasi-legal sport of prize fighting. As many as 15,000 men regularly packed it to see John L. Sullivan, the most popular sports celebrity of the nineteenth century, knock out all comers.

Parkhurst was by no means the first crusader against prostitution; nor was he the first minister to promise to shine light into the city's "subterranean mysteries." He was surely familiar with the sensational preaching style developed by his fellow Presbyterian Reverend T. DeWitt Talmage, probably the best-known American minister of the day after Henry Ward Beecher, the brother of the novelist who had been disgraced in an 1875 adultery trial. In the 1870s and 1880s Talmage had built a huge following at his Central Brooklyn Presbyterian Church with a highly physical and emotional style. Instead of standing before a pulpit, he would run around his platform, shouting, performing handsprings, and then leap off while bellowing, "Young man, you are rushing toward a precipice!" There would follow a sermon on the sinful temptations faced by young men in the city. Talmage specialized in warnings against the city's dangers, moralistic and titillating at the same time. In the fall of 1878 he delivered a series of sermons on "The Night Side of New York and Brooklyn Life" to overflow crowds attracted by detailed newspaper accounts. He based these on late night jaunts—always made in the company of policemen—in which he pretended to be a gentleman in search of stolen property. But his descriptions of what he saw in dance houses, gambling halls, and concert saloons (never brothels) were more general than specific, more sizzle than steak. He prefigured Parkhurst when he declared the existence of these places "can only be charged either to police cowardice or police complicity." Yet his approach was self-consciously bombastic, theatrical, even comic, recalling P. T. Barnum, complete with the broad winking at everyone's collusion in the fun. Mock threats evoked loud laughter and applause, as when, after noting that so many of the haunts of sin were supported chiefly by wealthy and prominent men, he declared: "I could call names and I may before I get through, though it wreck the fabric of society." He published his sermons in books and magazines. He scoffed at critics of his publicity-seeking, declaring it "the deliberate plan of my ministry to do what I set out to do in such a way that the devil will advertise me free gratis, for nothing." He took charges of sensationalism as a compliment, for the great battle to be fought, he argued, was not between Christianity and infidelity but between "honest Christian sensation and putrid stagnation."[6]

Parkhurst's style was the exact opposite—serious, scholarly, unemotional. Like many who challenged the long-established routines of the city's political class, its policemen, and its ordinary citizens, he came from the country. He was formed by the farms, small towns, and schools of western Massachusetts, growing up as he later recalled on brown bread and baked beans. Born near Framingham in 1842, Parkhurst traced his ancestry to Puritans who had left Surrey County, England, to settle in Watertown, Massachusetts, just outside Boston, in 1643. In 1855 the family, including Charles's two brothers and two sisters, moved about twenty-five miles west to Clinton, north of Worcester. His parents ran a prosperous farm there with arable land, woodlots, and a dairy managed by his mother. They were both educated and occasionally taught in local schools. Along with the routine chores of farm work, Charles received an early education at home and did not attend school until he was twelve. His lifelong ambivalence toward big city life—especially as a place to grow up—had its roots in what he remembered as an idyllic rural childhood. "After one has become an adult it is possible to be subjected to the artificialities of the city without serious detriment," he believed, "but they make poor soil for the nurture of the *young* roots of human life." After Charles began school, he also clerked in grocery and dry goods stores, selling molasses, dried cod, woolens, and hardware to local farmers.

He showed intellectual prowess early on, studying Latin grammar on the sly while his employers were not looking. With no desire to pursue either farming or sales, Charles decided to attend college. To prepare himself he trudged three miles each way to a tiny school in nearby Lancaster. In 1862, at age twenty and exempted from the Civil War draft on account of nearsightedness, he entered Amherst College. When Parkhurst graduated in 1866, a self-described "dig" (or grind), he had little sense of direction. He became principal of Amherst High School, but left after two years to travel in Europe and study philology in Germany. While abroad he learned mountain climbing in the Swiss Alps, the start of a lifelong passion. He returned to Massachusetts to teach Greek and Latin for three years at the Williston Seminary in Easthampton, and in 1870 published the scholarly study *Analysis of the Latin Verb: Illustrated by the Forms of the Sanskrit*. That year he married Ellen Bodman, his former high school pupil and daughter of a Northampton bank president, but his career plans remained unsettled. His old mentor, President Julius H. Seelye of Amherst College, urged him to balance his intellectual side with the more emotional demands of preaching and pastoral work.

In 1874, through Seelye's influence and connections in his wife's family, Parkhurst became pastor of the Lenox Congregational Church in the Berkshire Mountains. Diffident about preaching at first, and well aware of the suspicions among local Congregationalists that he was a closet Unitarian, Parkhurst quickly won the confidence and respect of his parishioners and warmed to the work. Lenox was a conservative Yankee town, and most of its roughly 2,000 inhabitants farmed or worked in the sawmills, quarries, and glassworks dotting the landscape. Parkhurst remained there for six years and might have spent his entire career in obscurity. But the Berkshire region had begun attracting wealthy families from New York and Boston, eager to build summer homes amidst the area's natural beauty. Parkhurst's preaching caught the attention of several prominent New Yorkers who summered there. In 1880, the same year that Amherst conferred upon him the Doctor of Divinity degree, Parkhurst accepted the call to become pastor at the elite Madison Square Presbyterian Church, which installed him with great fanfare. He arrived in Manhattan formed by the village ideal of western Massachusetts and he brought a firm belief, as he recalled many years later, in the church as "a center of influence and a power for good in the midst of the little community."[7]

In his first years Parkhurst threw himself into church work and avoided city politics. Madison Square had a long tradition of both foreign and domestic missionary work; in 1857 it had put up a separate building in the "gashouse" district on Third Avenue and Thirtieth Street. It built the Mission House "for the purpose of gathering in the ignorant & neglected children, & youth, in that vicinity for instruction on the Sabbath, & also to provide a place for public religious worship." Theodore Roosevelt attended Sunday school there as a boy. Women in the church's employment society brought garments to their poorer sisters at the mission, offered sewing classes, and paid them for their work. A loan relief society lent small sums of money, and offered medical help and legal aid "to those temporarily disabled by misfortune." Ellen Parkhurst served as president of the Ladies Association, which oversaw the social work of the church.

Meantime Charles Parkhurst looked to widen the church's (and his own) influence among the nation's Protestant clergy. He played a leading role at an 1888 New York conference of the Evangelical Alliance, a national group organizing Protestant churches to help solve urban problems and an early expression of the social gospel movement. Parkhurst's notion of "civic Christianity" for New York City demanded nothing less than a Christian revival, "a scheme for moving prayerfully, deliberately and concertedly upon this great Island, with all its heterogeneous population, whipping the devil into the river, and saving to the Lord this city where throbs the pulse of our American republic." Behind the talk of reclaiming the city for Christ lay an uneasy defensiveness among evangelical Protestants frightened by the city's new demography. In the densely populated Tenth Ward, on the Lower East Side, only two Protestant churches could be found among some 50,000 people. Across the city there were nearly twenty saloons for every Protestant church. And an estimated 80 percent of the city's people were either foreign born or children of immigrants.[8]

Parkhurst's effective leadership in the 1880s brought Madison Square more parishioners, more bricks and mortar, and a growing reputation for grappling seriously with the multiplying ills of city life. Among these was crime. In November 1890 Parkhurst accepted an invitation to join the Society for the Prevention of Crime (SPC), a private citizens' group led by his friend and fellow Presbyterian Reverend Howard W. Crosby. When Crosby died a few months later, Parkhurst succeeded him as president, radically altering the SPC's strategy and focus and turning it into a significant power base for himself. The Society had been founded in 1877 by a group of prominent New Yorkers, declaring its purpose as "the eradication of the sources and causes of crime and vice, by all suitable and legal methods." One focus was "tippling houses," meaning places that sold alcohol. With its fundamental premise that alcohol abuse was "the first cause of crime," the Society pressed for tougher police enforcement of (widely ignored) excise laws governing the saloon trade and the liquor industry. The SPC was not prohibitionist, and it distanced itself from the temperance movement, preferring legal and political action. "We have not used rhetorical appeals," Crosby insisted, "or spread before our readers heart-rending pictures of vice and crime. We wish to arouse something deeper than emotion or sentiment." With Crosby as president it lobbied vigorously for a so-called "high license" excise law that would drastically reduce the number of saloons by making licensing fees much more expensive. High fees, he argued, would reduce the city's saloons, the chief advantage of which would be to "permit the officials of the city to have complete surveillance over these dangerous sources of crime."[9]

Like other private preventive societies of the day, such as Anthony Comstock's Society for the Suppression of Vice (SSV) and Elbridge Gerry's Society for the Prevention of Cruelty to Children (SPCC), the SPC saw itself as the government's legitimate partner in that surveillance. While earlier reformers relied primarily upon moral suasion, these newer preventive societies effectively privatized law enforcement, operating sometimes in tandem with—and sometimes as rivals to—the city's police and courts. The SPC's charter, issued by New York State, bestowed vaguely defined law enforcement powers, including a limited right to issue arrest warrants. If the city and its police department could not control illegal saloons, brothels, and gambling houses, the SPC would take the job on itself.[10]

But while the SPC exerted its own parallel, quasi-legal police power, small victories and self-congratulations proved no match for larger trends. In 1890, for example, the Society's pressure brought 167 excise violations to trial and had 40 licenses revoked. SPC agents made over 200 visits to open gambling houses and pool rooms (off-track betting parlors), including one near police headquarters on Mulberry Street that reportedly made a profit of $72,000 that year (or approximately $1.9 million today). But the laws against them were ambiguous at best, and unenforced at worst, and even direct appeals to police inspectors often went unheeded. The city now had some 9,000 saloons, hotels, and restaurants legally selling liquor or beer and wine, paying nearly $1.5 million in license fees (roughly $39.5 million today). Thousands more never bothered with a license. Saloon-keepers in all parts of the city did a brisk Sunday business, as the demands of the immigrant working class and thirsty out-of-towners made a mockery of the law banning sales on the Sabbath. Many thousands of parents sent their children out to buy beer for the noonday meal, making it impossible to enforce laws against sales to minors.[11]

When Parkhurst succeeded Crosby as president of the SPC in April, 1891, he initiated a new strategy that combined elements of a religious revival, appeals to the fears of upper class New Yorkers, and sophisticated use of publicity, all bound together by a tough-minded political stance. Beyond the colorful and widely quoted epithets, these key themes stood out in that sermon of February 14, 1892. Part of what made Parkhurst's anti-Tammany outburst so sensational was that it was *not* an election sermon. It was not an appeal for votes but rather a call for an urban crusade, a throwing down of the gauntlet to New York's Christians. He reminded his parishioners of the origins of the word Protestant—"A man who protests"—and slyly compared himself to Martin Luther, "a grand stick of human timber, all afire with holy indignation." What New York needed was a more civic Christianity, as dedicated to saving itself as it was to saving heathen souls, action "taken directly in the teeth of the damnable pack of administrative bloodhounds that are fattening themselves on the ethical flesh and blood of our citizenship." He denied the charge of bringing politics into the pulpit, and declared the political stripe of a city administration to be none of a church's business.[12]

But the immediate aftermath of his sermon exposed Parkhurst's "apolitical" claim as naïve at best. He visited District Attorney Nicoll in his office, and the meeting was strained to say the least. Nicoll was young—elected DA at age thirty-five with the help of Tammany Hall—but he was no immigrant ward boss. Born into wealth, a graduate of Princeton and Columbia Law School, and descended from the first English governor of New York, he embodied the respectable wing of Tammany Hall and the Democratic Party. Parkhurst offered his Society's help in procuring evidence against the worst flouters of the excise laws, the saloons that routinely sold beer and liquor on Sundays. Nicoll refused to have any official communication with Parkhurst until he withdrew the charges made in his sermon, and threatened a libel suit unless the minister could substantiate them. On February 23, Nicoll brought Parkhurst before the grand jury. The minister offered no direct evidence of criminal acts or misconduct by the district attorney.

Parkhurst was at his East Thirty-Fifth Street home on March 1 when he learned of the grand jury's presentment. On the specific issue of the DA's allegedly lenient treatment of McGlory, the grand jury vindicated Nicoll and found that "the author of the charges had no evidence upon which to base them except alleged newspaper reports which in the form published had no basis in facts." "We desire further," the jurors concluded, "to express our disapproval and condemnation of unfounded charges of this character." Judge Randolph Martine, who had heard the presentment read in the court of general sessions, agreed, congratulating the jurors and condemning Parkhurst.

Press coverage, largely supportive of Parkhurst, focused on his personal feud with Nicoll, but it also recognized that Parkhurst's melding of old fashioned preaching and shrewd use of publicity signaled a new and effective strategy. Whatever injustice he may have done to Nicoll paled before the good achieved by naming a broader truth. "Nobody whose eyes are open and who walks the streets," asserted the *Tribune*, "can for one moment doubt that some police captains, police detectives, roundsmen and patrolmen must be shamelessly corrupt or utterly incompetent; and we know they are not incompetent." The minister later pointed to Nicoll's personal animosity toward him as the starting point of what would become the most famous and sustained crusade against officially protected vice in New York history. For Nicoll, the presentment put an end to the matter and confirmed his view that Parkhurst had "indulged in a lot of wild accusations on the strength of newspaper rumors." For Parkhurst, the rebuke was expected, but he promised not to back down. Instead of relying on the accounts of others, he would go and see for himself.[13]

And thus began Parkhurst's descent into New York's underworld. He let it be known that he would devote his March 13 sermon to a reply to the grand jury's presentment and Judge Martine's censure. He resolved to make his own tour of the city's nether side, "determined to acquaint myself with the worst thing that was to be known and seen." Parkhurst

consulted with David J. Whitney, a wealthy merchant and former superintendent of the Society for the Prevention of Crime, who had drawn
harsh criticism for his "system of espionage" in the early 1880s. Whitney,
chastened by the lumps he had taken as a "gentleman detective," urged
Parkhurst to make his tour in the company of a professional and introduced him to twenty-six-year-old Charles W. Gardner, a veteran "shadow"
who had recently begun working for the SPC.

Originally from Chelsea, Massachusetts, Gardner had worked as a
printer and a railroad detective before coming to New York. He opened
his own detective agency, which failed after one month, and after that he
spent five years with the Society for the Prevention of Cruelty to Children
at a salary of $20 per week. In 1890 he made an unsuccessful run for al-
derman as a Republican. He had also worked as a "steerer" for lawyers
seeking prostitutes as clients. There was no doubt that Gardner had intimate knowledge of the city's underside, but the notorious reputation of
his profession posed a problem for Parkhurst. Gardner's own checkered
career reflected the murky world of the private detective agencies, which
had flourished in the nation's big cities after the Civil War. Most of their
business came from large mercantile firms and railroads suspicious of employee theft, divorce cases, and robbery victims more eager for recovery of
their losses than for prosecuting thieves. Unregulated by law, the private
detective business and its system of rewards for the return of stolen property presented enormous opportunities for blackmail, extortion, and
outright partnership with criminals.

Private detectives had a reputation for double-dealing and for bearing
false witness in court. "Anxious always to furnish exactly what is desired,
their reports are often lies, manufactured to suit the occasion," an astute
observer of New York's private detectives concluded. "The tracking of a
criminal for gain by a person unauthorized to arrest him when found, breeds
indifference to the demands and forms of law, which is calculated to breed
contempt for the law itself." Though private preventive societies like the
SPC and the SPCC hired detectives on a salaried (rather than reward) basis,
they worried about the odor of disrepute emanating from these operatives. Parkhurst needed someone else for his explorations, a man whose
class position and pedigree would ensure acceptance of his testimony.

One of his parishioners, John Langdon Erving, a twenty-five-year-old
scion of the Van Rensselaer family, fit the bill perfectly. Through the intervention of his employer, telegraph magnate James A. Scrymser, Erving

volunteered his services to Parkhurst. Scrymser argued that Erving, "a lifelong New Yorker" and "a man of refinement and a gentleman," would provide the necessary moral ballast to a man like Gardner. The tall, good-looking, impeccably dressed Erving also embodied the innocent (and well-off) youth whose protection Parkhurst had identified as a key goal of his campaign. The plan called for SPC private detectives to gather information on Sunday law violations in saloons, while Parkhurst and his two companions experienced first-hand the city's lower depths.[14]

The story of Parkhurst's four-night underworld tour has achieved a legendary status, with comic overtones; indeed the myth-making began almost immediately. Details of what happened began leaking out to the New York press within days, and testimony taken at two criminal trials involving brothels the trio visited added more titillating specifics to the tale. Yet because of the subject matter, most of the newspaper coverage was cryptic, leaving a lot of room for imagination. Gardner's picaresque account, *The Doctor and the Devil, Or Midnight Adventures of Dr. Parkhurst*, privately published in 1894, has served as the main source for journalists and historians. But Gardner, who had many axes to grind with the SPC, the New York City police, and others, wrote a book full of dubious quotations and self-aggrandizing claims. His account resembled nothing so much as a briefer version of the "sunshine and shadow" guidebooks that had been a staple of New York publishing for a half century. Less important than the precise details of what the men saw and how they reacted was the geographic range of their explorations, the factual ammunition provided Parkhurst, and the new wave of sensational publicity given his cause.[15]

Gardner brought Parkhurst and Erving to his apartment, where he dressed them in loud, cheap costumes—black-and-white checked trousers, old shirts, and tattered flannel neckties—designed to make them look like out-of-towners in search of a good time. And indeed the first forays the trio made resembled the sort of highly ritualized slumming expedition already common and well publicized in city journalism and fiction. On their first three nights Gardner guided them through the cheap saloons, brothels, and hotels of the East River waterfront neighborhood—the oldest vice district in New York. Parkhurst, according to Gardner, mingled freely with young and old prostitutes, treated customers to nickel glasses of whiskey, and held his liquor surprisingly well, for a minister. He noted policemen in uniform in several places. Once the men paid five cents each to sleep in the lowest-grade lodging house—reputed to be a haven for illegal voters controlled by Tammany Hall—but they failed to last the night amidst the foul stench and bare canvas cots.

When they resumed the tour Gardner moved the party uptown. They took in a Bowery concert garden and a "tight house" brothel, where the prostitutes paraded their wares in flesh-colored tights, and where they also encountered a large contingent of soldiers visiting from Fort Hamilton, in Brooklyn. On the Lower East Side they visited brothels identified by the ethnicity of the owners and women, and where the madams would introduce the prostitutes as their "daughters." Just a couple of blocks from police headquarters they ran into a noisy, aggressive group of prostitutes who offered to take them to a nearby "boarding house" that serviced cops. In Chinatown, after a good dinner, Gardner and a Chinese interpreter, Lee Bing, brought Parkhurst to a very possibly fake "opium den"—the apartment of a Chinese man, his white wife, and their young son—where the doctor declined an offer to "hit a pipe." Gardner continued to highlight the ethnically exotic with visits to African-American brothels in "Coontown" (Sullivan, Thompson, and Macdougal Streets in the current-day Greenwich Village), and houses in "Frenchtown" (Wooster and Greene Streets in contemporary Soho). At the Golden Rule Pleasure Club on West Third Street, where male prostitutes catered to a bustling trade, Parkhurst evidently fled in horror after Gardner explained why the heavily made-up men sitting at the booths conversed in falsetto voices and referred to each other by female names.

Still, Gardner claimed, Parkhurst was not satisfied: "'Show me something worse,' was his constant cry." On the night of March 11 Gardner brought the party to Maria Andrea's brothel on West Fourth Street, a substantial three-story brick house with a uniformed cop standing on the front steps. The brothel was known as a "fancy house," and they paid a steep $16 each to see a "French circus" (nude can-can dancing) performed by four French immigrant prostitutes. But Parkhurst wanted not merely "something worse"—he pushed Gardner to shift the geography of his vice tour. So far the detective had limited their explorations to the older parts of the city, where vice exposés were old news, and to places that served a poor and working-class clientele. Although Parkhurst never admitted as much, he needed to see commercialized vice much closer to home for his story to have maximum impact with his well-heeled parishioners and the city at large. They headed uptown to the "Tenderloin" district, then emerging as the center of the city's more expensive vice economy.

Later that same night Gardner took Parkhurst and Erving to a lavishly appointed brothel at 31-33 East Twenty-Seventh Street, just three blocks from the Madison Square church and eight blocks from the minister's residence. The madam Hattie Adams and the eight prostitutes who lived there obliged the visitors with a "circus" that included nude dancing to the music of a blindfolded pianist and a game of naked leapfrog. This was evidently the last stop for Parkhurst, but Erving, Gardner, and another detective continued the tour, visiting dozens of brothels and gambling houses in the neighborhood. Parkhurst, Gardner, and Erving met at the minister's house the following day, Saturday, to review their notes and swear out affidavits against all the places they had visited. In addition, Gardner's four detectives produced a total of 254 affidavits drawn against saloons they had found in violation of the Sunday closing laws.

Parkhurst was now ready to go public. He let it be known that the March 13 sermon would offer specific and startling proof of the charges he had made four weeks previously. That morning, as they stepped down from their carriages, Madison Square's congregants found a huge unruly crowd around the church entrance, "eager for sensational preaching," as the *Sun* reporter put it. Ushers struggled to keep out all but regular pew holders amid the shoving, jostling, and cursing. When the doors finally closed the church was overflowing, with men and women jamming the aisles, the vestry, and even the pulpit steps. Thousands more stood outside. The *Times* reporter observed that even nearby Madison Square Garden would not have accommodated the throng. Those who managed to squeeze in listened intently and without interruption, though many turned red-faced and angry once Parkhurst got down to particulars. For his text he chose "The wicked walk on every side, when the vilest men are exalted" (Psalms 12:8). In place of the usual prayer books on his lectern, he had two thick piles of neatly typed affidavits. As usual, he read slowly and un-emotionally from his manuscript—but now he added emphatic gestures to his talk, waving the affidavits and pounding them on the pulpit railing, and pointing his fingers as a warning to his listeners.

This was the sermon that transformed his personal squabble with District Attorney Nicoll into a movement, as Parkhurst publicly worked through his own mixed feelings over the events of the previous month. He began by reviewing what he saw as Nicoll's personal animus against him—the refusal to speak with him in his office, Nicoll's heated charges that he had lied. Parkhurst resolved his defensiveness over his recent notoriety and the challenge to his motives by insisting that he really had no choice. It was not so much a question of defending his honor and character but of doing his job, for "I apprehend my function as a preacher of righteousness as giving me no option in the matter." The "purely moral intention of the crusade," he maintained, had nothing to do with politics; its "one exclusive aim was to expose the reality of sin." But it would be difficult for many to believe Parkhurst's claim to be apolitical when he went on to describe Tammany Hall as "the organization of crime," and to attack "the inherent tyranny of the civilized brigands who are despotizing over us."

Parkhurst made no specific mention of what he had seen in the downtown neighborhoods with Erving and Gardner. Nonetheless he offered particulars about the church's Tenderloin district to amplify the threat he saw posed to the moral condition of young men. He had never realized until his tour that there was "little advantage in preaching the Gospel to a young fellow on Sunday if he is going to be sitting on the edge of a Tammany-maintained hell the rest of the week." He waved a list of thirty brothels in the church's neighborhood—one of them "three blocks only from the spot where I stand now"—that he, John Erving, or Charles Gardner had visited. He stressed how easy it was for a young man of the Madison Square to get information about these politically protected places, "to pick out either a cheap or an expensive temple of vile fascination, where the unholy worship of Venus is rendered." He referred obliquely to his encounter with male prostitutes at the Golden Rule Pleasure Club— "iniquity in its vilest shape, for there is nothing in the first chapter of Romans, read this morning, that will outdo in filthiness the scenes which my eyes have just witnessed." The passage from Paul's Epistle to the Romans, excoriating the ungodly and the unrighteous, had been discussed during that morning's pre-sermon service. It might have also inspired Parkhurst's severe descriptions of Tammany:

> For this cause God gave them up into vile affections: for even their women did change the natural use into that which is against nature: And likewise also the men, leaving the natural use of the woman, burned in their lust toward one another; men with men working that which is unseemly, and receiving in themselves that recompense of their error which was meet.
>
> (Romans 1:26–7, King James Version)

Emboldened by his first-hand evidence, Parkhurst concluded his sermon with a full frontal attack upon the police department. Anyone who denied that "drunkenness, gambling, and licentiousness in this town are municipally protected is either a knave or an idiot." He mockingly quoted the rules and regulations of the NYPD requiring the superintendent, captains, and ordinary patrolmen to enforce the laws against gambling houses, brothels, and illegal liquor sales. "I am not making the definite charge," he noted, "that this proceeds from complicity with violators of the laws, but I do make the distinct charge that it proceeds either from complicity or incompetency. They can take their choice." Like most New Yorkers, he did not believe the police to be incompetent. With the legally certified facts he had presented that morning, "in behalf of an insulted and outraged public," Parkhurst insisted that the police enforce the laws. And with a final sardonic echo from the Tweed era, he challenged Tammany to act on the particulars he had presented: "Now, what are you going to do with them?"[16]

At first, Parkhurst's second sermon elicited the same mix of responses as the one delivered a month earlier. DA Nicoll challenged his motives and methods. "Doesn't it look really as if there was a little effort to create a sensation?" he asked. Some prominent clergy made similar criticisms. The Rev. Dr. Benjamin F. DeCosta, rector of the Episcopal Church of St. John, asked, "What need is there of respectable people, dressing in disguise and going around nights acting lies" to prove what everyone already knew? "This is simply sensational, nothing more."

The *Times* thought him an honest and brave man and the *Tribune* ran a long, highly favorable profile of Parkhurst as a "preacher of righteousness." The *World* criticized him as misdirected for insisting on enforcement of some laws that were "opposed by public sentiment—not vicious public sentiment, but sound and sensible public sentiment." And the *Sun*, the minister's most fervent critic among the city's press, noted that "if he had hunted for them, he would probably have found as many places of vicious resort in his precinct ten years ago as he found last week." The *Sun* underlined the ethnic and class tensions bubbling just under the surface: Parkhurst would have found then, as now, "thousands of respectable and self-respecting people, men and women, drinking beer in beer gardens on Sunday." It made what might be termed the cosmopolitan argument—vice and evil flourished in every big city, and no municipal government had ever succeeded in abolishing them. What mattered was preserving public decency.[17]

But on April 1 the same grand jury that had convened in March, after hearing testimony from Parkhurst, Gardner, and an assortment of police commissioners, inspectors, and captains, delivered a presentment that forcefully supported the minister. Its key finding closely paralleled Parkhurst's main argument: that the police were either incompetent or corrupt. It sharply criticized the police for selective law enforcement, contrasting its success in coping with violent crime with its lax approach to the vice economy. Although the grand jury believed police received "financial considerations in some cases for lax administration," it made no specific indictments for, as several of its members noted in press interviews, the testimony offered by police officials had been too vague and evasive for that. But in a public statement made a few days later, grand jury foreman Henry Taber charged that police collected annually between $7 and $10 million in tribute from brothels, gambling dens, and saloons (a staggering $187 to $263 million in current dollars).

This March grand jury report proved a decisive moment. A gratified Parkhurst, who had submitted the SPC's long list of affidavits to the grand jury, insisted he had no interest in indicting individual brothel keepers, gamblers, or saloon owners. The findings accomplished his goal to take police bribery and extortion out of the realm of doubt and conjecture—anyone could now see the NYPD was a fundamentally corrupt institution. And just as importantly for Parkhurst, the grand jury finding transformed his personal crusade into a popular movement, as it lifted his work "out of the region of crankism... and secured to it a dignity and a status." He received hundreds of letters of support from around the country, and a fundraising appeal made by the SPC to 2,000 New Yorkers brought a flood of contributions—some as large as $1,000 and many made anonymously.[18]

Police officials could no longer afford to dismiss Parkhurst as a faintly comical, ineffectual figure, and the gloves came off. Chief Inspector Thomas F. Byrnes, who would be elevated to superintendent of the force in a few weeks, threatened to resign over the grand jury report. Byrnes was the most famous policeman in America. Born in Ireland in 1842, he had arrived in New York as an infant, growing up near the Lower West Side docks. Byrnes had commanded the detective force since 1880. (In an uncanny historical coincidence, he had been appointed inspector on the same day that Parkhurst had been installed as pastor at Madison Square Church). Byrnes essentially invented the modern police detective service and did more to professionalize police work than anyone in city history. His 1885 book, *Professional Criminals of America*, made him the most celebrated detective in America, a reputation burnished by a fawning press and a popular dime novel series that fictionalized his exploits. Now Byrnes blasted the grand jury findings for lack of specific evidence and failure to distinguish the guilty from the innocent. "I say again," he told reporters, "it is an outrage to attempt to humiliate a body of men who are charged with the duty of protecting life and property in this great city." As for Foreman Henry Taber's accusation that police received millions of dollars every year in bribes, Byrnes thought his remarks "clearly indicate that he was more entitled to be shut up in a lunatic asylum than to be a member of a grand jury."[19]

If Byrnes was the prototypical detective, then Inspector Alexander S. "Clubber" Williams was the archetypal constable. Born in Nova Scotia in 1839, he had come to the city as a boy and was naturalized there in 1860, joining the NYPD in 1866. Williams personified a new breed of cop who sought out physical confrontations with criminals, thereby making streets and public spaces safer for citizens. His prowess with the hardwood locust baton earned him the nickname "Clubber" and contributed to high popularity both with reporters and rank-and-file cops.

Williams's response to the grand jury presentment and Parkhurst's crusade emphasized the department's success in reducing violent assaults against persons and property since the Civil War, as well as its success in making prostitution and gambling less visible. "It is a fact," he told reporters, "that a sober man or woman can walk through any streets of New York at any hour of the night, and, attending to business, neither be insulted or assaulted." Of course disorderly houses existed, but "they are more hidden and less of that vice is flaunted than in any other city in the world." In Williams's view, Parkhurst's disclosures would only make matters worse. He recalled his stint as captain of the Tenderloin in the 1880s, when he accompanied the Brooklyn minister Rev. T. DeWitt Talmage on his hunt for sensational material to enliven his preaching. "Never in their history," Williams claimed, "were the places he described so thronged by patrons, largely from Brooklyn, or so much money spent there for debauchery as after those sermons." Now, it was "the members of Dr. Parkhurst's and other churches who pay for the lace curtains, the plush furniture, and the panel mirrors of the disorderly houses, not the policemen." His "crusade" was nothing more than a way to draw crowds to his sermons.

As police officials had contended since the 1860s, Williams believed that *de facto* regulation and surveillance of prostitution in defined vice districts offered the most practical solution for a metropolis like New York. Attempts to drive out brothels led only to "scattering the infection all over the city" and made regulation impossible. While Parkhurst pounded away at the threat to his congregation's young men, Williams suggested that regulated vice districts could actually protect them. No matter what Parkhurst said, nothing could alter the fundamental reality of the modern cosmopolis. Williams pointed out that 30,000 strangers slept in New York every night and that they would go where they would. Parkhurst and his ilk had to look actively for vice whereas ten years ago, "it stared you in the face from every corner in certain sections of the city."[20]

Crime statistics for the Gilded Age are fragmentary at best, and in any era they are subject to conflicting interpretation and political use. During the Civil War years there was a sharp increase in the carrying of concealed weapons and in crimes of violence against New Yorkers. But by the 1880s both statistics and general perception supported the view that, whatever else might be true about the NYPD, it deserved substantial credit for reducing violent crime. Between 1885 and 1893, for example, the annual rate of robbery arrests per 100,000 population declined by fifty percent, from 30.6 to 15. And the city's annual homicide rate had also dropped sharply, from roughly 7 to 8 per 100,000 population in the 1870s to about 3 to 4 by the early 1890s.

But Parkhurst's campaign, enormously strengthened by the grand jury's second finding, had focused on protected vice, not violent crimes against people and property. Most newspapers agreed that the grand jury had uncovered nothing new, but its presentment gave official expression to prevalent opinion. For a large proportion of New Yorkers, the *Times* argued, the conclusion that the police protected vice for money "is more than a belief, it is a positive conviction. It is one of these things which many people *know* but cannot prove."[21]

The two-day civil trial of brothel keeper Hattie Adams in early April illustrated both the newly candid atmosphere created by Parkhurst and the frustrations presented by the legal system. Adams's landlord, embarrassed by the publicity, brought suit to evict her under a statute prohibiting tenants from using a house for illegal purposes. The houses at 31-33 East Twenty-Seventh Street had been identified in a front-page story in the *World* as one of the stops on Parkhurst's vice tour. The reporter had interviewed Adams and several of the house's "inmates," but offered few details as to what went on, finding it "impossible to say more here than that Dr. Parkhurst saw vice in all its nakedness." As city newspapers reprinted large portions of the public testimony of Parkhurst, John L. Erving, and Charles Gardner, all of whom faced tough cross-examination, the details of their March 11 visit emerged for the first time: how Gardner had brought them there because of his friendship with Annie DeVoe, one of the "boarders"; how Gardner and Erving arrived first, then left and brought in Parkhurst to witness a "circus"; how the three men drank beer while watching four girls perform a naked "can-can" to music supplied by a blindfolded piano player; how Erving danced with one of the women while, in a game of naked leapfrog, Gardner played the frog. This last image inspired concert saloon wags to sing a new version of the popular song hit, "Ta-ra-ra-Boom-de-ay":

> *Doctor Parkhurst on the floor*
> *Playing leapfrog with a whore,*
> *Ta-ra-ra-Boom-de-ay,*
> *Ta-ra-ra-Boom-de-ay.*

Both Erving and Gardner tried to shield Parkhurst, testifying that he never danced with the women or had one on his lap. But the patrician Erving—nervous, constantly blushing, and clearly mortified—made a weak witness, while Gardner faced a barrage of questions that flushed out his own dubious past and highlighted the deceit inherent in the detective business. Parkhurst, clearly the star witness, proved unflappable as he calmly and unapologetically offered his version of what happened that night. Adams's defense attorneys, like some editorial writers, tried hard to portray Parkhurst as a hypocrite who, instead of trying to save sinners had disguised himself to entrap them. In a strange scene, one of Adams's two attorneys, Isidore Hirshfield, asked Parkhurst if he was conversant with the New Testament and began reading from the Gospel of St. Mark. When an objection stopped his reading, he then asked: "Do you not think it is your duty as a Christian to follow the Saviour, who, when He sat down to dine with the publicans and the sinners, in answer to a comment, said: 'I come not to call the righteous but sinners to repentance?'" Parkhurst made no answer and the judge sustained the shouted objections of the landlord's attorney, putting a stop to this line of questioning.

Hattie Adams's defense relied upon the familiar claims of accused madams. A plump, nervous, fortyish woman, she had rented the two buildings, connected by a doorway cut through a wall, for five years. She maintained one as a private residence and ran the other as a respectable boarding house, one of the few ways a divorced woman could earn a living. She did not keep track of her boarders' comings and goings, as long as they paid the rent. Parkhurst's party had been let in only because Gardner had asked for Annie DeVoe by name, but she saw nothing of their carrying on. After reporters had come to interview her, she went to Parkhurst's house to demand an explanation from him, but wound up talking with his wife, and "I hadn't the heart to make the statement in Mrs. Parkhurst's presence I had come to make." The notoriety had caused her to lose all her boarders. She noted that there had never been any complaints about her house, and her attorneys called several witnesses from the neighborhood to say there had never been any disturbances there. On April 8, after two hours of deliberation, the six-man jury stunned courtroom observers by reporting they were unable to agree, evidently divided over the technical issue of whether the doorway connecting 31 and 33 East Twenty-Seventh Street made the two houses into one. The dispossess order covered only 31, but the "circus" took place in 33; in the eyes of at least two jurors, what took place in 33 had nothing to do with the other house. Mrs. Adams was free to stay put.

The *Times* described Mrs. Adams's testimony as "bald perjury," while the jury had "disregarded proved facts and ignored the law." Only prejudice against Parkhurst's crusade and his methods of conducting it could explain their failure to convict. But the sordid accounts of Parkhurst's adventures, splashed over the pages of every paper in the city, gave even the *Times*, one of the minister's strongest supporters until now, reasons to reconsider. For while "no right thinking person doubts the doctor's perfect sincerity, nor does any judicious person doubt that he committed a most deplorable blunder in pushing his quest for proofs of evil-doing to such extraordinary lengths," Parkhurst himself was unavailable for comment. He had left the city for a week-long vacation, whereabouts unknown, prompted by the strain of the past two months and the dozen or so anonymous letters he had received threatening to kill him or burn down his house.[22]

The criminal trials of brothel keepers Hattie Adams and, subsequently, Marie Andrea, threatened all the momentum Parkhurst had gathered.

Compared to the civil cases brought against the two women in April, these criminal proceedings promised even more explicit language and a much harsher tone, in court and in the press. On May 6, Hattie Adams went on trial for keeping a disorderly house. Her lawyers, Abe Hummel and William Howe, the city's most flamboyant and successful criminal defense attorneys, looked to shift attention from Adams and instead try Parkhurst and his companions with ridicule, sarcasm, and grandstand oratory. The judge barred women from attending, but there were plenty of lawyers, sporting men, clergymen, toughs, and businessmen—some watching the action with opera glasses—packing the court of general sessions.

Abe Hummel went right after the first witness, Erving, the young socialite whose discomfort and deep sense of embarrassment were evident to all. He forced Erving to re-enact the late night ramble at Adams's house, producing lurid exchanges such as the one reported in the *Times*, following Erving's description of the "leap frog" game and dancing with nude women:

"Did you have your arm around the woman?" asked Mr. Hummel on cross-examination.

"I do not remember," said Erving, getting red in the face.

"I believe you were once a Sunday school teacher?"

"I was."

"Will you swear that you didn't put your arm around her?"

"I don't think I did."

At Mr. Hummel's request, Erving stood up and illustrated his position in the dance. He said he took the woman's hand and put his other hand on her shoulder. He did not dance, he said, to please himself, but because he thought it was necessary. Dr. Parkhurst and [Charles] Gardner were present, but did not dance.

"Do you remember who proposed the dance?"

"I do not."

"Did you ever dance that way before?"

"No, Sir."

Parkhurst again made a more effective witness, calmly deflecting all attempts to impugn his motives. The sympathetic judge ruled many questions out of order, as when William Howe asked, "Did you deem it a part of your duty as a minister to go to these places and drink beer and contribute money for these sad and degrading spectacles?" Howe pursued this strategy in a bombastic closing statement, claiming Parkhurst's veracity was on trial. "It is for you to decide," he thundered to the jury, "whether this man went to this house and witnessed that dance for the object which he has stated or to gratify his lustful tendencies by looking on." Howe's bluster could not save his client. After two days of testimony the jury took two hours to return a guilty verdict. A bitter Hattie Adams, who received a nine-month jail sentence, lashed out at what she saw as Parkhurst's hypocrisy. "Why should Dr. Parkhurst pick me out? Why should he want to send me to prison?" A Presbyterian herself, Adams announced, "I'm done with all that church business—religion—now. Parkhurst has destroyed my faith. I am just done with it."[23]

Maria Andrea's trial followed immediately—but hers received much less coverage and a jury took only ten minutes to convict. Still, the sensational aspects of the case ricocheted around in ways damaging to Parkhurst. Several newspaper accounts found Parkhurst's sober demeanor and unemotional tone a jarring contrast with his testimony on "things too revolting for belief." He gave "the beastly details with precision," the *World* reported, "and as if he was a machine and had not the slightest possible interest in the matter." Charles Gardner introduced a newly vivid sexuality to the proceedings when he testified that Maria Andrea had told him that the steep $16 price for the "circus" would include going upstairs with the girls afterward. But little of this testimony found its way into press accounts, and Erving's turn on the stand created a much juicier story. In the midst of his testimony, described by one reporter as "the vilest ever listened to in a courtroom in this city," Erving suffered a collapse from "nervous prostration." In the middle of a withering cross-examination about who drank what, who kissed whom, and which naked girl sat on whose lap, a flushed and confused Erving turned to the judge and told him he could not continue, and fled the courtroom. Erving's father announced that his son's life would be endangered if he were forced to testify. He whisked John away to the family estate in Rye where the young man remained in seclusion.

The emotional ordeal of this wealthy, socially prominent, and good-looking young man—such a vivid contrast to the cool righteousness of Parkhurst and the disagreeable seaminess of Gardner—made Erving's story the most talked about aspect of the Adams and Andrea trials. Parkhurst's crusade had forced a new explicitness in the city's public life that could cut several ways. The trials, Parkhurst claimed, provoked "our enemies to a frenzy of affected loathing and hypocritical indignation." He reserved special disdain for the *Sun*, which blamed him for Erving's breakdown and railed against Parkhurst's "moral insensibility," as evidenced by "a story of unspeakable depravity, unparalleled in history, ancient or modern." But the trials also provoked sharp criticism from other city clergymen who applauded Parkhurst's goals but attacked his methods. Benjamin F. DeCosta, an Episcopal minister and leader of the White Cross Society, a group offering help to prostitutes and homeless women, made a public clemency appeal for Hattie Adams, calling her better than some of her accusers. Rev. Dr. Joseph H. Rylance of St. Mark's Church in the Bowery condemned "the caprice of Dr. Parkhurst and company," and worried about the disquieting effects of the publicity attending the trials. "What if our homes were to be flooded with reports of such doings for years to come? Think of the demoralizing effect!"[24]

Criticism of Parkhurst was not limited to rival clerics, the police, or Tammany Democrats. Ever since it had organized the nation's first Labor Day parade up Broadway in 1882, the Central Labor Union (CLU) had provided an influential voice for New York's unionized workers. Many of its delegates expressed sympathy for Parkhurst's anti-vice work, but not for his financial supporters in the SPC, mostly wealthy businessmen and attorneys. At a contentious and widely publicized meeting, CLU Secretary George K. Lloyd declared, "I have no respect for Parkhurst's society, which is supported by men who are driving girls to disorderly houses by working them twelve and fourteen hours a day for a few dollars a week." Women employed as waitresses, garment "sweaters," cigar makers, and other occupations in the grim world of tenement factories needed higher pay, not sermons about virtue. One study of 1,500 city prostitutes, done by the White Cross Society, revealed that more than 70 percent had earned wages of $4 per week or less "before their fall." The CLU agreed to support Parkhurst, but first wanted him to address the direct link between poverty wages and prostitution.[25]

Parkhurst now decided to create a new organization, the City Vigilance League, and he vowed to expand his New York movement into a national crusade. On May 12, at the Scottish Rite Hall, located just a few blocks from his church, Parkhurst addressed an invited crowd of several hundred on the theme, "How We as Young Men Can Make New York a Better City."

Most of them represented elite Protestant church societies from around the city and Brooklyn, and they listened avidly as Parkhurst claimed, "We are not working for next November. We long for nothing short of a purified municipality." But a purified New York could only be built on the ruins of Tammany Hall. Still, he paid grudging tribute to Tammany's effective organization, its relentless devotion to its cause. Only a parallel effort by "men with brains and hearts and consciences" could hope to defeat it. He urged the young men present to join him in a new group devoted to exposing protected vice, and over two hundred present signed cards pledging "to study the municipal interests of this city, and to do everything in my power to promote the purity and honesty of its government." The City Vigilance League would be methodically organized in imitation of Tammany, by assembly districts and city blocks, and dedicated to the moral surveillance of neighborhoods. This was not merely a New York campaign. "Our country's heart throbs here on Manhattan Island," Parkhurst argued. "Whatever problem is solved here is solved for all the country."

However, while Parkhurst invoked purity, morality, and civic obligation, there was no getting around the national political implications of his "nonpartisan" appeal. Republican president Benjamin Harrison had narrowly carried New York in 1888, and the upcoming 1892 election would most likely be decided again by the Empire State, and especially by the city's popular vote. "The fate of the great Democratic party of the whole Union," asserted the staunchly Democratic *NY Sun*, "is therefore in the keeping of Tammany Hall. The decisive battle of the campaign is to be fought here in New York and by Tammany Hall."[26]

On May 25, 1892, just three months after his first sermon, some 4,000 people jammed into Cooper Union's Great Hall for Dr. Parkhurst's political coming-out party. Perhaps half as many milled about Astor Place, unable to get in but eager to show their support. Inside, American flags and brightly colored streamers decorated the walls and pillars, and a life-size portrait of the late Dr. Howard Crosby, Parkhurst's predecessor as head of the Society for the Prevention of Crime, overhung the platform. Slipped inside each printed program was a copy of the grand jury's March presentment. The crowd itself was mixed and loudly enthusiastic. On stage sat more than a hundred prominent businessmen, clergy, bankers, lawyers, and other professionals, all of whom had endorsed the meeting and lent their names as "vice-presidents." The audience included large numbers of working-class New Yorkers, and perhaps a third of those present were women. Ex-judge William Arnoux, who presided as chair, defined the meeting's purpose as "the cause of virtue, temperance, manliness, and good government against the allied force of crime and intemperance." He praised Parkhurst for having accomplished more by his "bold, fearless conduct than all the rosewater reformers in ten years."

Organizers conjured the ghost of Boss Tweed from 1871. Former State Supreme Court Justice Noah Davis, who had presided over Tweed's trial twenty years earlier, drew cheers when he reminded listeners how "in this very hall the famous Committee of Seventy was appointed that fought that great battle for purity of government." Back then cartoonist Thomas Nast had done as much as anyone to topple the Tweed Ring with his ferocious illustrations for *Harper's Weekly*. Now, Nast cartoons from the *NY Gazette*, supporting Parkhurst and caricaturing the police department, circulated among the audience.

The crowd listened intently to a series of eight resolutions thanking Parkhurst and pledging united action against politicians, police, property owners, newspapers, politicians, and all others "who make common cause with criminals." But just as the crowd roared its approval, a tall woman dressed in black pushed her way down to the front, trying to get the attention of the chair. She was Charlotte Smith, a pioneering labor reformer best known as an advocate for laundresses and other low-wage women workers. "Before these resolutions are passed," she said in a voice quivering with excitement, "I want to ask why only we poor women are persecuted and prosecuted, and not the men who are responsible for these things?" She was greeted with a few hisses and then ignored as she retreated back to her seat. After more than three hours of speechifying the crowd was hungry for the entrance of its hero.

At 11:00 p.m. Parkhurst finally strode to the podium amidst a cheering, handkerchief waving ovation that lasted several minutes. He reiterated the central theme of his work, exposing "the league which exists in this city between our civic servants and the criminal classes." He did not question the honest intent of the new police superintendent Thomas Byrnes, appointed just a few weeks earlier. But he drew laughter when he reminded the crowd that "my detectives have been busy day and night, mostly at night"; he even read some choice details from their latest surveillance reports of disorderly houses running under the noses of beat cops. Parkhurst stirred his listeners by insisting their movement was at heart about the obligations and privileges of citizenship, a common plat-form uniting people across differences in party, religion, or ethnicity. The movement was nonpartisan, he insisted, with no political significance. If he was to be its engineer, with hand on the throttle, "I would rather let that locomotive burst than allow it to be switched off on to the side track of any political party." At the same time, no one should doubt that the eyes of the entire country were upon them and that they were "living and working where national history is made."[27]

2

. . . .

THE BUTTONS

The new superintendent of police looked resplendent on horseback, ramrod straight and bedecked with all his medals. He was a powerfully built man, just under six feet tall, with piercing brown eyes and a full mustache. On a sunny afternoon in late May 1892, Thomas F. Byrnes marshaled some 2,500 of his force in Battery Park at the south tip of Manhattan, and gave the order to begin the annual review and parade. Following the brass blare of the popular Seventh Regiment Band, five battalions of ten companies each marched in tight military formation from Whitehall Street to Broadway, and then to an inspection by Mayor Grant and the police commissioners at Forty-Second Street and Fifth Avenue. Patrolmen wore their new summer uniforms, topped by gray helmets. Their captains walked beside them, wearing long frock coats and white helmets decorated with gold bands. Four inspectors accompanied Byrnes on horseback. "The buttons," street slang for the police, were on full display.

The parade enjoyed a continuous ovation from spectators packed along the route; Superintendent Byrnes received so much applause that he periodically bowed his head in modest acknowledgment. The other crowd favorite was Inspector Alexander S. Williams, his muscular frame towering nearly six and one-half feet, a man known nationwide as the city's most fearless "clubber" of criminals. After inspection, the line reformed and passed before a formal reviewing stand at the Worth Monument (a memorial for a Mexican War hero), at Madison Square, just across the park from Reverend Parkhurst's church.

Only a week earlier Parkhurst had attracted an overflow crowd of supporters at Cooper Union for his speech, in which Byrnes and Williams had been singled out for criticism, accused of everything from negligence of duty and incompetence to personal corruption. Parkhurst's crusade, the resultant attacks against Tammany and the police, the heavily publicized court cases, the political rumormongering, the seemingly endless stream of sensational newspaper stories—all could be forgotten for at least one day as Byrnes, Williams, and their blue army basked in popular approval. The minister seemed to them just the latest in a long line of "reformers" determined to attack the police and remake the department. They had little reason to believe that Parkhurst or his campaign would show much staying power.[1]

Beyond the public adulation at the police parade, the two men had good reason to feel confident. The new superintendent was the most famous cop in America and, along with Allan Pinkerton, one of the nation's best-known detectives. In the public mind Byrnes, the prototypical detective, and Williams, the archetypal constable, stood out as the most imposing, influential, and feared policemen of the Gilded Age. Both belonged to a new generation of Civil War veterans who had reshaped the force along more strictly military lines and now dominated the NYPD brass. Along with tighter discipline and unquestioning obedience to superiors, the military model proved extremely effective for the escalating deployment of police against organized labor, strikers, and political radicals of all stripes in the 1870s and 1880s. Moral reformers like Parkhurst, fixated on rooting out gambling houses and brothels, and keen to enforce Sabbath "blue laws," saw a police culture shot through with bribery and corruption and a department that seemed to make its own laws. But the city's business elite, including bankers, real estate investors, merchants, and the owners of large hotels and theaters, revered a police force that had become much more efficient in the protection of life and property. For decades, Byrnes and Williams had led physical confrontations against strikes and riots, as well as commanding campaigns to clear the streets of thieves and violent criminals. Their careers reveal much about the sources of police authority, the shrewd cultivation of journalists and writers in creating larger-than-life reputations, and the deep historical connections between police careers and the intense partisanship of city politics.

Just six weeks earlier the board of police commissioners had announced the retirement of Superintendent William Murray and the appointment of Inspector Byrnes as his replacement. Byrnes entered office with an enormous reservoir of good will and a near-universal belief that he was the best man to root out corruption in the department and to repair the damage done to its image. Since 1880 he had headed the department's detective force, transforming it from an ineffective and decentralized corps into a centralized professional bureau. Byrnes had earned international fame and the fear of the city's criminals for his detective work. As he took office, Byrnes took pains to acknowledge the recent criticism of the department. He noted that he was free of party obligations, and that he was not, nor had ever been, a member of any political organization. (Although a Democrat, he was not affiliated with Tammany Hall.) "In the performance of my duty," he announced in his first public statement, "I shall have but one supreme object—the protection of life and property, the prevention and suppression of crime and, above all, the enforcement of the laws without fear or favor against whosoever are found violating them."

Despite the Reverend Parkhurst's flamboyant crusade, the March grand jury's scathing presentment, and the growing chorus of newspaper criticism, the police department's reputation and standing among the city's establishment had never been stronger. Commenting favorably upon Byrnes's promotion, *Harper's Weekly* expressed this view firmly. "However much the administration of the laws may have suffered in the hands of the police in some regards, in those affecting the safety of life and property and the preservation of the public peace they have always been not only trustworthy, but extremely zealous." The *Tribune* expressed the consensus views of the city's business and professional classes when it noted that during Byrne's command of the detective corps, "life and property in this community have been far safer than under any previous administration." And his reputation as a strict disciplinarian augured well, the *Times* thought, for the toughest job facing him: rooting out police corruption epitomized by the embarrassing spectacle of police captains "becoming too rich, and of retiring or dying with more money than the savings from their pay would amount to if they had saved it all."[2]

Parkhurst was having none of it. On the same day that the four-man police board swore in the new superintendent, Parkhurst released a blistering declaration to the citizens of New York, replying to his critics and promising to intensify his campaign. He reiterated the crucial motive behind his campaign, arguing that "the license which is municipally allowed to vice" constituted one of the greatest difficulties facing his church and his ministry. And he refused to apologize for his admittedly controversial tactics, except to say "it was the only method by which I could have cut to the quick of this whole corrupt business."

Still Parkhurst now made a significant shift in his attack strategy, from railing against Tammany's depredations to a new emphasis on the police department as the chief culprit—indeed, his statement made no mention of Tammany or any other political organization. He used incendiary language, calculated to arouse the ire of citizens and to taunt the new superintendent as well. Uninterested in convicting saloon and brothel keepers, Parkhurst claimed his only contention was with the "controlling powers of the police department, considered as the guardian of criminality." The NYPD itself was "the criminal par excellence." He urged New Yorkers to join him in fighting the true enemy. The repeated conflation here of the police with criminals anticipated Parkhurst's later coining of the phrase "organized crime," a term which obviously changed in meaning over the twentieth century.

An irritated Superintendent Byrnes struggled to ignore the bait. "What have I to do with Dr. Parkhurst or his address?" he asked a reporter looking for a comment. "I have no controversy with him. I am not Dr. Parkhurst's keeper. He is a clergyman and responsible only to himself for his statements. I don't care to discuss the matter any further."[3]

Parkhurst and his allies continued to cast the blame on what they saw as a hopelessly corrupt Tammany Hall political machine. However, long before Tammany Hall's rise to dominance in the Democratic Party, the police department had been the locus of the city's bruising political life. Even as Byrnes and Williams embodied the modern police—more militarized, more bureaucratic, more professional—they were both shaped by the traditions and fierce political infighting that had defined the force from its earliest days. By the 1890s, even after five decades of expansion and several major restructurings, key underlying continuities with the earlier era shaped police work. None was more important than the fundamentally political nature of appointment to and administration of the force.

New York City had established America's first full-time professional police force in 1845. Distinctively American notions about limiting and diffusing government power, alongside the emergence of universal white male suffrage, produced a very different model of police authority from those of other great cities, such as London and Paris. The belief that municipal institutions should be close to the people, strong antiprofessional sentiments, the republican fear of centralized power, a longstanding distrust of a standing army—all of these contributed to a police force caught up in partisan wrangling from the beginning. New York's first police were appointed for one-year terms, nominated by the aldermen in whose wards they served. By contrast, in London, which established its modern patrol in 1829, the police were an independent agency of the national government, run by commissioners appointed for life. The London force evolved under careful legal and institutional restraints aimed at creating professional public servants who answered to impersonal authority.

Not surprisingly, the city's partisan warfare between Democrats and Whigs badly compromised both police performance and public trust throughout the 1840s and 1850s. In 1853 authority shifted from wards to a city board of commissioners composed of the mayor and two judges, and the police now wore uniforms and could not be removed except for cause. Yet centralization made partisan control of the force easier. After his election in 1854, Democratic mayor Fernando Wood shrewdly exploited his power over police appointments and promotions in building the nation's first urban political machine. The prospect of a job on the force helped attract support from Irish immigrants pouring into the city to escape the Great Hunger. By the early 1860s contemporaries estimated the force of roughly 2,000 men to be half Catholic and three-quarters Democratic. In 1857 the Republican-controlled state legislature moved to curb Democratic power by establishing a new Metropolitan Police District, including New York, Brooklyn, and several surrounding counties, to be governed by a board dominated by gubernatorial appointees. Two police forces—the new Metropolitans and the Municipals, loyal to Mayor Wood—coexisted uneasily for several months. In June, when the Metropolitans tried to arrest the mayor for inciting a riot, a bloody confrontation broke out between the rival forces on the steps of City Hall, spilling over onto Broadway and ending only with the arrival of state militia. A month later the New York State Court of Appeals resolved the crisis by upholding the law creating the new state force.

The new city charter of 1870 returned control of the police to the city, granting the mayor power to appoint members of a four-man board of police for six-year terms. Municipal management of the force was a crucial part of the concerted drive, led by state senator William M. Tweed and a Democratic majority in Albany, to strengthen home rule (and the Democratic Party) in the city. The new charter assigned all real executive power in the department—appointments, promotions, department trials, and dismissals—to the board. In practice the reality of party politics severely weakened that executive power. The custom of maintaining a strictly bipartisan board, with two Democratic and two Republican commissioners, began in 1864 when the state legislature assigned the Metropolitan force control over the city's complex election machinery. Though not a legal requirement, this unwritten understanding acquired the force of law in city politics, guaranteeing further diffusion of power at the top. Rather than eliminate politics from police affairs by keeping the department out of the hands of a single party, the bipartisan principle had quite the opposite effect. It turned the running of the force over to both parties, making everything from appointments and assignments to promotion and punishment part of the spoils to be divided by the city's Democratic and Republican organizations.[4]

The bipartisan bargain brought stability to the force after 1870 and solidified the culture and practices of the NYPD, much of it still recognizable today. The attractions of the job for rank-and-file cops were clear: high wages, pension, and stability. The patrolman annual salary of $1,200 in 1875 (about $26,000 in current dollars) was roughly twice the annual earnings of an unskilled laborer and more than the average earned by such skilled workers as printers, painters, masons, or butchers. Policemen could also look forward to a half-pension after twenty-five years of service. Not surprisingly, applicants for the job far exceeded available positions, which only intensified the value of political "pull." The department attracted recruits with working-class backgrounds; two-thirds of these came from skilled, semi-skilled, and service backgrounds, greatly outnumbering men from the world of unskilled and casual labor. No wonder that by 1890 at least one-third of the force had been on the job for ten years or more.

The entrepreneurial element of police work had been present from the colonial era, through the early nineteenth-century growth of the city, and after creation of the force in 1845. Constables and watchmen had been paid by fees for serving warrants, detaining suspects, appearing in court, and providing special services for citizens. The explicitly political nature of appointment to the early force—at first made annually by the mayor upon recommendations of aldermen from each ward—reinforced the quid quo pro aspects of the work. The promise of doing business on the side no doubt appealed to many job applicants, coming from skilled trades and with business experience, attracted by the prospect of making a good living on the force. Although creation of a uniformed force implied full-time attention to patrol and station house duty, collecting rewards for the return of stolen property was a lucrative sideline, especially for detectives. Byrnes abolished this practice when he took command of central office detectives in 1881. But the custom continued at the level of ward detectives, loyal to captains and operating out of precincts.

The rank and file had already developed a distinctly Irish cast. An 1886 survey of the nationality of 2,936 policemen revealed that fully one-third (974) had been born in Ireland, and at least half of the 60 percent born in the U.S. (1745) were of Irish parentage. Germans (136) constituted the only other ethnic group of any substantial size. In the antebellum years, many middle- and upper-class New Yorkers expressed doubt about the loyalties of such a heavily Irish force in a city being transformed by poor and working-class Irish immigrants. The NYPD's heroic actions during the cataclysmic Draft Riots of 1863, featuring the effective deployment of small groups of cops against large mobs, laid to rest lingering questions about the force's discipline, devotion to the job, and its ability to maintain order. Among cops, collective memory celebrated police performance in those riots as the department's defining (and finest) moment. In 1870 and 1871 the police joined National Guardsmen in protecting Orangemen (Irish Protestants) parading up Eighth Avenue to commemorate the English Protestant victory at the Battle of the Boyne in 1690. These processions enraged Irish Catholics and provoked violent response. The bloody 1871 Orange riot left over sixty civilians dead, one hundred wounded, and a score of injured policemen. The fidelity and reliability of Irish policemen as a class would never again be seriously questioned. By the 1880s, Irish dominance on the force could be rationalized by invoking a comfortable stereotype. "Naturally enough," noted one *Harper's New Monthly* writer patronizingly in 1887, "those in whose constitution habits of subordination to authority have been ingrained by generations of servitude are most watchful and resolute when the enforcement of law is intrusted to their hands."[5]

Other factors distanced the police from their ethnic kin and neighborhood roots. Most police recruits came from the ranks of skilled workers and looked to dissociate themselves from the terribly insecure world of unskilled and casual labor. Frequent changes in precinct assignments meant cops were often strangers in the communities they patrolled. The combination of quasi-military structure and indefinite leadership at the top made the individual precinct captain the key figure and loyalty to him paramount for any cop's career. Finally, the working conditions of the post-1870 police produced an extremely insular job culture that continues to this day. The two-platoon system meant grueling hours and constant shuttling between home and the station house. A typical four-day work cycle meant thirty-six hours on patrol and twenty-eight on reserve; and any number of emergencies (riots, strikes, fires) or court appearances frequently interrupted home hours. Station houses by necessity served as dormitories, where men on reserve slept in spartan quarters and ate bad food, squeezed in among prisoners, homeless lodgers, and the endless bustle of precinct routine. New men learned the job not from the month-long training course or official manuals but from the accumulated experience and knowledge of veterans. Experienced cops honored physical courage and loyalty to other policemen above all and subjected recruits to extreme forms of hazing. The shared risk of death and injury, the feeling of isolation among hostile citizens and unreliable politicians, the sense that they were forever misunderstood—all these shaped the policeman's identity and the unique job culture of the force. So too did the Irish hatred of informers and overlords, exacerbated by centuries of English rule, that helped mold what later became known as "the blue wall of silence."[6]

By the time Byrnes took over in 1892, the NYPD numbered about 3,500 officers, including over 3,200 patrolmen, the overwhelming majority of whom never rose above that rank. They were commanded by 171 sergeants, thirty-seven captains, and four inspectors. Details of Byrnes's early life are sketchy. He was born in Ireland in 1842 and arrived with his parents in New York City as an infant or small boy. Orphaned early, he grew up in the Fifth Ward near the Lower West Side docks and apprenticed as a gas fitter. Like many working-class young men of the day he ran with a local volunteer fire company, quartered on Duane Street. When the Civil War broke out, Byrnes enlisted in the New York Fire Zouaves, a regiment raised from the city's firemen. Little is known about his Civil War service, and Byrnes himself hardly ever referred to it. But his Zouave experience may have taught him valuable lessons for the future. In 1859 Elmer E. Ellsworth, a poor young man of unknown background determined to make a career in the military, had organized the first Zouave unit in Chicago, modeling it after French light infantry that had fought in the Crimean War. Ellsworth's Zouaves adapted the costume of billowing red pants, open blue jacket, and crimson fez cap which supposedly made soldiers quicker and more effective in battle. Ellsworth taught his men highly gymnastic drills and began offering public exhibitions in Chicago to attract financial support. In the summer of 1860, Ellsworth's Zouaves embarked on a tour of twenty American cities, challenging local militia companies to drill competitions and creating a sensation with their colorful costumes and precise, rapid routines. They attracted tens of thousands of spectators, an enormous amount of newspaper coverage, and the ensuing "Zouave craze" spurred the creation of new volunteer Zouave units wherever they went.

When Abraham Lincoln took the White House, Ellsworth, who had clerked in Lincoln's law office, accompanied his friend and patron, the president-elect, to Washington as a bodyguard. After Fort Sumter, Ellsworth traveled to New York, where he raised a regiment of eleven hundred men, including nineteen-year-old Thomas Byrnes and his older brother Edward (made a company Captain), from the ranks of the city's volunteer firemen. They carried with them their reputation for rowdiness, fierce loyalty to their mates, and resistance to discipline. On April 29, 1861, the Fire Zouaves, dressed in fire-red shirts, red caps, gray breeches, and open gray jackets, received a huge and boisterous send-off in lower Manhattan before sailing to Washington, where they were sworn into the U.S. Army as the New York Eleventh Infantry Regiment. Not long after being mustered, the Fire Zouaves received orders to occupy the Virginia town of Alexandria—now a suburb of Washington—and on May 23, 1861, Ellsworth himself was shot dead while trying to remove a Confederate flag from a local hotel. Lincoln arranged for a White House funeral service and Ellsworth received eloquent tributes as the Union's "first martyr." Eight weeks later the New York Fire Zouaves found themselves in the middle of the carnage and chaos of the First Battle of Bull Run. Demoralized by a large number of casualties and desertions, the Fire Zouaves disbanded in the summer of 1862.[7]

Byrnes returned to New York when his regiment broke up and joined the police force as a patrolman in December 1863. Years later he replied bluntly to a reporter who asked his motive: "I became a policeman because it was the best way I saw of making a living." It was not merely the obsessive rigor of Zouave drilling that would serve Byrnes in good stead as a police commander. Ellsworth's canny exploitation of publicity and his cultivation of powerful political friends proved effective strategies for career advancement. Byrnes rose rapidly through the ranks, making sergeant in 1869 and captain the following year, commanding several different precincts over the next decade.

In October 1878 Byrnes confronted the defining case of his career. Burglars pulled off a spectacular robbery at the Manhattan Savings Bank on the corner of Broadway and Bleecker Street, taking over $2 million in securities (over $50 million in today's currency), $250,000 in negotiable bonds, and about $12,000 cash. The bank lay within the Fifteenth Precinct commanded by Byrnes, who was given control of the case by Superintendent George W. Walling. Byrnes identified several suspects by their *modus operandi* and had them shadowed by police detectives for weeks, but he had no evidence linking the conspirators. Eventually one of them, Patrick Shevelin, a bank night watchman, began to show signs of sudden wealth and was taken into custody. He refused to talk for several days, but as Byrnes gradually revealed all that had been learned about the case, and hinted that he knew a great deal more, Shevelin broke down and made a full confession.

The robbery was noteworthy for more than just the size of the haul. The New York police, at their own expense, had done all the work of tracing the robbery and capturing four of the burglars. "The present case," the *New York Times* reported, "is the first one in which men who have committed a bank burglary in New York City have ever been arrested." This startling claim may have been an exaggeration. Byrnes's success nonetheless stood out against the usual disposition of such cases, in which private detectives negotiated for the return of stolen property under circumstances suggesting their complicity. Indeed, a trustee of the Manhattan Savings Bank confirmed that overtures had been made from at least four different attorneys, presumably representing agents of the robbers, for the return of stolen securities. The thieves themselves, it was later shown, had each contributed $600 to pay for the services of a prominent lawyer to go to Washington and lobby Congress against passage of a bill that would duplicate the federal bonds stolen from the bank, which would have rendered worthless a large portion of the take. Nor were bank burglaries the only crimes that routinely went unsolved. Just days after the Manhattan Savings heist, New Yorkers were startled to learn that the coffin of A. T. Stewart, department store magnate and one of the nation's wealthiest men, had been stolen from the graveyard of St. Mark's Church. After two years of complicated negotiations the body was returned for a ransom of $20,000. No one was ever arrested for the crime.[8]

Captain Byrnes thus established himself as an exceptional detective whose achievement owed nothing to the reward system. On March 9, 1880, the board of police placed Byrnes in command of the central office detective force, and shortly after promoted him to the rank of inspector. (That very same day Madison Square Presbyterian installed Rev. Charles H. Parkhurst as its new pastor, a serendipitous portent of their future clash.) Byrnes immediately began a radical reorganization of the inefficient, decentralized system that assigned two plainclothes detectives, or "ward men," to each precinct house. Individual captains selected ward men, making them, in the words of one police official, "simply pliant servant[s] of the commanding officer of the precinct." Precinct detectives resented any interference from the central office and as one manifestation of their local clout frequently served as a captain's "bag man," or collector of bribes. Ward men were well known in the neighborhood by criminals and respectable citizens alike, making them useless for undercover work. Under Byrnes's new system, all ward detectives would be chosen by the Central Office and work under its direction, thus cutting their close ties to captains. In addition, Byrnes would command a new detective bureau from the central office, with handpicked men given the new rank of detective sergeant.

Byrnes's top priority in his new job was to win the confidence of the city's business elite, which understandably had little faith in police detectives. He wanted to establish the superiority of his men over the city's many private detective agencies, which either worked for rewards or charged clients *per diem*. City detectives also had to become in Byrnes's view a more physical presence in the commercial districts. He met with Brayton Ives, president of the New York Stock Exchange and subsequently the exchange's governing committee, and convinced them to subsidize an office at 17 Wall Street, with six to eight detectives stationed there. Every bank and brokerage house in lower Manhattan would be connected to it by telephone. Byrnes publicly announced a "dead line" on Fulton Street, promising to arrest any known thief who ventured below it, thus sealing off the financial district from professional criminals. Several years later Byrnes recalled telling the businessmen, "If I come here and do your work, and do it for nothing and be able to do it better than anybody else (and what I do I am responsible for) you will give me your work after awhile quicker than to a man who is responsible to nobody." Since that time, he boasted, "they have not lost a ten cent stamp in Wall Street by a professional thief; not a penny, not a cent."[9]

Byrnes invented modern detective practice, making crime detection as integral a part of city police work as crime prevention. He insisted his men be thoroughly informed about the lives and whereabouts of the city's criminals. He required detectives to keep diaries in which they recorded the names of all known crooks and their activities wherever they met them. The "morning parade" at Mulberry Street headquarters brought all persons arrested in the previous twenty-four hours before his detectives. Detective Sergeant Thomas F. Adams, one of Byrnes's closest aides, had devised the rotating photographic case familiarly known as the "rogues' gallery," widely copied in police stations around the country. Byrnes instituted the practice of photographing every person arrested in New York City, with the most notorious appearing in the rogues' gallery at police headquarters.

Perhaps most importantly, Byrnes struggled to reverse the negative perception of detective work by eliminating rewards and emphasizing his men's responsibility to the public. Private detectives, compensated largely through cash rewards, notoriously worked in tandem with thieves, blackmailers, kidnappers, and forgers. Byrnes revised the old adage that "it takes a thief to catch one," stressing instead empirical knowledge of the underworld. "The first thing that a detective officer ought to do after becoming a detective officer," he told an 1884 legislative committee, "is to familiarize himself with low criminals; without a detective officer knows criminals, he is almost useless; his knowledge of crime, the way it is committed, is what makes him a power in that business." Byrnes underscored the dangers posed by modern "professional criminals," particularly to the propertied classes, as well as the necessity for a careful typology of criminal methods and behavior. He thereby made the case for a professional detective force and pointed the way toward the twentieth century's redefinition of the primary police function as crime-fighting. He touted new quantitative calculations of success, using statistical comparisons as the surest measure of his achievements. Between 1876 and 1880, Byrnes testified, the detective bureau had made 1,943 arrests, leading to convictions totaling 505 prison years. During the first four years of his leadership, detectives had racked up 3,324 arrests resulting in 2,488 prison years.[10]

In 1886 Byrnes published the landmark *Professional Criminals of America*, featuring over 200 photographs reproduced from the rogues' gallery, mini-biographies, and elaborate commentaries on criminal techniques. Priced at $10, the book was aimed not for the mass market but rather at helping judges, district attorneys, U.S. marshals, and other policemen around the nation. Byrnes presented a kind of class analysis of the underworld, drawing distinctions between "the class of crimes dependent upon brains, adroitness, and address for their success" (forgery, confidence schemes, embezzlement) and "the criminal walks requiring brute force and nerve" (highway robbery, bank burglary, house thieves, pickpockets). Professional criminal life also provided opportunities for occupational mobility. One might begin as a general thief, willing to steal anything from a needle to a ship's anchor. "From that level," Byrnes argued, "he may rise, partly by the force of his own increased knowledge of the practice of crime, partly by his natural adaptability for especial methods of preying upon the community, partly by the advice and cooperation of older criminals with whom he comes into contact, whether at liberty or doing time in a prison."

Critics praised the book for its sober, scientific tone, and for its value to law enforcement. "There will be nothing but facts found in the book," wrote one reviewer, who also praised it for what it was not—"a cheap book with red paper covers and remarkable woodcuts purporting to reveal the lights and shadows of all the mysterious places in the great city of New York." Some also underscored the aesthetic quality of Byrnes's judgments, how "the work of a clever forger or safe burglar is as characteristic as the style of a well known author to a competent critic. Hence Inspector Byrnes's book will be to the police what a literary dictionary is to the student."[11]

Byrnes scoffed at the detectives portrayed in popular writing, dismissing the methods of the fictional Sherlock Holmes and the memoirs of the French criminologist Eugène Vidocq. The disguises in which they specialized were a waste of time. "All this fancied idea of whiskers and paint and things of that kind about detectives is all nonsense—nothing in it—not a thing on earth in it." Yet the world of detective fiction held attractions for Byrnes's keen instincts for publicity and self-promotion. In the spring of 1886, before the publication of *Professional Criminals*, he wrote to the dime novelist Ernest A. Young, offering to make his personal diaries available for "a series of what I believe to be interesting reading matter for the general public." Byrnes told Young he admired some of his books and invited the author to New York in May, offering to pay half his expenses. The two made an agreement that Byrnes would pay Young $500 for each of three projected books, after the writer submitted manuscripts for Byrnes's approval. Negotiations continued over the summer and fall, with Thomas Adams, Byrnes's longtime trusted aide, acting as his agent. The inspector, Adams wrote, insisted upon "the credit of being the author of the best work of the kind that has been produced in this country." After all, Adams told Young, "As you yourself have stated that this was the best material you ever worked upon for a detective story, it must be true." Young's first manuscript, tentatively titled "The Manhattan Bank Robbery," arrived in November and Byrnes found it acceptable and expressed eagerness to see it in print. However, Young's bad health forced him to withdraw from the project before anything was published.[12]

With his appetite for publicity whetted and Young now out of the picture, Byrnes turned to Julian Hawthorne, son of Nathaniel, for the job of ghostwriting. Hawthorne loved Edgar Allan Poe's detective tales and Byrnes struck him as a Poe-like hero. In 1887 and 1888, at the same moment that Arthur Conan Doyle introduced Sherlock Holmes, Hawthorne published five short novels, each carrying the subtitle "From the Diary of Inspector Byrnes." These were early examples of the police procedural or "true crime" fiction and enormously popular, selling more than one million copies combined. They were also each syndicated in some twenty newspapers, and translated into German, Swedish, and Dutch. Their descriptions of Byrnes at work no doubt represented the public face he wanted to project:

And there, at his desk, sits the inspector, examining, weighing, deciding, investigating, advising, reproving, encouraging; cheerful or grave, as the case may be, even-tempered, firm, suave, stern, penetrating, impenetrable; the depository of all secrets, the revealer of none; the man who is never hurried, yet never behind-hand; never idle, yet never weary; always patient, and always prompt. No position under the municipal government requires more tact than his, more energy, more courage, more experience.[13]

Byrnes cultivated this image with the journalists of his day as well, nearly all of whom ascribed his success to cool rationality and a genius for psychology. It's no wonder they did. With his strategic control over information, Byrnes held enormous power over reporters on the police beat, offering (or withholding) tips, always ready with a favor for cooperative writers. Thus the Byrnes depicted by journalists inhabited some ethereal region far removed from the gritty underworld, and he solved cases purely through logic, induction, and sympathy. An 1887 profile in *Harper's Monthly* declared, "Inspector Byrnes in manner is very gentlemanly, insinuating, and invitive of confidence. . . . Crime in his opinion is a fine art, and criminal detection a science." "Inspector Byrnes's imperturbable temperament and his keenness of intellect," another journalist gushed, "enable him to subdue the most obstinate and tenacious prisoner." An English journalist profiling New York's police told his readers that Byrnes and his men were "more of a terror to evil-doers than all the rest of the force—nay, than all the police in America." Even the pioneer muckraker Jacob Riis came under Byrnes's spell while covering the police beat in the 1880s. "The source of his success," Riis agreed, "is his knowledge of human nature and of the motives that sway criminals. It is partly the result of intuition, and partly of hard study." And when it suited his purposes, Byrnes would cast police news in the form of the pulp fiction he publicly scorned. Lincoln Steffens recalled such a moment when, as a cub reporter in the early 1890s, Byrnes announced arrests made in a Fifth Avenue burglary case: "[He] related a detective yarn which was so full of clews, thought, night reflections, and acute reasoning—it was, in brief, so perfectly modeled upon the forms of the conventional detective story, that the cynical police reporters would not write it." Steffens noted that Byrnes seemed to possess a dual temperament. He was affable, even courtly, with reporters, public figures, and businessmen, selecting his language with care. But when he needed to, he switched easily to the slang and profanity of the street, and the intimidating bearing that had served him well as a beat cop.[14]

The reality was far more sordid. Byrnes originated the so-called "third degree" treatment and made it an important part of police routine. He regularly beat prisoners, or ordered them beaten, and routinely engaged in what today would be considered psychological torture of suspects. George B. McClellan, Jr., the son of the Civil War general who later served as both a congressman and mayor of New York, described his method:

> Byrnes usually kept his victim in the cells for twenty-four hours, with nothing to read and very little to eat. He was then brought before the Inspector whom he found writing at his desk. After keeping him waiting until he became intensely nervous, Byrnes would rise, walk up to him, and knock him down. He would then be lifted to his feet and Byrnes would again knock him down. This process would be repeated until the prisoner had become thor-

oughly demoralized when Byrnes charged him with having committed the crime for which he had been arrested. If the prisoner confessed well and good; if not, the knocking down would begin again until the prisoner either confessed or was carried unconscious back to the cells.

Other sources corroborated McClellan's account, but none ever saw print while Byrnes was in office—independent investigative reporting of police methods would not become part of journalistic practice for many years. Euphemism was the rule of the day, as when newspapers reported that a confession had been "forced" from a suspect—the term used to describe how Byrnes himself had obtained the night watchman's admission of guilt in the 1878 Manhattan Savings case. Using journalists as his willing collaborators, Byrnes kept the public from knowing what it did not want to know.[15]

Over time, it was this symbiotic alliance between Byrnes and reporters that produced so many stories of his detective prowess. Consider the case of one of the most notorious murders of the era. On the morning of December 30, 1882, three burglars broke into the West Twenty-Sixth Street shop of Louis Hanier, a French immigrant wine dealer and saloonkeeper. Awakened by the noise, Hanier made it halfway down the stairway from his apartment above the shop, before one of the surprised thieves pulled a pistol and shot him. After staggering back upstairs and shouting for the police, Hanier fell dead across his bed, leaving a widow and seven children. A month later Inspector Byrnes announced the arrest of three young men, including nineteen-year-old Mike McGloin, who had fired the fatal shot and lived only a few blocks away. The case received more than routine press coverage for several reasons: the great outrage expressed by the French immigrant community, a fascination with the youth and callousness of McGloin and his mates, and the real-life detective work that had led to their capture. Three days later a canvass of city pawnshops turned up a revolver that had been hocked for $2 the day after the murder. The bullet taken from Hanier's body matched the gun. The pawnbroker provided a description of McGloin who had already served prison terms for theft and assault and battery. Byrnes learned that McGloin and his friends hung out at a West Twenty-Seventh Street saloon, where he kept them under constant surveillance. One night Byrnes instructed a uniformed officer to post a reward circular in the place. After he left, a detective overheard McGloin ask his companion, "Did I turn white when he hung that notice over my head?" thus convincing the police of his guilt.

Byrnes had the men arrested and held a private interview with McGloin. He gave the young suspect a detailed account of his actions since the murder, showed him the murder weapon, and then fitted the recovered bullet into the chamber. An unnerved McGloin broke down and made a full confession, taken not by Byrnes but by the coroner. Newspapers printed part of it, including a conversation McGloin said he'd had with a friend who had visited him at home the day after the murder: "'Were you there?' I said, 'Yes.' 'That Frenchman is dead,' he replied. 'Oh, go away,' I answered. 'Yes, and you're a "tough" now.' 'Well,' I said, 'a man can't be a "tough" till he knocks his man out.' I then got up and...and got my pistol and pawned it."

A jury took all of eleven minutes to convict McGloin of first-degree murder. His lawyer offered no defense, but sought to dismiss Byrnes's testimony on the grounds that the prisoner's confession had been coerced. The judge took Byrnes's word that he had used no threats or inducements; indeed the inspector had refused to hear the confession, calling for the coroner to take it. A year later, after exhausting all appeals, McGloin was hanged. His sneering attitude, utter lack of remorse, and celebrity status among the many young "toughs" who attended the trial and visited him in the Tombs provoked a great deal of comment. So too did the raucous crowd of several hundred young men and women waiting for McGloin's body at the wake held in his parents' apartment. He evidently maintained his "tough" pose until the end; the night before his execution he allegedly invited Byrnes to "'come over to the wake; they'll have a devil of a time.'"[16]

According to the contemporary sources, here was a case where methodical, patient detective work had captured a killer. Over the years, however, as numerous versions of the McGloin case and Byrnes's role circulated in print, writers routinely reimagined and reinvented it. In recounting the case in *Our Police Protectors*, his massive and highly flattering 1885 profile of the NYPD, Augustine Costello was not content to praise Byrnes's "good judgment, sagacity, penetration and energy." He needed a "eureka" moment. "Three glasses had been found on the counter," Costello wrote, "each containing a small quantity of brandy. The Inspector fastened on this one central clue. His first exclamation was 'It was Hanier's rum that killed him.... They broke into Hanier's saloon more with the expectation of finding rum than money. They drank deeply, and the brandy crazed their brain.'" No mention was made of the pistol found at the pawnshop. In 1892, ten years after the murder and upon the occasion of his promotion to superintendent of the force, Byrnes himself reminisced about the case. Speaking with a *NY World* reporter he emphasized a detective approach that had received no mention a decade earlier. "I got a woman to live with McGloin," Byrnes now recalled, "and through her obtained facts which strengthened my conviction, although he didn't confess to her. She was supplied with money and for a month or more McGloin was wearing my clothes."

In his 1901 autobiography, *The Making of An American*, Jacob Riis embellished the case to illustrate his quite plausible claim that Byrnes was "a great actor, and without being that no man can be a great detective." He had Byrnes struggling for six months to solve the crime (it had taken only a few weeks) before the climactic moment:

> Byrnes put McGloin at the window in his office while he questioned him. Nothing could be got out of him. As he sat there a door was banged below. Looking out he saw one of his friends led across the yard in charge of policemen. Byrnes, watching him narrowly, saw his cheek blanch; but still his nerve held. Fifteen minutes passed; another door banged. The murderer, looking out, saw his other pal led in a prisoner. He looked at Byrnes. The Chief nodded:—
>
> "Squealed, both."
>
> It was a lie, and it cost the man his life. "The jig is up then," he said, and told the story that brought him to the gallows.

By 1928, Herbert Asbury's classic work of pulp history, *The Gangs of New York,* had elevated McGloin to founder of the Whyos, "the greatest of the gangs which came into existence in New York after the Civil War." McGloin, according to Asbury, had killed Hanier with a slung-shot, and he had inspired the Whyo practice of "accept[ing] no man as a member until he had committed a murder." Luc Sante's 1991 bestseller *Low Life: Lures and Snares of Old New York* reiterated this story as part of its uncritical recycling of large chunks of Asbury's book. James Lardner and Thomas Reppetto's *NYPD: A City and Its Police* (2000), a more serious recent work of history, blends elements from both Riis and Asbury for its version of the McGloin case. It's impossible to know what actually transpired in the inspector's office between Byrnes and McGloin, or in any other case for that matter. By effectively coupling his innovations in detective practice to new opportunities for publicity available in the modern city, and through his innovative collaborations with journalists and novelists, Byrnes contributed as much as anyone to a tradition of blurring the boundaries between New York history and mythology and between police work and police fiction.[17]

If Byrnes embodied, at least publicly, the model detective, then his contemporary and rival, Alexander S. Williams, stood out as the city's—perhaps the nation's—most recognizable constable. "I am so well-known here in New York," he breezily told investigators in 1894, "that car horses nod at me mornings." Like Byrnes he astutely cultivated his own mythical persona, using it to advance his career, attract powerful friends, and punish enemies. Perhaps even more so than Byrnes, Williams's long and tumultuous career embodied all the contradictory practices and political intrigue required to police New York. Scratch the surface below the legend and the story of "Clubber" Williams reveals a great deal about the persistent tensions between physical courage and brutality, protected vice and anti-labor violence, disciplined loyalty and police perjury, and the advantages of being a stalwart Republican in a thoroughly Democratic city.

Born in Nova Scotia in 1839 of a Nova Scotian father and Scottish mother, Williams came to New York as a boy and was naturalized there in 1860. He apprenticed as a ship carpenter at W. H. Webb, the shipbuilding company whose yard stretched between East Fifth and Seventh Streets on the East River. The young Williams traveled extensively to Mexico, Japan, and other countries, before returning to work as a contractor for the U.S. government during the Civil War at the New York Naval Yard in Brooklyn. He went into partnership with a shipbuilder, but a ship carpenters' strike forced him out of business—an event that may well have influenced his later violent behavior against picketers and union activists. He joined the NYPD in the summer of 1866, assigned first to a Brooklyn precinct before moving to the Broadway Squad in 1868, a group including the most physically imposing men on the force. Well over six feet tall, broad shouldered, and a fighter by temperament, Williams quickly earned a reputation for physical toughness when he picked fights with some of the more dangerous characters around his post on Broadway and Houston Street. One story from his early years had Williams raiding a rough basement dive on Broome Street and single-handedly holding its thirty-eight occupants at bay with his revolver while another cop went for help. In one journalist's version of the scene, written a few years later, "The steady nerve behind [the gun] held sway over their brutal ferocity. It was a trial of nerve and endurance."

Whether accurate or embellished, the repeated retelling of these stories helped shape Williams's reputation and contributed to his rapid rise through the ranks. In 1871 he won promotion to sergeant and command of the mounted patrol; a year later he made captain, after less than six years on the force. Williams personified a new breed of cop, one who sought out physical confrontations with criminals, thereby making streets and public spaces safer for ordinary citizens. Williams's club, wrote one contemporary profiler, "enjoys the reputation among the roughs of being as hard, ready, and rough as themselves, and is certainly a notable instrument. Its owner is one of the most venomously hated, frequently tried, and most valuable of police officers." As a precinct captain Williams demanded strict obedience from his men—in 1878 the *NY Times* singled him out "the most conspicuously efficient disciplinarian on the force"—but he nonetheless enjoyed enormous respect and fierce loyalty from a rank and file that idolized his fearlessness and swagger.[18]

"Big Alec" embodied a masculine ideal both within and outside the department. In 1877 he founded the Police Athletic Club, outfitted in a gym on Thirty-Fourth Street near Third Avenue, and served as its first president. Some 500 members could get instruction in sparring, weight training, fencing, and running, and Williams himself was an accomplished boxer and wrestler. He organized regular public competitions featuring wrestling, boxing, fencing, and weight lifting, along with bicycling, and walking races. These popular exhibitions drew as many as 5,000 people, with proceeds going to the department's widow and orphan fund. Williams regularly won the most cheers from the thousands who lined the route of the annual police parade, and city politicos and businessmen loved to identify themselves with his legendary physical prowess. Toasting the police department at the annual captains' dinner in 1889, Democratic congressman W. Bourke Cockran typically exulted that "Capt. Williams's single club is equal in effectiveness to a regiment of infantry." Just the sight of his upraised locust, claimed Cockran, was enough to settle any disorder.[19]

Williams became closely identified with the Twenty-Ninth Precinct, which he commanded from 1876 until his promotion to inspector in

1887 (save for a stint as head of the Street Cleaning Squad). Notorious around the city and nation as New York's preeminent vice district, the "Tenderloin" was in fact much more than that. Before the Civil War it was a fashionable suburb where wealthier New Yorkers enjoyed life in elegant brownstones far away from the crowds and commercial bustle of downtown. After the war, however, the neighborhood's character changed dramatically as major commercial institutions—theaters, hotels, and department stores—moved north of Fourteenth Street, driving away many residents and catering increasingly to visiting businessmen, out-of-town shoppers, and patrons of the city's nightlife. By the 1870s and 1880s the Tenderloin included most of the city's leading hotels (Hoffman House and Fifth Avenue Hotel), prestigious social clubs (Union League and American Jockey), theaters (Metropolitan Opera, Daly's Theater), restaurants (Delmonico's), and high end shops (Tiffany's, Lord & Taylor). "No other command," wrote one police journalist, "approaches it in importance as the centre of civilization and all that makes nineteenth century city life agreeable.... Within it are the most frequented streets and avenues, and at night city life for the 'upper ten' alone exists within its boundaries."[20]

The neighborhood's commercial attractions also brought a steady stream of visitors who were rather far from the "upper ten." The biggest of these was Madison Square Garden, the largest indoor entertainment space in the nation and the birthplace of modern spectator sports. Occupying the entire block bounded by Madison and Fourth Avenues and Twenty-Sixth and Twenty-Seventh Streets, it was just around the corner from Reverend Parkhurst's church. With its sixty-five-foot walls and two towers looming hundreds of feet above street level, the Garden dominated the space around Madison Square. Originally the abandoned passenger station for the New York Central Railroad, the newly remodeled Garden opened in 1879, attracting as many as 15,000 people to see everything from dog shows to circus performances to week-long walking and bicycle races.

It was also the birthplace of commercial boxing, a sport it helped make popular despite its ambiguous legal standing. The laws that distinguished bare-knuckled prizefighting (illegal) from "scientific" and legal sparring exhibitions (the kind that the Police Athletic Club sponsored regularly) were fuzzy at best and subject to continuous legal challenges and police surveillance throughout the 1880s. Captain Williams was a familiar figure at

Garden boxing matches of the day, acting as a kind of super referee who had the power to stop a fight if it appeared that a legal sparring contest might degenerate into illegal "slugging," complete with bloody knockouts.

Of course, thousands of men (and a surprising number of women) regularly packed the Garden to see John L. Sullivan, the most popular sports celebrity of the nineteenth century, do exactly that. Sullivan had made his name by traveling cross-country and challenging any local fighter to last four rounds with him in the ring. Staging less frequent bouts before larger audiences proved far more lucrative and also meant less wear and tear. In August 1883, when he took on Herbert Slade, an Australian fighter hyped as the "Maori Giant," Sullivan attracted a huge crowd of over 13,000 described by one reporter as including "every class of the human male animal." The throng of gamblers, financiers, lawyers, pickpockets, bankers, working men, politicians, ex-convicts, and young boys required a force of one hundred police to maintain order. Amidst a blue haze of cigar smoke and dull yellow light provided by hundreds of gas jets, vendors hawked peanuts, lemonade, watermelon, and pictures of the fighters. White-aproned waiters took drink orders from patrons in the more expensive private boxes. Williams, "at whose glance the boldest 'crooks' trembled," ruled the scene with his locust club dangling from his wrist. In the third round Sullivan made one of his famous rushes, knocking Slade to the floor, where he lay with his body half outside the ring. Williams leaped into the ring declaring the fight over, as the frenzied crowd bellowed "Knocked out! Knocked out!" in unison. Disappointed audiences sometimes hissed Williams when he appeared at center ring; he was not only notoriously brutal with his club, he had the power to prevent fight fans from getting what they paid for.[21]

The often repeated story of how Williams named the Tenderloin district became part of the city's folklore. As Williams later recalled, when he was transferred to head the Twenty-Ninth Precinct in 1876 a reporter asked him how he liked the change. "I said, well, I have been living on rump steak in the Fourth precinct, I will have some tenderloin now; he picked it up and it has been named that ever since." According to H. L. Mencken's *The American Language* (1919), the word "tenderloin" described a "gay and dubious neighborhood." Mencken, writing four decades after Williams's encounter with the reporter, gave the quote as: "I've been having chuck steak ever since I was on the force, and now I'm going to have a bit of tenderloin." Whatever Williams actually said is impossible to determine. Mencken's definition became authoritative, even though it cited as its source a *NY Sun* editorial from 1913. Yet Mencken dropped "tenderloin" from later editions; he may have considered the term already archaic by the 1920s.

The origins of the term had been contested before Mencken. Augustine E. Costello, a journalist who knew Williams and wrote widely on police affairs, made a claim to authorship while testifying during the 1894 New York State Senate investigation into police corruption. "I was the author of the word 'Tenderloin'; that has often been disputed; I did not originate it; but it was I that first published it in the *World*." Perhaps Costello meant he was the first to publicize it. Whether or not he wrote about it in the *World*, his 1885 history, *Our Police Protectors*, included a discussion of the "Tenderloin Precinct" in which he mentioned vice briefly but emphasized other unique characteristics., noting that "it embraces nearly all the great caravansaries, parks, clubs, theatres, and stores." Abe Hummel, Costello's attorney and one of the best known criminal defense lawyers in the city, harked back to a bantering moment among a group that included himself, Costello, and Williams, where the captain "jokingly remarked that if I did not behave myself he would take me out of Delmonico's some evening, where he often saw me eating a juicy tenderloin steak. I quickly retorted that the Captain had a juicy tenderloin in his own precinct." Hummel recalled Williams and everyone present laughing heartily, with Costello writing up the incident for the *Herald*. Whatever the actual circumstances, Williams remained forever linked with the term "Tenderloin" and its double meaning as both a specific place and, more pointedly, the lucrative possibilities it presented for police shakedowns, bribery, and graft of all kinds.[22]

But even more than the Tenderloin, Williams's reputation for both physical brutality and personal corruption defined his career and public persona. By 1887, the year he was promoted to inspector, he had accumulated more citizen grievances than any man in the history of the force. His record included 358 formal complaints, 224 fines, 34 reprimands, and 18 departmental trials held before the commissioners. Williams's controversial record could not shake the extraordinary support he enjoyed from key business and political figures. Surviving accounts of Williams's public controversies, especially the highly contentious department trials held at police headquarters, reveal that political influence trumped evidence of wanton clubbing or bribe-taking. They exposed as well the sharp disagreements over the meaning and nature of police power in the expanding metropolis.

In April 1879, for example, Williams stood trial for "conduct unbecoming an officer," an umbrella charge involving five separate cases. The most controversial and serious one held that Williams had brutally clubbed a man and dragged him out of a sporting event without arresting him. On March 10 some 10,000 high-spirited fans packed Gilmore Garden (as Madison Square Garden was then called) for the start of a six-day walking race at the building, cheering, booing, and wagering on the athletes. Outside, a few minutes after the race's 1:00 a.m. start, another 5,000 fans charged the Madison Avenue entrance, broke through the outer doors, spilled into the lobby, and began climbing into the stands. Williams and a dozen of his men waded into the crowd, and, as one reporter described it, "the terrible blows of the clubs rained without mercy on heads and bodies, told at last, and the mob suddenly fell back until the lobby was cleared." William V. Blake, a pottery manufacturer from Trenton in the stands, claimed that he and some other fans had seen Williams club a man and they hissed at the captain, whereupon he climbed into the stands, clubbed Blake out of his box, called him "a damned sneak thief," and dragged him out of the building. Blake produced six eyewitnesses, while Williams countered with more than fifty witnesses of his own, including several police on duty at the time and the referees of the match. Spectators in the jam-packed trial room at police headquarters on Mulberry Street also included many cops in uniform and citizens' dress.

Appearing as Williams's counsel were two of New York's most influential Republicans: Colonel George Bliss was a highly successful corporate lawyer, former U.S. attorney for the southern district of New York, a Republican district leader, and an expert on city and state law. John I. Davenport was the U.S. commissioner and chief supervisor of elections for the southern district of New York, an attorney for the Union League Club, and the national Republican Party's longtime point man on the issue of vote fraud. The revelation that Blake had made his charges in collusion with Commissioner William V. Smith, a Democratic appointee who detested Williams, hurt his case, as did the fact that Smith had them published in the newspapers two days before bringing them before the board.

The most effective defense argument invoked the threat of riot. The police on duty, Bliss argued and many witnesses swore, faced a very unruly crowd; one of the race's judges testified he had asked Williams to put Blake out because he feared he was trying to create a riot. "It must not be forgotten," argued Republican commissioner Joel B. Erhardt in explaining his vote, "that every officer is entitled to credit for any riot he prevents, and that in this case prompt action and watchfulness alone prevented it." The board, on a 2–1 vote, adopted Erhardt's motion dismissing all charges against Williams. "This man Williams is a disgrace to the force," a disgusted *NY Tribune* commented, "and it is amazing to find the commissioners, whose chief concern it should be to preserve discipline, actually 'vindicating' him." The board's majority thought it more important to reaffirm the view, especially dear to most Republicans, that the crux of police power lay in maintaining social order, preventing mob violence, and quelling riots—and that routine brutality against citizens was a small, even insignificant, price to pay.[23]

As early as 1874 Williams had been accused of protecting vice, while commanding the Eighth Precinct (modern SoHo), a neighborhood then known for its large number of prostitutes and interracial couples. The board of education, acting on citizen protests against the close proximity of several brothels to public schools, asked Williams to provide detailed information about the addresses, occupants, and owners of these houses. As part of his regular duties, he had submitted a list of eighty-three houses of ill fame to the superintendent's office several months earlier. At a crowded public hearing Williams defiantly refused to share this information "for reasons best known to myself," and he declined to answer whether he was acting under instructions from police headquarters. He acknowledged only that he did not want to unjustly hurt the property owners who might have sold their holdings since the brothel census had been taken; more likely, he wanted to protect the reputations of prominent landlords who profited handsomely from the high rents paid by brothel keepers. The *Times* denounced his behavior as highly suspicious, against the public interest, and a forceful illustration of "that inordinate vanity and insolent officialism which promoted policemen are too apt to don with their captain's uniform."[24]

Police trials often hinged on the considerable power that police had to intimidate witnesses and to protect each other. In 1875, acting on a complaint made by John Groo, a sergeant who had served under Williams, the police commissioners formally tried Williams for protecting "panel houses" in the Eighth Precinct. Prostitutes would bring their tricks to these places where thieves, hiding behind hollowed-out walls, waited for the chance to rob them. Panel thieves counted on the reluctance of their victims, many of them out-of-towners, to press charges and face publicity; they changed houses frequently, maintaining a permanent floating presence. Groo testified that Captain Williams had instructed him not to enter panel house robberies on the precinct blotter, and not to visit them. Williams denied all this. The fact that Groo had been transferred out of the precinct at Williams's request suggested he had a revenge motive and tarnished his testimony. Williams, acting as his own counsel, took no chances and called over a dozen other cops to the stand, all of whom contradicted Groo's account and supported the captain. The "blue wall" could be effective against other cops as well as citizens.

Another, more troubling, witness against Williams was Ellen Brown, an African-American woman who for several years had occupied the bottom floor in a Mercer Street house before her landlord asked her to move upstairs to make room for a hatter business. The new tenants proved to be panel thieves who ran their scam for six weeks, sometimes escaping by running upstairs through the Browns' kitchen, leaping out the window and over a fence into a restaurant on Houston Street. Ellen Brown reported these goings-on to Captain Williams at the station house but he had ignored her. The next morning, one of the panel thieves knew all about the conversation she had with Williams, and repeated her words to him, adding that "she need not go again to the captain, as he knew all about the panel house." Perhaps the thieves lied about or exaggerated their connections with Williams to protect themselves; either way he tried to intimidate and discredit the witness. After her subpoena to testify against the captain, three men came to Brown and said "'it was no use for her to take any trouble,' as Captain Williams was cognizant of all their plans, and was paid well for not interfering with them." Williams also tried unsuccessfully to pay a friend of Brown's to attack her character by testifying that she had served time in jail and that Williams had once arrested her son for larceny. Williams was unable to shake her story despite an intense cross-examination that ended with him admitting, "You know too much for me; I have no further questions."

Three months later the police commissioners announced their verdict at a heated meeting. A motion to dismiss Williams from the force lost on a 2–2 tie vote. Two Republican members of the board, George Matsell and Abraham Disbecker, declared the charges unproved, while the two Democrats, John Voorhis and William Smith, found Williams guilty.

Matsell, a former superintendent of the force, said he would be sorry to lose an officer with Williams's physical courage and leadership ability upon the evidence of a woman like Brown unless it was fully corroborated. In response, Voorhis and Smith noted that Williams himself, in his 1874 census listing eighty-three brothels in the precinct, had described Brown's second floor apartment as occupied by a respectable family. The case seemed a clear example of how partisan politics could obscure the evidence. The fact that Mayor William Wickham, under public pressure to improve the morale and performance of the force, had just announced his intention to remove Matsell and Disbecker from the board (they vowed to fight it) only heightened the political tensions among the four commissioners.[25]

The board could never free itself of this sort of highly charged partisan wrangling because it operated as a thoroughly political institution. In 1872 the state legislature had given it a supervisory role over the city's election machinery, placing the bureau of elections under police department control. Commissioners selected polling places, established election districts, verified registry lists, and appointed inspectors and poll clerks. On Election Day police oversaw polling places and sent the results to headquarters. Police control over the nuts and bolts of elections had produced the unwritten agreement dividing the four commissioners equally between Democrats and Republicans. The political affiliations of police captains, roughly even in these years, were also of great import to the political parties, making promotions (and dismissals) subject to intense partisan maneuvering. An 1878 profile of the political affiliations of the force's thirty-six captains found thirteen outspoken Republicans, fifteen unequivocal Democrats, and the rest unknown.[26]

Williams was one of the most resolute Republicans on the force, and some of the city's—and the nation's—most prominent Republicans actively defended him against a never-ending stream of brutality and corruption charges. Williams's power and influence continued to grow through the 1880s despite the continual barrage of charges brought against him, often from the private preventive societies. In 1883, for example, agents for the Society for the Prevention of Crime, led by the merchant David J. Whitney, and the Society for the Suppression of Vice, headed by Anthony Comstock, tried to convince the grand jury to bring criminal indictments against Williams and another captain for failing to enforce the laws against gambling. Doubtful of the legality of such a move, the grand jury instead issued a strongly worded presentment, charging Williams with "lamentable incapacity or a shameful neglect of duty," which left it to "public spirited citizens to obtain the evidence which he ought to obtain through his own detectives."

A defiant Williams scoffed at the charges. "This presentment doesn't amount to anything. Why, d—— it, why didn't they make it an indictment? Why didn't they indict me, that's what I want to know." He also hit back by accusing SPC agents of trying to blackmail bartenders, shaking them down for money in exchange for not reporting alleged violations of the excise laws. "I'm not going around giving any information to Whitney or Comstock, or any men of that kind." Williams attacked what he saw as their hypocrisy, arguing that "gambling will always exist and all the police can do is to confine it within as narrow limits as possible." Besides, he sniped, "if they want to suppress gambling why don't they commence on Wall Street, where there is more open gambling done every day than in all the rest of the city in a month." Over the next decade Williams and others on the force, contemptuous of the preventive societies' quasi-legal claim to police power, kept up a steady campaign of harassment, arrest, and public maligning of their agents.[27]

By 1885 Williams's trials had acquired a ritual quality as public political spectacles, exposing the deep splits within the department, as well as the gap between law enforcement and the realities of cosmopolitan life. That year Williams faced trial for failure to suppress gambling houses in the Tenderloin, on charges brought by Superintendent George W. Walling. Williams's defense team now included two more powerful Republicans: Elihu Root, future secretary of state under Theodore Roosevelt and at the time U.S. district attorney for the southern district of New York, and Joel B. Erhardt, United States marshal and former member of the police board. In the trial's most startling moment, Frank Walling, a textile salesman and the superintendent's son, testified about his own Christmas season spree in Tenderloin gambling houses, during which he lost over $500 (about $14,000 in today's dollars). Young Walling went to his father for help and the superintendent evidently concocted a plan, using plain-clothes detectives, singling out Williams as the scapegoat for his son's transgressions. The bizarre circumstances made it easy for Root to declare the whole trial "not merely a prosecution, but a persecution." The *Tribune*, which had declared Williams a disgrace to the force only a few years earlier, now defended him, noting, "Life and property are more secure in his precinct than in some others in which gambling houses exist." More "peace-loving citizens" sympathized with Williams, despite his club-swinging reputation, because "he has made life and property conspicuously safe in his precinct."

As part of his defense Williams's attorneys presented a petition of support from 400 prominent residents and businessmen in the Twenty-Ninth Precinct, including Leonard W. Jerome, the financier and sportsman, Ward McAllister, arbiter of the elite "four hundred," and a long list of bank presidents, real estate brokers, attorneys, department store owners, and theater and hotel managers. They praised Williams's management of the precinct and protested against "any action which shall impair his efficiency by leading evil-doers to believe that he is not earnestly supported by his superior officers." The commissioners voted 3–1 for dismissal of the charges. Police board president Stephen B. French noted the difficulty in obtaining evidence against gamblers and the dubious legality of using plainclothes detectives. He declared, "No officer of the law is to be held responsible for the actual and entire suppression of all crime or of any particular crime." Williams, he argued, had to devote most of his time and energy to "a great multitude of other duties affecting the preservation and protection of life, person and property, and the general order and peace of the community fully as important as, and many of them far more important than, the suppression of gambling houses." After his acquittal, over 500 prominent Tenderloin businessmen and residents honored Williams with a lavish testimonial dinner and a gold-and-diamond-studded memorial album costing $1,500. Two weeks later the police board forced Superintendent Walling to retire.[28]

In the summer of 1887 Williams faced his last trial before the police board. The case resulted from a public campaign mounted against him by the Society for the Prevention of Crime and an allied organization, the Owners' and Businessmen's Association of West Twenty-Seventh Street, charging the captain with permitting brothels to exist on that street and two others nearby. The trial itself resembled a comic opera. Two African-American witnesses evoked derisive laughter when they claimed they could not recollect what they had sworn to in affidavits describing prostitution on West Twenty-Seventh Street. An elderly prosecution witness gave a detailed account of being accosted by streetwalkers on Thirty-First Street, including what they had said to him; but he was too deaf to hear the questions put by Williams's lawyer, Elihu Root. The Owners' and

Businessmen's Association turned out to be a dummy group that never met. Most damagingly, the group's organizer, Jules Chatelan, refused to testify after Root offered to prove that he owned two houses on West Twenty-Seventh Street that had once been leased for brothels, and that he had also provided bail bond surety for Frederika "Mother" Mandelbaum, the city's most notorious "fence" for stolen property. The commissioners refused to force Chatelan to the stand, but the damage to his case had been done. Williams meanwhile calmly summarized the record of hundreds of prostitution arrests his men made each year, and Root called the by-now-standard parade of solid citizens to tell how much Williams had improved the precinct since taking over. Root also called Superintendent William Murray to read a list of reputed disorderly places in the precinct furnished by Captain Williams, under a department rule requiring all captains to submit such lists every three months. Far from regarding this as evidence of negligence, Murray reaffirmed Williams's and the police culture's view that surveillance and quarantine offered the only realistic and efficient way to regulate (and left unspoken, to tax) the vice economy.[29]

That view infuriated the SPC and its allies. Their formal brief against Williams ended with a strident threat to the commissioners, opposing exoneration. "The effect of this course," they concluded, "would be to say to each police captain: 'You may allow vice to colonize in your precinct, to offend decency, to violate the rights of citizens, to interfere with worship, and even close thoroughfares to safe and peaceable travel; you may yourself violate the law which was made to control our force, and we will hold you blameless.'" The police board had different priorities. On August 9 the board considered the nine specific charges against Williams. They voted unanimously to drop two of them and on the remainder split 2–2 along party lines over Williams's guilt—so all charges were dismissed.

Immediately after this vote the board turned its attention to filling two inspector positions that had been vacant for a long time. They quickly worked out a deal whereby one Democratic commissioner, John Voorhis, agreed to support Williams for inspector in exchange for Republican support for Captain Peter Conlin, a Democrat. Voorhis defended his vote even as he acknowledged holding strong prejudices against Williams "aroused by charges that he used his place to advance his pecuniary interests." Yet, Voorhis continued, "I have never had any positive proofs of such charges, and I will not now let my prejudices stand against his long and valuable service." Elihu Root had argued in his brief that the real object of this latest round of charges had been to prevent the promotion. After fifteen years as the most controversial captain on the force, Williams was now one of four inspectors of police, assigned to the First District, covering the entire east side of the city south of 110th Street. The jubilant new inspector received enthusiastic congratulations from rank-and-file cops as well as nearly every hotel proprietor, storekeeper, and businessman in his precinct, who saw his promotion as victory for preserving law and order in the city.[30]

After a quarter century on the force both Thomas Byrnes, the Irish Catholic immigrant and Democrat, and Alexander Williams, the Scottish Protestant and Republican, found themselves at the top of the NYPD's uniformed hierarchy. Their careers reflected both the enormous changes and stubborn continuities marking the force's evolution since the Civil War. The tangled relations between political pull and police business, the local supremacy enjoyed by precinct captains, the symbiotic relationship between police work and the vice economy—these had not changed much since the 1860s, except in scale. The department was much bigger, of course, more bureaucratically ordered, and closer to the military model by the 1890s, and its detective corps had gained an international reputation for professionalism and efficiency. A new responsibility increasingly assigned to the NYPD during the Gilded Age cemented its status among the propertied and business classes and provided the ultimate shield against critics: providing the main bulwark against organized labor and radical activism in the city.

The respect and confidence that Byrnes, Williams, and the department as a whole had earned from these classes—stockbrokers, bankers, real estate developers, manufacturers, merchants, hotel and entertainment entrepreneurs, and many middle-class homeowners—derived from their ruthless, often brutal, suppression of unions and political dissent. During the 1870s the police often broke up political demonstrations deemed threats to the public order by elected officials and their allies on the police board. Police intervention on the side of capital escalated over the last quarter of the nineteenth century. In July 1877, as the great railroad strike swept through Pittsburgh, Chicago, and other rail hubs throughout the nation, the work stoppages and accompanying violence badly frightened the nation's political and business elites.

As exaggerated press accounts denounced the strikers as "communistic and law defying, against all law, order, and civilization," New York's

Workingmen's Party and other sympathizers prepared to demonstrate their support for the strikers at a July 25 rally in Tompkins Square. The city took on the air of an armed camp as the police board expressed fear that city cops might be overpowered by a mob. It deputized 200 employees of the New York Central Railroad as special police, while the mayor called up two National Guard divisions and the Seventh Regiment militia, to be stationed in the harbor and near Wall Street. Meanwhile, the day of the rally a contingent of 1,000 police took up positions near Tompkins Square, with hundreds more held in reserve. The rally itself turned out to be a tame affair, as the looming police presence dampened both the crowd's size and ardor. In the dim glow of calcium lights and gasoline lamps, several thousand people, including many children and bystanders, listened to English and German speakers express sympathy for the strikers, denounce the growing political influence of railroad corporations, and call for a new political party based on the workingman's vote. The *Tribune* seemed disappointed that "the resolutions were only half as inflammatory as it was anticipated they would be; the crowd in the Square was insignificant."

After two hours the meeting adjourned—and just then a force of 300 police led by Inspector William Murray, and another 150 led by Captain Thomas Byrnes, charged in, with no provocation, clubbing everyone in sight. As even the militantly anti-demonstration *Times* acknowledged, "The officers used their clubs rather more freely than necessary....the clubs fell so thick and fast that a large number must have been badly hurt." Still, the *Times* denounced city officials as "white livered demagogues" for even allowing "a pestilent and dangerous section of the population" the right to demonstrate at all. Both Byrnes and Murray received slight injuries from flying bricks. The police role in preventing a New York "commune" became part of departmental lore. Wildly overstating the threat to public order had its political uses as well. As class conflict intensified, growing more violent across the city and the nation, political and business leaders routinely summoned memories of the Draft Riots as justification for unleashing the police anytime they saw fit. Recalling the events of 1877 in a speech seven years later before the annual captains' banquet, former police commissioner Joel B. Erhardt—railroad attorney, U.S. marshal for the southern district of New York, future Republican candidate for mayor—invoked the specter of the Draft Riots when he praised the "power and discipline of the police force [for preventing] a second conflagration, and bloodshed which would have far exceeded the casualties of 1863."[31]

While the police actions in the 1870s largely involved suppressing free speech and the right of assembly in public spaces, by the 1880s the NYPD played a more direct role in crushing strikes, protecting scab labor, and spying on unions. Murray, promoted to superintendent in 1885 at barely forty years of age, was the youngest man ever to lead the force. With his lifelong friend Byrnes he had fought with Ellsworth's Zouaves during the Civil War, suffering a serious leg wound at Bull Run. He had an enviable record of physical courage and thief catching. But his meteoric rise through the ranks owed more to his reputation for instilling rigorous military discipline and his insistence on centralized command. Murray had abolished the old independent inspection districts, bringing the four inspectors to police headquarters as his aides-de-camp, and he established the first censorship of police news. Under Murray the force was much better prepared for confronting militant workers.

In March 1886, drivers and conductors on the Dry Dock streetcar line, desperate to reduce their workday to twelve hours and raise their daily wage to $2, went on strike. The company president immediately asked Murray to intervene. On March 4, thousands of angry strikers and their supporters filled Grand Street from river to river, determined to prevent the running of any Dry Dock streetcars. Murray mobilized nearly a quarter of the entire police force. He stationed 500 men along the street and personally commanded another 250 to accompany a lone horsecar from its East River stable across Grand Street, to the Hudson, and back. When a union leader pleaded with Murray to back off, the superintendent brushed him aside, saying, "I know my duty, sir, and I propose to do it. I mean to run a car across town and back if I live." As the car began to make its way slowly along, demonstrators blocked the tracks with overturned carts, ash barrels, and paving stones, while rocks and eggs rained down on the police from tenement windows. When they reached Allen Street, Murray suddenly yelled, "Charge!" and instantly hundreds of clubs came down on the heads and shoulders of everyone in sight, including well-dressed bystanders and women shoppers. The police, as one reporter put it, "zealously fought off would be intruders as though the Sub-Treasury, with all its millions, had been put on wheels and they had been guarding that." The beatings and street fighting continued for over two hours as the car completed its purely symbolic round trip. An exhausted Murray boasted of accomplishing his mission, and the *Tribune* praised the police for preventing "a pitched battle in our streets which might have revived the horrors of 1863." Others thought the police too lenient, ridiculing Murray's symbolic victory and calling him incompetent for failing to disperse the strikers, whom they lumped together with thieves and ruffians. "It was his duty," the *Times* insisted, "to put every one of them within reach of a club into the hands of the surgeon or the undertaker." Indeed, contemporary illustrations of the day's events, such as a two-page spread in *Harper's Weekly*, highlighted the ferocity of police clubbing in ghoulish detail—presumably what its genteel readers wanted to see. Two days later some 15,000 drivers, conductors, and stablemen from other car lines walked off their jobs in a sympathy strike, tying up the city's entire transportation system. The companies soon broke the union drive through indictments of union leaders and the continued massive police intervention.[32]

Three years later police commanders led by Inspectors Byrnes and Williams demonstrated even more forcefully how keenly the department responded to the needs of capital. On January 29, 1889, some 7,000 streetcar workers went out on general strike, a remarkable act of solidarity for the drivers, conductors, mechanics, and stablemen employed by a dozen or more independent companies. Although specific grievances varied on the different roads (some men earned less than a dollar a day and many worked more than the legal limit of ten hours), the Knights of Labor strike leaders made union recognition by the companies and state arbitration of all disputes their key demands. Even before the walkout, plainclothes detectives under Byrnes's direction infiltrated union meetings and provided Superintendent Murray with detailed information about leaders and planned actions. The superintendent confidently announced the police "can be trusted to keep the peace in the city if they have to fight seven days in a week," and he promised that "we will protect all the street cars in this city if the companies can find drivers and conductors to run them."

The greatest potential for violence was at the Forty-Third Street stables of the Sixth Avenue Company, where employees felt special hatred for a president who vehemently opposed arbitration or any dealings at all with the union. Also known as the "Shoppers' Line," the Sixth Avenue route was critical for the business of department stores, theaters, and other businesses catering to out-of-towners. When only a handful of its 550 employees showed up for work, and as strikers began overturning cars and blockading tracks, Inspector Williams appeared at the stables with a force of 200 police. He quickly sent squads of cops with batons flying into the crowds of picketers, and ordered police escorts on every car. Williams's own fearsome reputation had a quieting effect: "It was necessary only for him to descend to the sidewalk," wrote one reporter, "and the crowd would instantly move away." Ten cars managed to make the run from Fifty-Ninth Street to Canal Street that first day. The next morning the inspector arrived with even more police and delivered a blunt speech to give his men courage and intimidate the strikers: "I want three policemen to ride on the front platform and three on the rear platform. I want you to take this car to Canal Street and bring it back here. I don't want any policemen licked, remember that. Use your clubs if you have to, and make the blows tell. Don't bother about making arrests." Some newspapers published headlines that Williams had ordered his men to use their revolvers and "shoot to kill" if attacked by strikers. Back at headquarters, when questioned about these reports, he claimed to have information that some strikers planned to attack police. "I said to them: 'If the strikers attack you with clubs, use your revolvers.' I am not going back on those words."[33]

Inspector Byrnes was even busier. On the morning of February 2, he took a squad of about fifty police to the Central Crosstown Railroad stables at Twenty-Third Street and Avenue A, putting a man on each car. When a hostile crowd stopped the first car at First Avenue, pelting it with rotten vegetables and stones, Byrnes waded in, helping his men club everyone off the street. Later that afternoon Byrnes and a force of several hundred men arrived at the stables of the Belt Line on Fifty-Fourth Street and Tenth Avenue, determined to take at least one car on its normal route down the West Side to the Battery and back, Byrnes himself took his stand on the platform beside the driver, with about twenty policemen as the only passengers. Two patrol wagons with another fifty men provided an escort for the two-hour, thirteen-mile trip. Byrnes lined the entire route with bluecoats and plainclothes detectives, jostling against a thousand strikers and supporters. Obstructions had been removed from the tracks and the sullen crowds refrained from throwing anything—but organized police violence, no doubt exacerbated by days of street fighting and sleep deprivation, could be provoked by mere words. "The only things encountered that could hurt policemen's feelings," one observer of the scene reported, "were the hisses, cat-calls, and curses of the strikers and their sympathizers. The police are instructed to regard invectives as incitement to riot, and many a noisy striker was laid low by a blow from a detective before he knew what had hit him."[34]

On February 5, 1889, a week after it began, union leaders called off the great "tie-up," described by the *Tribune* as the "greatest fight...of organized labor which has ever occurred in this city, as far as the number of men is concerned." The refusal of company owners to negotiate or accept arbitration, the union's nearly empty treasury, the trickling back to work of some strikers desperate for work, the immediate hiring of strikebreakers—all these factors contributed to defeat. But the entire police force—on active duty or in reserve—loomed over it all. It was not simply the many hundreds of cracked skulls and broken limbs. In many instances policemen literally helped run the streetcars, managing the brakes while inexperienced scab drivers looked after the horse teams. Superintendent Murray curtly dismissed the striker's request for a rally at City Hall. "No matter how well disposed and law abiding you may be," he told their committee, "such a demonstration would be likely to provoke a disturbance." At company stables, police guarded the clusters of Italian and other strikebreakers, many of them literally just off the boat and escorted from Castle Garden, the immigrant receiving center in Battery Park. An angry committee from the city's Central Labor Union met with Mayor Hugh Grant, charging that "the police under orders from their superiors have used violence such as no other civilized country would tolerate." They saw nothing less than a conspiracy between the railroad corporations and police officials. "The police of the city," they argued, "are for the protection of life and property of the citizens generally and not for the purpose of intimidating law-abiding citizens or to aid private corporations in their private speculations to crush laboring people and force dividends for stockholders." The mayor politely dismissed the CLU men. He surely felt more comfortable with the report made two weeks later by Superintendent Murray, singling out the work of Byrnes and his detectives for special praise, and commending the intelligence, endurance, and courage of the entire force. "They were a unit in suppressing this trouble," Murray wrote, "nor can any disturbance be imagined during which they will not be fearless and loyal."[35]

As the careers of both Byrnes and Williams demonstrated, the essence of police power and prestige, and the invulnerability its leaders believed they enjoyed, emanated from three decades of increasingly efficient, militarized, and ruthless protection against "riot," broadly construed. In 1882

NYPD officers inaugurated the tradition of an annual dinner attended by captains, inspectors, the superintendent and a couple of hundred of their guests. It reflected the increasingly military outlook of an officer class, and their growing social distance from the foot soldiers/patrolmen under their command. A sumptuous affair held at Delmonico's, where as many as 600 bottles of wine might be drained, the dinner was also a ritual affirmation of the broad support the department enjoyed from the business and political elite of New York and the nation, an affair bringing together, as one reporter put it, "more men who are widely known than are gathered together at any dinner that is given."

At the 1892 dinner Chauncey M. Depew, president of the New York Central Railroad, soon to be senator from New York, and the most popular toastmaster of his era, underlined the historical foundations for confidence in the police. "In any emergency, however great," he intoned to long and loud applause, "in any danger, however imminent, in any crisis, however critical, in the history of this city, the New York police never have failed to do their duty and win a victory for law and order and public safety."[36]

Now, as the Rev. Charles Parkhurst launched his unprecedented attack on Thomas Byrnes, Alexander Williams, and the entire NYPD, the police and their allies would make sure to highlight that historic reputation as the most effective defense against charges of corruption, bribery, and brutality.

3

· · · ·

DEMOCRATIC CITY, REPUBLICAN
NATION

On June 1, 1892, just a few days after his triumphal appearance at the Cooper Union mass meeting, Charles Parkhurst, his wife, Ellen, and several of her relatives boarded the White Star liner *Germanic* for a three-month vacation. Parkhurst was an avid mountain climber and headed for the resort town of Vevey, on the northern shore of Lake Geneva. After six weeks amid the Swiss Alps—to which he made a pilgrimage every year—Parkhurst also visited Paris, London, Manchester, and Birmingham to investigate the social conditions in those cities. "There is no political significance to this movement, though it is a strong movement," he had insisted back in May, referring to what was called the City Vigilance League, founded as an organization of young men pledged to municipal reform and now claiming several thousand members. "Our object is to elevate the standards of citizenship and to educate men to those standards."

When Parkhurst returned to New York in late September he seemed oddly uncertain about his plans. He told reporters eager for a statement that he was not planning on going into politics, or turning the Civil Vigilance League into "a political machine." The League would not run candidates for office. "My fight is against the criminal collusion of police and other municipal authorities with the criminal classes of the city." Yet the minister also acknowledged that the battle could never be won except at the polls. And more pointedly, he maintained, it could only be won by a complete overthrow of Tammany Hall.[1]

Whatever complications Parkhurst faced in expanding his movement, one factor above all forced him to put it on hold: the upcoming 1892 presidential election. For almost six months—between his European vacation and the November polling—New Yorkers heard very little from Parkhurst. He essentially suspended his crusade, believing that the hyper-partisan politics of the era, defined by party identity and voter loyalty, could suck the oxygen out of any self-styled nonpartisan campaign. Parkhurst was not wrong. The 1892 national election, pitting former president Grover Cleveland against sitting president Benjamin Harrison, demonstrated the persistent grip of Civil War–era divisions on the nation's political life a full generation after Appomattox. Fundamental questions about who could vote and how those votes were tallied, especially in large cities like New York, only amplified partisan differences.

Most all Americans celebrated partisanship in the Gilded Age, and this was the most important political fact of the era. Partisanship meant loyalty to the two great parties and their histories, and a strong belief that government by party was the only way to hold people responsible for what they did in office. Republicans exulted in their heroic role during the Civil War, never missing a chance to hail the preservation of the Union or to honor Grand Army of the Republic veterans. Their key national concern was maintaining high tariffs to protect American industries like iron, steel, mining, and sugar refining, thereby guaranteeing (so they claimed) a high standard of living for workers. Republicans also defended the gold standard and "hard money" as critical for national prosperity and defending the interests of banks and other lenders. They opposed growing calls to expand the nation's currency by using silver along with gold to back the dollar. Currency reformers, including some Democrats and the new Populist Party, believed that "free silver" would put more money in circulation and spur inflation, thereby relieving the many farmers and small businesses anxious for debt relief.

For Democrats the national focus was on free trade (which they claimed would lower prices for all), as well the spirited defense of "personal liberty," limited government, and local autonomy. Democrats were badly divided regionally, and once the Republicans abandoned voting and civil rights for African Americans after 1877, "the race problem" became a

Southern one, best handled by white Southerners, nearly all Democrats. The axis of politics, especially in big cities, was more closely tied to ethnocultural identity than to what we would today call "issues." Both Democrats and Republicans believed in the power of patronage as the lifeblood of party organization: jobs, appointments, the spoils of victory in exchange for votes. Election campaigns, especially presidential contests, reinforced partisan identity through highly ritualized public displays: torchlight parades, "monster" rallies, and endless speechmaking. All these activities received highly detailed coverage in the nation's newspapers, most all of which were either subsidized by or maintained close editorial ties to one of the two parties. No wonder that party regulars reviled proponents of nonpartisanship (like Parkhurst). For them party loyalty trumped all, and "Mugwumps" who sat on the fence—their Mug on one side, their Wump on the other—invited challenges to their patriotism, their loyalty, and their manhood. They were political amateurs who rejected the grand traditions of the two-party system.

Partisanship informed every aspect of political life, including the critique of so-called "machine politics." Generations of journalists and historians, focused on exposing the often-colorful excesses and depredations of Tammany Hall, have obscured a larger truth: In New York "machine" politics was a bipartisan affair. The use of the term "machine" to describe political organizing dated from the 1840s, when the confluence of industrialization, mass immigration, and white manhood suffrage reshaped urban political life. It was most often used as a pejorative expression by people unhappy with the growing voter clout of recent immigrants and working-class men. Criticism of "machine politics" became a common rhetorical practice, reflecting the sharp partisan differences of the era: we have an organization, you have a machine; we have leaders, you have bosses. There were in fact two parallel machines in Gilded Age political life. The familiar machine, the one whose power and influence have been traditionally demonized, was Democratic, city-based, with a largely ethnic and working-class clientele organized around municipal patronage. The other machine, rural-based, with a middle-class, Protestant (including African-American) clientele organized around federal patronage for everything from post office appointments to Civil War pensions, was Republican.

The 1892 presidential contest would reveal two trends in New York politics. One was the transformation of Tammany Hall into the enduring face of the Democratic Party. Electing and re-electing a mayor in 1888 and

1890, winning control over the main municipal offices, expanding its influence throughout the judiciary and city bureaucracy, and perfecting a more centralized and efficient approach to getting voters to the polls, Tammany effectively ended a half century of factional strife among city Democrats. Beyond the city, Tammany looked to expand its influence over the state and national Democratic Party. The second trend, which magnified New York City's growing clout on the national scene, was New York State's emergence as the country's ultimate swing state. In an era when the two major political parties were very closely matched, and razor thin margins often determined presidential elections, the state's thirty-six electoral votes were decisive. The contest between incumbent Republican president Benjamin Harrison and former Democratic president Grover Cleveland epitomized the extremely tight partisan balance of Gilded Age politics and the pivotal role of New York.

In 1884 Cleveland, the first Democratic president elected since before the Civil War (and one of only two Democrats elected between 1856 and 1932), had carried New York State by fewer than 1,200 votes out of more than 1 million cast. In 1888 Harrison defeated Cleveland despite losing the national popular vote. His narrow margin in New York—13,000 votes out of over 1.3 million cast, an edge of less than one tenth of one percent—meant victory in the Electoral College. New York State's strategic importance meant a reversal of the old adage: in New York City, all politics was national. And since the NYPD supervised the bureau of elections, partisans of all stripes viewed police politics as inseparable from the national contest. Both Superintendent Byrnes and Dr. Parkhurst quickly discovered how far Tammany's tentacles reached into everything from police appointments and promotions to the regulation of saloons and the wider vice economy of the city.

By 1892 Tammany Hall was already a century old and had finally built itself into the city's dominant political force. Critics such as Dr. Parkhurst might assert that it existed only for "plunder and corruption," a judgment shared not only by many of the minister's contemporaries but also by the preponderance of journalistic and historical accounts. Yet the Tammany "machine" was a far more complicated phenomenon. To consistently win city elections, make policy, and control patronage required disciplined organization, creative financing, multi-ethnic and -class appeals, popular campaign techniques, and strategic alliance building. Tammany success owed a great deal as well to the peculiarities of American politics and the yawning gap between what city government could offer and the desperate needs of too many New Yorkers. Its enemies argued that Tammany's hold on power had always been rooted in consistent and widespread vote fraud. Yet that explanation ignored Tammany's appeal to voters and its expanding influence in the city and state.[2]

Founded in 1789 as a patriotic and fraternal organization, the Tammany Society had been named for a mythical seventeenth-century Delaware Indian, and it adapted pseudo-Indian rituals and terms in its affairs ("braves" for followers, "sachems" for leaders, "wigwam" for its headquarters). It entered the political arena in 1800 by supporting Aaron Burr for president, as well as several local Democratic politicians. When the society applied for a state charter as a charity, critics objected to its political activism. In response, the society created a separate political organization, the General Committee of the Democratic-Republican Party (later just Democratic Party). It quickly became better known as Tammany Hall, after the building it met in. The Tammany Society and Tammany Hall were technically two organizations sharing a home, one an exclusive club, the other open to all voters who wished to join. The society controlled access to the building, but the real power lay with the general committee and the leader it selected.

In the 1840s Tammany aggressively courted the Irish emigrants fleeing the horrors of the Great Famine. Between 1845 and 1855 some 1 million Irish perished from starvation, malnutrition, and disease. Another two million left the country for good, including roughly 1.4 million to America, the vast majority settling in East Coast cities. The famine is now understood as a profoundly international catastrophe that, among many things, transformed New York City's working class and political culture. By the mid-1850s about 85 percent of the city's laborers and three-quarters of its domestic servants were Irish-born. In 1855 immigrant Irish constituted one-quarter to one-half of the total population in sixteen of New York's twenty-two wards; more than a quarter of the total population in both Manhattan and Brooklyn was born in Ireland. By the 1880s a full 40 percent of New Yorkers were of Irish extraction, either immigrants or first-generation Americans.[3]

Tammany determined to make good Democrats of them all. It did this by encouraging naturalization for the Irish and by fighting back against the city's deep currents of nativism and anti-Catholicism, often erupting in the form of gang warfare in the streets. It opposed calls for immigration restriction, supported universal white male suffrage, and demanded the abolition of imprisonment for debt, thereby winning the lasting loyalty of generations of Irish New Yorkers. Searing memories of the Great Famine also pushed Tammany to demand a greater role for government in protecting the poor from starvation and eviction, and to act as an informal hiring hall for job seekers.

The use of the term "machine" to describe political organizing dated from the 1840s, when the confluence of industrialization, mass immigration, and white manhood suffrage reshaped urban political life. It was most often used as a pejorative expression by people unhappy with the growing voter clout of recent immigrants and working-class men. In 1854 Democratic merchant Fernando Wood became the first mayoral candidate to harness the Irish vote, winning election and re-election largely on the strength of the immigrant working class. He appointed Irishmen to the police force and other patronage jobs, called for aiding the unemployed with public assistance and public works, and opposed state efforts to impose prohibition and ban Sunday drinking. After a falling out with Tammany and its new rising star, William M. Tweed, in 1858 Wood founded a rival Democratic organization, Mozart Hall, the first of several factional challenges to Tammany's dominance.

Indeed the bitter factionalism that wracked the city's Democratic Party throughout the 1850s benefitted the nascent Republican Party, particularly upstate. Intraparty disputes and personal feuds among aspiring politicians fueled a never-ending procession of party primaries, nominating conventions, and mass meetings. Organized violence frequently marred contests for the array of local elective offices, from aldermen and assembly district leaders to judges and congressmen. The instability, strong-arm tactics, and ever-shifting alliances all stemmed from the bedrock Democratic belief that all men (at least all white men) deserved equal rights. No matter what faction they might belong to, Democrats celebrated what they saw as their Jacksonian heritage: local autonomy expressed through frequent elections and a limited executive power, a weak judiciary, and belief in the wisdom of public opinion for guiding political behavior. Small wonder why the political game attracted so many ambitious young men, especially immigrants, in a city where economic and physical growth rapidly outran the weak, decentralized grasp of municipal governance.[4]

During the Civil War, William M. Tweed rose to "boss" of the Hall. Born in the city in 1823, the last old stock American to lead Tammany,

Tweed and his small army of district leaders, block captains, and neighborhood heelers appealed directly to Irish Catholics, feeding, clothing, and housing poor immigrants and the unemployed. He looked to expand the reach of municipal government by building more orphanages, public baths, almshouses, and hospitals, while fighting in Albany for greater home rule for New York City. The Draft Riots of July 1863 constituted the most violent and destructive civil rebellion in the nation's history, including at least 105 people killed, many millions in property damage, and brutal attacks upon the city's African-American population. In the aftermath, Tweed brokered a bipartisan deal that helped restore social peace. As a member of the Board of Supervisors, Tweed administered a $3 million bond issue (nearly $58 million today) raised to buy substitutes for exempted conscripts, including poor men with dependent families and municipal police, firemen, and militia members.

A large new red brick, marble-trimmed Tammany Hall opened in 1868 on Fourteenth Street near Third Avenue, symbolizing its growing influence in city, state, and even national affairs. That summer, decked out in spectacular bunting and decorations, the Hall hosted the Democratic National Convention, which nominated New York governor and former "Peace Democrat" Horatio Seymour to run against Ulysses S. Grant. Seymour went down to defeat, but managed to carry the state by a margin of exactly 10,000 votes. Tammany's candidate for governor, Mayor John Hoffman, won by a huge margin, as did its mayoral candidate, A. Oakey Hall. Tweed himself won re-election to the Board of Supervisors (to go along with his seat in the state senate), and, more importantly, a unanimous vote as the grand sachem of the Tammany Society, cementing his hold over both the political and social wings of the organization. Tweed had also amassed one of the largest real estate empires in the city. With control of the mayor's office, a governor in Albany already being touted as Grant's opponent in 1872, Tweed and Tammany enjoyed unprecedented influence, extending far beyond lower Manhattan. None of this was lost on Republicans. After electing Grant, capturing both houses of Congress, and setting in motion what came to be known as Radical Reconstruction in the defeated South, the Republican Party looked to deploy federal power to rein in Tammany.

The election of 1868 featured unprecedented levels of organized vote fraud by New York Democrats (as suggested by Seymour's margin of victory). Shortly after the election the Union League Club (ULC), which had begun investigating fraudulent naturalizations in the city, petitioned Congress to launch a broader inquiry. Founded in 1863 to support the Union cause, the ULC quickly emerged as a political and social base for the city's wealthy and mostly Protestant Republicans. The House appointed a special committee led by Ohio congressman William Lawrence that held hearings in the city and throughout the state in December and January. In late February 1869 the committee presented the most highly detailed account to date. The Lawrence Committee defined and documented a wide range of fraud in New York politics. Its report employed hyper-partisan language that both echoed Civil War–era divisions and reverberated over the next generation and indeed into the twenty-first century. As a result, the charge of "vote fraud" became a kind of permanent "bloody shirt" in American politics.[5]

The most startling finding was that more than 41,000 people had received naturalization papers from municipal and state courts a few months before the 1868 election, and as many as 68,000 may have acquired papers illegally or inappropriately. In the previous twelve years the courts had naturalized about 9,000 new citizens annually. One court "processed" some 2,000 new citizens daily, and thousands of aliens received citizenship papers without a hearing of any kind. The report detailed "every known crime against the elective franchise": aliens receiving illegal or fraudulent certificates of naturalization; certificates of naturalization granted to fictitious persons; many hundreds of voters engaged in "repeating"; names voted and counted illegally in the canvass of ballots. It duly noted the national implications, as "election frauds in one great city may decide the political majority of a Congress, of a State, or of the nation in a presidential election." The report saw nothing less than conspiracy on the part of Tammany and the entire Democratic Party, "a systematic plan of gigantic proportions, stealthily prearranged and boldly executed, not merely by bands of desperadoes, but with the direct sanction, approval, or aid of many prominent officials and citizens of New York."[6]

These allegations were never subjected to cross-examination or common-law rules of evidence, and no judicial hearing or official legal judgment ever established exactly how many illegal certificates were issued. The witnesses, records, and documents produced at the hearings closely followed the Union League's own private investigation, and Tammany officials did not cooperate with the committee. The Democrats' minority report overlooked the Republicans' findings, offering instead a racialized perspective on partisan motives. It contrasted the "spirit of hostility to persons of foreign birth, and of opposition to their free admission to the enjoyment of citizenship and suffrage" to Republican support for the freed people of the South. White immigrants were "in intelligence, industry, morality, capacity for self government, and even loyalty, immeasurably superior to the emancipated negroes of the south." If blacks could be advanced in a single leap from slavery to suffrage, "Let the Irish and German immigrants be treated with at least equal liberality. The most effective guard against fraud in naturalization and voting is to throw open the door of welcome to them." Thus the Democrats answered accusations of racism with charges of nativism.[7]

From the Republican perspective, the badly compromised city and state courts and the failure of state and municipal voting laws demanded congressional action, a national approach to curbing the excesses of Tammany. This led directly to a new federal elections law that established the power of the national government to regulate voting. The Lawrence Committee recommended far-reaching changes in the nation's election and naturalization laws, and these became a vital part of the so-called Enforcement Acts passed by Congress between 1870 and 1872. The emerging Republican majority designed these laws to protect the constitutional rights of freedmen under the newly enacted Fourteenth and Fifteenth Amendments to the Constitution. But Republicans also wanted to weaken Democrats in their urban North strongholds, especially New York City, and they included new federal regulations over elections to achieve this end. The first Enforcement Act, passed in May 1870, defined false registration, repeating, ballot box stuffing, and preventing eligible voters from voting as federal crimes if committed in congressional elections. In July 1870 Congress passed a Naturalization Act, aimed at curbing the traffic in illegal naturalization papers. That law also gave U.S. Circuit Court judges and U.S. marshals authority to appoint federal election supervisors and deputy marshals in congressional elections if a request were made for them.

After the 1870 elections, with New York Democrats re-electing Governor Hoffman and Tammany Hall tightening its grip on municipal and state offices, the Republican Congress moved to strengthen federal regulation. A second Enforcement Act in February 1871 (also known as the Federal Elections Law) authorized each federal circuit court, upon petition of two citizens, to appoint as chief supervisor of elections a United States commissioner for each judicial circuit. As the only permanent, year-round office created, the chief supervisor would be the real administrator: creating a federal registry list of eligible voters, observing elections, challenging voters thought to be ineligible, and scrutinizing the counting of ballots. To these ends, supervisors were given the power of arrest and the assistance of U.S. marshals and their deputies. All violations found, whether of state or federal laws, were considered federal offenses under the jurisdiction of federal courts. Crucially, these new federal election laws applied only to cities with more than 20,000 people. And with sixty-one of the sixty-eight American cities of that size located in the North, the new federal election regime thus created a powerful mechanism for Republican regulation of the largely Democratic urban vote.[8]

The key "enforcer" was John I. Davenport, who until the law's repeal in 1894 presided over a vast and well-funded Republican federal election machine. Like the Enforcement Acts themselves, Davenport embodied a combination of fierce partisanship and idealism rooted in antebellum abolitionism. Born in Brooklyn in 1844, where his pastor was Henry Ward Beecher, Davenport proved something of a boy wonder, working as a stenographer, court reporter, and newspaper correspondent while still in his teens. He studied law and during the 1863 Draft Riots volunteered as a special deputy to help keep the peace. That year he also covered Lincoln's Gettysburg Address for the *NY Tribune*. In 1864 he was commissioned as lieutenant in the First U.S. Colored Cavalry and then became an aide de camp to General Benjamin Butler. Davenport had impressed Union commanders with his careful and accurate reports on the enemy's strength. Reviewing one of Davenport's estimates on the condition of Robert E. Lee's army, General Grant called it "a more accurate roster of the strength of Lee's army than I believe Lee himself has." After the war, admission to the New York bar, and work for several leading Republican politicians, Davenport served as attorney for the Union League Club and lead investigator for the 1868 Lawrence Committee inquiry into New York vote fraud. He in fact wrote large portions of the Enforcement Act statutes relating to voting in the cities, and in 1871 a federal judge appointed Davenport U.S. commissioner and chief supervisor of elections for the southern district of New York.[9]

For the next twenty-three years Davenport's work demonstrated an entrenched prejudice against cities and urban voters, creating a political dynamic that turned the fight against vote fraud into the act of voter suppression. Davenport openly expressed his contempt for the city's voters, routinely contrasting the largely Republican voters of upstate New York—"plain, temperate, substantial farmers, possessed of intelligence, discrimination and industry"—with the mostly Democratic voters in the neighborhoods of lower Manhattan, whom he described as "degraded, intemperate, ignorant and criminal in character." Between 1871 and 1894 federal appropriations for elections officers approached $5 million (more than $100 million in today's dollars), one half of which went to New York State alone. Early on Davenport focused on creating a federal registry in New York City, and in 1872, to complete that task, he convinced President Grant to transfer $34,000 (nearly $700,000 in today's dollars) from a Secret Service fund, originally appropriated as part of the Ku Klux Klan Act. (The Act had expanded the president's power to suppress the KKK and its attacks upon Southern black voters.) In addition to overseeing a federal registry every two years, Davenport concentrated on identifying and challenging an estimated 24,000 bogus certificates of naturalization still in circulation from the 1868 frauds. He might summon individuals to appear before him or publish in the city press names of those holding questionable certificates. By 1878 Davenport claimed to have reduced the number of illegal naturalization certificates in circulation to 12,000, estimating that only 1,200 were used for illegal voting that fall. Most provocatively, before every election Davenport would prepare warrants and announce that those holding false certificates would be arrested at the polls. If anyone tried to vote in defiance of Davenport's order, he would be hauled off and stripped of his naturalization papers. Over the years, these biannual rituals of false arrest, detention, and voter intimidation also played to Tammany's strength as self-styled protector of the city's immigrant, working-class voters.[10]

Tammany had its internal crises as well, none greater than in the summer of 1871. Newspaper revelations demonstrated that William M. Tweed had amassed a huge personal fortune and concentrated enormous political power by holding multiple offices and surrounding himself with a small coterie of allies known as the Tweed Ring. He made bitter enemies both within Tammany and outside of the Democratic Party. After the sensational exposures of the Ring's corruption—mostly through kickbacks from construction projects and city bond issues—Tweed fell from power. Forced to resign his city positions and replaced as Tammany's leader, Tweed was eventually convicted of embezzlement. After years of legal wrangling and a brief escape from the Ludlow Street jail, Tweed was recaptured and died in prison in 1878.

In the aftermath of the Tweed scandals, Tammany Hall reorganized under the leadership of "Honest John" Kelly, an educated, genteel son of Irish Catholic immigrants. He worked with reform-minded "swallowtail Democrats" (nicknamed for the long frock coats they wore), such as corporate attorney and future presidential nominee Samuel J. Tilden, iron manufacturer Abram S. Hewitt, and the banker August Belmont, in an effort to cleanse Tammany of Tweed's taint. Kelly established a new framework for the Tammany machine, at least in theory. At the top was "the boss," chair of the executive committee comprised of district leaders from each of the city's assembly districts (or ADs), the key unit for Tammany's organization. Every AD was subdivided into election districts, each with roughly 400 voters, and these in turn were broken down into individual blocks and even tenement houses. The district leader appointed election district and block captains, who were expected to know and serve the needs of voters and families under their charge. District leaders, theoretically elected but in practice appointed by "the boss," used the power of the organization to make or break elected officials—everyone from aldermen and assemblymen to state senators, judges, and congressmen. The prospects of ambitious election precinct and block captains rose or fell on their ability to meet the needs of their constituents, as reflected in election results. Thus Tammany grafted the world of rural Irish villages—tight boundaries, stable social relations, and constant surveillance of village elders—onto the work of New York's precinct politics. "Only men from such a background," as Daniel Patrick Moynihan, the scholar and senator, once observed, "could make an Assembly district their life's work."

To finance campaigns, Kelly systematized the collection of an annual percentage of the salaries of officeholders and required an "assessment" from candidates seeking election. To strengthen party finances Kelly pursued alliances with real estate developers, contractors, and other businessmen, such as the wealthy importer W. R. Grace, who in 1880 was elected as New York's first Irish Catholic mayor. Most importantly, Kelly separated the purely political work of the Tammany Hall from the social and fraternal activities of the Tammany Society, and he tightened Tammany's hierarchical structure along the lines of the Catholic Church, another American institution dominated by the Irish. (Kelly's marriage to the niece of New York's Cardinal John J. McCluskey made the connection flesh.) Yet Tammany's chain of command was never as disciplined or cohesive as critics claimed. During his fifteen years as leader Kelly could not prevent ambitious local leaders emboldened by Tweed's fall from bolting from Tammany. Powerful rival groups within the city's Democratic Party, such as the Irving Hall, Mozart Hall, and County "Democracies," effectively prevented Tammany dominance. And especially during gubernatorial and presidential campaigns, it was all too easy for local leaders to "knife" Democratic candidates by failing to support the top of the ticket. Tammany was not yet synonymous with the Democratic Party.[11]

The creation of a more dominant and efficient Tammany was the legacy of Richard Croker, who succeeded Kelly after his death in the spring of 1886. A Protestant Irish immigrant raised in an East Side shantytown, a machinist by trade, a fearsome pugilist by reputation, and a Democratic Party "shoulder hitter," he had been elected alderman in 1869 and coroner in 1872, a position with potential yearly fees of $25,000 (approximately $500,000 in today's dollars). But Croker's political career stalled after his indictment and imprisonment for an election-day murder committed at the close of Abram Hewitt's 1874 congressional campaign. After a controversial trial that ended in a hung jury, Croker began a slow climb to the top of Tammany Hall. He became Kelly's most trusted aide, and held a series of appointed offices, including collector of taxes, city marshal, fire commissioner, and city chamberlain (responsible for maintaining financial records).

A taciturn man with a forceful personality and a violent past, Croker redefined the profession of politics in New York during the 1880s and 1890s. Under his direction the tradition, common to Democrats and Republicans alike, of financing campaigns by "assessing" candidates for office gave way to a more centralized system of contributions from corporations, contractors, and liquor dealers. Alliances with major segments of the city's business community, especially public utility companies, expanded the domain of jobs at Tammany's disposal. A greater emphasis on capturing government sinecures and controlling what came to be known as "honest graft"—that which made use of inside information—gave the organization an even greater stake in top-down control and discipline. A city-wide network of local Tammany clubs, begun in the late 1880s and modeled on the techniques of Henry George's 1886 United Labor campaign for mayor and the city's socialist sub-culture, increasingly tied political loyalties to the social and family lives of members. Croker's accomplishments could be measured in a number of ways: He enjoyed unprecedented success in electing Tammany candidates to city and state offices; he destroyed Tammany's rival factions; he was the politician most reviled by the largely anti-Democratic press of his era; he made a fortune largely through real estate speculation; and he died in 1922 a multimillionaire horse breeder in his native Ireland.

Croker strengthened Tammany with two key strategies. One was to decentralize patronage among the two dozen district leaders, ensuring greater personal loyalty to him and tamping down potential rebellions. The second was his commitment to "pushing young men to the front," as he put it, thus making membership in Tammany an attractive path to upward mobility. By encouraging young men, Croker argued, "all the smartest lads will crowd around you, and naturally. You are giving them the chance they want today, while the other fellows only promise it next week." More broadly, Croker claimed for Tammany the critical (and conservative) role of turning urban immigrants into Americans. "Think of the hundreds of thousands of foreigners dumped into our city. They are too old to go to school. They are alone, ignorant strangers, a prey to all manner of anarchical and wild notions....And Tammany looks after them for the sake of their vote, grafts them upon the Republic, makes citizens of them in short; and although you may not like our motives or our methods, what other agency is there by which such a long row could have been hoed so quickly or so well?"[12]

In an 1892 *North American Review* essay, "Tammany Hall and the Democracy" (probably ghostwritten by the Tammany lawyer and orator Bourke Cockran), Croker scoffed at the Hall's many critics and hammered home the theme of politics as "aggressive warfare." Tammany owed its electoral success to efficient organization, common purpose, respect for chain of command, and loyalty of the troops. Administering the vast complexities of New York required skillful men who must be compensated. "The principle," Croker argued, "is precisely the same as that which governs the workings of a railway, or a bank, or a factory....Now, since there must be officials, and since these officials must be paid, and well paid, in order to insure able and constant service, why should they not be selected from the membership of the society that organizes the victories of the dominant party?" Croker's analogy here underscored the Tammany creed that politics was a business, a profession demanding seven days a week, year-round attention to the needs of voters.[13]

One of the young "hustling" politicians Croker pushed to the front was Timothy D. "Big Tim" Sullivan, who embodied the popular style and political success of Tammany. Born in 1862 to parents who had fled the Irish famine, Sullivan grew up in the worst tenements of the Five Points and the East Side's Fourth Ward. At age seven Sullivan started working at the old *Commercial Advertiser* on Nassau and Fulton Streets, bundling papers for delivery at a $1.50 per week. He also worked as a bootblack in the 4th Precinct police station house on Oak Street. By age eighteen he was a wholesale news dealer, handling five different newspapers, establishing connections all over the city, and gaining a local reputation as a leader and patron of poor newsboys. Politics beckoned as a natural career choice for the ambitious teenager who had spent so many of his days and nights roaming around City Hall, Newspaper Row, the Tombs prison, and the local police station. His intimate knowledge of the streets at the center of New York's government and commerce made him a useful errand boy to the local Democratic leaders. Six feet tall and weighing two hundred pounds, with a handsome face, bright smile, and piercing blue eyes, Sullivan's physical presence was an asset in a day when local political careers frequently began as extensions of masculine prowess or athletic skill.

Sullivan began his political career in 1886 not in Tammany but in the rival "County Democracy" faction, winning election to the state assembly from the second district at age twenty-four. The County Democracy had been founded in 1881 by politically active merchants, bankers, and lawyers prominent in the city's economy. Known as "Swallowtails"—after their fondness for frock coats—their leaders included nationally prominent men such as financier William C. Whitney (later Secretary of the Navy under President Cleveland) and the iron manufacturer and congressman Abram S. Hewitt. Tammany and County Democrats sometimes traded off support for their respective candidates, and Sullivan, with his strong local following and the support of these two factions, easily won election and re-election to Albany. Ethnic pride (and resentment) propelled Sullivan and many other New York Irish into the Tammany orbit in the late 1880s. In the highly charged mayoral campaign of 1886, Abram S. Hewitt, running with the support of both county and Tammany Democrats, had defeated Republican Theodore Roosevelt and United Labor Party candidate Henry George. Once in office, however, Hewitt committed a series of political blunders, marking him as anti-labor, anti-immigrant,

and elitist. In particular, he outraged New York's Irish community by refusing to follow the tradition of reviewing the annual St. Patrick's Day
Parade. Unhappy with the County Democracy's re-nomination of Hewitt
in 1888, Sullivan joined a growing number of public officials who bolted
to Tammany. That year, the Hall elected Richard Croker's close friend
Hugh J. Grant, a wealthy liquor dealer, to the first of two terms as mayor,
and the disintegration of the County Democracy cemented Tammany's
hold on the city's Democratic Party.

Big Tim's rise also owed something to a public spat with Police
Inspector Thomas Byrnes in 1889. Angered by Sullivan's opposition to an
assembly bill that would have given police the power to jail on sight any
person who had ever been arrested, Byrnes denounced the young politician in the press, calling him the boon companion of thieves, burglars,
and murderers. Sullivan angrily and tearfully defended himself on the
Assembly floor, increasing his standing with downtown voters. In later
years Sullivan would proudly recall how Byrnes's attacks "made a man
of me."

In 1892 Richard Croker made Sullivan the leader for the new Third
Assembly District, a populous, polyglot area, bisected by the Bowery, and
not previously a Tammany stronghold. Sullivan won election to the State
Senate in 1893, and concentrated on creating the powerful fiefdom that
would dominate lower Manhattan. By 1895, the *Tammany Times* hailed
him as "the political ruler of down-town New York," and "the most popular man on the East Side." Tammany's enemies grudgingly acknowledged his district to be "the most perfectly organized and the strongest in
New York." Power in Tim Sullivan's machine emanated out from "the Big
Fellow" himself and a tightly knit group of literal and figurative kin, each
of whom became a political force in his own right. Big Tim's election to
the state senate in 1893 solidified the Sullivan machine's control of the
Bowery district, a sprawling, multi-ethnic area of some 300,000 people
crowded into the tenement-lined streets surrounding lower Manhattan's
busiest boulevard. Late-nineteenth-century observers had long noted the
distinctly German flavor of Bowery life, but other languages, increasingly
heard in the theaters, tenements, and shops, reflected the new immigration to Manhattan's Lower East Side: Yiddish, Italian, Chinese, Greek.
Tammany Hall remained distinctly Irish, as reflected in the overwhelming
number of Irish district leaders and patronage appointees, but how to organize new immigrant voters and make them regular Democrats in the

face of strong Republican and Socialist appeals was the central political task facing the Sullivan machine.[14]

Operating out of a modest three-story clubhouse, Sullivan hitched electoral politics to the commercial flash of the Bowery. His organization effectively socialized portions of the vice economy, particularly gambling and the alcohol trade, to support welfare activities in his district. Carnivalesque summer "chowders" gave tenement dwellers a much appreciated escape to the country. Although these summer excursions were by no means invented by Sullivan, he transformed them into extravaganzas, remembered by future presidential nominee Al Smith and others as always the biggest Tammany affairs of the year. As many as 10,000 five-dollar tickets might be sold; but the great majority of those who came did not pay, obtaining their tickets from saloonkeepers, businessmen, and others who bought them in large bunches as campaign contributions. In the depression winter of 1893–4 Sullivan also started the tradition of offering the poor a free Christmas dinner. Later he began giving away shoes and wool socks every February to as many as 6,000 people, who lined up for blocks around the Bowery clubhouse. Sullivan's charity was famous for making no distinction between the deserving and the undeserving, no home investigations, no questions asked. "Help your neighbor, but keep your nose out of his affairs," Sullivan said, explaining his creed. "I stand with the poet of my people, John Boyle O'Reilly, against the charity that only helps when you surrender the pride of self respect: 'Organized charity, scrimped and iced/ In the name of a cautious, statistical Christ.'" And as a successful entrepreneur invested in vaudeville and burlesque theaters, amusement parks, and later, motion pictures, Sullivan amassed a personal fortune by pleasing his public in entertainment as well as in politics.[15]

Sullivan thus established his base among those New Yorkers most vulnerable to the worst economic and social insecurities of metropolitan life. But Sullivan's operation was not all bread and circus. It meticulously organized the Bowery neighborhood, using scores of loyal election district captains, each of whom might be responsible for an area containing hundreds, even thousands, of people. A large number of the captains were Germans, Jews, and Italians; many were attorneys, liquor dealers, merchants, or other prominent members of the community. Big Tim himself often led groups of workers on early morning treks to uptown public works sites, making sure men got the employment he had promised them. He regularly visited the city prison and local police courts, offering bail money, the promise of a job, or simple encouragement to petty thieves, vagrants, and others down on their luck.

Sullivan's machine, like Tammany itself, rested upon a version of the American work ethic and a notion of service that turned the ideals of genteel reformers upside down. The Sullivans were nothing if not dedicated businessmen, political entrepreneurs eager to chalk up success to individual initiative. "All this talk about psychological power and personal magnetism over man is fine business for pretty writing," Big Tim observed, "but when you get down to brass tacks it's the work that does the business." The Tammany leader was successful precisely because he worked at his business on the Fourth of July and Christmas, tending year-round to the personal obligations that translated into votes on election day. As his chief lieutenant and cousin Timothy P. "Little Tim" Sullivan once explained it, "The kind of political activity that shows itself in public letter writing, in personal exploitation, in speechmaking, does not appeal to the 'common people,' to the man who wants to work, to the family in trouble, to the neglected widow, to the children sentenced to 'half time' at school, to the homeless stranger, to the young man on the threshold of life with so much against him, to all the strugglers against the hard conditions of competition."[16]

These were the New Yorkers for whom the Democratic machine provided at least some relief from the harsh realities of city life. Through the post–Civil War years of dynamic population growth, Tammany thrived by capturing the votes and loyalty of a large fraction of the newcomers pouring in from Europe and from American towns and farms. It was strongest in the sprawling tenement districts that had grown up on Manhattan's Lower East and West Sides, in neighborhoods that matured around railroad and ship yards, factories, gas works, and other magnets for immigrant labor. By 1880 over 600,000 New Yorkers lived in 24,000 tenements, each of which housed anywhere from four to a hundred families. Overcrowding kept getting worse, as in one Mulberry Street tenement that housed nearly two hundred people in a building meant for twenty families. Thousands of tenements were in terrible sanitary condition, with defective plumbing, and often no ventilation or sewer connections. Above the first floor, water was unavailable in many, contributing to the scourge of diarrhea, which every summer killed over 3,000 children below the age of five. By 1890, the housing reformer Jacob Riis reported, as many as 1.2 million of New York's 1.6 million people lived in 37,000 tenements. "The other half" had grown into the "other three-quarters."[17]

For the city's propertied elite, the problem lay in universal manhood suffrage itself. As recently as 1877 an alliance of capital-owning New Yorkers had banded together to support an amendment to the state constitution that would have in effect disenfranchised about half of New York voters. Their ranks included many pillars of the city's wealth and respectability: iron manufacturers Peter Cooper and John B. Cornell, corporate lawyers William M. Evarts and Simon Sterne, bankers Joseph Seligman and Levi P. Morton, merchants William E. Dodge and John Jacob Astor, and conservative intellectuals like the journalist E. L. Godkin and the historian Francis Parkman. Governor Samuel J. Tilden had appointed twelve men from the state's business and legal elite to a bipartisan commission charged with proposing reforms in the structure of municipal government. They recommended an amendment to the state's constitution, creating a board of finance to oversee all taxation, expenditures, and debt, and elected by New Yorkers who paid taxes on property with assessed value of at least $500, or who paid yearly rent of at least $250. In a city where even skilled workers could expect to take home between $400 and $600 a year, with less than 20 percent going to rent, as many as half of the laborers, mechanics, clerks, salesmen, and small shopkeepers would be excluded from municipal voting. Tammany and the city's burgeoning labor movement led the opposition to the amendment, which failed to pass the New York state legislature in early 1878.[18]

By the 1880s Tammany's opponents had abandoned efforts to restrict the franchise through legislative or legal means. But attacks upon the urban vote generally and Tammany in particular would continue for many decades to come. At the same time, critics from among the elite excoriated genteel New Yorkers for remaining above the political fray. As Henry W. Bellows, a leading Unitarian minister, as well as founder and president of the United States Sanitary Commission during the Civil War, put it: "The ignorant and vulgar, the lawless and violent classes in America, are not so much to blame for their injuries to the American character and the hopes of free institutions." Rather, the failure was due to the "indolence and fastidiousness" of the upper classes. "They expect the blessing of good government without being willing to expend the care it demands." Bellows, a founder of the Union League club during the Civil War and a staunch Republican, also expressed a racial dimension of the municipal vote. "If none but self-seekers or aspirants to office are to be interested in elections," he warned, "what can keep us from falling into the hands of a race not our own?" For Bellows and his allies, fear of the Irish vote and Irish-dominated urban machines ran as deep as any white Southern planter's horror at the prospect of former slaves possessing the franchise.[19]

The conflation of Tammany with "the ignorant and vulgar, the lawless and violent" hardened into the rhetorical maxim of anti-Tammany politics. E. L. Godkin, who had been a member of Tilden's reform commission, put it most baldly when he declared in 1890 that the most important issue of the age was how the country's great cities would manage under universal suffrage. He distilled the views of many propertied New Yorkers and elite opinion-makers—the sort of people who made up Parkhurst's congregation—when he condemned the emergence of "criminal politics" in urban centers. Godkin, an Irish Protestant lawyer and journalist, had emigrated to America in 1859, founded *The Nation* magazine in 1865, and later edited the *New York Evening Post*. A leading voice of conservative principles—laissez-faire economics, limited government, the gold standard, civil service reform—Godkin had become a relentless critic of Tammany Hall. Godkin's definition of the criminal class included not only thieves, burglars, fences, gamblers, and brothel keepers, but those "who share political spoils with them . . . and are willing to profit in politics by their activity." Tammany Hall's strength—and that of every other urban Democratic political machine—lay, according to Godkin, in "the control it exerts over the ignorant, criminal, and vicious classes."

Even influential reformers had to acknowledge the hard political realities of New York life, and Godkin was not above offering bribes himself. Just before "Criminal Politics" appeared, the *Evening Post* had published *Tammany Biographies*, a pamphlet purporting to catalogue the criminal connections and shady pasts of several dozen Tammany leaders and elected officials. Civil judge Peter Mitchell (accused of being a "fence" for stolen goods) and Bernard F. Martin, deputy commissioner of public works (portrayed as a boon companion of thieves) both obtained warrants to have Godkin arrested for criminal libel. When a policeman showed up at the editor's house one Sunday morning with a summons to appear in court, Godkin impulsively offered him $5 to go away and return later. The grand jury refused to indict Godkin, and responses to his actions reflected the sharp partisan divisions of the day. Godkin, claimed the *New York Sun*, "has more than once been exhibited as a mendacious and malicious slanderer." The *Evening Post*, according to the *New York Tribune*, had "performed a valuable service when it photographed our municipal rulers for its rogues gallery." Nor was Godkin so high-minded when it came to trimming his own political sails. In 1892 he threw his support to Democrat Grover Cleveland for president, and the *Evening Post* stopped publishing any Tammany biographies.[20]

The larger point here is not Godkin's hypocrisy but rather the disconnect between anti-Tammany rhetoric and the Hall's resilience. Even the most upstanding, genteel, and wealthy New York Democrats—"Swallowtails" like Abram S. Hewitt and William C. Whitney—understood the political necessity for allying with Tammany, both for business and political purposes. Without Tammany's formal endorsement and organizational muscle, Hewitt would have not been elected mayor in 1886, defeating the insurgent labor candidate Henry George and the young Republican Theodore Roosevelt.

Some critics offered a more structural view of the problems posed by "machine politics," an analysis based on the peculiarities of the American electoral system rather than emphasizing the supposed criminal or racial character of Tammany's constituents. William M. Ivins, a prominent attorney, former city chamberlain, expert on New York's financial affairs, and a leading figure in the anti-Tammany County Democracy, demonstrated how election laws had in effect turned political parties into permanent legal entities subsidized by public funds. Writing in 1887 he noted that the 1872 state law regulating the registration of voters had evolved into a long and complex statute with 92 sections. The law directed the police board to establish and oversee a bureau of elections charged with enforcing the intricate rules and regulations. These included preparing the registry of voter names and addresses; dividing the city into election districts (EDs) containing roughly 250 voters each; and furnishing the necessary registers, books, maps, forms, oaths, certificates, and ballot boxes. Every year the police board also appointed four inspectors of election and two poll clerks for each ED, to be divided equally between representatives "of different political faith and opinion on State issues."

This system produced substantial patronage opportunities. Inspectors and poll clerks received $7.50 per day (more than $200 today) for their work during registration periods and on election day. The city paid for all of these expenses, and for the election of 1886 Ivins estimated the total cost to be $242,000 (about $6.4 million in current dollars). During presidential election years, the amount approached a half million dollars. Although statutes covered the apparatus and costs of conducting elections, the law said nothing about the printing and distribution of ballots at the polls. This was the private affair of parties, not the business of the state, an enormous expense and a practical deterrent to independent movements for reform.[21]

In the months leading up to the 1892 election, as he responded to Parkhurst's campaign, Thomas Byrnes aggressively tried to put his own stamp on the police force. On the eve of the minister's May 25 "monster rally" at Cooper Union, the new superintendent surprised the police board and everyone else with a report detailing his successful enforcement of the laws against gambling, drinking, and disorderly houses (brothels) during his first two months in office. Byrnes offered a barrage of statistics: nearly 150 brothels raided, over 200 gambling houses and policy (numbers) shops closed, some 756 arrests for excise law violations. He credited his new system, requiring inspectors and captains to submit daily and weekly reports directly to him. At the same time, he delivered a report to the police board in which he challenged both the efficacy and moral basis of the laws regulating New York's vice economy, publicly voicing the disdain of the police subculture toward enforcing the unenforceable. Was it really a good idea to close brothels and thus scatter prostitutes among the respectable people of the tenements? "It might be better for the health and morals of the city," Byrnes argued, "to localize houses of this character in certain well recognized quarters where the evils could be regulated by police supervision, as is now the case in some of the leading cities of Europe."

Did current excise law, especially the ban on the Sunday saloon trade, have any real meaning when it was unpopular with so many New Yorkers "who entertain the belief that it interferes with their rights and privileges?" How could uniformed patrolmen be held responsible for the persistent lawbreaking of licensed liquor sellers when the courts and magistrates routinely failed to punish them? High-stakes public gambling houses might be eliminated, but what of the small time bookies, numbers runners, crap games, and floating card games in thousands of beer saloons, cigar stores, and neighborhood groceries? Unwilling to stir up more controversy by considering the so-called "continental" (or European) system for controlling vice, the police board received Byrnes's report in stony silence, filing it without discussion.[22]

The police board preferred a less controversial way to counter Parkhurst's attacks. A week after the new superintendent took office in April it announced, with Byrnes's consent, the transfer to new precincts of every one of the 35 captains, and the remanding of 44 ward detectives, to patrol duty. The press described the "Great Shake-Up" as the biggest since the department's founding and emphasized its nonpolitical nature; every captain, regardless of his political affiliation, would be reassigned. And by demoting the majority of ward detectives, who traditionally served as collectors, or "bag men," for their captains, Byrnes simultaneously struck against the most visible neighborhood symbols of police graft and furthered his goal of controlling all detective work from the central office. Still, even some who expressed high hopes for the new superintendent viewed these moves skeptically. Parkhurst's crusade centered not on excise law violators, gamblers, madams, and prostitutes per se but on the systematic, regular police toleration of lawbreaking in return for tribute. And that practice, as the *Times* argued, "could not have attained its present proportions without having countenance from the powers that are above the superintendent."[23]

Byrnes himself soon discovered this truth. He ordered tighter enforcement of the excise laws and on April 24, the first Sunday of the new regime, police arrested 120 saloon owners and bartenders for illegal sales. If nothing else the crackdown revived the intense debate, dormant for some years, over excise laws and the contradictions of enforcement in a modern cosmopolis. The new arrests were all well and good, doubters pointed out, but the district attorney's office already had a backlog of some 5,000 indictments for excise violations, gathering dust in office pigeonholes. Many of these arrests, observers noted, were made by plainclothes cops despite the fact that seven months earlier the Police Board had passed a resolution banning the controversial "spy system." Reporters wandered through the city to see if they could get a drink, filling newspaper columns with colorful tales emphasizing how "those in the know" might be whisked through locked side doors to hoist a few—as long as they were personally known by edgy saloonkeepers. At the fashionable hotels and restaurants, waiters insisted those looking for a drink order food to make their drinking legal. A large contingent of German workers and their families crowded the ferries to Hoboken, forced to flee the city to enjoy the traditional Sunday outing at the beer garden.

The new crackdown was therefore met with cynicism on all sides. One Tammany alderman and saloon owner underlined the resentment felt by many working-class New Yorkers. "You can get a drink on Sunday at the Union League Club, the Manhattan Club and at the Broadway hotels," he complained, "but you cannot get a swallow of beer on the east or west side of the city." Many thought that the element of danger and sport now involved in getting a dram increased rather than decreased the amount of drinking. "Even the members of Dr. Parkhurst's church," the *Sun* sneered, "could share in the exhilaration by patronizing the bars of their clubs, and the strangers who went to take a look at the sensational preacher were able to brace themselves up at their hotels on returning from the exhibition." When questioned about Sunday enforcement, one bemused police captain explained that only two people out of eleven went to church at all in New York, "and one of those is a Catholic, who goes only in the forenoon. Most of the nine and the Catholic in the afternoon propose to enjoy themselves on Sunday, and they will have something to drink. How in thunder the one man who believes in praying and singing and sitting in the back of the house with the blinds closed all day Sunday is going to hold the other ten in check I don't see."[24]

Popular skepticism over excise laws could not alone explain why Sunday arrest totals dropped from 120 to 70 and then 52 over the next two weeks. Byrnes's zeal for law enforcement brought him smack up against the powerful political influence of liquor dealers and saloon owners. The city had over 9,000 licensed liquor sellers and through various organizations they wielded enormous clout, especially within Tammany Hall. If, as nearly everyone conceded, each seller could be counted on to furnish three votes besides his own, that meant a solid bloc of 36,000 votes—roughly 12 percent of the city's total of 310,000 voters. And the saloon business had a valuable ally in James J. Martin, president of the board of police commissioners and Tammany leader of the so-called "silk stocking" Twenty-First Assembly District in midtown.

A classic Tammany professional politician, the bald and mustachioed Martin shared a similar background with Byrnes. He had been born in Ireland in 1846, arriving in the city with his family as a toddler. Educated in public schools and by the Christian Brothers, Martin quit school at age fourteen to work as a Wall Street law clerk. Shortly after the Civil War broke out Martin, all of sixteen, ran away to join Hawkins's Zouaves (New York Ninth Infantry Regiment), one of the many Zouave units that had sprung up in imitation of the Ellsworth's Zouaves with which Byrnes had served. Some sources later claimed that Martin returned to the city with his unit and helped suppress the Draft Riots in July 1863. But since his regiment was mustered out in May 1863 this seems unlikely. Even if false, the story's persistent retelling is itself noteworthy: The claim that Martin had helped put down an insurrection closely identified with the immigrant Irish poor could go a long way toward establishing respectability for a politically ambitious, Irish-born Tammany Democrat.

While many professional politicians of his era began as "shoulder hitters," exploiting their muscle and physical prowess, Martin chose a different path to power. Working during the war at the New York headquarters of General John A. Dix, Commander of the Department of the East, he made himself a professional clerk. After the war he joined the anti-Tweed forces within the Democratic Party and became a protégé of John Kelly, Tweed's successor as leader of Tammany Hall. Martin held a series of appointed clerkships within the city's growing financial bureaucracy, sinecures that allowed plenty of time for political work: second deputy controller, secretary to the board of commissioners for the revision of assessments and taxes, and deputy register. Martin also served as Tammany's chief lobbyist in Albany. By the time Mayor Hugh Grant appointed him to the police commission in 1889 he had emerged as part of the small group of insiders that dominated the Hall's affairs. That appointment had itself both reflected and reinforced Tammany's growing ascendancy in city politics. By naming Martin to replace Republican commissioner Stephen B. French, Mayor Grant violated the unwritten law, observed for twenty years, that ensured a balance of two Republicans and two Democrats on the police board. Martin's appointment gave Democrats a three-to-one advantage.[25]

Byrnes's determination to enforce the excise laws during his first weeks in office as superintendent produced what would be the first of several high-profile clashes with Martin. On Saturday, April 30, with Byrnes out of town on business, Martin met with Chief Inspector Henry Steers, acting temporarily as executive officer of the force. Martin reminded Steers of a resolution adopted the previous fall by the commissioners, forbidding the use of plainclothes police to get evidence of excise law violations. Martin had pushed the resolution through in response to pressure from organized liquor dealers who alleged that plainclothes cops routinely resorted to extortion and blackmailing their customers. The resolution expressed disapproval "of any action on the part of the force partaking of the character of sneaks or spies, or of acting in a surreptitious manner in the discharge of its duties" and forbade the police from taking bribes. Steers dutifully assembled all the captains and related these instructions, which they understood as an order to ease back from the aggressive campaign enforcing the ban on Sunday drinking.

Upon his return Byrnes struggled to balance indignation over Martin's devious maneuver with his reluctance to challenge superior authority. Byrnes told reporters that withdrawing plainclothes cops set up "a great hindrance to the strict enforcement of the excise law." Yet he denied any rift with Martin or the Board and promised that the police would enforce every law, "in uniform if they can; if not, otherwise." Newspapers pounced on the story as proof that the superintendent and the president of the police board were at loggerheads, and as disturbing evidence of Tammany's intention to achieve unprecedented control of the NYPD. Byrnes received strong support from the press. The anti-Tammany *Tribune* contrasted him with Martin: one a brave, determined public servant, a "man of commanding ability [who] could double his salary any day by entering the service of private employers," the other "one of the worthless and shabby crowd of dependents upon the bounty of Tammany Hall who would starve to death if they were not supported by the city treasury." After several days of this sort of pounding, Martin publicly backed off. Following a long meeting with Byrnes, Martin disavowed any intention of interfering with the superintendent's power, and claimed that the resolution banning the use of plainclothesmen in excise cases was not an official order but merely advisory in character. Byrnes also maintained that there was agreement. His training, temperament, and military background made him wary of openly bucking the power of the police board, as well as the wider Tammany organization, especially as he had only been on the job for a few weeks. This first confrontation between Byrnes and Martin ended in a stand-off at best.[26]

The entire affair offered a clear reminder that a half-century after its creation, the New York City Police Department's legal lines of authority remained ambiguous. Could an individual member of the police board, or the board as a whole, give direct orders to the force or its members? Martin clearly thought so. Charles F. MacLean, another Democratic commissioner, argued that while the law authorized the police board to formulate rules, orders, and regulations, the board as a whole (let alone an individual commissioner) had no authority to give orders to the force. In the wake of this controversy MacLean moved to rescind the so-called "spies resolution." Martin and John C. Sheehan, another of the Tammany commissioners, argued that the resolution was not intended to interfere with enforcing the excise laws but rather to discourage police blackmail. John McClave, the lone Republican on the board, noted that even if the resolution had been intended to improve discipline on the force, the public clearly believed it interfered with enforcement of the law. The motion to rescind lost on a 2–2 tie vote. Immediately afterward, just in case anyone doubted the political ramifications of all this, the Tammany General Committee of the Seventh Assembly District announced that Commissioner MacLean's name had been stricken from its rolls for failure to pay dues. Reporters asked the man who proposed MacLean's expulsion to explain its meaning: "Construe it as you please," replied Bernard F. Martin, Tammany leader of the district and brother of police board president James J. Martin.[27]

The confusion over who had ultimate authority in the NYPD—the superintendent or the police board—hovered over the national political landscape. The extremely close partisan balance of Gilded Age politics was never clearer than in the contest between incumbent Republican president Benjamin Harrison and former Democratic president Grover Cleveland. As in 1884 and 1888, the New York vote promised to be both close and pivotal. Now, as Election Day 1892 neared, a violent clash between municipal and federal authority loomed. The old partisan oppositions of the Civil War–era, refracted through the new realities of urban life, threatened to explode once again at the city's polling places and on its streets. Some 8,000 U.S. deputy marshals, operating under the authority of federal election inspectors, stood ready to challenge a 3,500-member police force increasingly dominated by Tammany Hall. Neither Parkhurst nor Byrnes, no more than the city itself, could escape the national implications embedded in New York's local politics and by extension its underground economy.

By the time Reverend Parkhurst had returned from his vacation in late September 1892 the presidential campaign was in full swing. With reporters pressing him for his plans, Parkhurst gamely insisted he remained apolitical even as he called for "the complete overthrow of Tammany Hall." This was the only way, he argued, that the city could end "the system of protecting the criminal classes by the very men who are put in office to suppress them." He now left the daily operations of the Society for the Prevention of Crime to others so he could concentrate on building his newly created City Vigilance League (CVL). The idea was not to run candidates for office but rather to enlist thousands of young men serious about "civic responsibility" and elevating "the social, political, and general tone of the city." In effect, Parkhurst proposed a moral surveillance of the city's officeholders. He maintained that no politics were involved. He was simply after the truth about how the city worked.

Like others, Parkhurst envied Tammany's organizational genius and its careful attention to every one of the city's 1,137 election districts. He outlined a plan whereby the CVL assigned at least one "supervisor" to each of those districts. They would prepare lists of residents; chart the saloons, brothels, and gambling houses in any district; and investigate the local police relations with them. By late October Parkhurst claimed some 10,000 members for the CVL. Even if that number were accurate—and it was certain to have been an exaggeration—there was little evidence of CVL activity during the election season; the organization seemed more an idealized future goal, a way for Parkhurst to claim a moral high ground far above the rough and tumble of electoral politics.[28]

While Parkhurst had been climbing the Alps that summer, Tammany Hall geared up to demonstrate just how crucial it was to the national Democratic campaign. From his days as Buffalo's mayor, Grover Cleveland had made his name as an anti-Tammany Democrat, unwilling to bend to patronage demands or make routine policy promises. Tammany had bitterly opposed his successful run for governor in 1882, and the anti-Tammany boast of Cleveland supporters at the 1884 national Democratic convention—"we love him most for the enemies he has made"—had not been forgotten. Tammany operatives had been widely suspected of "knifing" Cleveland in the city in both the 1884 and 1888 elections by, for example, encouraging voters to focus on local contests or scratching Cleveland's name off of the paper ballots they distributed. The organization had favored Cleveland's rival, New York governor David B. Hill, for the 1892 presidential nomination. Yet after Cleveland secured the nomination, Tammany leader Richard Croker, determined to cement the Hall's place as the only credible Democratic organization in the city and eager to extend its national influence, made sure that Cleveland received the full support of every building, block, and election district captain in the city. With New York City boasting a record voter registration of 310,000 (an increase of roughly 25,000 over the 1888 figure), and with Harrison weakened by unhappiness over his protectionist tariff policies, Croker confidently predicted Cleveland would carry the city by 75,000, more than enough to offset the traditional Republican advantage upstate. Democrats were united as never before, Croker noted, and Republicans hoping to carry New York state "must not depend upon Democratic disaffection."[29]

The Republican machine mobilized its own resources. For the past twenty years John I. Davenport had used the authority granted him by the Federal Elections Law to challenge Tammany's power. He kept the specter of Tweed era frauds alive as a "bloody shirt" waved over New York City politics. Davenport had brought his enormous energy, stamina, and organizational talents to his dual role as chief supervisor of elections for the New York southern district and United States commissioner. Davenport by 1876 had created an extraordinarily detailed federal registry of New York City voters, a continually updated set of 4,000 "block books," with a 42 volume index, to be used by federal election supervisors every two years to purge illegal voters from the rolls. He aggressively pursued illegal naturalization certificates as well. In early 1878 Davenport estimated that over 12,000 New Yorkers still voted using bogus 1868 papers; by the fall of that year he had gained possession of all but 1,200 of them. Davenport's operation was a thoroughly partisan one. The circuit courts, which oversaw the Federal Elections Law, required four election supervisors for each election district, evenly divided between Democrats and Republicans, and selected from lists submitted by the party state committees. But enforcement of the law was in the hands of U.S. deputy marshals, nearly all of whom were active Republican party workers.

Most provocatively, before every election Davenport would prepare arrest warrants and announce through the press that anyone caught voting illegally would be arrested at the polls. If someone tried to vote in defiance of Davenport's order, he was arrested and stashed in Davenport's infamous "iron cage," a cramped and dank temporary jail set up in the old post office building next to City Hall. But the evidence from numerous congressional investigations and other testimony shows that many of those routinely arrested or warned by mail to stay away from the polls— victims of Davenport's "bulldozing" as Democrats saw it—included perfectly legitimate city voters: Civil War veterans who held naturalization papers issued by courts after their discharge from the Union army; men who had lost their naturalization papers; and other citizens, both naturalized and native born, who had attempted to vote legally. Davenport's critics noted that after elections ended, virtually no one was ever tried or convicted of illegal voting. By the 1892 election the biannual rituals of false arrest, detention, and voter intimidation also played to Tammany's strength as protector of its immigrant, working-class constituency.[30]

What Democrats mockingly called "Davenportism" took a central place in the political platforms and national campaigns of both parties, closely linked to the heated partisan battle in Congress over what became known as the "Force Bill." In 1890, responding to the escalating suppression of the black vote in the South and the increasing number of contested congressional elections around the nation, Northern Republicans had introduced a variety of measures to strengthen federal supervision of congressional elections. Rep. Henry Cabot Lodge of Massachusetts introduced a bill (authored by Davenport) that would have effectively empowered federal circuit courts to oversee every congressional election in the country. Most Northern Republicans supported the Lodge Bill, though the dwindling numbers of Southern Republicans, aghast at the thought of black election supervisors and deputy marshals, did not. When the bill passed the House in the summer of 1890 by a 155–149 vote, not a single Democrat supported it. And in 1891 the bill lost in the Senate, where Republicans, some of whom wanted to see the "Negro question" removed from politics so as to focus on tariffs and the silver issue, could not overcome the solid Democratic opposition. For its supporters, especially men like Massachusetts senator George Frisbie Hoar, struggling to keep alive the fading idealism of Radical Reconstruction, it marked the last great attempt to protect suffrage rights for African Americans.[31]

After defeating what they dubbed the "Force Bill" in Congress, Democrats looked to exploit the issue for the 1892 presidential campaign. The re-election of Republican president Benjamin Harrison, they charged, would mean its reintroduction and guarantee passage. Opposition to federal control of elections united Northern and Southern Democrats, as well as both high-tariff and low-tariff proponents. The 1892 Democratic national platform opened with a denunciation and a warning: "[T]he policy of Federal control of elections... is fraught with the gravest dangers, scarcely less momentous than would result from a revolution practically establishing monarchy on the ruins of the Republic." The Republican platform asserted that "the party will never relax its efforts until the integrity of the ballot and the purity of elections shall be fully guaranteed in every state." In urban Democratic strongholds like New York, opposition to the Force Bill dovetailed with the longstanding hatred of Davenport and the federal election regime, producing an eerie reprise of the Civil War–era alliance between the Democratic South and a Democratic New York City. Charles Dana's *NY Sun*, for example, ran an article every day from June to November with the headline, "No Force Bill! No Negro domination!" "Better vote for the liberty and the white government of the Southern States," Dana warned, "even if the candidate were the Devil himself, rather than consent to the election of respectable Benjamin Harrison with a Force Bill in his pocket!"[32]

Opposition to the Force Bill helped unite city Democrats as never before in 1892, and political observers noted the stark contrast to the party's disarray during the 1884 and 1888 presidential campaigns. Tammany leaders sensed an opportunity to bolster their claim as the only true Democratic organization and to project their influence onto the national stage by delivering the city and the state for Grover Cleveland. Except for the Force Bill, national issues took a back seat to the perennial local questions about who could vote, by what authority, and which political organizations could get the most people to the polls. New Yorkers heard little about tariff policy, the pros and cons of bimetallism, the industrial violence wracking the steel mills of Homestead and other manufacturing centers, or the prospects for the newly minted Populist Party, a growing third party force in the West and South.

In early October David Martin, Republican National Committee member from Pennsylvania, arrived in New York, declaring that the biggest danger the Republican Party faced in New York was vote fraud in places like New York and Brooklyn. He alleged widespread colonization of illegal voters in the cheap hotels and lodging houses of lower Manhattan, more crowded than they had been in thirty years, a "floating vote" of aliens, repeaters, and criminals that Tammany would use to pile up a huge majority in the city. Martin and others fed the newspapers with the names and addresses of these places. Democratic newspapers countered with interviews of their proprietors. One of them was Thomas F. Foley (for whom Foley Square was later named), who ten years later would sponsor and launch the political career of Al Smith. He kept a saloon and lodging house on South Street, where, he told the *NY World*, his clientele was small, regular, and that "No strangers have lived here within six weeks." Others noted the large numbers of deck hands, sailors, teamsters, and other working-class men who made up their regular trade, often staying for months or years, and distinguishing them from transients. For their part, Democrats crowed when police detectives uncovered a Republican colonization scheme in the hotly contested new Eighth Assembly District on the Lower East Side, arresting sixteen men (including numerous African Americans) for inducing men to register illegally for $2 each. Republicans dismissed this as a Tammany diversion carried out by police loyal to the Hall.

Beyond the rhetorical sniping, ambitious local operatives from both parties worked the system. There were many ways to swell registration rolls or the election day vote, and both sides used them all: importing men from New Jersey and Philadelphia; stashing others in canal boats and barges on the waterfront; bargaining with Italian "padrones" who could pressure immigrant workers to register illegally; offering freedom to men held by police courts; or registering inmates and orderlies from Bellevue Hospital.[33]

For John Davenport the stakes in 1892 were especially high. After two decades as chief elections supervisor his position now looked wobbly. The defeat of the force bill, which he had largely written, had emboldened Democrats to call for repeal of the 1871 Federal Elections Law, a sure prospect if they carried the White House and the Congress. In September the Democratic House appointed a select committee led by Tammany Democrat Ashbel Fitch to investigate the elections law. Democrats, sensing a political advantage, had vowed to resist further expansion of federal supervision over elections, and the Fitch Committee arrived in New York ready to expose its workings. It subpoenaed Davenport in mid-October, but he refused to appear before the election, citing his work as chief supervisor. Testimony centered on how Davenport used federal funds to line his own pocket (in addition to his $3,000 salary as chief supervisor, as a U.S. commissioner he received $1 for every arrest warrant issued). But nothing much came out of the committee's work except to underscore the intractable partisan divide over Davenport's work and the entire election supervision apparatus.[34]

Davenport, wobbly or not, remained undeterred. Thousands of New Yorkers in the fall of 1892 received letters like the following from his office: "Sir: Your right to register and vote in the Thirty-First Election District of the Sixteenth Assembly District of the City of New York has been questioned. By calling at this office you may be able to satisfactorily explain the matter and thus avoid further trouble." Tammany Hall lawyers responded through the press, announcing "Counsel and bondsmen will be provided, without expense, to all persons who are entitled to vote, and whose right to vote is being unjustifiably challenged by Mr. Davenport." The chief supervisor upped the ante in early November when, acting with the U.S. attorney, he sent deputy U.S. marshals to arrest two charities and corrections department commissioners, Edward C. Sheehy and Charles Simmons, both Tammany appointees. A federal grand jury indicted them for encouraging scores of paupers and inmates of the hospitals on Blackwell's and Randall's Island to cross the East River and register illegally. Some fifty-seven were arrested. The commissioners and their attorneys argued the men in question were not inmates but unsalaried employees. For years the department, which had over 18,000 people under its care, hired former inmates, veterans, and other unemployed men desperate for a living, paying room and board for menial labor and odd jobs around hospitals and other institutions. And lawyers also noted that the previous year Davenport had at first challenged their right to vote but then relented and allowed their ballots to be counted. Commissioner Sheehy dismissed Davenport's dragnet as "the last kick of a dying horse.... They know they have lost New York as sure as they're alive and they're making this play so they can cry 'Fraud!' It won't work." The commissioners quickly made bail and, as typical in most of Davenport's cases, charges were dropped after the election.[35]

Davenport's activity only escalated attacks upon federal election supervision. "If the force bill becomes a law," roared Tammany congressman John D. Warner to a packed campaign rally on Third Avenue, "a revolution by arms will be required to dethrone the Republican Party!" With the election only days away, Lt. Gov. William Sheehan, chair of the Democratic state campaign committee, fueled the fire with a circular to party workers. Sheehan insisted that neither election supervisors nor U.S. marshals had the right to stand inside the guardrail at polling places while voters completed their ballots, implying that these federal officials would be subject to arrest by city police or sheriff's deputies. Thomas Carter, chair of the Republican National Committee, promptly warned that "broken heads and prison cells will be the sure reward" if Sheehan's instructions were followed. Republican officials, including Davenport, United States Attorney Edward Mitchell, and United States Marshal John W. Jacobus all took legal issue with Sheehan, citing numerous court decisions that had upheld the legal superiority of federal election supervisors and deputy marshals over local authorities in election disputes. Democrats like Sheehan may have been more interested in firing up their base than in provoking an actual physical confrontation. But Tammany also won an important legal ruling against Davenport just before Election Day, when the Republican U.S. attorney general William Miller held that men could not be arrested before they had cast their votes if they were willing to "swear in" their vote, taking an oath that they voted legally.[36]

Where was the NYPD in all this? Dr. Parkhurst's crusade and the ensuing criticism of the department seemed a distant and unimportant distraction, and Superintendent Thomas Byrnes's standing had never been higher. In October he earned universal praise for his skillful handling of the quadricentennial of Columbus's landing, a week-long celebration that had attracted the largest crowds in New York history. He had banned the use of clubs by his men, unless absolutely necessary for self-defense, proving that order could be maintained without resorting to brutality. Now he prepared for an election day amid expectations of violence between competing federal and local authorities.

On Sunday, November 6, two days before the election, Byrnes convened all 36 captains at headquarters to review plans for enforcing the law and preserving the peace. He was joined there by police board president James J. Martin, the Tammany leader with whom he had earlier clashed over enforcement of the liquor laws. In a tense scene, Byrnes spoke first, reviewing his orders on maintaining calm at the polls. Then Martin addressed the captains and undercut Byrnes by suggesting that the prerogatives of the police were superior to those of U.S. marshals and election supervisors. As Martin later recalled, "I said that if any disorder was committed or any breach of the peace at the polls by any person, whether citizens or United States marshals, that I thought they should be arrested for it." An angry Byrnes quickly responded, telling the captains he disagreed with the board president and advising his men against interference with the marshals. He reiterated his position in a typewritten order and in press interviews, in which he downplayed the prospect of violent clashes, stressed "the protection of all citizens in their legal rights," and predicted a peaceful Election Day. The Republican *NY Tribune* commended Byrnes for refusing "to be made the tool of Tammany and the promoter of violence and crime," calling him "the most popular man in New York City." Nonetheless the combination of swirling rumors in the partisan press (that U.S. Marines were stationed on the East River; that Davenport was poised to issue 7,000 arrest warrants against illegal voters) and the unprecedented deployment of some 7,900 deputy U.S. marshals and

2,300 federal election supervisors at the city's 1,137 polling places created enormous apprehension as Election Day dawned.[37]

In the end Byrnes's prediction proved correct and the election unusually quiet. Davenport and his marshals arrested fewer than 200 men, most of whom were discharged after showing that they had been falsely accused or were victims of clerical error. The real story was the Democratic landslide. Cleveland carried the city by 77,000 votes (almost exactly what Richard Croker had predicted) and the state by 47,000. Democrats also elected Tammany sachem Thomas F. Gilroy as mayor, won every assembly district for the first time ever, took every seat on the board of aldermen, and also took control of both houses of the state legislature in Albany. There was political insight, if not wisdom, in the pre-election thinking of the Tammany worker who had dismissed all the talk about floaters, illegal registration, and vote fraud: "You see, Tammany is so sure of the city that we would be foolish to put ourselves in a position to be jumped on needlessly." Nationally, for the first time since before the Civil War, Democrats controlled the White House, the House, and the Senate. In early 1894 they finally repealed the Federal Elections Law, ending a quarter-century regime, and legislating John Davenport out of his job. By the time he died in 1903, impoverished and suffering from mental illness, Davenport had been all but forgotten.[38]

Amid all the excitement, hardly anyone noticed that just a few days earlier Reverend Charles H. Parkhurst had won re-election as president of the Society for the Prevention of Crime. He ran unopposed. Asked by a reporter whether he intended to continue attacking vice, he replied, "I make it a point not to say beforehand what I am going to do."[39]

4

....

ANARCHY VS. CORRUPTION

With the bruising 1892 presidential election season finally over, Reverend Parkhurst—newly re-elected as president of the Society for the Prevention of Crime—lost little time pushing ahead with his reform movement. Over the next year his campaign escalated into all-out warfare against the police department and Tammany Hall, against which he would wage a series of battles on the streets, in the courts, and on the pages of the city's newspapers. At the same time, the onset of economic hard times ravaged millions of families across the nation, throwing unprecedented numbers out of work and into despair. As the nation's banking center and its largest manufacturing city, the growing depression hit New York with special force. The swift and intense economic downturn complicated Parkhurst's fight, but it also opened up new political possibilities.

A financial panic in early 1893, triggered by the collapse of the Philadelphia & Reading Railroad and then the failure of the National Cordage Company, a trust manufacturing most of the nation's rope and twine, spiraled into the worst industrial depression in American history. By the end of the year over 15,000 businesses had failed, with liabilities over $350 million. Over 600 banks, including sixty-nine national banks, went under or suspended business, freezing the nation's credit system and making it impossible for cash-strapped companies to meet their payrolls. By the winter of

1893–94, the national unemployment rate approached a staggering 20 percent, with much higher numbers in large cities and manufacturing towns. Politicians, economists, and journalists debated the pros and cons of maintaining the gold standard, reforming the currency, raising tariffs, and other policy measures. They could agree on only one fact: The swift pace and depth of the crash reflected how much more integrated and industrialized the American economy had become since the last depression of the 1870s.[1]

The depression highlighted the failures of Tammany rule and mismanagement, deepening disillusionment among settlement house workers, organized labor, and ordinary voters. On the Lower East Side, rowdy, sometimes violent, demonstrations by the immigrant unemployed, led by socialist and anarchist agitators like the twenty-five-year-old Emma Goldman, brought a new militant spirit to the streets. The police, invoking their historic role in putting down riots and guaranteeing social peace, tried to use the "anarchist threat" as a shield against Parkhurst's attacks on corruption and brutality. And the department, including the police commissioners, bitterly resisted the challenge to its monopolies over surveillance, detective work, and control over arrest warrants—indeed, objected completely to the whole project of civilian "policing" as embodied by the Society for the Prevention of Crime.

Parkhurst defied the police commissioners, the top brass, the courts, and the political establishment by exposing individual captains and appealing directly to public sentiment. By the end of 1893, as Democrats watched their historic electoral gains melt away, Republicans gained control of the legislature in Albany and offered Parkhurst a powerful new weapon in his battle: a special State Senate investigation—the Lexow Committee—created to probe and expose corruption in the NYPD. With the support of the city's Chamber of Commerce, the state senate thus created an opportunity for Parkhurst's crusade to escape the confines of municipal politics. But the road to the Lexow Committee, the climax of his efforts to attack corruption in the city's police department, was anything but straight and narrow.

On November 24, 1892, Parkhurst spoke to a crowd of 400 men at Judson Memorial Hall on Washington Square, the first recruits for the City Vigilance League (CVL). He proclaimed that he had purposely waited until after the heat of the campaign had subsided, "so that we might frame a platform big enough and square enough for every decent man in the city to stand upon, whatever his creed, nationality, politics, or condition."

It would be distinct from the Society for the Prevention of Crime, which had no membership other than the nine prominent Republican businessmen and attorneys on its board of directors. The CVL, as Parkhurst envisioned it, would be a grassroots organization devoted to moral surveillance, "a protracted watch meeting" meant to "keep our eyes on the men who are pretending to govern us." Each of New York's 1,137 election districts would have a CVL supervisor responsible for detailed mapping and tabulations: the position and character of every house and building, together with the names and social status of the occupants; a list of voters, noting their nationality and whether they were native born or naturalized citizens; and side remarks as to inhabitants' "moral standing." Special attention would be given to saloons and whether they operated within the law. Gambling houses, policy shops (numbers), pool rooms (off-track betting parlors) and "disorderly houses" would be watched, along with the police officers and captains of each district.

"Wherever the administrative blood beats in this city," Parkhurst declared to the new recruits, "the finger of the Vigilance League shall be upon it, counting the pulsations. These officials are not our masters," he insisted, to hearty applause, "though they may think they are. They are our servants." While "nonpartisanship" might have been his watchword, Tammany Hall provided the model for the CVL. The 1,137 supervisors would constitute the general committee; they would report to the thirty assembly district supervisors who constituted an executive committee. He was emulating the very organization that he was attacking.[2]

Parkhurst's broadened campaign, unsurprisingly, enraged Police Superintendent Thomas Byrnes. He had made his reputation as the nation's foremost detective by creating new and more effective surveillance techniques intended to control the criminal underworld and infiltrate labor unions and radical groups. Byrnes now looked to reassert the police monopoly on these practices by going after Parkhurst's Society for the Prevention of Crime. Since 1877 the SPC had invoked vaguely defined law enforcement powers, conferred by its charter from New York State, to obtain arrest warrants from police justices or other municipal judges. Sometimes its agents arrested brothel owners, prostitutes, saloonkeepers, and gamblers without any judicial cover. In the fall of 1892 SPC agents made a flurry of raids on brothels and gambling houses, including several near Parkhurst's East Thirty-Fifth Street home, using bench warrants obtained from sympathetic Republican police justice Charles Taintor in Yorkville (the Upper East Side, above Seventy-Sixth Street). Byrnes demanded that the police commission reign in the SPC's quasi-legal activities, and in early December the board of police justices issued a new rule forbidding the issue of warrants "except to persons authorized by law to execute warrants." Parkhurst dismissed the new rule as meant solely to harass him and the work of the SPC. "There is no common ground between us," he said of Byrnes, "and he antagonizes us, and we mean to keep our eyes on him." For good measure, Parkhurst added, "we have the majority of the better class of people on our side."

Byrnes drew attention to recurring reports of SPC agents—or men claiming to work for the Society—blackmailing prostitutes and their madams. In one such case, Marie St. Clair, proprietor of a brothel on West Thirty-Third Street, told a police justice that her refusal to pay an SPC agent $25 a month for "protection" had led to a raid on her place. Charles W. Gardner, the private detective who had famously arranged Parkhurst's sensational underworld tour the previous March, now directed the daily operations for the Society. Appearing before the same police justice, Gardner vehemently denied these charges, insisting that the woman was either lying or had been swindled by impostors.[3]

On December 5, Byrnes made an even more startling announcement: The police had arrested Gardner and charged him with blackmail against the complainant, Mrs. Lillian Clifton, who ran a brothel on West Fifty-Third Street. Clifton's story, a highly detailed, at times lurid account of her dealings with Gardner, put Parkhurst's crusade back in the news and revealed Byrnes's determination to go on the offensive. Her deposition described how Gardner, whom she had met through an ex-SPC agent in October, told her she was on a list of persons to be indicted. She was to pay him $50 a month for protection. She had met numerous times with Gardner, she said, including several lengthy drinking bouts in saloons all over town. She even visited his apartment on Lexington Avenue, where she met his nineteen-year-old wife, Florence, to whom she gave gifts of a gold necklace and a dozen silk handkerchiefs. Gardner had taken Clifton after hours to the SPC's office in the United Charities Building, on Fourth Avenue and Twenty-Second Street, where, as they drank wine, Gardner showed her a stack of envelopes which he claimed were indictments. One of them had her name on it. After Gardner demanded another $150 to "fix" her case, Clifton went to her local precinct captain, William S. Devery, to complain of the shakedown. Devery and Inspector William S. McLaughlin provided Clifton with $150 in marked bills. After Clifton gave Gardner the money at his home, they took a cab together to a saloon on Twenty-Fourth Street to celebrate. As Gardner got out of the hack, Devery and another policeman arrested him, while Gardner tried to throw the marked bills upon the sidewalk. When searched at headquarters, Gardner had $1,500 in cash on him (about $40,000 in current dollars).

Byrnes, longtime master at manipulating reporters and controlling information through his office, used Clifton's statement as the basis for the narrative he gave out to the press. The damning details of Clifton's story made Gardner appear not just corrupt but utterly cynical about the SPC's work and his unlimited expense account. While draining a bottle at the Society office, Clifton recalled Gardner turning to her to say, "Lil, what do you think of these psalm singers here? I blew $300 last week; but that's no matter. I suppose I'll get it back." When he told her she could avoid an indictment by paying Gardner $50 per month, he added "there were a hundred other school teachers such as myself on the list."

At his hearing before Police Justice McMahon, Gardner, dressed in a dark cutaway suit and vest, patent leather shoes, and expensive overcoat, faced a withering examination. Society lawyers and Parkhurst gamely defended Gardner, declaring him the victim of police entrapment and innocent until proven guilty. But the judge denied their motion to dismiss charges, set bail at $7,500, which Gardner could not raise, and then ordered him to the Tombs prison to await trial. Byrnes told reporters that he had received a number of complaints against Gardner, more evidence of the abuse arising from allowing private societies to serve warrants. "My experience," he said, "is that within the society is practiced a regular system of blackmail and that many of the men live by extortion and dishonest dealings."[4]

Parkhurst and the SPC had real doubts about Gardner's behavior and character, but they had to bury them now that war had broken out with the NYPD. It was clear that Byrnes was going to use Gardner as a cudgel. Two days after Gardner's arrest, Byrnes summoned reporters to his office for a gloves-off, highly personal attack on Parkhurst's motives and integrity. The minister's crusade against the police, he asserted, originated in a divorce suit involving the daughter of one of Parkhurst's congregation. She had married a prominent member of the "Four Hundred"—referring to New York's most elite families—but sued for divorce when she discovered her husband had a "kept woman" in a brothel. According to Byrnes, when a member of the police force refused to swear to certain facts in the case, the enraged mother of the young wife went to Dr. Parkhurst for help. An investigation against the brothel, motivated by revenge, followed, and then broadened into a campaign to defame the entire police force. The mother had asked a friend, yet another woman, for assistance as a go-between. But unbeknownst to her or to Parkhurst, the friend went to Superintendent Byrnes, became his ally, and eventually gave him some twenty letters she had received from the mother of the woman who won the divorce suit. A visibly angry Byrnes claimed to have these in his possession, and he charged that all the police persecution dated from the divorce suit. They showed that Parkhurst had "resorted to methods which are dishonorable, through the intrigues of women, to gather evidence compromising."

Byrnes made other disturbing claims. Parkhurst had used SPC detectives to "shadow" eleven city officials, including the mayor and the district attorney. The letters also revealed that Parkhurst had asked one parishioner to procure a set of "indecent French pictures" for use in the Marie Andrea trial the previous April. Parkhurst was afraid that when he appeared in court he would be embarrassed if called upon to describe his notorious tour of brothels; the French pictures would help to illustrate what he saw. But he had the parishioner send them to him anonymously through the mail so that he could claim he received them from an unknown source.

Parkhurst was most indignant about Byrnes's charge of insincerity. He ridiculed the idea that the divorce case had anything to do with his attacks on the police, accused the superintendent of "colossal impudence," and charged Byrnes with "trying to blacken me as a means of whitewashing himself and his department." He quoted the law requiring police to identify gambling dens and brothels, and "to repress and restrain all unlawful or disorderly conduct or practices therein." At least, Parkhurst noted, the battle lines were now definite and clear. "It is an issue between criminal rule on the one side and honest rule on the other. It is a battle between purity and lechery. It is a fight between true citizens who pay honest money for the administration of a Municipal Government and the criminals, in and out of office, to whom Government means nothing but an opportunity to feed and fatten on the common treasury and the general life."

Parkhurst nonetheless had to concede the truth of some of Byrnes's claims. He acknowledged having a "French picture" in his pocket at the Andrea trial, which he planned to show the jury. But when his turn to testify came, "I judged that oral evidence would do the work best, and the picture was withheld." Still Parkhurst wasn't backing down from the other charge. He proudly confirmed that while he was off mountain climbing in the Alps over the summer, SPC detectives had indeed shadowed city officials during the summer—"that was done and well done." He claimed the right to it as a citizen, and added "if I think the circumstances are such as to require it, I shall put a detective on Mr. Byrnes."[5]

Reporters could not identify the mysterious female parishioner who had helped gather information for the SPC, nor could they pinpoint the divorce case Byrnes had discussed. They clamored to see the divorce case correspondence. Byrnes refused to make the letters public. Instead, in a prepared statement, he charged that Parkhurst "is not trying to suppress gambling or to repress the social evil. He is in the field to attack the police." Parkhurst's SPC detectives were "as great a set of scoundrels as ever misled a reputable man into slandering the fair name of the city which he makes his home." Byrnes cited statistics to refute the claim that police ignored vice. In his seven months as superintendent, he announced, he had closed 440 brothels and 86 gambling houses, while imprisoning over 2,500 prostitutes and over 300 gamblers. He challenged Parkhurst's Christian charity, wondering how many prostitutes he and his society had given shelter to. The two solutions to prostitution were suppression or licensing. Neither was realistic in New York, according to Byrnes. And therefore the police followed a middle course, "to thrust the evil as far as possible out of sight, hide it from public view where it cannot corrupt the morals of our growing youth. That is all the police can do, and that they are doing to the best of their ability." To follow Parkhurst's strategy and break up houses of ill fame would simply scatter more prostitutes through tenement and apartment houses, bringing them into closer contact with decent citizens and their children.[6]

The city's press eagerly followed every charge and retort. "I loathe the man with unutterable contempt," Parkhurst said in a statement to reporters. Noting the superintendent had acknowledged the existence of a brothel close to the Madison Square Presbyterian Church, he challenged Byrne to do the right thing and shut it. He mocked Byrnes's invoking of the Gospel and Christian charity: "You had better quit the evangelical business and attend to your legitimate concerns." A disgusted Byrnes fired back, "Why don't he stick to theology and leave police business alone"[7]

In the city's courthouses, saloons, shops, and streets, the Byrnes-Parkhurst controversy was now the hottest topic of discussion. Press coverage reinforced the sense that it was really a battle over public opinion, as reporters sought the views of prominent attorneys, clergy, reformers, and businessmen. Parkhurst's strongest supporters were fellow Protestant clergy and veteran women moral reformers like Elizabeth Grannis of the Social Purity League and Francis Willard of the Women's Christian Temperance Union, who dismissed concerns about his methods while praising his honesty and sincerity. Martha Van Marter, secretary of the Methodist Woman's Home Missionary Society, defended Parkhurst's aggressive tactics, noting "the only way to curb vice and crime is to make them as hard a road to travel as possible." Most prominent men, on the other hand, remained wary of taking sides, and reacted like the railroad attorney Chauncey Depew, who threw up his hands when questioned by a reporter. He said, "I am not in it. I have nothing to say."

Partisan politics hovered above all the talk about vice and morality, inflamed by the revelation of SPC agents spying on city officials. Those officials, the *Sun* argued, had just "received a verdict of approval and confidence more emphatic" than in any election in the city's history, despite the fact that Parkhurst had been harassing them. The *World* ran a detailed profile of the nine directors of the Society for the Prevention of Crime, all Republicans, all wealthy merchants and lawyers. But the paper, which had given qualified support to Parkhurst's crusade, expressed the widespread dislike for spying and the blackmail that seemed to flow inevitably from it. The *World* editorialized that if one used hired hands to police the police the result would be men like Gardner—"irresponsible hired detectives"—and everyone would be worse off, whether or not Parkhurst's accusations were true.[8]

By Christmas 1892 both Parkhurst and Byrnes announced they had sworn off press interviews and public statements. This was no truce, for their war continued on other fronts. Parkhurst began exploring the possibility of getting bench warrants issued against police officers engaged in the same sort of blackmail schemes that had led to Gardner's arrest. His meetings with his ally, Yorkville police justice Charles Taintor, fueled the rumor mill. Byrnes, meanwhile, looking to repair his own reputation as an effective commander, went on the offensive against some of his own subordinates. On January 12 the superintendent presented formal charges against two of his inspectors, Alexander Williams and Thomas McAvoy, and three police captains, for neglect of duty and failure to enforce the law against several gambling houses and opium dens in their precincts. (A

Charles H. Parkhurst, c. 1872, when he taught Latin and Greek at the Williston Seminary, Easthampton, MA. This previously unpublished photo depicts Parkhurst twenty years before his controversial sermons at Madison Square Presbyterian Church in New York City made him famous. (Courtesy Williston Northampton School Archives)

A formal portrait of Dr. Charles H. Parkhurst, 1893. (Collection of the New York Historical Society)

Madison Square Presbyterian Church, where Parkhurst preached from 1880 until the building's demolition in 1906. (Collection of the New York Historical Society)

The first Madison Square Garden, located a couple of blocks from Parkhurst's church, was a mecca for prize fighting and the birthplace of modern professional sports. (Collection of the New York Historical Society)

Thomas F. Byrnes, c. 1885, when he was Inspector of Police in charge of the Detective Bureau. (Courtesy of the Police Museum)

Alexander S. Williams, c. 1885, Captain of the 29th Precinct, the notorious "Tenderloin" district so named by him. (Courtesy of the Police Museum)

Inspector Thomas F. Byrnes and Inspector Alexander S. Williams, the two most influential police officials in Gilded Age New York, 1888. These portraits, part of a "Police Inspectors and Captains" trading card set put out by Buchner Tobacco Company, reflect the celebrity status enjoyed by NYPD leaders.

William S. Devery, the corrupt police captain whose political connections ran so deep that he re-emerged in 1898 as New York's Chief of Police. (Courtesy of the Police Museum)

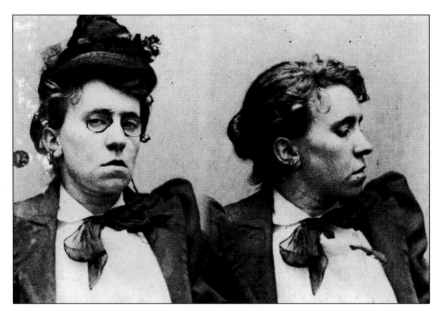

Emma Goldman, the charismatic anarchist speaker and organizer, in a mug shot taken by Philadelphia police, August 31, 1893. NYPD detectives arrested her there on charges of inciting a riot in Union Square. (Rogues Gallery, Department of Records, City of Philadelphia, in Candace Falk, ed., *Emma Goldman: A Documentary History of the American Years*, Berkeley, 2003)

Swedish born illustrator Thule de Thulstrup captured the police violence routinely used against organized labor in this depiction of a streetcar strike in March 1886. (*Harper's Weekly*, March 13, 1886)

Richard Croker, c. 1886. The former prize fighter and machinist led Tammany Hall from 1886 to 1901, when he retired to breed horses in England and Ireland.

Timothy D. "Big Tim" Sullivan as an Assemblyman in 1886, at the beginning of his political career. A protégé of Richard Croker, Sullivan became the most powerful Tammany leader in lower Manhattan and made a fortune from his investments in theater and the early movie business. (*NY State Assembly Red Book*, Albany, 1886)

Thomas Collier Platt, 1892, two-time U.S. Senator and Gilded Age leader of the Republican Party in New York State. (From *The Autobiography of Thomas C. Platt*, NY, 1910)

John I. Davenport, c. 1890, U.S. Commissioner and Chief Supervisor of Elections for the Southern District of New York. One of the most influential partisan Republicans of the Gilded Age, for 25 years Davenport led efforts to tamp down the Democratic vote in New York City. (From Benjamin Butler, *Autobiography and Personal Reminiscences*, Boston, 1892)

Josephine Shaw Lowell, leader of the Charity Organization Society, in 1880. She believed charity should rehabilitate recipients, not merely relieve their suffering. A bitter opponent of Tammany Hall, she founded the Woman's Municipal League in 1894 at Dr. Parkhurst's urging, encouraging women to get active in that year's mayoral campaign. (Schlesinger Library, Radcliffe College)

third inspector, Peter Conlin, received a very public dressing down.) Byrnes had used a squad of central office detectives to gather evidence, thus violating an unwritten law among New York City policemen against interfering in precinct management. The men would now be brought before the board of police commissioners, which had never tried such a large group of high officials before and had never heard charges against an inspector.

The proceedings on January 16 attracted a large crowd to the third floor trial room at police headquarters on Mulberry Street. With the four police commissioners seated up front, witnesses, patrolmen, reporters, and others huddled together on plain wooden benches, forced to keep their overcoats on as the steam radiators did little to warm the room. The most dramatic moment in the three-hour session featured a confident Williams facing off with his commander and old rival Byrnes. The two men sparred over everything from the reliability of captains' reports, to the fine points of anti-gambling statutes, to respect for the chain of command. Williams dismissed most of the gambling in the city as penny-ante, low-stakes games. Then he asked Byrnes, "Can gambling be suppressed in New York?" "No. It can never be wholly suppressed," Byrnes replied. Williams then quoted from one of Byrnes's own recent interviews answering Dr. Parkhurst, in which the superintendent said never in the history of the city was there so little gambling, and he applied this defense to his own case. Byrnes had to smile and acknowledge this was a good point against him. In the end, both inspectors were found not guilty of failure to suppress gambling because their inspection districts were so large that inspectors were forced to rely upon reports from the captains under their command. The three captains were found guilty of neglect of duty, but received only censure and reprimand from the board.

The police trial had revealed, once again, how ambiguous lines of authority within the department served to protect captains, inspectors, the superintendent, and the police commissioners themselves from even (or especially) the most serious charges. Byrnes had gone after the inspectors and captains vigorously, particularly his longtime nemesis Williams. But did he really want to break them? The entire proceeding had resembled a highly ritualized dance, performed by a department resistant to any disciplinary action imposed by outsiders. Afterward, when asked his opinion of the verdicts, Byrnes told a *World* reporter, "Well, of course, my charges as to the extent of those places were correct," but then added, "The decision's all right." Parkhurst took a dimmer view of departmental tribunals. "Does anyone think that these trials are serious? I don't," he told a journalist visiting his house. Still, at least the proceedings revealed a city so rotten that "you cannot stick a fork in the crust without releasing a foul stench. Exposing more rot and appealing to the public conscience was the only way forward."[9]

On January 31 Parkhurst's chief detective Charles W. Gardner went on trial for extortion, and for eight days the case exposed plenty of rottenness of a different sort. The proceedings attracted enormous attention because the press and the broader public saw the case as, according to the *Times* "a battle royal" between Parkhurst and Byrnes. Presiding over the case was Frederick Smyth, the city recorder, an elected judge who oversaw criminal cases in the Court of General Sessions. Gardner's lawyers, provided by the SPC, were two well-known former assistant district attorneys, John W. Goff and William Travers Jerome. Goff, a fiery Irish nationalist, had a longstanding hatred of Tammany Hall and had been active in the anti-Tammany County Democracy. Jerome, nephew of the financier Leonard Jerome, more closely resembled the well-heeled Republican members of the SPC and Parkhurst's church than Goff. Both the defense and prosecution, led by assistant DA William Wellman, closely questioned prospective jurors as to whether they held any opinions on Parkhurst's methods and whether they could believe the testimony of a brothel keeper like Lillie Clifton. The defense argued that the police had engaged in a conspiracy against Gardner, aimed at putting Parkhurst and the SPC out of business. Goff made several motions for dismissal, insisting that since Clifton had acted in collusion with the police there could be no criminal extortion, which the law defined as requiring the threat or the use of force. Gardner had merely been acting upon orders from the SPC executive committee to obtain affidavits against George C. Grant, an ex-SPC detective whom they suspected of blackmailing prostitutes under the Society's auspices. As Parkhurst noted in his deposition, the SPC "instructed [Gardner] that he should use such means as he saw fit in order to secure such affidavits."

"Such means" evidently included a great deal more than the SPC bargained for. Lillie Clifton testified at length about the long drinking excursions and meetings she had with Gardner, and the defense was unable to shake her. A parade of prosecution witnesses, including policemen, hack drivers, private detectives, saloonkeepers, and even a bowling alley operator, corroborated nearly all of what Clifton said. More damning, they depicted Gardner as a charlatan with a history of blackmailing prostitutes and dime museum operators, going back to his days working for the Society for the Prevention of Cruelty to Children. Gardner himself acknowledged that while working for the SPC he "also made money showing parties around the town in the beer dives and houses of prostitution." The Society covered all expenses in his work. Gardner's SPC salary was $100 per month. But at his arrest he carried more than $1,500 in cash (roughly $40,000 today), and at the trial he admitted to owning real property worth more than $11,000 (roughly $290,000 today). The prosecution hammered away, asking how the twenty-seven-year-old had come into all that wealth.

Goff, Gardner's lead defense attorney, focused his summation on what he alleged was a police conspiracy against Gardner, Parkhurst, and the SPC. Goff's repeated confrontations with Recorder Smyth over procedure and interpreting the law, however, may have done Gardner more harm than good. At one point, after the judge asked Gardner to stand so that a witness could identify him in court, Goff objected and got into a prolonged shouting match with the judge over his client's constitutional rights. The judge then ordered court officers to physically lift Gardner up for identification.[10]

After eight days of testimony, the jury deliberated for six hours and found Gardner guilty of attempted extortion. Recorder Smyth sentenced him to the maximum penalty of two years hard labor at Sing Sing. The state prison that opened in 1826, 30 miles up the Hudson River, was the most famous in the nation, due in large part to its notorious reputation as a tough place to do time. Smyth shocked the court by also charging Goff with contempt, giving him a choice between a $200 fine or thirty days in jail. Goff reluctantly paid the fine. Most of the press coverage agreed with the *Times* reporter who observed, "The weight of evidence to prove Gardner's bad character was so great that the jury convicted him on it." Gleeful Parkhurst critics like the *Sun* argued that the minister had effectively trained Gardner in the art of blackmail, producing "moral perversion glorified as holy zeal." More temperate voices zeroed in on the inherent limits of private detective work, noting that the professional detective had one marked advantage over the amateur: He was a sworn officer of the law. Gardner was not a public officer and was under no bond.

And the accumulated weight of trial testimony reinforced the low opinion most New Yorkers held of the private detective business. "It is manifest," the *Times* editorialized, "that Gardner exploited Dr. Parkhurst and the society for his own pecuniary behoof, and told Dr. Parkhurst whatever lies promised to serve his turn, with unquestioning faith in the good man's credulity." But even if the police had in effect framed a guilty man, Gardner's case suggested another approach to rooting out police corruption. One of the main arguments used against Gardner—that he must be guilty because he grew wealthy on such a small salary—might also be turned against police officers who had amassed wealth far beyond their salaries. A case as conclusive as the one against Gardner brought against a police captain, the *Times* argued, "would be a far more important public service than any the society has succeeded in rendering under the presidency of Dr. Parkhurst."[11]

Badly shaken by the conviction of his chief detective, Parkhurst went into seclusion at his home on East Thirty-Fifth Street, refusing to speak with reporters. On the first anniversary of his historic sermon, the minister's movement had seemingly stalled. Gardner's trial had proved a public relations disaster, baring the sordid world where private detectives too easily slid into the blackmailing business. The recent police trials had once again shown the unwillingness of police commissioners to punish Inspector Williams and captains for neglect of duty. The vigorous defense mounted by John Goff and William T. Jerome had resulted in highly unusual contempt citations for both men.

Yet Parkhurst resolved to move forward in the spring and summer of 1893, improvising new strategies to keep the heat on the police. The City Vigilance League, now with roughly 600 active members, stepped up surveillance on saloons violating laws against Sunday openings and sales to minors. In the especially active Harlem chapter, for example, led by SPC attorney Frank Moss, some fifty members of the League produced a steady stream of reports on saloons along the main thoroughfares 125th Street and Second and Third Avenues. They detailed the comings and goings of Sunday patrons, including women and children, and noted the failure of beat cops to stop them. In the Tenderloin, where many prostitutes had begun abandoning brownstone brothels closed by the police or by too much publicity, League members collected evidence against "disorderly women" and landlords who now rented them small apartments. Parkhurst insisted that they were not detectives but promoters of municipal pride among New Yorkers. But Leaguers were also urged to conceal as far as possible the fact that they were members.

Parkhurst regularly leaked reports of these campaigns to the press, keeping his work in the public eye and attracting a swelling flow of letters supporting his work. Supporters began calling on Parkhurst at his home, eager to report stories about protected vice or police oppression in their neighborhoods. The stream of strangers who came calling became such a distraction that Parkhurst had a hole drilled in the floor of his second floor study that allowed him to look down to the front hall below and screen out the cranks from more legitimate visitors.[12]

On the legal front, the SPC pursued a new strategy, one that took to heart the suggestion made by several newspapers during the Gardner trial: Aggressively investigate individual police captains and expose the protected vice under their control. The first target, unsurprisingly, was William S. Devery, who, after the Gardner trial, had been transferred to the Lower East Side's Eleventh Precinct. Even aside from his key role in Gardner's arrest and conviction, Devery embodied everything that Parkhurst and his allies detested about the police force. Born in 1854, the son of Irish immigrants escaping the famine, Devery had grown up in the rough East Side "Gashouse" district. As a teenager he went to work for his uncle, Steve Geohegan, a Tammany-connected owner of a string of saloons. Devery became a loyal Tammany man himself, joined the force in 1878, and had made captain in 1891 with the help of his good friend Richard Croker. A physically imposing figure at just under six feet and weighing over 225 pounds, Devery earned a reputation for physical bravery, combined with a quick sense of humor. These traits, along with his well-known "pull" with Tammany officials, made him popular with his men and his superiors. He personified the politically connected cop who put loyalty to the force above all else.

Parkhurst and his allies believed Devery presided over the most shameless precinct in the city. A newly beefed up corps of Society for the Protection of Crime detectives—not City Vigilance League volunteers—devoted weeks to visiting alleged criminal resorts, talking with residents, and reviewing letters of complaint. On August 10 the SPC made public a list of addresses for fifty-three disorderly houses and fifteen gambling spots it claimed Devery protected. "His precinct," Parkhurst charged in a press statement, "swarms with boys and girls; it is a sort of devil's seminary in which the vicious negligence of Devery constitutes him a kind of first trustee." In a letter to the board of police president Martin, the SPC reiterated its insistence that the law required the police to repress and prevent crime. "No option is accorded you as to what classes of crime you shall repress and what not. The department is executive, not legislative. . . . Your function is to act, not to philosophize." Devery dismissed the charges and used the traditional police argument of citing statistics in his defense. Since he had taken command in March, 3,832 prisoners had been brought to the Eldridge Street station, including 424 women, and twenty-one disorderly houses had been raided. Higher police officials offered no comment on the charges. The list and the letters sent to police officials and the mayor had been prepared in June, but for reasons he never made clear Parkhurst held off on sending the letters or releasing them to the press until August, when he was away on his annual Swiss Alps vacation. Perhaps Parkhurst sensed that the issue of police corruption had begun to pale next to the swift deterioration of the economy.[13]

By the summer of 1893 mounting unemployment, evictions for nonpayment of rent, and a growing homeless population were nowhere more evident than on the Lower East Side, Devery's precinct. The depression would ignite a more militant response from hard-hit immigrant workers demanding more radical solutions. Anarchist and socialist activism also reflected the profound demographic transformation of a neighborhood in the midst of the largest influx of Jewish immigrants in New York history. For the police department, a summer of street confrontations with the unemployed, striking workers, and their radical allies brought an opportunity to deflect Parkhurst's campaign. By cracking down on combative workers, exaggerating the threat of anarchism in the city, and playing upon anti-Semitic fears over the burgeoning Jewish population, police officials believed they could erase the stigma of Parkhurst's revelations.

Unemployment in the garment industry, the city's largest single employer, threw tens of thousands out of work, as hundreds of small shops dotting lower Manhattan closed up. Cigar makers, construction workers, printers, and the restaurant and hotel trades all reported record numbers of men and women out of work. In December 1893 Mayor Gilroy commissioned a census of the city's unemployed, tabulated by police going door to door in their precincts, and supervised by Seth Low, president of Columbia College. The police found that some 49,000 families, consisting of 207,000 people, reported that one or more members of the household were out of work, for a total of about 67,000 unemployed. Nearly a quarter of these were women. Others estimated the number unemployed to be 85,000, with another 20,000 or so comprising a permanent "floating" population of the homeless and jobless. Reliable statistics on unemployment, declining wages, business failures, and other economic markers were still hard to come by in the 1890s.[14]

The human toll of the depression was evident everywhere. With an estimated 20,000 homeless in the city, police precinct basements, the last option for homeless New Yorkers, turned away crowds every night. Lodging houses licensed by the board of health and temporary shelters set up by charitable societies also reported unprecedented overcrowding. Less visible was the suffering in tenement apartments, detailed by charity workers. One nurse tersely described a not untypical scene with a family of eleven: "Father a tailor out of work ten months. Eldest daughter (eighteen) out of work two months, other children out of school for lack of shoes. Wife ill, the rooms bare, and the usual pile of pawn tickets." Another investigator discovered an Italian immigrant, "his three children lying on the floor moaning for food." Food was provided, but one child was too exhausted and died of starvation. An unemployed Jewish tailor, recently widowed, broke, and living in one room on Suffolk Street, had no choice but to send his four children to live in orphanages.[15]

The depression spurred a variety of relief efforts, accompanied by fierce wrangling over which methods were effective, "scientific," or simply made matters worse. During the brutal winter of 1893–94 unemployed New Yorkers belonging to one of the few strong unions—typographers, cigar makers, carpenters—might receive cash relief of $5 a week, underscoring the skilled worker's pride in self-sufficiency and mutual help. But they made up only a small fraction of the city's working class and most had to look elsewhere for aid. For the first time, daily newspapers, motivated by a mixture of social responsibility, self-promotion, competitive spirit, and a sense of their growing influence, entered the relief field, raising over $120,000 (about $3.2 million in current dollars). The *Herald* gave away free clothing; the *World* distributed 5,000 loaves of bread each day for three months; and the *Tribune* ran a coal and food fund. Philanthropist Nathan Straus, the founder of Macy's, spent about $100,000 of his own money establishing several depots where New Yorkers could buy coal, bread, sugar, flour, coffee, and tea below cost.

Tammany Hall raised a relief fund of $70,000, largely by collecting one day's profit from hundreds of saloonkeepers. Roughly the same amount came from a levy on city officials and employees. As always, Tammany offered assistance largely through its district organizations, distributing coal, groceries, and work tickets to loyal voters and party workers. Some in Tammany embraced a more inclusive approach to charity. Big Tim Sullivan, elected to the state senate in 1893, began the tradition of feeding as many as 5,000 poor people at a free Christmas dinner at his Bowery clubhouse. Later he would begin giving away shoes and socks to thousands more, priding himself on providing charity with no strings attached. "I never ask a hungry man about his past," Sullivan declared. "I feed him, not because he is good, but because he needs food. Help your neighbor but keep your nose out of his affairs."[16]

Those committed to "organized charity" sharply criticized all these relief efforts. Their most influential champion was Josephine Shaw Lowell, who founded the New York Charity Organization Society (COS) in 1882, an ambitious effort to coordinate and make more efficient the jumble of philanthropic organizations, some of which dated back to the colonial era. The depression pushed Lowell to organize the most ambitious response to the city's suffering, the East Side Relief Work Committee (ESRWC), which brought together representatives from Catholic charities, the Hebrew Emigrant Aid Society, social settlement houses, and the Society for Ethical Culture, all working under the direction of COS-trained social workers. The committee raised more than $100,000, mostly from wealthy businessmen, with an eye toward providing work rather than relief to the East Side's unemployed. Men earned a dollar a day for cleaning streets or whitewashing tenements. Tailors received sixty or seventy cents for a day sewing clothes donated to poor African-American hurricane victims on the Sea Islands off South Carolina. Over four months, the committee managed to employ some 5,000 men and women, though rarely more than 1,000 at any given time.

Lowell was a complex figure who blended strains of traditional Protestant charity work with a devotion to statistics, belief in professional bureaucracy, and support for the labor movement. Despite the unprecedented magnitude of distress—Lowell estimated 50,000 to 60,000 unemployed Jewish clothing workers on the East Side alone—she could not shake the old-fashioned assumptions shaping relief efforts. The committee's work with the unemployed, she noted, had been guided by "a deep rooted determination that their moral character, their souls, must not be sacrificed in the effort to save their bodies." And for more long-term solutions to the congestion and poverty on the East Side, she still clung to an old bucolic reform fantasy: encouraging urban workers to take up farming, in order to relieve the congestion of the cities.[17]

Others, growing in number and visibility, had different ideas about what needed to be done. As the city's economy contracted during the summer of 1893, Jewish trade unionists and unemployed workers, many of them socialists or anarchists, maintained a steady drumbeat of protest in the streets, parks, and meeting halls of lower Manhattan. The extraordinary upsurge in Jewish immigration that began with the assassination of Russian Czar Alexander II in 1881 had already begun transforming New York's politics and culture. In 1880, New York's Jewish population had numbered roughly 60,000, or less than 5 percent of the city's inhabitants. By 1890 some 200,000 Jews, largely from Russia, Poland, and Austria-Hungary, called New York home, making up about 13 percent of the city's people. The vast majority clustered on the Lower East Side—bounded by Houston Street (North), Catherine Street (South), the Bowery (West), and the East River—comprising the largest concentration of Jews in the world. With population a density of 334,000 per square mile, or 522 per acre, this was also the most crowded neighborhood in the Western hemisphere.[18]

On August 17, 1893 the frustrations of the unemployed erupted into full-fledged riot. A crowd of 5,000, including out-of-work cloak-makers, garment cutters, tailors, bakers, carpenters, and upholsterers, gathered for a morning "hunger demonstration" at the International Labor Exchange on East Tenth Street. Many faced eviction for nonpayment of rent, or had already been thrown out on the street. Demands included work for the unemployed, "bread for our families and children and a place whereon to lay our head," and the withholding of rent "until our miserable condition is relieved." Only a fraction of the crowd could squeeze into the building and a cry went up to head for a bigger hall. In a pouring rain, the crowd marched down First Avenue, and then to Walhalla Hall on Orchard Street, a popular working-class gathering spot for dances and political meetings. Jacob Fliegman, manager of the saloon on the ground floor, refused to open the doors unless the demonstrators paid a rental fee of $10. Incensed by this demand, a group broke through the locked doors and smashed a window with paving stones, allowing several hundred to pour in and take possession of the hall. Joseph Barondess, the popular socialist leader of the cloak-makers union, urged the crowd to disperse and warned against destroying property. More militant voices argued for keeping the rump meeting going, denouncing capitalism, the police, and Fliegman, who looked on helplessly. A small contingent of police arrived and arrested a few men, but failed to clear the hall. Finally, at around three o'clock, Captain Devery, the man who had arrested Gardner and now commander of the

Eldridge Street precinct house, arrived with a force of forty cops, entered through a rear door, and cleared the hall amidst a violent melee of cracked heads, thrown bottles, and smashed furniture. They then charged the crowd on the street with clubs swinging, as some of the protesters shouted "Kill the police." Devery kept a reinforced patrol at Walhalla until midnight. Barondess, acting as an intermediary with the police, arranged bail for the fifteen men arrested.[19]

Parkhurst's effort to expose Devery faded against the threat to social peace. The Walhalla riot triggered a burst of protest meetings among Lower East Side activists, and press coverage combined breathless, often distorted, accounts of anarchist and socialist speechmaking. Reporters wandered the streets, conflating the neighborhood, radicalism, and the burgeoning Jewish presence. The *Times*, for example, described the area as "Anarchy's Dingy Stronghold," populated by, "Hordes of pinched and frowsy foreigners, with the squat, swollen faces, the harsh beards, and the deep-set furtive eyes ... the air was full of what seemed to be menaces in Hebrew characters, leveled against the peace and order of the community." Sectarian political disagreements among and between anarchists, socialists, and trade unionists produced attacks more virulent than any aimed at the capitalist order. While these distinctions received detailed attention in foreign language radical papers such as the *New Yorker Staats-Zeitung*, *Die Freiheit*, and the *Freie Arbeiter Stimme*, they were usually lost or ignored in English newspapers.

One figure came to embody the radical threat: Emma Goldman. The twenty-five-year-old Russian Jewish anarchist had arrived in 1889 in New York, where she became a disciple of the German-born editor Johann Most, the first anarchist in the U.S. to publicly advocate *attentat*, or political assassination. Goldman herself had become well-known in 1892 after her lover Alexander Berkman had failed spectacularly to murder Henry Clay Frick, top executive for the Carnegie Steel Corporation, during the tumultuous Homestead strike in Pittsburgh. Goldman had begun shaping her own hybrid version of anarchism, one that combined denunciations of capitalism, inequality, and the wage system with a deeply felt appeal to personal liberation. She made herself into an effective and dynamic speaker who connected emotionally with audiences composed largely of immigrant Jews. She folded her attacks upon all forms of institutional oppression—capitalism, the sweatshop system, orthodox religion, even marriage—into a call for a new social order where personal freedom and liberty would be untrammeled by man-made law.

By August 1893 Goldman was a ubiquitous presence on the Lower East Side, delivering public lectures on anarchism and addressing meetings of strikers and the unemployed in German, Russian, and English. Two days after the Walhalla riot, she spoke at Golden Rule Hall, a nearby anarchist stronghold, where one newspaper quoted her as telling the crowd: "If you are hungry and need bread, go and get it. The shops are plentiful and the doors are open." On August 21 she addressed a crowd of several thousand in Union Square amidst a heavy police presence. Superintendent Byrnes, who believed in keeping tight surveillance on radicals and labor activists, had assigned a German-speaking detective, Charles Jacobs, to monitor her speech. According to Jacobs, Goldman encouraged the audience to armed revolt: "Go to the houses of the capitalists and demand your rights, and, if you are refused them, take them by force. You will be attacked by the militia and the police. You must be prepared to defend yourselves with clubs and stones." Tipped off that she might be arrested after the Union Square rally, Goldman fled the city, creating intense newspaper speculation on the whereabouts of "Red Emma."[20]

Lower East Side labor activists now faced a broad police crackdown. Captain Devery ordered every hall proprietor in the Eleventh Precinct to report immediately any application for meetings by anarchists, socialists, or the unemployed. In several instances, determined demonstrators ignored the captain's order and the pleas of frightened proprietors, occupying meeting halls on Grand, Orchard, and Stanton Streets. Devery led squads of several dozen club-wielding cops to clear them out. "Where Do Anarchists Riot?" the *Times* headlined rhetorically—"Not in Capt. Devery's Precinct." With Devery's precinct shut tight to them, demonstrators looked to hold meetings elsewhere. When a group of some 500 unemployed met in the Chasam Sopher Synagogue on Clinton Street, Captain Jacob Siebert of the Thirteenth Precinct marched in with a dozen men and quickly cleared them out. Echoing Devery, Siebert announced that he would break up any similar meetings. Striking longshoremen on the East River waterfront received much the same treatment. Hundreds of men had walked out in protest against a reduction of pay from thirty to twenty-five cents an hour. When shippers brought in Italian immigrants as strikebreakers, some under police protection, violent confrontations flared up along the riverfront. Inspector Alexander S. Williams, still physically imposing at age fifty-four and animated by a longtime hatred of unions, personally led a large force of cops to clear picketers from South Street, shoving strikers off sidewalks and forcing everyone to move on. Dismissing the strikers as "loafers," Williams told a reporter: "I do not intend to stand any more nonsense from these men.... They have no right here."

In this climate, more moderate union leaders had trouble distinguishing themselves from radicals. Samuel Gompers, president of the American Federation of Labor, led a delegation to meet with Mayor Gilroy, hoping to discuss relief measures for the unemployed and hungry. Gompers urged the mayor to consider funding more public works projects, declaring it would be the city's safest course. "I don't know whether you mean that as a threat or not," Gilroy replied icily. Gompers replied that he had not, but that "no community can be entirely safe where a large body of the people are without employment." The mayor dismissed the proposal for more public works, agreeing only to do what he could as a private citizen—raising relief funds from wealthy individuals. Gompers, embarrassed that the mayor interpreted his request as a threat and eager to distance himself from radicals like Goldman, issued awkward apologies to the press.[21]

On August 23 the police board finally got around to considering the charges the Society for the Prevention of Crime had made in June against Devery for protecting gambling and prostitution in the Eleventh Precinct. Devery, Inspector Williams, and Acting Superintendent Conlin (Thomas Byrnes was on vacation at his summer home in Red Bank, New Jersey) all submitted reports dismissing the allegations. Each man claimed to have personally visited the places named and failed to find any breach of the law. They noted that most of the places named were licensed saloons, respectable restaurants, coffeehouses, and tenements. Others were closed or simply did not exist. The police board voted to file these reports and send copies to the SPC. "Captain Devery does not stand well with Dr. Parkhurst's Society," the *Commercial Advertiser* editorialized, "but the fact that the Anarchists flee before him is much to his favor."[22]

While Parkhurst remained on his Swiss Alps vacation, Byrnes returned early from his summer home to, as the *Herald* put it, "Shut anarchy's mouth." He immediately ordered captains to watch all places where incendiary speeches were being made and report to him the exact language used and the speakers' names. He promised to stop "this business of a lot of cranks running around as if they owned the town and frightening law abiding citizens." On September 1 he announced the capture and arrest in Philadelphia of Emma Goldman, brought back to New York by his detectives on a warrant for inciting to riot at her Union Square speech.

How did he find her? There is evidence that Byrnes applied his famous "third degree" technique to none other than Johann Most, Goldman's first anarchist mentor, who now had only glowing praise for the superintendent and his men. Bringing in Goldman put another feather in Byrnes's cap, and he touted his surveillance methods. "You can say," he boasted, "that not a single move is even thought of by the New York Anarchists that is not reported to me within an hour after the thought has become an intention."

Long considered a national authority on identifying and capturing professional criminals, Byrnes now fashioned himself an expert on dealing with anarchism. His definition of the term was so loose as to include socialists, militant unionists, and just about all of the labor and political protest sweeping America in response to hard times. He attacked the "industrial armies" movement of unemployed men marching to Washington to urge funding of public works—"the menace of Coxeyism"—as "the most dangerous this country has seen since the Civil War." In New York, as the *Recorder* confidently put it, Byrnes "may be relied upon to nip anarchy in the bud . . . and to spank the simpering Goldmans of the platform until they cry for the mercy they would not show to others."[23]

On October 5 Emma Goldman went on trial for incitement to riot, a dramatic coda to the summer's anarchism panic. Newspapers paid extraordinary, largely unflattering, attention to detailing Goldman's physical features and clothing. Her mouth, the *Sun* thought, defined her character: her lips "are thick and hard, and the under lip is forced beyond the perpendicular line of its mate by a square, projecting, defiant under jaw." There was no shortage of nicknames. She was the queen of East Side firebrands, the evangel of disorder, the fiery anarchist, the feminine firebrand, a strange woman, a dangerous woman. Superintendent Byrnes made sure to assign extra police security around City Hall to clamp down on any demonstrations by her supporters. Goldman's defense counsel was former mayor A. Oakey Hall, at sixty-seven a white-haired relic from the city's past. Several papers found it ironic that as district attorney in 1863 Hall had prosecuted the "anarchist" draft rioters. He served as mayor from 1868 to 1872 before becoming entangled in the Tweed scandals. Though indicted for corruption he had never been convicted; his reputation ruined, Hall spent many years in London before returning to the city.

The prosecution's case rested upon the testimony of several German-speaking plainclothes detectives that Byrnes had assigned to watch over radical activists. Goldman had addressed the Union Square crowd on August 21 in both English and German. When she switched to German, the detectives testified, her language had become incendiary, reinforcing the image of anarchism as a secret alien conspiracy. Hall made a spirited defense, challenging police witnesses and invoking free speech rights. The rally against unemployment and starvation, Hall noted, had the necessary permits (obtained by socialist union leader Joseph Barondess), and the crowd was entirely peaceable. One defense witness thought that Goldman had spoken more in the manner of prophesy than incitement. Hall put Goldman and several German language experts on the stand to challenge the police version of what she said, arguing that the detectives deliberately distorted her words. When one detective explained how he circulated among the listeners while she spoke, Hall asked if they broke the peace. No, he admitted, but added, they acted as if they'd like to do a great deal, and only lacked a leader. Assistant DA Robert McIntyre's closing remarks effectively conflated anti-anarchist prejudice with fears of immigrant hordes. "She was there," he told the jury, "to influence the minds of that crowd of aliens who might run a knife into you or blow you up with a dynamite bomb."

After a two-hour deliberation the jury found her guilty, and Judge Randolph Martine sentenced Goldman to a year in prison on Blackwell's Island. A satisfied Byrnes pronounced the verdict a great triumph of police justice. The Parkhurst campaign, he implied, could never eclipse the historic duty of the NYPD "as a bulwark against riot, strife and bloodshed, which are the sure results of the lawless teachings and speeches for which [Goldman was] convicted."[24]

Parkhurst himself had returned from his three-month vacation in late September, rested and eager to resume his crusade. However, recognizing that the anti-anarchist crackdown gave the NYPD a big boost from the press and with the broader public, he kept a low profile until the conclusion of the Goldman trial. He touted a new strategy for the fall: exposing individual police captains and their conversion of crime into a source of revenue. "Our society," he explained, "does not say, 'Stamp out the social evil.' It does not say, 'Close the saloons.' But it does say, 'Stop the police from turning immorality into corner lots.'" He also made his sharpest attacks yet on Tammany Hall, but not as a branch of the Democratic Party. Tammany, he declared, "is an organization that does not deserve any political name. It is simply 'a superbly organized band of brigands.' ...We have no hope of anything better until it is rooted out, and all self-respecting men, both Republicans and Democrats, ought to combine against it."[25]

Two days after Goldman's conviction Parkhurst and the SPC renewed their offensive against Captain Devery, reviving the charges made in August. Any anarchist threat, in their eyes, paled beside vice run rampant in the Eleventh Precinct, as Society agents found that protected gambling houses and brothels continued to operate openly on the Lower East Side. Parkhurst released to the press letters he had sent to the mayor and police officials documenting the failure to close down brothels and gambling houses. Devery, Parkhurst charged, ran his precinct "in a manner which made profligacy an open fact, the whole region pestilential, and youthful escape from foul contagion a physical and moral impossibility." Yet just a week later, on October 20, the board of police commissioners rejected all of the SPC's charges against Devery. The board had reports from investigations by Devery, Inspector Williams, and Superintendent Byrnes: All of them dismissed once again, as they had in August, the SPC's allegations. Williams angrily denounced Parkhurst for pursuing a personal vendetta against Devery, called the accusations false in every detail, and concluded that Parkhurst "has no regard for truth or his moral obligations." After some talk about a possible libel suit against Parkhurst, the board endorsed and filed the reports exonerating Devery. For Tammany police commissioner John Sheehan, Parkhurst's frequent denunciations of the Hall revealed a partisan political motive rather than a moral one. He urged the board to ignore any future communications from Parkhurst or the SPC and stated that the minister's speeches should get no more attention than a Republican stump speaker "howling for the destruction of the Democratic Party." Parkhurst dismissed the findings as a whitewash and declared that by failing to act against Devery, Byrnes, and Williams, the police commissioners had now made themselves defendants in the case.[26]

Much of the press believed the anti-police crusade had suffered a severe setback—"a knockdown blow," as the World called it. Still, Parkhurst and the SPC pressed on, convinced now that they must ignore the police commission and expect nothing from the force's highest officers. Instead, they would sidestep the police, use the courts, and appeal to the broader public. SPC agents began obtaining warrants to arrest brothel keepers in Devery's district, and the Society's lawyers explored bringing charges against Devery himself before the grand jury. On October 26 SPC lawyers appeared in the Essex Market police court for the arraignment of five brothel keepers, all immigrant German women, arrested on bench warrants issued on the testimony of SPC agents. In a faintly comic reprise of the famous underworld tour Parkhurst had made in February 1892, SPC agent John Lemmon testified about visits he made to the house of Matilda Berger on Forsyth Street. "I acted as if I was a young man about town out for a good time," he told Judge Voorhis. "I invited all the girls to drink with me." A second visit, made with the SPC's new chief of detectives, Alexander Wishart, included a "little high kicking party," as three young women in short skirts tried to kick his hat, held as high as he could above his head. In yet another visit Lemmon claimed he danced with Mrs. Berger while someone played a waltz on the piano. SPC lawyers complained to the judge that the women had been tipped off by the police about the arrest warrants.

Testimony continued the next day, Friday, October 27, and the judge remanded the five women to the Tombs pending trial. The proceedings had attracted a big crowd to the Essex Market court, neighborhood supporters of the accused women, and the tense scene inside spilled out onto the streets. What happened next was hotly disputed. When SPC agents and lawyers left on Friday afternoon, they found themselves surrounded by a group of jeering men, cursing and hooting at them, as they tried to make their way to streetcars. When the SPC men reached the corner of Bowery and Broome Street and boarded a streetcar, several crowd members jumped on after them and roughed up a Society detective and a conductor before several policemen appeared and broke up the scene. Sensational newspaper accounts—"Mobbed By Thugs," "Parkhurst's Men Stoned"—exaggerated the size of the crowd, the violence, and the unwillingness of the police to intervene.

For Parkhurst and the SPC it seemed a perfect illustration of Devery's true character and of broader police collusion with the criminal underworld. Three men were arrested and held for rioting. They were released when Society officials declined to press criminal charges, arguing that the burden was on the police to either prove they were not delinquent or to prosecute the offenders. Superintendent Byrnes made a detailed report to the police board, based on a large number of sworn affidavits, and he found no dereliction of duty by police. Inspector Williams's report tartly dismissed the whole affair as inflated by the SPC as a way of getting sympathy and money, "in order that their paid agents may continue to lead lives of confessed adulterers and would-be blackmailers unless restrained by the police."[27]

Williams's sarcasm no doubt reflected the predominant view within the police department, but it could not deflect the growing support for

Parkhurst's campaign on the Lower East Side. One of his prominent new allies was Stanton Coit, a leader in the emerging social settlement movement. A graduate, like Parkhurst, of Amherst College, Coit went to work for Felix Adler and his Ethical Culture Society. After earning a PhD in Germany, Coit returned to New York, eager to put into practice Adler's ideas connecting personal ethics to social reform. In 1886 he founded the Neighborhood Guild on Forsyth Street, America's first settlement house. Breaking with the older tradition of "charity work," Coit stressed living with neighborhood residents, providing a variety of free educational and cultural clubs, and helping the community organize to improve housing and sanitary conditions. In 1891 Coit reorganized the Guild into the University Settlement, and now voiced support for Parkhurst in the name of the "public conscience" of the city. In Devery's precinct, vice "flares and flaunts itself in the face of honest men with an impudence which seems to say: 'We know we are safe. We have arranged that. No one dare molest our work of corrupting the young men in Capt. Devery's precinct!'" Another new Parkhurst backer in the neighborhood was the Reverend William Hamilton, minister of the Allen Memorial Church on Rivington Street, a Methodist outpost amidst the city's most heavily Jewish district. Both men would testify repeatedly before grand jury investigations as supporters of Parkhurst's "war on the captains."[28]

Through November Parkhurst's campaign gained more momentum. On November 13 the five German women arrested by SPC agents in Devery's precinct stood trial in the Court of Special Sessions. All were convicted of keeping disorderly houses and paid fines of $250, after which they were released with a warning that a second conviction would mean imprisonment. Five days later the state supreme court reversed the conviction of former SPC detective Charles Gardner and ordered his release from prison. The court found that no crime of extortion had been committed because there had been no use of force or fear by Gardner in his dealings with Lillie Clifton. An elated Gardner, locked up in the Tombs since early February, received a congratulatory letter from the SPC's executive committee—but no offer of reinstatement. He was too well known and too controversial to be taken back in.

Good news for Parkhurst kept rolling in. On November 29 the grand jury, using the evidence gathered by SPC agents, indicted Captain Devery on four counts of willful neglect of duty in failing to close disorderly houses. As Superintendent Byrnes negotiated Devery's surrender without an official arrest, a jubilant Parkhurst vowed to continue his war on the captains.

Asked when he would finish, he replied, "Not 'til we have covered Manhattan Island." Devery, released on $5,000 bail, faced substantial jail time and fines if convicted. The significance of his indictment, however, was much bigger. A high official of the police force had at last been charged with neglecting to suppress certain classes of vice for the purpose of private gain. Byrnes and the police commission declined to suspend Devery, insisting on his right to presumption of innocence. They reassigned him to the First Precinct's Old Slip station house and announced the transfer of a dozen other captains. Inspector Williams, who had accompanied Devery to his bail hearing, curtly dismissed reports that he might be the next target of a grand jury indictment. "I shall not lose any sleep on account of Dr. Parkhurst, and I enjoy my meals as usual. I will bet $4 that I have sent more men to jail than Dr. Parkhurst has to heaven."[29]

Williams's words were more than bluster. Parkhurst's string of victories—conviction of the East Side brothel keepers, the reversal of Gardner's conviction, the indictment of Devery—had not shaken police officials' confidence in their own power and resources. Byrnes still enjoyed wide admiration, both as a crime fighter and as the scourge of radicals. The *Times* marked the thirtieth anniversary of his appointment to the force in 1863 with a flattering profile headlined, "He Rules Through Fear." His "master work," built largely on an elaborate system of espionage, had been "ridding the city of the organized gangs of burglars, thieves, and forgers with which New York was infested not more than a dozen years ago." Police Commissioner John McClave invoked the anarchist threat while dismissing Devery's indictment and the sensational news coverage around it as unfair distortions of the force's effectiveness. McClave, whose family had made a fortune in the lumber business, was the police board's lone Republican, and he had served as its treasurer since his appointment in 1884. Not only could any decent man "go anywhere at any hour of the day or night and be perfectly safe," many who had made fortunes elsewhere moved to the city because they could be "certain that their lives and property will be safe." Still McClave warned that a dangerous element was growing and would test the police, who would respond by driving "every Anarchist in the city into the river." With Byrnes as their leader, "the policemen would fight until they dropped dead." For his part, Byrnes declined to comment on Parkhurst, Devery, or any accused officers. Instead, he proudly reiterated his view that "there is less open vice, less crime, less gambling and less disorder in this city than in any other large city in the world."[30]

The key word here was "open." To underscore his point, Byrnes ordered all the city's disorderly houses closed and the women inhabitants evicted into the cold December streets. Hundreds of prostitutes poured out from the Water Street dives in the city's old waterfront red light district, up through the fifty-cent houses on the Lower East Side, to the "French houses" around West Third Street and the African-American brothels off Bleecker Street, and to the Tenderloin brownstones lining Sixth Avenue and Broadway. Police warned hotel keepers not to take them in or risk being raided. The drunk and loud women congregated on street corners, in saloons, and in all-night restaurants. The scene grew especially rowdy in the heart of the Tenderloin, around Broadway and Thirtieth Street, where respectable men and women, on their way home from the theaters, ran the gauntlet through clusters of intoxicated and singing women who had no place to go for shelter. Byrnes moved the women like "wretched pawns," said the *Commercial Advertiser*, to play on "the public sympathy, the public indignation, the public fear that the contagion will spread to the home and the family."

The Tenderloin, the very heart of midtown Manhattan's hotel, shopping, and tourist district, received the most attention. Real estate prices and rents—for brothels and anything else—were substantially higher than downtown. In fact hundreds of prostitutes and madams already operated out of apartment houses in the district bounded by Fourteenth and Fifty-Ninth Streets, Sixth and Eighth Avenues. Everyone agreed that the very worst kind of resorts ran right in the middle of families and children. One West Side realtor, disgusted by police hypocrisy, told a reporter, "It is a pretty late day to talk about dissolute women taking possession of flats." Press accounts were full of examples of reputable citizens caught up in the police net, thrown out of their homes, and forced to appear in court. Many of them rented rooms in large brownstones broken up into apartments, with no clue as to their "mixed use." A large double brownstone at 40-42 West Twenty-Fourth Street, kept by a madam, Anna Cummings, also housed such respectable tenants as variety actor Fred Pettengill and Wall Street clerk Frank Edwards. They shared a jail cell until getting bailed out by the famous vaudeville impresario Tony Pastor. Police arrested other innocent victims from the same house, including an irate, fez-wearing forty-five-year-old Greek Egyptologist, Demetrius Mosconus, just back from lecturing at the Chicago World's Fair. "I lodge there and I am known from all the world," he protested in broken English, and after hearing his story a judge released him and his wife. The carnival atmosphere on mid-town streets, the arrests of innocent citizens, the raucous scenes in police courts were all part of the police strategy: to show just what kind of place New York would be if the laws against disorderly houses were actually enforced. Newspapers wondered just how many prostitutes worked in New York, citing estimates ranging from 25,000 to more than 50,000.[31]

Parkhurst tried to turn the situation to his advantage. As evicted women wandered the streets, languished in jail, looked for shelter from charities, and even appeared on the minister's doorstep, SPC agents took scores of affidavits detailing payoffs to police. They uncovered an informal licensing system for Tenderloin streetwalkers, the lowest class of prostitutes. Patrolmen to whom they paid protection issued identification cards that allowed women to move from street to street with impunity. Parkhurst expressed sympathy for "these poor women" and invited them to stop by his house or the new United Charities Building near Union Square, offering assistance "providing they desire to abandon their disreputable work and lead respectable lives." He objected to being called callous and un-Christian; his target was the system of police blackmail, not the prostitutes themselves.

But a December 8 interview with the *NY Times* called Parkhurst's compassion into question. He would not address the low wages and grinding poverty, exacerbated by depression, that drove so many women into the trade, including thousands who engaged in irregular casual prostitution. He acknowledged that only a small fraction would embrace the opportunity to reform their lives. And the others? "I do not care whether they starve or freeze on the streets, so long as they are starved or frozen into a healthier way of thinking and living." He intended to "follow them down, to keep them moving, to hunt them out of the city." The reporter asked Parkhurst to repeat his statement, to make sure he had heard correctly, which he did. The page one story, under the headline "Let Them Starve or Freeze," led with the quote uttered by Parkhurst "seated in his warm and comfortable dining room, from which a trim maid had just cleared away the remnants of a substantial luncheon."

Parkhurst angrily objected to the story, the headline, and the lead quotation as "misrepresentation of the worst sort." Follow-up interviews only seemed to reinforce what critics saw as hard-heartedness. "My real remark," he gamely explained, "was that if these women did not change their way of life, but only expressed a desire for help until such time that circumstances may enable them to resume their nefarious traffic, it would not be right for us to do anything for them, even if they were to starve or freeze." Well-known women reformers, most of whom considered Parkhurst an ally, attacked him for upholding the double standard and for insensitivity to the economic realities facing women in the city. "If Doctor Parkhurst wishes to suppress this great evil," suggested pioneer suffragist Matilda Joslyn Gage, "he should turn his attention to the men. . . . He can have every disorderly house watched, and every man entering it arrested, fined, and his name published. That would put a stop to it speedily." Novelist and journalist Lillie Devereux Blake, president of the New York City Woman's Suffrage League and a founder of Barnard College, thought Parkhurst had "done the cruelest thing in the world," and argued that only financial independence for women, single and married, could end the social evil.[32]

By mid-December a somewhat chastened Parkhurst had begun rethinking his strategy. The controversy over the *Times* interview reminded him that, as that paper editorialized, "his exceedingly aggressive attitude arouses much animosity, most of which is creditable to him, but which nevertheless makes mistakes by him unusually dangerous." He indeed received a score of threatening letters promising to kill him before Christmas, most of them written by rousted prostitutes. He paid no attention to them, he said, but they worried his wife, Ellen; he no longer went out alone at night, and SPC agents now provided personal security. The Society had launched investigations of several other precinct commanders, as Devery awaited trial on his indictment for neglect of duty. As Parkhurst now knew, the so-called "war on captains" was a hard slog, fought on uncertain legal and political terrain, with no predictable outcome. Byrnes managed to remain above it all and still enjoyed wide support in the press and business community. And the recent crackdown on brothels and eviction of thousands of prostitutes reminded everyone of the enormous street level power enjoyed by the police. Parkhurst needed somehow to shift the ground beyond the city limits.[33]

The beleaguered minister dismissed the latest spasm of police raids as theatrical. Going after corrupt captains like Devery, the protracted skirmishes with Williams and Byrnes, the ritualized trials before the police commissioners, the recalcitrance of District Attorney DeLancey Nicoll— none of this could produce true reform. The department was organically rotten from top to bottom, he declared, and "no improvement can be worked in this city," he told a *World* reporter at his house, "until Tammany Hall is downed." The system, he argued, had become perfectly efficient, funneling money to the political masters at the top. Police management of the city's vice economy was the key element in Tammany's growing power, "for Tammany lives on money—the money sapped from the integrity of men and the virtue of women."

Parkhurst added an attack on "bossism," one from which many New Yorkers caught a whiff of nativism. Addressing a meeting of the City Vigilance League at his Madison Square church, he noted that "while we have no objection to men coming from abroad and settling with us, we would have them become Americans." Bossism meant "men willing to sublet their civil rights to a boss," leading to the current situation where New York was controlled by Tammany chief Richard Croker "of whom it has been trenchantly said that his natural wages are $15 a week." And striking a chord that would become common in reform circles, Parkhurst reserved his greatest contempt for the respectable citizens who allowed such things to happen. He now talked about developing a broader reform approach that prefigured the core of political progressivism: Teach children to love America, separate national from municipal elections to limit Tammany's power over state and national affairs, and elect men who would be nonpartisan and govern on sound business principles. At the close of the meeting he sat down at a piano and led his audience in singing "My Country, 'Tis of Thee."[34]

The political field now looked much more promising. Parkhurst noted the growing opposition to Tammany and imagined a united front among several groups: "We have the German organization, the Union League, the City Club, my own [City] Vigilance Committee. Now the only way to overthrow Tammany is for these organizations to get together.... [W]e must fight fire with fire and organization with organization." Most importantly, the Democratic sweep of only a year earlier seemed a distant memory as the depression had reshaped the political landscape of the city and state. In November 1893 Republicans took control of the state legislature in Albany and every statewide office, ushering in thirteen years of GOP dominance.

Parkhurst seized the political moment, floating the idea of asking the senate and assembly in Albany to appoint a special committee to investigate the police commissioners and the entire police department. He continued to insist that he was not a politician but saw that a Republican-dominated legislature would help his crusade. He promised to furnish such a committee with all the evidence SPC agents had collected over the past two years. Several newspapers supported the idea of an independent investigation as well. The Republican *Tribune* thought the most important business for the new legislature would be a law making the police board a nonpartisan body, "thus compelling the restoration and maintenance of the practice which was held sacred for nearly twenty years." In other words, legalize the unwritten agreement that the four-member board would include two Democrats and two Republicans. This practice had been in effect from 1873 to 1889, before Mayor Grant had tipped the balance by appointing a third Tammany police commissioner. The *Tribune* gave more attention to how a Tammany-dominated board meant control of the election machinery than to police management of the vice economy. Republicans in the city and in Albany evinced more interest in this side of the equation, especially as there had been an unusually high number of arrests for vote fraud during the 1893 election season.[35]

Any hesitation Parkhurst may have felt toward supporting an outside investigation dissolved by New Year's. An extraordinary grand jury, meeting during the last week of December, had declined to indict Inspector Alexander Williams or Captain Max Schmittberger on charges of neglect of duty, citing insufficient evidence. Both Williams and Schmittberger, Williams's former ward detective in the Tenderloin and now the captain of that precinct, had been in the SPC's sights for months. Parkhurst and the Society lawyers were especially eager to get at Williams who, they argued, had protected Devery and other captains by regularly endorsing the reports made to him, and in his own reports to Superintendent Byrnes. The imperious Williams had airily dismissed rumors of an indictment and, as usual, expressed contempt for Parkhurst and his methods. Despite his high rank and his Republican politics, Williams prided himself on understanding the gritty, multifarious reality of city streets in ways Parkhurst or his agents never could. In his latest report to Superintendent Byrnes, discussed before the grand jury, Williams made a point of minimizing the vice in lower Manhattan's dense neighborhoods. Most of the places identified by the SPC as immoral or lawbreaking were licensed liquor stores, or "the resort of seafaring men, longshoremen, laboring men, and the poorer classes of people who live in the vicinity; they are also frequented from time to time by respectable women and by women of questionable character."[36]

Parkhurst issued a blistering attack on DA DeLancey Nicoll, detailing how he had repeatedly failed to use the grand jury to get indictments against rogue captains or higher-ups. Nicoll, Parkhust charged, had mort-gaged his judicial sense to his political allies and friends in Tammany and the NYPD. The city, he concluded, could expect no more than a "carica-ture of justice" until "at the polls some of the joints and ligaments have been broken that knit our municipal government into a compact body of brigandage and defiance." Nicoll, now out of office, issued his own spir-ited denial of these charges, defending his relations with the grand jury as upright and legal. Parkhurst had "allowed his zeal to run away with his discretion and common sense."[37]

Fear of the "anarchist threat," which intensified with the economic depression, had played a crucial role in the failure to indict more police officials. The foreman of the July grand jury and the December extraordi-nary grand jury was Richard J. Cross, a prominent banker, and partner in the Wall Street firm of Morton, Bliss, and Co., founded by former Republican vice president and future governor Levi P. Morton. Both Cross and Nicoll had adamantly opposed indictments over the summer, arguing that the police should not be attacked because "labor riots" were expected in September. Throughout the fall they had continued to invoke what Nicoll called "the disturbed condition of the city" to defend the status quo and shield police officials like Williams from indictment. At the annual captain's dinner held January 22 at Delmonico's, Mayor Gilroy exploited the same threat as he tried to defend the department and take a swipe at Parkhurst. "Passing through such an emergency as we are today," the mayor warned the crowd of 300 police officials, businessmen, and political figures, "with the pov-erty and distress around us breeding the dissatisfaction that is its natural result, it is neither the part of wisdom nor of policy to hold the police up to ridicule or contempt before the public."[38]

Despite the efforts and rhetoric of Gilroy and others, a week later leg-islative leaders in Albany announced creation of a special state senate com-mittee, chaired by Sen. Clarence Lexow (R-Nyack), to investigate the NYPD from top to bottom. If nothing else, the inquiry would take the issue of police corruption out of the city's political hothouse. It might even put to rest the playing of the anarchy card. The news was widely hailed as a tri-umph for Parkhurst's movement. As he would discover, however, the fe-rocious realm of partisan politics presented a bigger obstacle to reform than anarchism ever did.

5

· · · ·

A ROCKY START

As he sat in a parlor of the Metropole Hotel on Broadway and Forty-Second Street, awaiting his turn to speak at the first preliminary meeting of the new state senate investigating committee, Reverend Charles H. Parkhurst could feel his anger rising. Just days before, the newspapers had hailed Albany's passage of the bill authorizing an inquiry into the New York City police as a personal triumph for Parkhurst, a capstone to his two-year-long crusade. The bashing he had incurred from confrontations with outraged police officials, irate political partisans, and frenzied press coverage had only deepened his sense of purpose. In his recent New Year's sermon reviewing that campaign, Parkhurst had evinced a confidence about the future, a genuine optimism based on the power of conscience. "Conscience is not a lost art," he had told his Madison Square parishioners. "In the last analysis, that is the hope of humanity, it is the hope of our country, and it is the hope of our city."[1] But as the senators, who had arrived February 2 on a late train from Albany, began to organize themselves, no one seemed too interested in conscience. None appeared to have any idea where to start or what line of inquiry to adopt.

Along with Parkhurst, the committee had invited two pillars of the city's commercial establishment to its organizing session, Charles Stewart Smith, president of the Chamber of Commerce and Darwin R. James, president of the board of trade and transportation, both of which groups had lobbied for a senate investigation of the NYPD. Committee chair Clarence Lexow, a Republican from the small town of Nyack, about thirty miles north of the city on the Hudson River, asked Smith and James to first address the most pressing question: Who should act as counsel for the committee? A man of medium height and build, with a short beard and mustache, Lexow was an attorney with a precise manner and a reputation for honesty and efficiency. He had deep roots in the city's German community; his father, Rudolph Lexow, had fled Germany during the 1848 revolution. In New York he had edited the *New Yorker Criminal-Zeitung und Belletristisches Journal* (Crime Reporter and Belletristic Journal), a leading German American newspaper and a rival to the city's largest German newspaper, the *Staats-Zeitung*.

Reflecting the gentleman's club atmosphere of the proceedings, Lexow directed Smith to act as the committee's agent and contact Joseph Choate, perhaps the nation's leading trial lawyer and corporate attorney, whose clients included Standard Oil, the American Tobacco Company, and Bell Telephone. One senator asked if a representative from the Union League Club might be invited to attend future sessions. The committee came to the city believing they could rely upon the Chamber of Commerce and Parkhurst's Society for the Prevention of Crime for the presentation of evidence. Some senators, believing they would complete their task in a few weeks, pushed to start taking testimony the next day.

When Chairman Lexow finally asked Parkhurst his opinion, the minister fought to contain his ire. His voice tense, Parkhurst pointed his forefinger at the assembled senators and in a tone that bordered on sarcastic, reminded them that, unlike the other groups represented, the Society for the Prevention of Crime "has expressed no wish that such a committee as yours should come down from Albany." His Society had been acting independently for two years, it had made its own charges, and it had verified them. Nor did he think testimony could begin before counsel—Joseph Choate or whoever it would be—had had a chance to do a good deal of background work. And that testimony, his experience had shown, needed to be made in secret sessions, in the manner of a grand jury. Potential witnesses rightly feared police retribution. "Publicity," he declared, "will close their mouths; secrecy will make them communicative, and I am convinced that the more secret this investigation is, the more effective it will be."

At this there was considerable coughing and hemming. Secret sessions would be impossible as every word of testimony would in the end have to be printed and sent to the legislature. Lexow denounced the policy of secrecy as "a star chamber proceeding which would not be tolerated." Anxious to get started, and noting the committee had been directed to deliver a report in only three weeks, several senators asked the minister if he had charges ready that they might take up the next day. Parkhurst grimly shook his head and sat down. Before adjourning, Lexow named a three-member subcommittee to resolve the issues of counsel, secrecy, and work schedule. These would not be easy to work out, because with its very limited time frame, the Special Committee Appointed to Investigate the Police Department of the City of New York (its official title) looked like it might go out of business before it even started. The only thing clear, reported the *Times*, "was that the committee is absolutely at sea as to the course it will pursue."[2]

A series of follow-up meetings between Parkhurst and the subcommittee produced only widening disagreements: Precisely what was the Lexow Committee, as newspapers quickly dubbed it, supposed to accomplish? Parkhurst, while still at the center of things, was no longer alone in his anger in this new, larger, and more crowded field of play. Tammany Democrats had borne the brunt of the minister's attacks for two years, and a Republican legislature had dutifully pushed through an investigation of New York City affairs, as it had repeatedly done in the past. Parkhurst now confronted a very different challenge from those earlier investigations: Could his moral crusade against police collusion with the vice economy be translated into an official investigation inevitably shaped by partisan politics? Put another way, could a movement for moral reform coexist with the Republican Party establishment in New York State? Parkhurst had made powerful allies among the city-based Republican "reform" elite, notably the Chamber of Commerce, the Union League Club, and various "good government" groups. They believed the Lexow inquiry would produce testimony supporting the two reforms they thought most crucial: separating the NYPD from politics with a nonpartisan, single commissioner, and divorcing the police from the bureau of elections. But in Albany, Republicans more focused on patronage and expanding their power base ran the show. Their vision for revamping the city's police centered on a bill requiring a bipartisan police commission of four, two from each party—in effect, making legal the informal arrangement that had been in place from the 1860s until 1889, when Tammany mayor Hugh Grant had tipped the balance to three Democrats and one Republican. It was this deep split between Parkhurst-led reformers and the statewide regular GOP that led to six weeks of protracted, often difficult negotiations over the nature and scope of the inquiry.

Legislative investigations of New York City driven by partisan politics and the settlement of personal scores had long been part of the state's political landscape. Committees were formed, briefly explored issues, provided a vague recommendation or two, and then disbanded, content that they had done their job and the people's business. That history was known to all and it allowed Democrats and other skeptics to dismiss the new Lexow inquiry, intended to last three weeks, out of hand. It would follow the course of all the others and end up doing nothing. But in 1894 a combination of circumstances created a very different climate for the investigation. New York's political significance nationally as the crucial swing state ensured that this would be more than the usual wrangling between Republican upstaters and city Democrats. The deepening economic depression, especially in the city, had already weakened Democrats, turning their unprecedented sweep of 1892 into a distant memory. For a growing number of New Yorkers the economic crisis exposed as well the failures of the two-party system. A newly aggressive press generated extensive coverage, much of it graphically illustrated, as newspapers touted their own investigative powers and their influence on the committee. Prosecution of election fraud cases and the highly publicized court trial of Captain William S. Devery provided counter-narratives, tributaries creating a rising tide of interest. The city would elect a new mayor in November. A brief review of these factors helps explain not only the formation of the Lexow Committee, but its singular inner contradictions, and its evolution into the first sensational political investigation of the modern era.

While Clarence Lexow quickly became the committee's public face, he was merely a lieutenant for Thomas C. Platt, the state's Republican Party leader. Born in 1833, Platt had risen from running a drugstore in Owego, Tioga County, to make himself one of the most influential political players on the national scene. As a young man he had led torchlight parades for Abraham Lincoln, and for the rest of his life Platt treated party loyalty as a faith. A former and future U.S. senator, Platt embodied the "Stalwart" faction of Gilded Age Republicans, men fully committed to the politics of party patronage, opposition to civil service reform, and absolute loyalty to the GOP. Indeed in 1881 Platt had resigned as U.S. senator from New York, following the lead of his mentor Senator Roscoe Conkling and other "Stalwarts," in protest against the "Half-Breeds" of the Hayes administration who had refused to honor the Stalwarts' nominations for federal offices in New York. Although out of office until his return to the U.S. Senate in 1897, Platt expanded his political influence throughout the state. As president of the U.S. Express Company, created to handle the special delivery business of the Erie Railroad, Platt used his strategic position to dispense favors to rural editors, politicians, and legislators in upstate counties where the Erie did business. He centralized corporate funding for Republican candidates, ensuring that executives from certain big businesses—utilities, insurance, banking, transportation—enjoyed regular access to political representatives. From his apartment in the Fifth Avenue Hotel, just across the street from Parkhurst's church, Platt helped direct every Republican election campaign in New York State and the nation for over three decades. For several years, he was even a member of Parkhurst's Madison Square congregation. Newspapers dubbed him "the Easy Boss," but in an interview with journalist Nellie Bly he expressed abhorrence for a term he thought only appropriate for describing Democrats. When she asked, "What do you want to be called—a leader?" Platt replied tersely, "No. I only want to be called a Republican."[3]

As the Lexow Committee tried to organize itself, Platt found himself in an uncomfortable alliance. He complained bitterly to Lexow about "constant delays and unceasing concessions to the Parkhurst Party." (In his autobiography, published in 1910, Platt's account of the Lexow Committee's origins and its work made no mention at all of Parkhurst.) Platt, his eye always upon the national implications of New York politics, thought the most important goal of the investigation would be procuring testimony in support of the bipartisan police bill. For Platt and the Republican establishment, recent events in Washington gave special urgency to a legally bipartisan police board. On February 9, 1894, President Cleveland signed the bill repealing the Federal Elections Law, marking, as the *Times* put it, "the close of a most important and at times exciting period in the history of the country since the war." For the first time since before the Civil War, Democrats controlled both the legislative and executive branches of the federal government, and they had finally put John Davenport and the entire federal election regime out of business. And for the first time in a generation, New York Republicans would be unable to rely upon federal marshals to help tamp down urban Democratic turnout. The city's bureau of elections was still in the hands of the NYPD. The hard-fought election of 1892, with its near violent confrontation between city police and federal authority, was fresh in everyone's minds.

But the economic depression helped Republicans take back the New York State legislature in the fall of 1893 and national prospects looked brighter as well. Party allegiance would be more important than ever, as was invoking the specter of Democratic vote fraud. Senator Lexow expressed the Republican view with a vivid image that captured the essence of the upstate/downstate split. "We are not willing," he said in a speech supporting the bipartisan bill, "to march down to the Harlem [River] with a magnificent majority representing the lawfully cast and honestly counted vote of two-thirds of this state to find that majority overcome and the will of the people undermined by a larger majority south of the Harlem cast in corruption and counted in fraud." While he expected Democratic opposition, Lexow reserved special scorn for reformers like Parkhurst, "who desire a single headed department—framed upon the standards of European experience & who bow reverently at the shrine of everything foreign and un-American—because it's English you know." He dismissed as well the Union League Club and Chamber of Commerce as out-of-touch political amateurs who ignored the issue of vote fraud. "Do they represent the wishes of the average American citizen? They represent only themselves. It is impossible for them to appreciate ordinary everyday conditions of life." Regular Republicans described Mugwumps variously as "the delicate, dainty few," "Anglomaniacs," "Miss Nancys," and "political flirts." As one critic put it, "A neutral in politics is like a neutral in sex." Real men stood by their party, as they did their country.[4]

Throughout February the Lexow Committee met with representatives of the "Parkhurst Party," from the Society for the Prevention of Crime, the Chamber of Commerce, the Board of Trade and Transportation, and the recently formed City Club, devoted to efficiency and honesty in municipal government. Nearly all the members and activists in these groups were socially prominent and longtime Republicans (more than half of the City Club's members were listed in the *Social Register*), but they took pains to distinguish themselves from professional politicians like Platt. Negotiations produced some real give and take. Lexow agreed that the committee would need to sit for much longer than the original three-week time limit. President Smith of the Chamber of Commerce, along with the senators, emphasized the critical need to get testimony from high-level expert witnesses—current and former police commissioners, judges, ex-mayors—who could discuss the best ways to reorganize the police force. They had little appetite for putting victims of police blackmail or seedy figures from the city's underworld on the stand. Sessions would be open to the public, but the committee reserved the right to ban reporters and go into secret session when, as one senator put it, "the testimony was of such a nature as that which was so freely printed concerning Dr. Parkhurst's much talked-of expedition."

Joseph Choate, the consensus pick, declined to serve as committee counsel. He probably anticipated a leading role at the upcoming New York State constitutional convention. (Choate had been elected as a delegate and he was eventually elected as president of the convention.) With Choate out, deliberations broke down. The chief counsel could be a powerful force in shaping any investigation, or he might be simply a figurehead doing the committee's bidding. Behind the scenes, Platt pressed Lexow to get the hearings rolling and to procure testimony that would help get his bipartisan police bill through the legislature as quickly as possible.[5]

Parkhurst continued to push his agenda in meetings and correspondence. But unlike Platt, who shunned publicity and preferred summoning Lexow and other Republicans to private strategy sessions at his Fifth Avenue Hotel apartment, Parkhurst also conducted a highly public campaign asserting his movement's independence. "I wish we could get rid of politics," he told the City Vigilance League at a meeting held on the Bowery. Parkhurst struggled to control his emotions as he expressed special scorn for Republican partisans. "Men who appear to be in favor of moral reform," he told the crowd, "have been under the rule of Plattism, doing their best to defeat this work." Given a choice, "I would rather be run by a Tammany Hall boss than a Republican boss, for the more pretensions to decency a boss makes the more dangerous he is." Only a thorough investigation, with enough time and adequate preparation, could dig as fully as he wanted into the main issue of police department corruption and its routine collusion with criminals. And to buttress his insistence on nonpartisanship over bipartisanship, Parkhurst repeatedly referred to the failures of previous investigations that were prematurely "called off" when they had threatened to shake up or embarrass the political status quo.[6]

New Yorkers understood Parkhurst's point about those previous investigations. Over the last twenty years three major legislative inquests, all run by Republicans, had revealed as much about partisan practices as about how the city actually operated. An 1875 assembly committee examining the increase of crime held six months of hearings at City Hall. It described the police as "a corrupt force" that was hugely demoralized. Police captains were "absolute monarchs" over the criminal classes, and ran roughshod over the lower classes. Half were either untrustworthy or unfit for their jobs. Ward detectives were notoriously corrupt. The 1875 committee heard testimony about the alleged immunity enjoyed by some gamblers and brothel keepers, as well as claims that personal safety and the security of property for respectable citizens had worsened. It exposed corruption and inefficiency within the detective system, the city's prisons, the district attorney's office, and the board of excise. Its main recommendations called for enlarging the force (at that time patrolmen covered beats of two miles or more), creating a centralized secret detective police, and licensing and regulating prostitution. However, none of these reforms gained traction. Instead, Mayor William H. Wickham used the report to oust two commissioners, his political enemies, from the police board.

The second was an 1884 assembly investigation led by the twenty-six-year-old Theodore Roosevelt (the only New York City resident on the committee) that examined charges, made by the Union League Club and others, against city officials for gross neglect of duties, fraudulent construction bids, and large increases in tax levies. It also took testimony on the court system, prisons, the sheriff's office, and the board of public works. The investigation burnished the reform credentials of its energetic young chair and Roosevelt managed to push through some municipal reform bills in Albany. But it refrained from looking hard at the police. One explanation—widely repeated among politicos—maintained that the committee's final report deliberately held back criticism of the NYPD to protect one of its upstate members. He had been caught with a prostitute in a city hotel while the committee was in session.[7]

The third major pre-Lexow investigation was the 1890 Senate Committee on Cities, which dug into the murky world of municipal governance and administration: the collection and assessment of taxes, revenue collection, and bonded debt. Led by upstate Republican J. Sloat Fassett, the committee seemed more intent on trying to embarrass prominent Tammany leaders like Mayor Hugh Grant and Richard Croker by grilling them about Democratic Party fundraising and their own personal finances. The Fassett Committee final report included support for several important reforms, including greater self-government for cities and a commission to bring order to the chaos of New York City's ordinances, regulations, and aldermanic resolutions. But it never investigated the police department, no doubt because it knew that the police commission had been run as a bipartisan body since the 1860s. Shortly after the committee's final report appeared, President Benjamin Harrison appointed Fassett as collector of the port of New York, one of the juiciest patronage positions in the entire federal government. He held the post for only two months, resigning to run (unsuccessfully) as Republican candidate for governor in 1891.[8]

In early March 1894 it appeared the Lexow Committee would repeat this pattern of cronyism and toothless recommendations. Two sticking points remained: where the committee would focus its first formal hearings and who—now that Choate had declined—would act as its chief counsel. Moreover, Platt and Lexow had established a narrow line of inquiry: the investigation would center on alleged police interference with elections and alleged offenses by policemen at the polls in recent general elections. The fiercely Democratic *Sun* mocked "these bucolic statesmen from Nyack, Clyde, Peekskill, and other centres of intellectual activity," arguing that, as in the past, a partisan motivated investigation would backfire. "For the purpose of making recruits for the Democracy in New York city," the paper predicted, "the Republican investigating committee cannot begin its labors too soon or stay too long." Nonetheless Platt and Lexow took comfort in the recent spate of publicity that once again put vote fraud on the political front burner.

In late February the district attorney's office issued indictments against seventy-two election officers for illegal conduct during the 1893 elections, the largest group of election fraud cases in the city's history. Newspapers detailed the charges, trials, and sentences for the offenders, the worker bees of the city's political system. Democratic inspector James Dooley was sentenced to five years hard labor for conducting a false canvass, whereby all 271 eligible votes counted in his election district were Democrat. A prize of a gold watch had been offered to the leader of the election district casting the largest number of Democratic votes in proportion to the number of votes cast; second prize was a patronage job paying a salary of $1,800. A Republican inspector, Michael Fay, was sentenced to five years in prison for collusion with his Democratic counterpart. Lesser offenses—swearing falsely, repeating—brought jail terms of thirty days. The stiff sentences and wide publicity prompted many of the indicted, eager to avoid trial, to jump bail or plea bargain. Francis Wellman, the assistant

DA who had supervised the indictments, noted that none of Tammany's prominent leaders or office holders, such as Richard Croker or Mayor Thomas Gilroy, protested the vigorous prosecution, or made any effort to defend the accused. Loyalty to the organization counted for little with this sort of very public heat.[9]

These vote fraud cases reinforced Platt's view that the Lexow Committee needed to focus on alleged police interference with voters and election officials, provide support for his bipartisan police bill about to be debated in the state senate, and finish its work before the legislature adjourned. To that end, Platt settled upon William A. Sutherland, a prominent Rochester attorney, as lead counsel. After considerable bickering the committee also agreed to name Parkhurst's candidate, John W. Goff, as co-counsel. The committee reached a wobbly understanding whereby Sutherland would take charge of the first part of the investigation, the political part, with Goff later directing a broader inquiry into the police department. Sutherland knew nothing about New York City's police department, but he was a member of the Republican National Committee and the party's nominee for state attorney general in 1891—in short, as reliable a stalwart as Platt could wish for. Goff, by contrast, knew the city's underside and its police as well as any lawyer in New York. It's easy to see why Parkhurst pushed so hard for his appointment. Goff had forcefully defended Charles Gardner, Parkhurst's former chief detective, in his extortion trial the previous year. Working as counsel for the city bar association, he had also helped prepare the recent vote fraud indictments. But more importantly, Goff represented the sort of independent political spirit prized by Parkhurst and his allies.[10]

Goff had been a notable figure in New York legal, political, and Irish circles for many years. Born in County Wexford, Ireland, in 1848, he had immigrated to New York as a boy, clerking in a dry goods store while working his way through night classes at Cooper Union, and then earning a living as a journalist and telegraph operator while studying law. Like so many New Yorkers of Irish descent, he moved easily between the volatile politics of Irish nationalism and the infighting among city Democrats. Goff had been active in the Clan-na-Gael, a secret society dedicated to liberating Ireland from English rule by force. In 1875 he played a leading role in the daring rescue of six Fenian prisoners held in a British penal colony in western Australia. Goff raised money to outfit the *Catalpa*, a New Bedford whaling ship used for the raid, which became popularly known as "Goff's Irish Rescue Party."

In New York Goff's hatred for Tammany Hall led him to the County Democracy, the last meaningful challenger to Tammany's dominance within the Democratic Party. Goff disliked Tammany's efforts to promote the careers of lawyers and judges in exchange for their political loyalty. After serving a term as assistant district attorney, Goff ran unsuccessfully in 1890 for DA on the County Democracy ticket, losing to Tammany-backed DeLancey Nicoll. Goff had returned to a lucrative private practice but remained active in anti-Tammany circles, where he came to know and work with Parkhurst and the Society for the Prevention of Crime. He had earned a reputation for relentless and effective questioning of witnesses in court, as well as a temper that, as in the Gardner case, could lead to charges for contempt of court. In fact, even as Chairman Lexow publicly announced appointment of the two co-counsels, Goff and the committee continued a messy public quarrel over terms of his appointment. Goff insisted on the right to name his own associate counsel (William Travers Jerome and the SPC's Frank Moss), and in a speech before the Bar Association asserted that he should direct the scope of the investigation, free to pursue all lines of inquiry. It was a clear slap at the narrow agenda set by Republican leader Platt. Chairman Lexow bristled at this demand and responded that his committee "will direct its own course of inquiry, no matter who is its counsel."[11]

With the first public session of the Lexow Committee set for March 9, a sense of confusion and uncertainty loomed over what it might actually do. Goff, though named as co-counsel to William Sutherland, made it clear he was not yet on board. A fuming Parkhurst announced he would not attend the first public session. "Why should I go?" he asked a reporter. "I don't know what they are doing or what they are going to do." For two difficult, often lonely years, he had tried to keep focused on the heart of the matter: "Do the police levy tribute and are they guilty of criminal negligence?" The committee appeared set to launch a much more restricted probe. "It is repulsive," Parkhurst declared, "to get aside from that issue and turn to such a side show as the behavior of police at election time. In other words, we started in for big game, and did not look for small-fry sport."

Beyond the disputes over counsel and the tensions between Republican regulars and "the Parkhurst Party," the Lexow Committee would not be operating in a vacuum. It would have to contend with two powerful city institutions that had their own ideas about how to best investigate and reform the police department. One of these was the NYPD itself. Superintendent Thomas Byrnes still possessed potent resources unavailable to any state senate committee. Even more importantly, the New York City press was a much more aggressive player than in previous investigations into police corruption and city scandals. Newspapers now competed more intensely than ever to establish their own claims as the most effective investigators and the true champions of reform. Whatever direction it took, the Lexow Committee would have to contend with a police leadership and an assertive city press that were both determined to challenge its authority and bend the investigation to their own ends. A brief overview of these competing factors helps clarify the complexity and difficulties faced by the committee on the eve of the first public hearings.[12]

Unlike the highly politicized four-man police commission, Superintendent Byrnes remained quite popular with the Chamber of Commerce and others in the business elite that he had served so faithfully since reorganizing the detective bureau in 1881. The Union League Club, divided over how to best reorganize the police department, nonetheless supported giving the superintendent more power as the best way to clear up the blurred lines of authority. Journalists and political insiders regularly touted Byrnes's unmatched knowledge of the department and believed Byrnes could enlighten the Lexow Committee as much as anyone. And with the investigation pending, Byrnes also demonstrated that he was as skilled a bureaucratic infighter as the NYPD had ever produced. Throughout January and February he directed a series of highly publicized moves against brothels, saloons, and other public places. On January 21 some fifty police, led by Inspector Alexander Williams, swooped down on the notorious McGurk's Saloon on the Bowery, arresting the owner and four bartenders for running a disorderly house. They also arrested 211 men and women there as "disorderly persons," in what reporters described as the biggest single police raid in the city's history. (Everyone except John McGurk was bailed out or discharged within two days.) Byrnes used the raids to gather evidence against police captains without their knowledge, causing a sensation within the department.

He took a page from Parkhurst's playbook by bringing charges for neglect of duty against three captains (including one who ran the precinct where Parkhurst lived). In the departmental trial held before the police commissioners, Byrnes sounded just like Parkhurst when he told one captain, "It is a remarkable thing that your people cannot find out the character of these houses when I can." Byrnes asserted his autonomy from the board as well. Annoyed by board president James J. Martin's persistent sarcasm and objections during the police board trial related to the McGurk raids, Byrnes finally challenged him sharply: "You had better put me out if you do not want me." Regardless of what Parkhurst or others thought, Byrnes expressed no fear of the Lexow Committee and tried to position himself as an independent force for reform within the NYPD.[13]

The Lexow Committee would operate in a more sophisticated and competitive media environment than any of its predecessors. In 1894 New York City's daily newspapers were in the midst of an expansive transformation as profound as any since the 1830s. The daily newspaper and New York had grown up together, and by the 1890s metropolitan journalism was as venerable and defining an institution of city life as the police department or Tammany Hall—and more influential on the national scene than either. Jammed into the area just south of City Hall at the junction of Park Row and Nassau Street, newspapers had made Printing House Square the crowded hub for publishing and printing for over a half-century. In close proximity to key sources of news—City Hall, the courts, Wall Street, the harbor—the area routinely attracted large crowds eager for the latest news during crises or straining to see up-to-the minute election results posted on newspaper buildings. In 1894 plenty of New Yorkers could still recall the early days when Benjamin Day and James Gordon Bennett created the first "penny press" dailies and carved a new approach to urban journalism. Day, a job printer, founded the *Sun* in 1833 with just a few hundred dollars and a hand-cranked flatbed press capable of printing 200 four-page copies per hour. Relying upon street sales and classified advertising rather than subscriptions or subsidies from political parties, the "penny press" expanded the concept of news beyond trade and commercial affairs to include accounts of street life, court cases, crime, the exotic, and the trivial, reflecting New York's emergence as the nation's commercial and cultural capital. Several of those original papers were still on the scene six decades later.

By 1837 the *Sun* printed 30,000 copies a day, attracting readers with crime reporting and by printing the names of major and minor criminal offenders. Bennett founded the *Herald* in 1835, at first simply imitating the *Sun*'s use of sensational material. But Bennett quickly outdid his rival by combining more comprehensive coverage of city life—finance, sports, a letters column—with an assertive policy of investigative reporting that placed the paper itself at the center of crime stories. As no journalist before him, Bennett claimed to be looking and listening for the public, visiting and revisiting crime scenes, interviewing and cross-examining witnesses, badgering the police, assembling the raw data of a detective story and then challenging his readers to solve the puzzle. Bennett's journalism promised to reveal a general pattern of moral decay in New York and the nation, giving his readers knowledge of "the secret springs of actions which regulate society in this corrupt and overgrown city." Bennett routinized the linkage between crime news and the reform impulse in journalistic practice; and he made the *Herald*'s success and his own "genius" the most important ongoing story of all. By 1860, the *Herald*'s daily circulation of 77,000 made it the world's largest daily newspaper.

In 1841 Horace Greeley started the *Tribune* as a more conservatively edited penny paper, one more attentive to literary culture, moralistic editorials, and, eventually, Greeley's passion for the antislavery cause. The most solidly Republican of all the city's papers, the *Tribune* never reached the daily circulation of the *Sun* or *Herald*. But none of its rivals could match the enormous success of the *Tribune*'s weekly edition. Read in small cities and towns around the country, it made Greeley a household name, selling 200,000 copies a week by 1860, demonstrating how a New York paper might achieve regional and national influence. In 1846 the *Sun*, *Herald*, and *Tribune* had been founding members of the Associated Press, exploiting the potential of the telegraph by sharing news and dividing expenses. As the telegraph system matured, the AP made news a lucrative commodity by selling dispatches from Europe, Wall Street, and Washington, DC, to daily newspaper customers all over the country. After the Civil War, AP's tight alliance with the Western Union Company strengthened New York's position as the nerve center of American news. By the 1890s hundreds of small newspapers and magazines, mostly Western and Southern, had New York representatives based in the *Tribune* building.[14]

In 1894 the *Sun*, *Herald*, and *Tribune* were still influential players in the city's journalistic scene. [See Table of Circulation Figures.] There were now, however, no fewer than sixteen English language newspapers published daily in New York, competing in a world where the rules had been redrawn by the popular "new journalism" created by Joseph Pulitzer. A Hungarian Jewish immigrant who had first made his mark editing the *St. Louis Post-Dispatch*, Pulitzer took over the moribund *New York World* in 1883, and quickly made it the most widely read and imitated paper in the city. Pulitzer fused sensational coverage of crime, financial and political scandal, and human interest stories with relentless self-promotion of the paper. Various "crusades" reflected Pulitzer's identification with New York's immigrants, his sympathy for the poor and organized labor, and his distrust of the vast personal fortunes so characteristic of the Gilded Age. He deployed his news staff to investigate garment district sweatshops, the dismal health conditions in the city's tenements, the lack of school opportunities for women, and the failure of the very rich to pay their taxes. He promoted highly publicized campaigns to keep the newly opened Brooklyn Bridge free for people who crossed it to get to work, and for raising money to put a pedestal under the Statue of Liberty. Writing for the *World* made Nellie Bly (Elizabeth Cochrane) one of the first celebrity journalists: Readers eagerly followed her race to beat Jules Verne's fictional *Around the World in Eighty Days* (she made it in seventy-two), or her harrowing account of how she feigned insanity to report on the awful conditions inside a New York asylum.

Pulitzer invested in new technologies (high-speed presses, color supplements) and lucrative Sunday editions. His banner headlines, oversized cartoons, and liberal use of illustrations made the *New York World* the most visually exciting paper. Against the charges that he violated good taste or lowered the moral tone of his readers, Pulitzer sounded a good deal like Dr. Parkhurst. "The daily press," he argued, "publishes vice, no doubt, but it does not idealize or palliate it. It publishes also the inevitable consequences of vice." In 1890 the new World Building opened on Park Row, the tallest structure in the city, higher than Trinity Church, its gleaming gold-finished dome visible for miles around. That same year failing eyesight and nervous exhaustion forced Pulitzer's retirement from active editing. New challenges to the *World's* supremacy would come just a few years later, when William Randolph Hearst took over the *Morning Journal* in 1895 and Adolph Ochs began his historic reinvention of the *New York Times* in 1896. But in 1894 the *World* remained the city's most popular and widely imitated daily.

The *World* was steadfastly Democratic in national politics, sympathetic to organized labor, and positioned itself as the voice of the city's vast immigrant working class. But unlike the *Sun*, its suspicions about Parkhurst and his movement had faded and its criticism of Tammany Hall and police corruption, always populist in tone, grew sharper. By early 1894 the *World's* ramped up coverage of Parkhurst's movement included frequent cartoons and portraits of principal players and extensive interviews with witnesses and key political figures, all wrapped in the self-assurance that the newspaper itself was now the greatest agent for change. The lead for one front-page story in December 1893, about an alleged plot to oust Superintendent Byrnes, illustrated this tone: "As the *World* investigates deeper and deeper into the police department, the more evidence piles up that the real captains of the department are not the captains in uniform of the precincts, but the Tammany leaders of the assembly districts." The grandiose sense of its own importance would continue throughout the proceedings of the Lexow Committee. But more importantly, the newspaper that most closely mirrored and spoke to the city's immigrant, working-class Democratic majority had thrown its considerable weight behind Parkhurst's movement.[15]

Other newspapers touted their own investigative strengths and promised to provide full coverage. The *Herald* looked to outdo the *World* with extensive illustrations, and its historic rival the *Sun* with deeper investigative reporting. These three papers would present the most comprehensive and detailed accounts of the committee's work. Some papers, like the *Tribune* and the *Evening Post*, made no effort to present detailed transcriptions of testimony or racier sidebar stories. But even a smaller daily like E. L. Godkin's conservative and Republican *Evening Post* could make a splash. In 1890 Godkin, a longtime enemy of Tammany, created his own sensation by publishing *Tammany Biographies*, a highly unflattering collection of sketches detailing the alleged crimes and personal depredations of the machine's leaders. Godkin's bios, revised each year and published separately as a pamphlet, anticipated much of Parkhurst's attack on machine politics and police corruption. Godkin acknowledged that "in the case of men leading, as so many of these do, vicious subterranean lives, complete accuracy is difficult to attain." And much of their history "is absolutely unfit for the columns of a respectable newspaper." But no matter, as all was in service to exposing Tammany as "simply an organization of clever adventurers, most of them in some degree criminal, for the control of the ignorant and vicious vote of the city in an attack on the property of the tax payers."

To cover the Lexow investigation, Godkin assigned a recent addition to his staff, the future muckraker Lincoln Steffens. Like most young journalists of the day, the twenty-seven-year-old Steffens had literary ambitions. A recent graduate of the University of California and son of a wealthy businessman, he worried that his assignment as the paper's first-ever police reporter might degrade his "literary touch." Writing to his father in California, Steffens described his beat as "beastly work, police, criminals and low browed 'heelers' in the vilest part of the horrible East Side amid poverty, sin, and depravity." Still, he was eager to learn about New York politics and he sensed that police reporting might be the best way to grasp how the city actually worked.[16]

Cracks in the formerly impregnable walls of party affiliation also contributed to a more aggressive investigative journalism. The "Mugwump" phenomenon of the 1880s had helped push formerly Republican journals like the *Times* and conservative editors like Godkin away from partisan orthodoxy. The term originally referred to Republicans who had deserted the scandal-tainted Republican presidential candidate James G. Blaine for conservative Democrat Grover Cleveland in 1884. Although most newspapers retained strong party identification, the bonds were not nearly as strong as they had been a decade or two earlier. Political independence in journalism could now demonstrate strength rather than weakness or "unmanliness," a charge often leveled against Mugwumps.

Compared with their role in earlier police investigations, then, New York's newspapers in March 1894 promised to be more competitive, more visual, more engaged. Yet even the fullest newspaper coverage would have to summarize and edit down large chunks of testimony, offering highly selective, often incomplete accounts. A comparison of the official Lexow Committee transcript with newspaper stories reveals varying degrees of accuracy in reporting what people actually said. Nonetheless, these stories achieved their own kind of facticity—widely circulated public accounts that might bend the story and turn the investigation in unpredictable ways.

The two tables below summarize circulation figures for NYC newspapers in 1892 and 1900. Although notoriously unreliable and often manipulated by publishers like Hearst and Pulitzer, these figures reflect the extraordinary growth in newspapers' readership during the 1890s, the emergence of fat Sunday editions, and the spreading influence of the New York press beyond city limits.

The Lexow Committee's first public meeting on March 9, 1894, proved anticlimactic in every respect. After two years of Parkhurst's crusade, months of partisan squabbling over its creation, weeks of internal disagreement about its true purpose, how could it not? Clarence Lexow gaveled the seven senators to order that morning in the Court of Common Pleas, a small, dingy, and uncomfortable room overlooking Broadway on the third

New York City Daily Newspaper Circulation, 1892

Morning Papers (Political Affiliation)	Daily Circulation	Sunday Circulation
Herald (I)	90,000	100,000
Morning Advertiser (R)	70,000	39,000
Morning Journal (I)	130,000	75,000
Press (R)	100,000	
Recorder (R)	59,000	96,000
Sun (D)	80,000	110,000
Times (D)	30,000	40,000
Tribune (R)	75,000	85,000
World (D)	192,000	260,000
Evening Papers		
Commercial Advertiser (R)	23,000	
Daily News (D)	179,000	83,000
Evening Post (R)	22,000	
Evening Sun (D)	50,000	
Evening Telegram (I)	20,000	
Evening World (D)	183,000	
Mail & Express (R)	25,000	

(Adapted from N. W. Ayer & Son's *American Newspaper Annual* (Philadelphia, 1892); Moses King, ed., *King's Handbook of New York City*, 2nd. ed. (Boston, 1894), "Journalism and Publishing," pp. 609–38 (political affiliation). Figures rounded to the nearest thousand.

New York City Daily Newspaper Circulation, 1900

Morning Papers (Political affiliation)	Daily Circulation	Sunday Circulation
Herald (I)	140,000	366,000
	(93,000 Local	(207,000 Local
	47,000 Country)	159,000 Country)
Journal (I)	275,000	508,000
	(172,000 Local	(170,000 Local
	103,000 Country)	338,000 Country)
Press (R)	115,000	42,000
Sun (D)	120,000	150,000
Times (D)	103,000	48,000
Tribune (R)	70,000	75,000

Morning Papers (Political affiliation)	Daily Circulation	Sunday Circulation
World (D)	251,000	402,000
	(203,000 Local	(215,000 Local
	47,000 Country)	185,000 Country)
Evening Papers		
Commercial Advertiser (R)	21,000	
Daily News (D)	178,000	83,000
Evening Post (R)	25,000	
Evening Sun (D)	100,000	
Evening Telegram (I)	NA	
Evening World (D)	NA	
Mail & Express (R)	NA	NA

(Adapted from N. W. Ayer & Son's *American Newspaper Annual* (Philadelphia, 1900); "Daily and Sunday Comparative Statement" for *World, Journal, Herald*, Box 1900, September–December, NY World Collection, Columbia University; Moses King, ed., *King's Handbook of New York City*, 2nd. ed. (Boston, 1894), "Journalism and Publishing," pp. 609–38 (political affiliation). Figures rounded to the nearest thousand.

floor of the New York County Courthouse. (The building remains familiarly known as "the Tweed," the most striking architectural achievement of urban graft.) The members squeezed themselves behind the small judge's dais at the front. Alongside Lexow sat four upstate Republican senators largely unfamiliar with New York City: Charles T. Saxton (Wayne County), Edmund O'Connor (Broome County), Cuthbert W. Pound (Niagara County), and George W. Robertson (Westchester County). Daniel Bradley, an independent Democrat from Brooklyn, and Jacob A. Cantor, a Tammany loyalist from Manhattan, rounded out the committee. At the attorneys table, William A. Sutherland served as lead counsel. Beside him, in something of a surprise, sat ex-district attorney DeLancey A. Nicoll, who asked to be recorded as counsel for the police board. Neither Dr. Parkhurst nor John Goff attended, conspicuous absences that reflected their unhappiness with the committee's focus on election fraud cases over police complicity in vice.

For its first six weeks the Special Committee Appointed to Investigate the Police Department of the City of New York failed to gain much traction with a largely skeptical public and initially blasé press. The committee held twelve meetings before adjourning its first session on April 17. At the time, a variety of related diversions seemed far more pressing: a battle in Albany over a law mandating a bipartisan police law; a nasty internal war among New York's Republican Party; and the unprecedented jury trial, for neglect of duty, of Captain William Devery.

The main purpose of the investigation seemed, as the *Times* put it, "to find an excuse, not for taking politics out of the police board, but for getting more politics into it." Committee counsel Sutherland set the tone on the first day with a florid 3,000-word defense of the exclusive focus on alleged police intrusions at the ballot box. Their interference, he argued, made the police part of a grand conspiracy. They were "active participants in attempts at every election to overthrow the sovereignty of the citizens of New York, to bring about a result, not that desired by the voters, but that desired by the masters of the police." Addressing procedural questions raised by defense counsel DeLancey Nicoll, Chairman Lexow made a key distinction: The hearings were not trials bound by courtroom rules of evidence; nor would the committee bring indictments. It was, rather, an investigation into whether the police power of the state was properly administered, and its aim was to gather facts that could inform new legislation. He thereby revealed that he intended to keep Nicoll, skilled and experienced at cross-examination, on a very short leash. Over the course of the next six weeks Lexow consistently ruled against Nicoll's attempts to question witnesses' political views, challenge their motives, or have their testimony thrown out as hearsay.[17]

These early sessions thus lacked the drama and news value of courtroom confrontations or grand jury proceedings. Instead they mostly presented stories told, in numbing detail, by Republican political operatives about the abuse they received at the polls in Democrat-controlled New York City. The testimony focused less on the actions of policemen—virtually none of whom were actually named or identified—and more upon allegations that they followed the orders of Tammany district captains rather than the dictates of the law. Much was made of the 1893 ballot law, passed while Democrats controlled the state legislature, which reduced the number of inspectors, poll clerks, and ballot clerks in each New York City election district from four to three, giving Democrats control of most election boards. Republicans had tried to counter with poll watchers, appointed by the Bar Association and the Republican County Committee, and charged with checking the names and addresses of voters. The litany of violations was a long and familiar one, with policemen accused of looking the other way, poll watchers roughed up by Tammany ward heelers for challenging the votes of repeaters or the falsely registered, Democratic voters receiving illegal help while marking their ballots, physical assaults by Tammany men outside the polling place. Otto Kempner, a former Tammany man who ran for assembly as County Democrat, accused patrolmen of forcing shopkeepers to remove his lithograph from their store windows.

Some testimony revealed long-simmering feuds in local election districts. Robert Strahl told the committee he had been assaulted by a Tammany operative looking for payback: In 1892, as a deputy U.S. marshall, Strahl had ordered the same man out of an Attorney Street polling place. A great deal of attention went to the Third Assembly District, along the Bowery, formerly controlled by Republicans but now a Tammany stronghold under the leadership of newly elected state senator "Big Tim" Sullivan. Harry Cunningham, a Republican election captain and former deputy U.S. marshal, told how after having a man arrested for illegal registry, "Senator Sullivan came into the polling place with several others and caught me by the collar of the coat and pulled me outside...they pushed me out into the street and Senator Sullivan said to me, 'If I wasn't running for senator I would' do so and so."

There was occasional comic relief. Jacob Subin, a Republican watcher in the Third AD, described how a policeman refused to intervene as some twenty-five men "who looked like Irishmen" voted illegally, using Jewish names. He knew "that they were not Hebrews, because they could not pronounce their names, not to save their souls."[18]

Stories like these had been told for decades before investigating committees of the state and of Congress. They were an established part of the rough and tumble of politics, impossible to separate from partisan motive. And they revealed again how at the street level so much of machine politics—in New York and other large cities—relied upon an entrepreneurial model that rewarded ambitious election district captains with cash prizes or city jobs for bringing in the biggest vote. The Lexow Committee was less interested in whether they were true than with getting them on the record. In any case there was nothing new in them. And only a few weeks earlier the district attorney's office had prosecuted scores of election fraud cases that had actually sent quite a few people, including Republican election officials, to jail.

Only a few committee members, often arriving late and drifting in and out, attended these early sessions of the Lexow Committee. Newspaper coverage, stressing the monotony and dullness, looked anywhere for a humorous angle, often finding it in the evident unfamiliarity that Sutherland and the upstate senators had with the city. "The Spectacular Investigating Machine in Operation," mocked a typical *Herald* headline, "But the Results Are Only Meagre." "Merrily the Play Proceeds," the *Times* reported, and the show was merely "an amusing farce." Even the Republican *Tribune*, eager to document Tammany strong-arm tactics, used theatrical metaphors, describing defense counsel DeLancey Nicoll as "the court jester of the proceedings," his cross-examination of witnesses meant "to turn the hearing into a great joke."

Reverend Parkhurst occasionally appeared at the proceedings but rarely stayed very long when he did. He and his allies privately lobbied the committee for John Goff to join the legal team. On March 17 the committee announced Goff had given up on his demand for control of the extent and direction of the investigation, and had agreed to join the legal team after completion of the election cases. But precisely when and what Goff might do, and his relationship with Sutherland, remained hazy.[19]

The truth was, the real action unfolded elsewhere. While the first meetings of the Lexow Committee were taking place at the Tweed Courthouse, in Albany, Senator Lexow himself was leading the floor fight for the so-called bipartisan police commission bill, which would require a board composed of two men from each major party, to be named by the mayor. Hearings before the committee on cities drew large audiences to the senate chamber, as prominent speakers testified for and against. Charles S. Smith, president of the thousand-member Chamber of Commerce, speaking "in the name and by authority of the commercial class of the City of New York," argued strongly against the bill and in favor of a single police commissioner. The goal was to get politics out of the police department, but the bill "would make it always a partisan and political concern." "I don't believe," Smith concluded, "that it is possible to have an impartial board of police commissioners when both sides are bidding for patronage."

Parkhurst attracted the biggest crowd for his prepared remarks, and he pulled no punches. "Permit me to say that for two years I have been fighting a mercenary, criminal, and conscienceless police department, and the greatest difficulty that I have had to encounter has been that I have never been able to pin responsibility and accountability at a fixed point.... You cannot fasten anything anywhere, and you never can as long as there is any plurality at the point of supreme responsibility." Proponents of the bill included Edward Lauterbach, chairman of the New York County Republican Party and a close ally of Thomas Platt. He did not see how any Republican could oppose the bill, for it offered the best chance for honest elections, especially with the demise of the Federal Elections Law. ("The only check against crime at our elections is gone.") His closing remarks revealed as well the deepening split among Republicans. Lauterbach, one of the most prominent Jews in the GOP, attacked the Union League Club for opposing the bill and questioned why anyone should listen to its political views. The club had recently blackballed the Jewish attorney Theodore Seligman for membership, even though his father, the banker Jesse Seligman, had been one of its founders. "No club that manifests the spirit of bigotry and ostracism that we have seen," he declared, "can voice the sentiment of the people on any subject."[20]

The "spirit of bigotry" hovered over Republican infighting and it threatened to undermine any challenge to Tammany Hall. At the end of March, the Committee of Thirty, a coalition of elite city Republicans challenging the rule of Thomas Platt, attracted a loud, banner-toting, boisterous crowd to a rally at Cooper Union. Led by men from the Union League Club, the Chamber of Commerce, and several former cabinet members, the Committee looked to revitalize the city's Republican Party by actively enrolling new voters and running primary candidates against Platt's men. They hammered away at what they viewed as Platt's too-cozy relationship with Tammany, and they stressed attracting independents and "Mugwumps" to oust it.

The most newsworthy remarks came from the featured speaker, eminent attorney and former Union League president Joseph H. Choate, the man who had refused the position as chief counsel on the Lexow Committee. In the midst of his speech reviewing the historical depredations of Tammany Republicans, Choate drew wild applause with the following: "I am tired of the despotic control of a handful of foreigners who have no stake in the soil and who are using the treasures of this city for political purposes, if not for personal purposes." Choate's nativist language dominated news coverage and underlined one of the enormous obstacles facing any movement to overthrow Tammany. Ethnic pride and sensitivity to slights were a combustible feature of city politics. Only a few years earlier Mayor Abram S. Hewitt, elected with Tammany support in 1886, effectively ended his political career after refusing to honor the tradition of flying the Irish flag over City Hall on St. Patrick's Day. He was not re-nominated for a second term.[21]

Back at the Lexow investigation, the committee finally heard from its first important witness, James J. Martin, president of the police board and Tammany district leader. "The senators from up country," the *Times* wryly noted, "scanned him as though he were a great curiosity. Here was a real, live Tammany tiger, the first genuine example of the type that had been before the committee." Clad in a tight-fitting, tailor-made suit, expensive overcoat, and silk hat, the bald and mustachioed Martin looked every inch the part: a Tammany professional politician. The committee hoped Martin's testimony, taken over several sessions, might revive waning interest in the investigation. It mostly confirmed a core complaint, long leveled by Parkhurst and other reformers: Vague lines of authority made it virtually impossible to fix responsibility or blame, while also accelerating Tammany's influence in recent years. Martin blandly acknowledged many of the claims made by committee counsel Sutherland. He freely admitted that of the 300 or so men he had appointed to the force over five years (from civil service eligible lists), 85 to 90 percent had come from recommendations made by Tammany leaders. He agreed that allowing policemen to join political clubs was a bad practice—but instead of issuing an order to stop it, he appealed to his fellow Tammany district leaders to voluntarily curb the practice.

Martin also played down his numerous disagreements with Superintendent Byrnes, claiming he never said that police authority would be superior to that of U.S. marshals during the heated 1892 election. When Byrnes began using plainclothesmen to gather evidence of excise violations, Martin had issued an order prohibiting the so-called spy system. He acted not on behalf of liquor dealers, he testified, but rather to eliminate bribery and blackmail by police in civilian dress. Martin took every opportunity to emphasize Byrnes's role as head of the uniformed force. Alleged police interference in elections, investigations into police collusion with criminals, neglect of duty by captains—in all these he deferred to the superintendent. When asked if he could give the committee any recommendations for improving the efficiency of the force, and especially the detective service, Martin declined to offer any at all beyond hiring more men and increasing salaries.

A frustrated Chairman Lexow wondered about Martin's lack of initiative, asking, "was it not also your neglect of duty in not seeing that the captains performed their duty?" No, Martin replied calmly, "I do not think the law impresses upon the board of police commissioners the necessity of personally making examination of those matters." Defense counsel DeLancey Nicoll, in his cross-examination, underlined the statutory limits on Martin's power, including a review of civil service eligibility lists. The police commission's responsibilities were those of administration, government, and discipline; the duties imposed upon the uniformed force included preserving the peace, preventing crime, arresting offenders, suppressing riots, and inspecting places of public amusement, licensed saloons, brothels, gambling shops, and so on. Nicoll's leading question summarized this view: "Q: So that the law, while it imposes a general duty of government, or administration, or discipline, upon you, imposes the specific duty of executing the powers I have mentioned upon the police force; that is as you understand it? A: That is as I understand it; yes sir."[22]

Sutherland had fallen short with Martin. The Rochester lawyer's unfamiliarity with city politics and relevant statutes was evident to all, and critics pointed to his overreliance upon press clippings and unsubstantiated stories to get at Martin. What did come out was largely old news: the tensions with Superintendent Byrnes, the fact that some cops belonged to Tammany clubs, the importance of political "pull" for getting a job. All this, as the *Herald* noted, had "long been a matter of common notoriety." Some policemen shared responsibility for election frauds, the *Times* noted, but there was no evidence that "the department intended or upheld such action on the part of the police." The resolutely Republican *Tribune*, which ran detailed page-one coverage throughout these sessions, likened Sutherland questioning Martin to a man "pick[ing] up a globule of mercury with his fingers. He eluded the grasp again and again." Police interference in elections may have aided in keeping some Republicans from voting and in the casting of hundreds of fraudulent Tammany ballots. But these amounted to rather small potatoes in a city with over 300,000 voters.[23]

Martin's testimony failed to generate much fresh information. Nor could it compete for public attention with the highly anticipated criminal trial of Captain William S. Devery, held the very same week. For the first time in city history, a police captain faced jail time and a stiff fine if convicted in a criminal trial. The previous year Devery had been a key figure in the conviction of Charles W. Gardner, Parkhurst's chief detective, for extortion. The tables were now turned. Devery had been indicted the previous November on four misdemeanor counts for neglect of duty while he commanded the Eleventh Precinct on the Lower East Side. Held in the Court of Oyer and Terminer, in the same building where the Lexow Committee met, Devery's case provided high-stakes drama so far missing from the senate investigation. It promised a compelling confrontation between Parkhurst's crusade and the police department, complete with undertones of revenge.

Unlike the Lexow investigation, the Devery trial did not disappoint. Led by Assistant District Attorney William Weeks, the prosecution elicited highly detailed testimony from Society for the Prevention of Crime detectives who had made numerous visits to brothels operating in Devery's precinct. They continued to run despite SPC complaints and orders from superior officers to shut them. But Devery's defense counsel, Colonel E. J. James, effectively damaged their credibility by, as the *Times* reported, "bringing out the character of the witnesses for the people whom the prosecuting society is forced to employ to secure evidence." Like most private detectives, the men had unsavory careers and they admitted to their checkered pasts: various arrests, fines, and failure to hold down steady jobs. Indeed Charles W. Gardner, Parkhurst's original detective, had been back in the news two weeks earlier, arrested for public drunkenness while trying to jump from the rear end of a Bronx trolley car. Because he was unable to pay the $3 fine, a judge ordered him jailed.

James played to the popular suspicion of private detectives, hammering away at how routinely their work required using aliases, making false representations, and deceiving people. Their accounts of what happened in an Eldridge Street brothel, complete with drinking, holding prostitutes on their laps, even getting kissed, turned into a farcical echo of Parkhurst's notorious brothel tour two years earlier. SPC detectives, James thundered, were self-confessed liars, "lower in the grade of decency than the poor creatures whom they were sent to spy on." Parkhurst himself testified about his crusade and vigorously denied that the SPC's campaign against Devery was payback for the arrest and conviction of Gardner. He repeated his view that his movement was "directed against what I understand to be the criminal collusion between the police department and the criminals." But he also admitted that the criminal collusion included the district attorney's office, thus embarrassing and undermining the prosecution. Superintendent Byrnes, cool and imperturbable on the stand, described Devery's reputation as generally good. He defended his own role, expressing confidence in numerous reports made to him by his detectives and Inspector Williams, all of which absolved Devery, and which he dutifully summarized to the police board.

Colonel James subpoenaed 150 patrolmen and detectives as defense witnesses; large patches of blue colored the crowded courtroom, surrounding halls, and side streets. In the end, however, James decided against calling any witnesses for the defense, declaring that the prosecution had failed to show any willful neglect. Instead, he made a two-hour closing argument impugning the SPC's "vagabond detectives" and Parkhurst's movement as a whole. He emphasized Devery's brave and prompt work suppressing radicals the previous summer, "snatching the black flag from the hand of anarchy." After an eight-hour deliberation, the jury returned just before midnight on April 9 with a verdict of not guilty. "A great cheer," the *Sun* reported, "which might have been heard in Park Row and fairly made the building tremble, went up from several hundred lusty throats." Most of those cheering were policemen, including many captains, men who understood that a conviction would have meant an unprecedented blow against their way of working. They no doubt shared the acid opinion expressed by Inspector Williams: "No jury in the land would convict a mad dog, much less a man, on the testimony of the witnesses of Dr. Parkhurst's society."[24]

Parkhurst expressed no surprise at the verdict. "I am not disappointed. It was just what I expected," he told the press. Two days later the defiant minister spoke to a New York conference of the Methodist Social Union, addressing 3,000 people packed into Harlem's Calvary Methodist Church on Seventh Avenue and 129th Street. Roughly the same number milled outside the doors in a steady rain. The crowd, which included many women and young girls, greeted Parkhurst with a noisy "Chautauqua salute," waving white handkerchiefs and hats, and cheering his name. His subject was "Perils and Opportunities" and he challenged his audience by invoking their shared religious history. "Are we the sons and daughters of Protestants? ... Yet we dare not stand on our own feet! That is a thing to be thought and prayed over." He served up a review of his crusade and a hint of what might come next. More than two years after his campaign began, he saw no real change in the police department. "Tonight," he told his audience, "it is exactly as vicious, exactly as disposed to convert the innocence of children and the virtue of women into corner lots." Superintendent Byrnes's testimony had saved Devery, according to Parkhurst. Nor could citizens expect justice from the district attorney's office, for it had not put its heart into the prosecution. Did Devery deserve all that credit for suppressing anarchists? Parkhurst turned the assertion around: "I claim that the entire department from Commissioners up to patrolmen are anarchical. They enforce the law just as far as they see it to their advantage to enforce it." To sustained applause, Parkhurst made his most explicitly political appeal yet. It was all about ending "the damnable influence" of Tammany Hall. Until that happened at the polling place, there was no hope for the cause. Infuriating as it was, Devery's acquittal, he later wrote, "was a boon to our cause for which we shall never cease to be profoundly grateful."[25]

Three days after Parkhurst fully embraced overthrowing Tammany at the ballot box, the Lexow Committee abruptly adjourned amidst a nasty internal dispute, leaving the city to wonder if it would ever reconvene. Long-simmering tensions between Sutherland and Goff spilled over into public for all to see. Goff and Parkhurst thought Sutherland had injured the cause of police reform by his weak handling of James J. Martin and they worried about a repeat performance as Sutherland prepared to question the other Tammany police commissioner, John C. Sheehan. Using leaks to newspapers, Goff accused Sutherland of trying to obstruct subpoenas for Captain James Price and Inspector Alexander Williams to appear before the committee.

On April 14, at a heated closed session, Goff, Parkhurst, and SPC attorney Frank Moss delivered an ultimatum to committee members to replace Sutherland with Goff before any more damage was done. A brief twenty-minute public session followed, with Sutherland bitterly denying Goff's charges. Chairman Lexow then announced adjournment *sine die* until after the state legislature ended its current term. A humiliated Sutherland hit back at Goff and Parkhurst, insisting, "I received nothing of the evidence they boasted of.... I believe confidently that they have been trying treacherously to undermine and break me down." The *Tribune* criticized both men: Sutherland for trying "to dignify such chatter by an elaborate refutation," and Goff, who "has taken himself a little too seriously from the outset." An embarrassing clash of egos, splashed across the newspapers, now threatened the future of the investigation.[26]

Parkhurst left no doubt that his own work would continue, now including the electoral front. And on April 17 the state senate voted to extend the Lexow Committee into the next legislative session, setting a new deadline of January 1895 for its final report. But the inability to generate much new information about police collusion with electoral frauds, continued political maneuvering around the bipartisan police bill working its way through the legislature, and the messy and unplanned adjournment all reflected the Lexow Committee's failure as an instrument of reform. Its future looked dim and the question of whether it could ever transcend politics-as-usual remained open at best.

6

· · · ·

MANAGING VICE, EXTORTING
BUSINESS

The abrupt adjournment of the Lexow Committee in mid-April 1894 left most New Yorkers dubious about the investigation's future. They deemed it unlikely to ever escape the confines of partisan politics that had restricted so many previous inquiries. But for Dr. Parkhurst, resumption of the committee's work, set for May 21, could not come fast enough. Despite his intense and vocal disappointment with the first phase, he was confident that shifting the focus from alleged electoral frauds to the sordid details of police blackmail would supply irrefutable proof that the charges he had made for over two years were based on fact. Testimony would be made not in secret grand jury–like proceedings, or before unsympathetic police commissioners, or delivered from his own pulpit to the congregation, but, rather, in the full public glare of the city's press.

Parkhurst grasped the political opportunities such exposure might provide for defeating Tammany Hall, with the upcoming November mayoral contest providing a first real test. While he insisted that he had no political agenda of his own—and he dismissed repeated suggestions that he stand for mayor himself—Parkhurst began pushing for a nonpartisan movement to oust Tammany. He frequently shared platforms with regular Republicans and speakers unafraid to voice their nativist and anti-Catholic prejudices. His own rhetoric, particularly in denunciations of Tammany, sometimes included more than a hint of these. Yet Parkhurst had evolved toward a more inclusive political strategy: a reform movement open to all regardless of religion, ethnicity, class, or previous political affiliation. The "civic Christianity" model shaped in the small towns of western Massachusetts required a more expansive vision of democratic citizenship to succeed in the cosmopolitan city.

In the spring of 1894 Parkhurst seemed to be everywhere. He spoke all over the city, energized by cheers from people inhabiting very different worlds from his wealthy parishioners at Madison Square Presbyterian. At the old Church of Sea and Land on the Lower East Side's Henry Street, founded in 1819 as Dutch Reformed, Parkhurst attracted an overflow crowd of working-class and immigrant New Yorkers, eager to hear more about his crusade and its larger implications. He answered the question in his lecture's title, "Whose City Is This?" by proclaiming, "We want a clean city government. We don't care if it is administered by Republicans or Democrats, as long as it is clean." Nonpartisanship in city politics could reshape the future because the cities determined the character of the whole country. In a trade union hall above a German lager beer shop on East Tenth Street, he assured an enthusiastic crowd of cigar makers that "we shall pull ourselves out of the hole that we are in on the next election day." His views on citizenship drew sustained and loud applause, as he appealed to the union men's sense of independence. "Citizenship here," he told his listeners, "does not depend upon a man's ancestry or the amount of brainpower he possesses, or upon the size of his bank account; it depends upon the fact that he is a man [applause], and we want to stand up and realize this fact and exercise the prerogatives that belong to manhood." Before a Baptist Social Union dinner held at the Windsor Hotel on Fifth Avenue, Parkhurst spoke on "The Citizen in City Politics." He did not ease up on his anti-Tammany rhetoric: "There is no city administration on the face of the globe as thoroughly rotten as ours." The city's only hope lay in destroying Tammany Hall, "the historic impersonation of the evil one."

Parkhurst nonetheless managed to avoid the sort of anti-immigrant posture assumed by other speakers on the dais that night. Wheeler Peckham, prominent attorney and founder of the City Club, decried the growing influence in national politics of immigrants "who know nothing about politics, and who are 'voted' and do not vote." State Senator Charles

Saxton, a Republican member of the Lexow Committee, argued that respectable and native-born citizens must take a more active role in politics, "or we will be governed not by the people, but by the bosses."[1]

Parkhurst believed the city had the greatest chance for genuine reform if only "self-respecting men" could put aside personal interests and political labels for the sake of the collective good. Demonizing Tammany provided the only reliable glue for such a coalition and any reform hinged on utter destruction of the enemy. Speaking after a dinner held in his honor by the City Vigilance League, Parkhurst's language had never been more colorful, sarcastic, or direct. "We are trodden under the dirty heels of a pack of lecherous, drunken, blood-stained, mocking villains, by the side of whom the South Sea Islanders, from the very fact that they have never known anything better, are crowned seraphim and harping angels, and this at the end of the nineteenth century." Parkhurst was flushed with conviction that reform must be based upon a political platform "broad enough for Republican or Democrat, Prohibitionist, Catholic, or Hebrew."

That platform, however, was not broad enough to include women. As New York State prepared for its first constitutional convention since 1867, suffragists in the city had been active for months, holding meetings and circulating petitions to grant women the vote. Parkhurst declined to support them, urging women instead to focus less on suffrage and more on their power "to exert an influence that man cannot." When pressed by a reporter, he acknowledged his old-fashioned views celebrating women's rule in the domestic sphere and protecting their "femininity": "There is something about it that I do not think is fitted for the rough and tumble of political and mercantile life." A more practical concern contributed to Parkhurst's sensitivity about femininity: A great majority of New York City women would surely support Tammany and Democratic candidates if they gained the vote. Moreover, feminists sharply criticized Parkhurst's anti-prostitution stance. Lillie Devereux Blake, a novelist, lecturer, and campaigner for women's rights, rejected the "separate spheres" doctrine and criticized what she saw as Parkhurst's hypocrisy. As she told told a Greenwich Village meeting of the New York City Woman Suffrage League (she served as its president), "We are not astonished to find him in a crusade that sends women to the penitentiary, while it lets the men go free who drag them down." Parkhurst was unwilling to embrace the vote for women or to include them in his coalition beyond appealing to their influence over husbands and brothers. He nonetheless confidently expected that the next round of Lexow hearings would only strengthen support for a nonpartisan political approach to municipal reform.[2]

Just a few days before the Lexow Committee prepared to reconvene on May 21, however, Democratic governor Roswell P. Flower wielded two defiant vetoes, reminding everyone that nonpartisanship remained a distant dream. First he vetoed the legislature's $25,000 appropriation (about $700,000 today) for the committee's work. A Democrat from upstate Watertown who had made a fortune in the jewelry business and then as a banker, Flower's election in 1891 reflected the party's growing strength outside New York City. But the economic collapse of 1893 and Republican resurgence in the legislature had made veto power Flower's main political tool, one that he wielded in the name of traditional Democratic values: support for personal liberty, negative government, and local autonomy. His veto message deployed all the rhetoric of Gilded Age partisanship. The Lexow investigation was "a misuse of public money and of legislative power for the manufacturing of political capital or the division of political patronage." Legislative "reform" investigations only targeted Democratic strongholds like New York City. Taxpayer money "should not be used to pay the campaign expenses of the political party." He mocked the investigation—a "junketing committee"—and said that the $25,000 figure would be enough either to satisfy the "avaricious appetites of counsel or to accomplish the bribery of witnesses."[3]

Senator Lexow, enraged by such language, vowed to continue the committee's work by raising private funds. Charles Stewart Smith of the Chamber of Commerce immediately announced his intention to raise the money through private donations. The chamber had played a leading role lobbying for the committee's creation back in January, and its committee on municipal legislation had maintained a close working relationship with both Lexow and Parkhurst. Smith thought the governor's message would galvanize people to donate and organized a "Fund for Police Investigation." Over the next several months at least 101 Chamber of Commerce members donated just under $18,000 to cover the Lexow Committee's expenses. The contributors included some of the biggest names from the city's banking, merchant, and insurance sectors, many of them prominent Republicans. Seven contributors put up $1,000 each (nearly $30,000 in current dollars), including Drexel Morgan Co., Cornelius N. Bliss (treasurer of the Republican National Committee), and the chamber's new president, investment banker Alexander E. Orr. Most of the funds went directly to the committee's attorneys, after Clarence Lexow had endorsed their invoices. (In October 1895 the state legislature appropriated money to refund these private contributions.)[4]

Flower's second veto came a day later, blocking the bipartisan police bill that had finally passed the legislature in amended form. It would have terminated the current four police commissioners and provided for the appointment of four new ones, two Democrats and two Republicans. The bill would have also greatly increased the powers of the superintendent, expanding his authority to assign and transfer members of the force, and to punish them for offenses previously tried before the commissioners. It thereby weakened the arbitrary power of the captains. Amendments giving the superintendent more control had been a compromise response to the strong objections raised by Parkhurst, the Chamber of Commerce, anti-Platt Republicans, and other voices advocating a single-headed commission and abolition of the four-man board. Governor Flower's veto message objected to placing too much power in the superintendent's hand, as well as to removing the forty-year-old legal principle, dating back to the creation of the NYPD, that no policeman could be punished without a formal examination of charges against him. Flower also opposed the "making of a new office for a particular person," namely Thomas Byrnes.

Parkhurst, eager for the next round of Lexow hearings, pronounced himself glad about the veto and reiterated his opposition to any bipartisan board as merely an "opportunity for trading and dickering, which is the bane of municipal government," making it impossible to fix the point of responsibility and accountability. Yet he gave Governor Flower no credit, describing him as "narrow, partisan, vicious, and conscienceless, a creature of the machine and the tool of Tammany Hall." For Senator Lexow, the bill's chief legislative sponsor, the governor was "acting as chief ringmaster in the Tammany circus," his veto a measure for "securing to an un-American organization continued existence, based upon the violation of the most sacred rights of citizenship." The resolutely Republican *Tribune*, like Lexow, kept the focus on alleged election fraud and believed a bipartisan board necessary because "Tammany systematically stole elections in the city through the connivance of the police." But unlike Lexow, who needed to maintain his shaky alliance with Parkhurst, it blamed the bill's defeat upon the minister and the amendments demanded by "the treacherous and malignant clamor of the professional 'reformers.'"[5]

Right after Flower's veto of the bipartisan bill, Tammany mayor Thomas Gilroy provided a revealing coda. The term of Police Commissioner Charles Maclean, an independent Democrat, had expired, and to replace him Gilroy shocked many of his Tammany colleagues by appointing Charles Murray, a staunch Republican and member of the Union League Club. Murray was Republican leader of the Third Assembly District along the Bowery (Big Tim Sullivan's counterpart) and he had offered some of the most detailed and damning testimony before the Lexow Committee alleging police collusion in vote fraud. He was close to Thomas Platt and Democrats had dubbed him "Murray the Depopulator" for his work as supervisor of the 1890 federal census in New York City. Murray's census had put the city's population at just above 1.5 million; a police census done later that year came up with a total of over 1.7 million, a difference of over 12 percent. (Despite protests, federal census officials refused to perform a recount.) Gilroy's appointment of Murray took the sting out of Governor Flower's veto for Republican politicians and silenced their criticism. It also allowed the mayor and Tammany Democrats to tout their support for bipartisanship without inscribing it in law, and it provided them some defense against future attacks on a "Tammanyized" police. In other words, it precisely embodied the "dirty bargain for spoils" that had so frustrated reformers.[6]

The governor's vetoes and the related maneuvering could not stop the investigation from moving forward. The Lexow Committee did indeed reconvene on May 21, now led by a new legal team determined to put partisan divides on hold in the service of exposing police corruption. John W. Goff replaced William Sutherland as the new lead counsel, assisted by two men, Frank Moss and William Travers Jerome. The thirty-five-year-old Moss was Parkhurst's closest ally, serving for years as attorney for the Society for the Prevention of Crime and as a member of its executive committee, an inside player in all its legal battles against police corruption. A Union League Republican and devout Methodist, Moss was an active anti-vice crusader in his East Harlem neighborhood. His rambling, idiosyncratic three-volume history of New York City, *The American Metropolis* (1897), reflected his view that most of the city's current ills could be laid at the feet of recent immigrants, especially the Irish, Jews, Italians, and Chinese. Jerome came from a family of prominent New York attorneys, and his cousin, the noted beauty Jennie Jerome, later became Lady Randolph Churchill, mother of Winston. Jerome, also thirty-five and an independent Democrat, had already served as deputy district attorney, successfully prosecuting several high profile cases against Tammany politicians accused of bribery and protection of gambling. Unlike Sutherland, Goff, Moss, and Jerome had all gotten their hands dirty in the city's legal and political underside, and none was identified with the regular Republican Party. This was a legal team much closer to Parkhurst's agenda than that of Republican boss Thomas Platt.

Goff quickly emerged as the dominant figure in the investigation. Tall and thin, with piercing eyes, a full head of prematurely white hair and a nearly all white beard (he was only forty-five), Goff brought an extraordinary intensity to his work both in and out of the courtroom. Parkhurst had become close to Goff ever since watching him defend SPC detective Charles W. Gardner in his extortion case the previous year. The state senators took longer to come around, but by May, after the widespread criticism of the committee's lackluster first sessions, they had to agree with Parkhurst. Goff's political independence, his reputation as an effective and relentless prosecutor while assistant district attorney, his well-known commitment to Irish self-rule—indeed his very Irishness itself—made him the ideal lead attorney. Personal experiences fueled Goff's animus toward Tammany. As a young lawyer he had resented the machine's regular interference in the legal system and its promise of lucrative clients if only he would become a Tammany man. His experiences in the Irish independence movement offered an alternative model and set of ideals for political activism. And Goff's temperament valued self-autonomy above all— he was always his own man.

In the twenty-three days of testimony held between May 21 and summer recess on June 29, Goff produced unprecedented revelations. "It was during these twenty-three days," as the *World* put it, "that there was for the first time in the history of the city actually spread before the people of New York positive evidence of the systematic collusion of the police with thieves, prostitutes and gamblers, of the methodical and elaborate system of blackmail which is levied by the police at certain fixed and graded rates upon merchants of all kinds."[7]

Goff lost no time getting down to the business of erasing the partisan divide. As his first witness he called Police Commissioner John McClave, the Board's treasurer, its longest serving member (originally appointed in 1884), and a Republican. Goff's withering examination of McClave, he later wrote, "convinced the public that the Committee was in earnest, and that they would uphold the counsel in all their efforts to get at the condition of affairs." McClave, 55, was short, slender, broad shouldered, with black mustache and gray hair. He looked every inch the prosperous businessman he had become through his lumber dealership. But he was utterly unprepared for Goff's aggressive approach. On the first day Goff startled the witness and the crowded courtroom by subjecting McClave to a barrage of questions, often moving quickly from one topic to another. How much had his personal net worth increased during his time on the board? Had he benefitted in business from his position? How did he explain deposits of suspicious amounts into his account—in particular one check for $3,333.33, exactly one-third of the rumored price of $10,000 for promotion to captain? Had the commissioner commingled his personal bank accounts with that of the police pension fund that he administered? This last inquiry had a furious McClave pounding his knee with his fist in denial. He and his attorney, DeLancey Nicoll, expressed outrage that a gentleman would be subjected to such detailed questions about personal business.

Things got even more personal when, in the middle of that same first day, Goff asked McClave to step down so that the committee could hear from the commissioner's son-in-law, Gideon Granger, a shady real estate agent in the middle of a messy divorce from McClave's daughter. A nervous and uncomfortable Granger testified that he had acted as a go-between for his father-in-law, collecting money from men looking for promotions and appointments to the force. McClave grew increasingly red-faced listening to Granger. Finally he jumped up from his seat, pointed his finger at Granger, and shouted, "I want to say to you that this man on the stand here is a drunkard, a liar, a thief, and a forger, and it is too bad that he should give testimony!"[8]

It was clear now to one and all that the entire tenor of the Lexow investigation had changed. Granger's testimony and McClave's outburst dominated coverage of the session, described by the *Herald* as "the liveliest ever held by the committee" and by the *World* as "dramatic, and at times intensely sensational." The next day, with Granger scheduled for cross-examination, "men fought like football players to get into the narrow passageway that leads into the small courtroom used by the Lexow Committee." Three policemen fought to keep the crowd back, as several hundred managed to squeeze into a space that might hold fifty people comfortably. But Granger never showed up, and Goff and Nicoll exchanged accusations over why he failed to appear: either police intimidation or fear of being exposed as a liar and forger. As McClave's testimony continued, Chairman Lexow struggled to keep order amidst repeated outbursts of applause and hisses. More conservative voices, like the *Tribune*, worried about Goff's tactic of "so abrupt an attack through the medium of so disreputable a witness as Granger." Yet as Goff and Chairman Lexow repeatedly noted, the committee was not a court of law and not bound by legal rules of evidence; it was a legislative investigation searching for information that might require listening to hearsay or common rumor. In fact, calling McClave to the stand had been a risky move meant to grab attention and strengthen the committee's hand. "While there was no definite evidence to accuse him of corrupt practices," Goff later wrote, "yet there was sufficient to satisfy reasonable men that corrupt practices existed, after Mr. McClave had got through." Under friendly cross-examination by Nicoll, McClave gamely tried to salvage his reputation, disparaging Granger and insisting that his practice of following the recommendations of Republican politicians merely mirrored that of the two Tammany members of the board. Following his four-day ordeal, McClave abruptly left the city with a case of "nervous prostration" and eventually resigned his post in July.[9]

Goff's skewering of Commissioner McClave had broken the ice. It also established the new routines for the committee's work. Individual senators would occasionally ask questions or press points with witnesses, and Chairman Lexow himself ruled on points of procedure. But Goff now ran the show, including which witnesses to call and in what order. As with McClave, he frequently subjected witnesses to a stream of questions, jumping from topic to topic, probing for weaknesses and ignoring social standing or political status. He sometimes began sessions by questioning minor figures before moving on to bigger fish. He was cagey with reporters about his strategy, keeping everyone guessing about who might be called next or which new lines of inquiry might be pursued. Goff's improvised approach allowed him to act as circumstances required.

Now that Goff had put the committee's work squarely back on the front pages, more New Yorkers sought him out with their own stories of blackmail, oppression, and abuse by the police. Goff's private law office on Broadway and Chamber Street, just across the street from the Tweed Courthouse, became the command center for the investigation. A corps of clerks handled the hundreds of letters pouring in relating to the Lexow investigation. A small army of private detectives and subpoena servers kept busy hunting up new witnesses and taking depositions. Goff and the committee relied upon agents of Parkhurst's Society for the Prevention of Crime for this work. The SPC's detective branch was now led by Arthur Dennett, a tall, gangly detective who also ran a summer hotel on Lake Winnipesaukee in New Hampshire. An energetic true believer in Parkhurst's work, Dennett had become a familiar figure around town; city cops referred to him as Goff's "long Yankee detective."

As effective as Dennett and Goff were, the fear of retribution remained a challenge to persuading people to testify in public. Chairman Lexow repeatedly reminded everyone that witnesses enjoyed immunity from prosecution for their testimony. Yet many subpoenaed witnesses simply refused to show up or fled the city. As one Bowery concert saloon owner told a reporter, "The Senate committee goes away, but the police remain. I would be ruined were I to tell all I know."[10]

As Goff prepared to charge ahead, the city first took in a strange interlude. On May 31 the NYPD mounted its annual parade, from the Battery up Broadway, across Forty-First Street to Fifth Avenue, and then down past a reviewing stand of dignitaries at Madison Square. Superintendent Byrnes, riding a bay horse and with two rows of medals on his chest, led 2,500 police in tight formation, five battalions of ten companies each. Despite all the negative publicity and the Lexow Committee's new vigor, hundreds of thousands cheered the men unstintedly and young boys shouted the names of their favorites. The *Sun* called it "as impressive a spectacle as our 'finest' have ever offered," and the rest of the press agreed. The exhibition of precision marching and disciplined drilling, the mounted police formed like cavalry, the many Civil War veterans wearing their Grand Army of the Republic medals—all exhibited Byrnes's success at creating a more militarized NYPD. The loudest and most enthusiastic ovation greeted men carrying the colors that had been presented to the department for bravery in the 1863 Draft Riots, emblazoned with its motto, "Faithful Unto Death." "It is a good idea," the *World* thought, "to show New Yorkers once a year just what it has to rely upon in case of a riot. It would be hard to find a body of men of better military appearance." Was there no sign or acknowledgement of the Lexow investigation? On the reviewing stand filled with politicos, one journalist reported (or perhaps imagined): "Someone around the corner of the stand yelled 'Goff,' and several of the shiny hats were ruffled the wrong way, but their owners smoothed them and themselves down when the alarm was found to be false." But all in all the bluecoat parade seemed to support the *Tribune*'s view that "New Yorkers are honestly proud of their police force, which, despite all criticisms of the police department, is vigilant, active, and well disciplined."[11]

There might have been fewer accolades had the parade been held a week later. Having started at the top with Commissioner McClave, Goff switched direction during the first week of June, calling a series of witnesses from the bottom: brothel keepers from the Lower East Side who could testify directly about police blackmail and protection. The committee—and the city—now listened as voices previously unheard, mostly women and German immigrants, revealed intimate details of police supervision of and collusion with the vice economy. Charles Priem, a stocky middle-aged German, proudly wore his Grand Army of the Republic button as he testified unwillingly, under subpoena. He had emigrated from Berlin at age eighteen in 1863, joining the Union Army shortly after arrival. Trained as a bookkeeper but unable to find work due to lack of English, he worked as a bartender and waiter, and then moved into the boarding house business. His marriage proposal to his wife included a business proposition—they would run a brothel together—and the couple leased a place at 28 Bayard Street in 1888 under her name. One cost of doing business was a $500 "initiation" fee paid indirectly to each captain, along with $50 collected each month by his ward man (plainclothes detective). Priem estimated paying over $4,300 (roughly $120,000 in current dollars) to the police over six years. The $500 and $50 arrangement appeared nearly universal. Rhoda Sanford, a middle-aged blond and another unwilling witness, had drifted from housekeeping into running a "furnished room house" at 49 Bayard Street. She gasped when Goff produced her personal account book, stolen from her home by an SPC detective, and reluctantly acknowledged a list of payoffs identified only by initials.

Some of these witnesses testified eagerly. Katie Schubert, a pink-cheeked, bleached blond in her early thirties, stylishly dressed in black and wearing diamonds in her ears, disarmed everyone with her smile. She had run a house at 144 Chrystie Street for two years. Goff displayed the advertising cards she had printed. He also showed her the health certificates signed by a neighborhood doctor, attesting that individual women were free of venereal disease. She told how she gave the local ward man $500 in ones, twos, and fives. "He said I would be protected, to run along quiet and not make any disturbance, fighting, or any noise; just to run my business quietly." Schubert also testified that Captains William Devery and Adam Cross had personally visited her place to collect their $500 fee.

SPC agents had raided her place the previous fall, and after paying a $250 fine she had left the business. Over two years she estimated paying $2,900 (about $80,000 today) to the cops.

Lena Cohen was brought to testify from the Tombs, where she awaited trial for keeping a disorderly house. A stout, small, twenty-eight-year-old native of Berlin wearing an old calico gown with a black shawl over her head, Cohen practically ran to the witness stand when called. She had opened a "fifty cent house"—the bottom of the brothel world—on E. Houston Street in 1893. A local butcher introduced her and her husband to the two ward detectives. She recalled telling them about her place: "I am keeping it for the purpose of a disorderly house, will you give me a permit, gentlemen, and they said yes, I will give you a permit, only you have to know by going in and opening a house like that, what you have got to pay." She borrowed $500 from a jeweler her husband knew, at 100 percent interest. When she fell behind on the monthly $50 fee demanded by the ward men, they had her arrested. She visited the captain in February 1894, pleading for help:

> I said, "Captain, will you be kind enough to allow me, I have paid out all the money I had, and I am broke, and I want to open it again for a month or so to pick myself up, and have a few dollars"; and he said, "I don't know; I will give you a permit until the first of April; I will give you a permit"... "You had better, Mrs. Cohen, don't have so free open, be careful a little and see who they let up; don't let up any of Dr. Parkhurst's men;" I said, "You need not take me for a child. I can consider a person, I can consider a workman from an officer," and he said, "All right, you can open up until the first of April."

The talk of needing a "permit" startled the committee and the press. It demonstrated the belief, widespread among immigrants, that, as the *Times* put it, "she could procure a license to carry on a vicious and disorderly resort." She supposed, in other words, "that the plan of licensing disorderly houses, which has been adopted in a good many European communities, was in operation in New York." After her appearance before the committee, the indictment against her was dismissed.[12]

The most detailed and damning testimony from this line of inquiry—names, dates, places, amounts—came from Mrs. Augusta Thurow, whose lengthy answers to questions by Goff about police graft revealed more than the committee bargained for about women in the prostitution business. A large, heavy-set, middle-aged woman dressed in black silk, Mrs. Thurow had emigrated with her family from Germany when she was a small child. She worked as a dressmaker and married her husband Ernst, a baker, in 1882. To supplement their income, they took in boarders in their house at 23 Second Avenue, some of them workmen he knew from his job. For five years they ran it as a "straight" house, renting rooms to married couples and to single men and women. When hard times hurt Ernst's trade and also made it harder to find regular tenants, Mrs. Thurow began taking in single women, who often said they were actors or married, charging them $3 or $4 a week for a room. Though she knew some of these women occasionally brought men up at night, she did not consider herself a brothel keeper, and she continued her dressmaking business, aided by some of the women who boarded with her. Working prostitutes gradually made up more of her tenants.

As the police came around to collect, they also encouraged Mrs. Thurow to expand so she could afford to pay them more. "Well, where this house stands you can never put a church," she testified that one ward man had told her, "and you can go on in business and I will see you in a month." She claimed that growing police demands for protection money pushed her to expand her involvement with prostitution—but she no doubt saw the potential for earning more money from her "unrespectable" tenants. This gradual transition from "straight" to "disorderly" boarding house was a common one for the women who kept them, especially during economic hard times. Although tenants frequently came and went, she enjoyed amiable relations with the mostly German-born women, sharing household tasks and sometimes dressmaking work.

Mrs. Thurow's testimony, detailing her gradual movement into the trade, the widespread practice of casual prostitution, the ethnic ties between prostitutes and other workers, and the constant police harassment for more money, contradicted most of the moralistic, conventional assumptions explaining the commercial sex trade. Mrs. Thurow and the women she rented rooms to were much more than helpless, innocent, "fallen" women, victims of seduction or weak family structure. Unlike many other brothel keepers, Mrs. Thurow had not worked her way up as a prostitute herself. She was an independent, skilled, and savvy woman for whom the switch to running a brothel made good business sense. Her story illustrated how running a house of prostitution was often the best business opportunity open to women. And she had moved into brothel-keeping not as a result of a broken family, but rather quite the opposite: to help keep her own family together after her husband could no longer find work.

Mrs. Thurow's account demonstrated as well the autocratic power of the captains and how they leveraged the fear of raids from both central office detectives and Parkhurst's men. Captain Michael Doherty told her at the Fifth Street station house "he had orders from the central office to close all house in the precinct, and for me to keep on doing business very carefully, and not to let any lady friends in, and not take money myself, and if I took money, I might get in trouble, and they might raid me from the central office." Captain Doherty told her, "I am not supposed to take money but you can give the money." He then handed her a pencil and envelope and instructed her to write the ward man's name on it, and after she put in $25 in, he placed it in a pigeon hole.

During a flurry of raids by the Society for the Prevention of Crime, another captain advised Mrs. Thurow to run her place under the cover of a cigar store or café until the heat passed. She recounted how three different captains had called at her house to receive their $500 "initiation fee." She learned how to bail out arrested women by paying $10 to the desk sergeant, who would then allow her to provide surety bond though she owned no property. But the protection money did not protect Mrs. Thurow or her prostitutes. She found some relief by having her husband visit George Roesch, the Tammany district leader and a state senator, paying him a $100 "retainer fee" to have the ward men called off. She nonetheless endured continued harassment from ward men, who often lied to their captain to line their own pockets. After yet another raid, she maintained that she complained bitterly to a ward man: "I said, 'This is a nice deal; I am at home, always ready with my money,' and he said, 'You don't hitch with the boss, and that settles it, and that is the reason.'" In early 1894, furious over her continued persecution, she learned from her lawyer that she might have to serve time in prison. "I felt so angry...and I felt revengeful, and I told Dr. Parkhurst all about it."

No wonder Mrs. Thurow proved such an enthusiastic and effective witness. Goff and his associate counsel used the long affidavit she had given to the SPC, along with police blotter records, to corroborate the specifics of her charges against at least twenty different police officers. Her testimony, the *World* reported, "was astonishing even to those who have been most firmly convinced of police corruption and blackmail."[13]

The cumulative weight of the brothel keepers' testimony was unprecedented in city history. The *Sun*—no friend to Parkhurst or the committee—said it "reveals a condition of depravity and corruption in the department of police almost beyond human belief...the foulest moral cesspool that has ever been exposed in the history of a community." Enough testimony had already been heard, the *Times* editorialized, "to establish that the blackmailing of criminals by the police pervades the whole force and the whole city." Goff's aggressive strategy neutralized the traditional objections to the moral character of witnesses. Attacking the bad reputations and criminal pasts of witnesses had long been a staple used by attorneys in open court. DeLancey Nicoll had certainly taken this tack in cross-examining Lexow witnesses. But he largely failed to impeach their credibility. Goff employed a settled principle in the law of evidence to establish the credibility of brothel keepers, prostitutes, and political fixers on the stand—that testimony given against a person's own interests had a higher value than testimony given in support of those interests. "When the keepers of disreputable houses testified against the power which they had for years been slaves to," Goff argued, "they testified against their own interests. They testified without hope of reward, and with all the dangers and risks of tradition staring them in the face." Goff's success also brought a new upsurge in private contributions to the Chamber of Commerce fund, laying to rest any concerns that the investigation might end for lack of funding.[14]

By the end of the first week, Parkhurst pronounced himself highly gratified by the investigation's revelations. There was certainly no need to put off his annual three-month vacation climbing the Swiss Alps. As Parkhurst and his wife, Ellen, prepared for their June 6 departure aboard the White Star ship *Britannic*, he expressed confidence that his presence was no longer needed. The detailed testimony of the brothel keepers provided "an absolute vindication of the ground we have taken for the last three years." Like everyone else, he believed "that woman Thurow could never have invented such a story as she told." Parkhurst heaped praise upon Goff and his "peculiar genius for 'gimletting' the reluctant truth out of a witness who wants to lie." Yet he worried about the ultimate effect of all the exposures unless political action followed.

Parkhurst remained fixated on blaming Tammany Hall alone. He imagined a highly centralized and disciplined arrangement secretly controlled to fill its coffers. Despite plenty of evidence implicating a Republican police commissioner and numerous Republican captains, as well as the revelations that police blackmail flourished historically regardless of who was mayor, Parkhurst described police corruption as "merely the expression of the viciousness inherent in the entire criminal Tammany Hall system." The NYPD was only "the gastric center where the food of Tammany Hall is digested. It is the stomach into which the material enters which goes to build up that organization." If a coalition of anti-Tammany forces could unite around one man in the fall mayoral election, he predicted, it could destroy the cause of corruption. But that man would not be Parkhurst himself, as he dismissed those floating the idea of "Dr. Parkhurst for Mayor."[15]

Meanwhile, various elements within the police department tried to deflect the glaring light of negative publicity generated by the committee hearings. Superintendent Byrnes followed the testimony closely and gamely promised to confer with the police commissioners. "If it is untrue," he told reporters, "it is a malicious libel on the department. If it is true, and can be substantiated in a court of law, the accused officers ought to be sent to jail." The commissioners at first directed Byrnes to investigate the charges made against police captains. They quickly called off any inquiry after Chairman Lexow met with the superintendent and warned him that any such effort would hamper and prejudice the investigation. "The accused officers"—police captains named before the committee—typically made laconic denials that, perhaps unwittingly, illuminated the enormous power of their command and the insular job culture that went with it. Responding to accusations made by Katie Schubert, for example, Captain Adam Cross simply told a reporter, "My sixteen years of service on the force should protect me against the false accusations of a woman whose testimony betrays its falsity."[16]

Goff's probing had begun revealing, layer by layer, the historical persistence of the problem. The entrepreneurial element—and attraction—of police work had been present from the colonial era. By the 1890s, as Lexow testimony revealed, the profits to be had from managing the city's vice economy dwarfed all other police entrepreneurial activity. Throughout June Goff continued to call witnesses who exposed the far-flung reaches of that entrepreneurship. Testimony from Bohemian saloonkeepers, for example, showed how the city's poorer and more insular immigrant communities were especially vulnerable to police "protection." Most of New

York's roughly 60,000 Czech speakers lived and worked in the Yorkville neighborhood on the Upper East Side. In 1889, local ward detective Samuel Campbell—who was also the Republican district leader—advised Bohemian saloonkeepers to form an association for their mutual benefit. Joseph Pospisil, a former president of the Bohemian Liquor Dealers Association, nervously recounted how each of its thirty-five members paid weekly dues into a fund that paid Campbell $100 every month, along with cash gifts to precinct Captain Daniel Strauss. In exchange, members could routinely break the Sunday excise law (remaining open after 1 a.m.), and they received early warnings of occasional police raids. Goff brought into evidence the organization's books and circulars, all written in Czech, with frequent references to payments made to the "pantata." A lively row broke out over the precise English equivalent of the term, variously translated as "father-in-law," "head man," or "captain." Pospisil eventually settled on "ward detective," and "pantata" instantly became a new addition to the city's slang.[17]

Even more disturbing was the testimony that exposed police collusion in the so-called "green goods" business: protection of the lucrative sale of counterfeit currency. On June 14 the committee and an overflow crowd of spectators heard from George Appo, a reluctant witness under subpoena. His strange physical appearance and picaresque life story embodied the contemporary definition of a career criminal. "By nature, by heredity, by instinct, by association, and by training," the *World* noted, "he has been an habitual violator of the ten commandments and the laws which govern civilized communities." A slightly built man in his late thirties, Appo's right eye had been shot out during a fight in Poughkeepsie and replaced with glass. His face and hands bore ugly scars from knife fights and he was nearly deaf. Appo was also of mixed race, "a pale, sallow little man," as the *Herald* put it, "whose high cheek bones and black hair and slanting eyes showed clearly his Mongolian origin." His father, Quimbo Appo (originally Lee Ah Bow), was a Chinese immigrant who had made his way from San Francisco to the city's small Chinatown where he became a tea merchant. He married an Irish Catholic woman, Catherine Fitzpatrick, who gave birth to George in 1856. But Quimbo was sent to prison in 1859 for murdering his landlady (the first of two murder convictions), and shortly after that Catherine abandoned young George, leaving him effectively orphaned in the harsh world of the Five Points. There he learned how to be a pickpocket, for which he was convicted and sent to prison at age sixteen, the first of several jail terms.

Appo's unprecedented and minutely detailed account of the "green goods" business, given in soft-spoken, nearly inaudible tones, kept the committee, the courtroom crowd, and reporters straining forward for some three hours. Most New Yorkers were familiar with the ancient practice of swindling greedy "countrymen" by selling them a satchel of counterfeit bills that turned out to hold bricks or sawdust. Stories of such cons had long been a staple of city guidebooks, urban melodramas, and cartoons. But few people understood just how highly organized and lucrative the green goods game had become by the 1890s. Appo had been in it for nine years and he laid out how the business worked, describing the specialized roles in the argot of the trade. A "writer," using names and addresses from credit rating agencies such as Bradstreet or Dun, would send out circulars all over the country announcing that counterfeit money made from stolen government plates could be had cheaply. These might be accompanied by bogus press accounts describing the robbery of such plates, a real $1 or $2 bill, and a blank telegraph form for reply.

If someone expressed interest, he would be instructed to come to a hotel in a town outside the city, where he would be met by a "steerer" (the role Appo played for years), who would use a preset code phrase such as "How are you, speedy fortune?" The "steerer" then brought the "guy" to a saloon in the city, where he introduced him to the "turner" and his father, known as "the old gentleman." They then went to a small storefront fitted up to "do the trick." The "turner" showed the "guy"—the mark—a package of five or ten thousand dollars in genuine bills (provided by a "backer"), and asked him how much he wanted to purchase on a ten to one basis: $300 would buy $3,000. The real money was then put on a shelf near a desk. Once the "guy" named his amount he was asked to sign a form. The "turner" opened up the desk, briefly obscuring the shelf holding the package of real bills. A "ringer," sitting behind a partition, then quickly substituted an identical package of worthless paper for the good money just shown to the "guy." A "tailer," usually a large menacing man, then accompanied the victim to the train station or ferry, warning him not to open the package until he had left the city and to be on the lookout for treasury detectives and New York cops. In a more recent variant of the con, Appo described how the switch might be made in a cab. Most victims never returned or filed complaints to the police. Those who did would be threatened with arrest (or worse) by the police, who would also warn green goods gangs of any such gripers. The police would also come down hard on any freelancers engaged in "stealing guys"—"working on their own hook"—from protected gangs.

Goff and the senators were most interested in the police connections. Green goods swindling had been around since paper currency had entered the economy during the Civil War. In his *Professional Criminals of America,* published in 1886, Thomas Byrnes himself included detailed descriptions of green goods (also known as the "sawdust game") and related cons. But while Byrnes emphasized the skill and cleverness of the city's con men, he made no mention of the importance of police collusion. Appo insisted that in New York, unlike any other city he knew, the entire business thrived under police protection. When challenged on how he knew this, Appo contrasted his experiences as a pickpocket with his work as a "steerer." "If I passed by any of them [police] and tried to pick a pocket they would see me pretty quick, but it seems that when I passed by them with a victim they never saw me." He noted that his criminal past made him well known to the cops and pointed out the window in the direction of police headquarters. "Why don't they arrest me?...My picture is up in the rogues' gallery in the central office, and they pass by me in the street and I have a victim alongside of me, and they bow and look and all that sort of thing." There was no comparison to stealing watches on a streetcar. Appo estimated that the city's biggest "backer," James McNally, had thirty-five men working for him, earning in one day as much as $8,000 (roughly $220,000 today). The "writer" and the "backer" (who supplied the real money for show) split the profits 50-50, paying the other accomplices out of their end. The green goods business also had men working in the post office and Western Union to help with distribution of the circulars. New York, Appo told the committee, was the only city in the country where green goods men could buy police protection that guaranteed them immunity from arrest.

Appo's tale also spelled out the structural basis for so much police entrepreneurship: the exploitation of out-of-towners looking for easy money, sex, or other services unavailable at home. Appo's friend, Frank Clarke, a veteran gambler, three-card monte dealer, and "bunco" artist, testified about his long criminal career in the Fourth Ward, near the East River waterfront. He confirmed Goff's statement that "the understanding was that you were allowed to do business on condition that you were not to beat any citizen of New York." People caught in compromising situations or victimized by their own greed feared publicity and very rarely pressed charges or appeared as witnesses. By the 1890s lining one's pockets via the weaknesses and avarice of visitors to the city had become part of police routine. Appo's account demonstrated the highly theatrical nature of the green goods swindle, with its precise roles, stock characters, and colorful slang. Not surprisingly, with all the publicity and sensation generated by his Lexow appearance, Appo himself became a vaudeville attraction. In December 1894 he appeared as the star of the melodrama *In the Tenderloin*, performed at the People's Theater on the Bowery, one of the city's largest playhouses. Appo's role augured a more ambiguous portrayal of the underworld, one that became commonplace in the twentieth century: the criminal as celebrity, as much a heroic figure as a villain.[18]

Appo, appearing under subpoena, declined to name specific police officers in his testimony. Nonetheless, the city's newspapers strained to outdo each other in underscoring its significance. As the *Herald* noted, "No one who read it can fail to be convinced that, whatever Appo's motive may be, his story contains a startling amount of truth." The *Times* declared it "the most startling, the most appalling, that has yet been submitted," asking rhetorically, "Does anybody suppose that he could possibly have fabricated the complicated story?" Even the city's veteran legal observers found Appo's testimony shocking, the *Sun* reported, "a story experienced lawyers pronounced one of the most remarkable ever told in a court room in New York City." The *World*, always looking to connect local stories with national politics, led with how Appo revealed a situation akin to the hated (for Democrats) protective tariff. Immunity under the privilege of police protection "is shared by a few wealthy capitalists in the sawdust game. Small individual operators who invade the high tariff precincts secured by the wealthier scoundrels are driven out ruthlessly, sometimes at the pistol's point." Yet convincing as Appo's testimony had been, his physical scars, mixed-race features, and long career as a pickpocket and green goods steerer marked him as a lifelong criminal. His testimony, like that of the brothel keepers, came with the odor of the city's lower depths. Looking for links between police corruption and more respectable citizens, the committee expanded its range of witnesses.[19]

A few days after Appo's testimony, a stocky, gnarled old man with a ruddy, weatherbeaten face reluctantly climbed into the witness stand. Unlike Appo or the brothel keepers, Harry Hill had been a genuine New York celebrity long before his Lexow appearance. For over thirty years he had operated Harry Hill's Variety Theater on the corner of Houston and

Crosby streets, one of the best known—and controversial—entertainment spaces in the city. A combination of saloon, dance house, restaurant, and theater, the two-story wooden structure and its proprietor had been profiled, satirized, denounced, and celebrated in newspapers, guide books, variety sketches, and magazines. Hill was a central figure in the male sporting world centered around boxing and horse racing, serving as stakesholder and referee for some of the biggest sporting events of the century. Indeed Hill's place virtually defined male sporting culture both locally and through national media and was also known for dissolving, at least temporarily, social boundaries. Over the years Hill had moved toward greater respectability, straddling the city's bachelor male subculture and the emerging sphere of more respectable commercial entertainment. But by 1894 he had been reduced to poverty and anonymity, running a tiny restaurant in Rockaway Beach, Long Island. How had such a wealthy, successful, and famous man come to so pathetic an end? Friendly relations with the police department had been crucial to Hill's historic rise—and, as his Lexow testimony revealed, when those connections went sour Hill's fall was swift.

Hill's career and life story help explain the significance of his Lexow appearance and underscore the parallel evolution of the police force and New York's commercial entertainment over the second half of the nineteenth century. He was born sometime in the late 1820s in Leatherhead, England, in Surrey, where he spent his boyhood apprenticed to an uncle who was a prominent horse trainer at the Epsom Downs race track. While working there young Harry became acquainted with a wealthy American sugar merchant, George M. Woolsey, who engaged Hill to come to America in 1850 and take charge of his private stables in Astoria, Long Island. Hill soon opened his own livery stable on Third Avenue, selling horses to the Third Avenue Railroad Company and driving the first car of that line himself. He drifted into the saloon trade and opened a combination grocery store, barroom, and stables at Houston and Crosby Streets in 1854. Around this time Hill also gained a reputation as a boxer and wrestler when he defeated a local champion for the then-enormous stakes of $2,500 (about $67,000 today). Hill's fame as a prizefighter no doubt helped him to build his place up, but so too did shrewd attention to politics and police affairs.[20]

Police headquarters at 300 Mulberry Street was literally around the corner. In 1857, after the Republican state legislature created the new

Metropolitan police force to supersede the old Municipals, controlled by Democratic mayor Fernando Wood, the two groups edged toward a violent confrontation. When a riot between the rival police forces broke out on the steps of City Hall on June 16, 1857, Hill volunteered himself and a group of men as deputies in support of the Metropolitans, and his place served as a shelter for the wounded. The courts ruled in favor of the legitimacy of the Metropolitans. In backing the winning side Hill began a thirty-year period of essentially friendly relations with the police department. George W. Matsell, chief of the Municipal Police and therefore on the opposite side from Hill in the 1857 riot, nonetheless praised him as "a square man." During the 1860s, on Matsell's recommendation, the Pinkerton National Detective Agency used Hill as an informant for news about criminals who might have hung around his place. The agency also recruited operatives there for its New York office.

By the Civil War era, although no longer a prizefighter himself, Hill had become a central figure in the increasingly popular and commercialized world of boxing. He served as a referee for the first international heavyweight championship bout between the Irish-American John C. Heenan and the Englishman Tom Sayers, held in Farnsborough, England, in April, 1860. Arguably the most publicized sporting event of the nineteenth century (it ended in a chaotic draw), the Heenan-Sayers fight resonated with powerful ethnic and nationalist overtones. Widely reported and long celebrated in popular songs and poems, the match greatly expanded public interest in boxing and added to Hill's own reputation. For twenty-five years he reigned as the premier stakeholder, matchmaker, and promoter of boxing in New York (possibly in the United States), enjoying wide respect for his fairness, honesty, and expertise in the "science" of pugilism.[21]

By the late 1860s Hill's place on Houston Street had become more than just an unofficial office for conducting the business of the boxing fraternity. It featured a barroom and restaurant on the ground floor and a variety theater and dance hall upstairs. Men paid twenty-five cents for admission to the upper floor, while women were admitted free of charge through a separate entrance. Stage entertainments included comic singers, ventriloquists, blackface minstrels, dancers, burlesque sketches, and male and female boxers. Groups of small tables and chairs surrounded the dance floor, where patrons danced to music provided by a small orchestra. Lithographs and paintings of stage personalities and boxing matches adorned the walls, alongside quaint sayings touting the benefits of drink:

"Punches and juleps, cobblers and smashes,/ To make the tongue waggle with wit's merry flashes." What made Hill's unique was its reputation as a place where classes and sexes mixed, where the underworld met the upper world on more or less equal terms. On any given evening, distinctions between the wealthy and the working class, the criminal and the policeman, the countryman and the urbanite, the rough and the respectable, disappeared or at least blurred. Female patrons and performers included prostitutes but also single working-class women with their friends and male dates as well.

Hill's attracted not only a large number of customers, but also the attention of a host of journalists and observers who criticized, satirized, and celebrated it depending upon their view of the activities. Many post–Civil War guidebooks documenting the "sunshine and shadow" contrasts of New York life devoted at least a chapter to Hill. In the most widely read and evangelically oriented version of these books Rev. Matthew Hale Smith noted that "it is the pride of Harry Hill that judges, lawyers, merchants, politicians, members of Congress and of the legislature, doctors, and other professional men, visit and patronize his place. And no public resort of any description in the city is better known." Hill himself, quick with his fists, maintained the peace: "He keeps the roughs and bullies in order; he keeps jealous women from tearing out each other's eyes; he keeps the noisy drunkard quiet." The contrast of the rather dingy room, its sawdust floors and hard benches crowded with a mostly well-dressed clientele, made Harry Hill's "look as if upper New York, in their best outfit, had taken possession of a low dwelling at Five Points for an evening." By the early 1880s, when the London fashion for "slumming" reached New York City, Harry Hill's was a regular stop on the tours given to visiting society types and celebrities.

If Hill's place developed fundamentally as a bastion of male camaraderie based on the sharing of sporting gossip and drinking, it had a more ambiguous policy toward women than did most concert saloons. Hill did not employ "waiter girls," nor did he hire prostitutes to provide dance partners, as did the waterfront dance houses. Prostitutes undoubtedly mixed in the crowd, but it was precisely the fact that other, respectable women could be found there that worried Reverend Smith:

A sadder story of New York life cannot be written than that connected with this place. Girls of great promise and education; girls accomplished, and fitted to adorn any station; girls from country homes, and from the city; missing maidens; wives who have run away from their husbands; girls who have eloped with lovers; girls from shops and factory, from trade and saloon, can here be seen in the dance. The only child of a judge, the wife of an eminent lawyer, showy, flashy, and elegantly dressed, and women of a lower degree, all mingle. They come and go as they will.

Other writers agreed that the real danger of Hill's lay in its owner's claim to run a "respectable house." Voyeuristic accounts of the activities there, accompanied by illustrations, concluded with moralistic warnings to readers: "Visits from curiosity are dangerous. Stay away. To be found on the Devil's ground is voluntarily to surrender yourself a willing captive to him." Edward Crapsey, police reporter for the *Times* and chronicler of "the nether side of New York," described Hill's as a "dance-house for prostitutes, a resort for prizefighters and the idling ruffians who hang upon the edge of the roped ring, a rendezvous for the vicious of all classes, and a place where the potations are interspersed with suggestive dancing and the performances of the lowest type of a 'variety show.'" Despite (and because) of Hill's "square" reputation, his boast of including the political and economic elite among his regular customers, the "Houston Street hell" was "the most demoralizing place to be found in the city...there is nothing in the country to compare with it in its malign influences."

Descriptions like these helped make Hill's a booming tourist attraction. He distributed cards at hotels and saloons advising visitors how to find his place: "Strangers, ask any hotel clerk, policeman or conductor, where Harry Hill's is, and they will direct you. If they don't know, they are not fit to hold their position in this great city." Mark Twain lampooned Hill—and his profilers—in his "Travels with Mr. Brown," a series of sketches written for a San Francisco newspaper in 1867. Passing through New York bound for Europe, "It was in my head somehow that Harry Hill's was where the savants were in the habit of meeting to commune upon abstruse matters of science and philosophy." Twain's naïf expected to find men of renown like the naturalist Louis Agassiz or the inventor John Ericsson. "I felt in a reflective mood, and said I would like to go to Harry Hill's and hear those great men talk much better than to trifle away the time in the follies of gayer localities." Twain's narrator spends an evening observing the goings-on "so out of keeping with the grave characters

I had thought all philosophers possessed." He concludes with a jibe aimed at himself and journalists as a whole. "When I found that I, as a newspaper man, had been drawn into such a place as that, my indignation knew no bounds, and I said we would go and hunt up another one."[22]

Hill received his most favorable publicity in the *National Police Gazette*, in which he advertised regularly and with whose publisher, Richard Kyle Fox, he often partnered in arranging boxing matches. By the late 1870s Fox had turned the *Gazette* into an extremely popular illustrated weekly, featuring coverage of sports, theater, crime, and the urban demimonde. An 1879 description of a visit to Hill's neatly paralleled the appeal of the *Gazette* itself: "Seeing a great city after the lamp lighter has gone his rounds has always been a favorite amusement with those sportsmen who combine a keen desire to hunt the elephant with a natural disinclination to wander away from the comforts of home." Fox's magazine offered America's young men a mediated safe tour of the urban underworld, a similar if more vicarious chance to "hunt the elephant"—explore the New York demimonde. At Hill's they could find sporting celebrities, politicians, criminals, women, drink, and entertainment all in a protected environment. "That is the great charm about Harry Hill's place. There is nothing vulgar or obscene said on the stage, and no disorderly conduct is permitted. No one can be robbed there." The press regularly sought out Hill's expert opinion for their expanding coverage of professional boxing. Hill, "the sporting man," his gold chains and diamond pins described by reporters in minute detail, testified regularly in much-publicized court battles involving prizefights of the day. He and *Gazette* publisher Fox cooperated in promoting the career of John L. Sullivan, the greatest sports hero of the Gilded Age. They took him (and professional boxing) out of the dingy realm of taking on all comers in whistle-stop towns—$50 for whoever could last four rounds with John L.—and into the big money to be had by staging fewer, heavily promoted bouts in large arenas. Sullivan made his New York boxing debut at Hill's theater in 1881, and Hill often served as stakeholder and matchmaker in Sullivan's fights, even as he backed and helped train his opponents.

Hill grew very wealthy by domesticating and sanitizing the city's vice economy, becoming a national celebrity in sporting circles and beyond. Through it all, the police settled distinctions between the licensed and the licentious. Thus in 1879 Mayor Edward Cooper routinely renewed Hill's theatrical license, based on the favorable report made by Police Inspector

George Dilks. Dilks described the male patrons as "usually of the better class of citizens and strangers, who are attracted there generally from motives of curiosity." Female patrons "are all women of doubtful character, but who conduct themselves with propriety while visiting there." Most importantly, "no disturbances have occurred calling for the interference of the police." At its height, Harry Hill's Variety Theater took in thousands each night, mostly from liquor sales. He kept a country estate in Flushing with fine horses and cattle; he bought his own yacht and a private steamboat that he leased to friendly police commissioners. He gave large amounts of money away to charity and friends. On Sundays he presented "Grand Sacred Concerts" in his theater, sometimes making it available for temperance meetings. On February 19, 1884, Hill presented a "Grand Fancy Dress Ball" honoring inventor Thomas Edison and inaugurating "the Edison Electric Light" in the theater. Plugging in to the new Pearl Street generating station, Hill's thus became the city's first electrically lit entertainment space, the beginning of what would soon become, further uptown, the Great White Way.[23]

By the time he testified before the Lexow Committee and John Goff, Hill had been largely out of the public eye for a decade, though he cut a striking figure and could still make news. Short and powerfully built even as he approached seventy, his thinning hair white, his neck bronzed from sun and sea air, dressed in a salt-and-pepper tweed suit, Harry Hill, the *World* observed, "came back like a ghost from the graveyard of old New York." Behind him sat state senators who "had dreamed of his place when they were boys, and now as great statesmen studied him carefully." He had been subpoenaed at 3:00 a.m. on June 20, just as he had come off a fishing smack on Flushing Bay. Hill reminded Goff and the committee that he appeared unwillingly and he pleaded to be permitted to go home, gather relevant papers, and come back another time. After some initial jousting, however, he agreed to testify, if selectively. "I am not going back on any good friends that did me kindness," he declared, "but them that did me an injury, I am going back on them."

Once settled in, the old man played to his audience with theatrical flair and comic timing. He recalled how detectives often came to his place with sightseers in tow. "Harry, we have some suckers, we are showing them around New York, but make them pay for the wine." Then waving his soft brown felt hat at the committee sitting behind him, he added, "like it might be the senators here, hayseeders." A roar of laughter erupted from the crowded courtroom, including the committee members themselves. Hill pretended not to understand what the hilarity was all about. When one senator offered Hill a drink of ice water, he got more guffaws when he declared with a straight face that it was "the first time I ever drank a glass of water in my life."[24]

Hill told a colorful and convincing tale. After more than thirty years on Houston Street an ungrateful and greedy new police captain had forced him out for refusing to pay regular tribute. He acknowledged voluntarily giving thousands of dollars over the years to policemen, mostly $50 or $100 gifts at Christmas or New Year's. Pressed for details, however, he refused, claiming "I was making so much money I didn't keep accounts." In 1886 Hill helped arrange for the transfer of a new captain, Michael Murphy, to his precinct. Soon after, Murphy and his ward man, James Moran, "struck" him for regular monthly payments of $50, intermittent payoffs up to $1,000 each, and endless freeloading visits to drink his wine. Hill objected to the regular collections established by his erstwhile friend Captain Murphy. "I said I was not a thief...I don't want to put up any protection; if I meet a good friend, I am willing to give $50 or $100, but I will not fall in line." Hill had been assured that his money "landed right" at police headquarters around the corner, but he no longer trusted Murphy. He met with then-superintendent William Murray and Inspector Henry Steers, both of whom he had known for many years. Murray demanded to know how much Hill was paying, appealing to him as a fellow Mason and promising to keep his confidence. "They played me as a hayseed, to tell the truth...I gave my guts away; after they got that, then they made use of it; they called me squealer after pledging their word." The police commission transferred the insatiable Captain Murphy far uptown "among the goats" and forced the resignation of Wardman Moran.

Because he had informed, "gone back on the buttons," Hill found himself hounded by the police as never before. In the fall of 1886 yet another new captain, providing a report for Hill's theatrical license renewal, wrote dryly that "said place is frequented by dissolute characters of both sexes...and in my opinion said place is not a proper one to receive an amusement license." In desperation, Hill wrote directly to Mayor William R. Grace. Hill noted that he had received licenses before from Grace, and he appealed to him as a fellow businessman (Grace was a wealthy shipowner and merchant.). "By a strict attention to business, and building up a reputation for honesty," he had written the mayor, "my place is and has been the resort of business men and people of respectability, who desiring to pass a few moments of recreation after the fatigues of business, have come to my theater where they can see a better performance for less money than any other place in the city."

But Hill could not persuade the mayor. His license gone, the police repeatedly raided his place and arrested him for giving illegal theatrical performances. In the spring of 1887, his famous resort now under court injunction brought by Grace's replacement Mayor Abram S. Hewitt, Hill left Houston Street for good. He tried opening places in Harlem, on Broadway, and in Brooklyn, but he found himself "backcapped" by the police wherever he went. With the money raised by a benefit put on at a Bowery theater, Hill bought a small hotel in Rockaway Beach, where he finally found some peace. When he died two years later, in 1896, the city's press was in full nostalgic mode for Hill and "that queer resort which trod so closely on the border line of respectability."[25]

Harry Hill was the Lexow Committee's most famous and effective witness to date. His tale underscored the police power to make or break even the most celebrated and successful men in the world of commercial entertainment, particularly those who depended upon theatrical and excise licenses. If he had straddled the worlds of the demimonde and respectable society, he still represented a higher class of witness than a brothel-keeper or green goods sharper. Yet by late June, there was a strong sense that the committee's revelations had become redundant. Hill's testimony would have been considered truly sensational only a few weeks earlier. Now, as the *World* put it, "it is only cumulative and confirmatory of the proof, already abundant, that the police have systematically made themselves partners in the business of vice and crime." Hill's relations with the police, dating back to the early 1850s, reinforced rather than introduced the view that the department's internal codes of loyalty and silence protected blackmailing. Even if some payoffs went "around the corner"—to inspectors or the superintendent or police commissioners—there was plenty of room for, even expectation of, freebooting and individual schemes among captains, wardmen, and patrolmen. The problem could not be reduced to a rapacious Tammany, despite Parkhurst's claims. After all, as the *Times* noted, Hill's testimony "related to a period when we enjoyed the blessings of a bipartisan police and the Republicans had their share of the wages of sin."[26]

By the last week of June, as temperatures inside the stifling courtrooms of the Tweed reached 100 degrees, the committee began discussing adjournment for the summer. John Goff urged suspension of the hearings over July and August, telling the senators that he was physically unfit to go on without a rest. The oppressive heat at the hearings was only part of it. After sessions, Goff would head back to his office to work late into the night, interviewing witnesses, drawing up subpoenas, and poring over evidence. The grinding routine of sixteen- or even twenty-hour days could not continue.

Tammany Democrats, like committee member Jacob Cantor, and their allies in the press, argued for continuing sessions through the summer so that accused officers might have a chance to testify and clear their names. With so many reputations at stake and worry over morale on the force, "Is it proposed to leave the police force in this state all the rest of the summer?" asked the Democratic *Sun*. But the opponents of a summer recess included a good many Republican and conservative voices as well. The committee had not yet heard from any of the accused officers, and the distrust of testimony from known criminals remained widespread. The *NY Recorder*, a Republican organ, urged fair play for the police and described the accusing witnesses as "mainly and extremely disreputable. They are habitual and professional lawbreakers of the lowest and most degraded character." And some accusing witnesses were clearly motivated by revenge. Reflecting a commonly held view among the city's business and commercial classes, the *Recorder* compared the police force of 1894 favorably with that of any other period in city history. With regard to law enforcement, "New York today is a paradise to what it was only a dozen years ago."[27]

The committee agreed to a summer recess starting June 30. Goff and his associate counsel, Moss and Jerome, wanted to use the final days of June to refute claims that the word of lawbreakers could not be trusted. They called a seemingly endless procession of legitimate businessmen who testified about payoffs to the police, and along the way opened up whole new lines of inquiry to be pursued come September. Produce dealers and grocers, peddlers and bootblacks, dry goods merchants and steamship lines, builders and box makers: blackmailing operations extended everywhere. James D'Olier, agent for the White Star Steamship Company, told how he had paid a regular salary to policemen on one of its piers for twenty-five years. Produce dealers and grocers on Washington and Greenwich Streets paid $25 or $50 every month to wardmen for the privilege of blocking the sidewalks with their barrels, boxes, and hand trucks. Some, like John H. Sweester, a large dry goods merchant on lower Broadway, blithely acknowledged that police payoffs were simply a cost of doing business, a way to avoid prosecution for obstructing sidewalks: "I paid it in the same light that I would any other servant that did work for me." Thomas J. Roberts, a fruit seller on Reade Street, objected to the word "bribe": "We didn't look at it as a bribe, it was a matter of business; we had to do it or get out of business." Only one prominent businessman, the building contractor Edward Kilpatrick, testified that he had successfully resisted police shakedowns while putting up the Edison Building on Broad Street. Kilpatrick spoke defiantly; the press and the committee praised him as a rare heroic figure.

No occupation was too low to escape paying tribute. William Mayston, who peddled scissors from his pushcart on Fulton Street, told how police would not allow anyone to sell on the street unless they paid $3 every month. When Mayston complained to a precinct desk sergeant, he found himself hounded by police throughout lower Manhattan. Francisco Scholastico, an Italian immigrant with a bootblack stand also on Fulton Street, had to cough up $10 regularly to stay in business.[28]

Once again, the cumulative weight of such testimony proved damning. "It was generally understood that vice and crime bought immunity," the *Tribune* noted, "but few were prepared to believe that honest industry was intimidated and blackmailed." But not everyone saw innocence despoiled. The law held the briber and the bribed as equally guilty. Senator O'Connor, the Republican from Binghamton, declared he had no more respect for the merchants than for the police who blackmailed them. "Every one of them is as deserving of punishment as are the policemen who received money from them." The *Times* saw a broader crisis of civic pride and bad citizenship, equating the behavior of merchants and storekeepers with "precisely what the keepers of saloons and brothels are doing." A police force could not be so rotten without the public's help. "We all have to take to ourselves some share of shame for the corruption which had been shown to permeate the police." The *World* thought prosperous businessmen who paid bribes were far worse than brothel keepers and prostitutes. "Every man of them, had he chosen, could have secured independence by a plucky fight, but paying blackmail was easier and more to their taste."[29]

Regardless of where one stood on the ethics of New York's citizenry, troubling new questions seeped out during the final days before adjournment. Patrolman Charles Beeck, a twenty-two-year veteran of the force, admitted to being part of the "envelope gang" that kicked payments up to superior officers who ran the Steamboat Squad, which had the status of a separate precinct. This was the first time a member of the force had acknowledged before the committee making regular payoffs to a superior officer, though in this case that superior was a mere sergeant. Calls for questioning captains, inspectors, the superintendent, and all the police commissioners echoed throughout the newspapers. Yet there would not be enough time before adjournment to fully explore how the police brass fit into blackmailing. Instead, committee counsel made sure to call a few witnesses whose disturbing testimony would be revisited in September.

One target was Inspector Alexander Williams. Lincoln Steffens, covering the Lexow investigation for the *Evening Post*, believed the committee would eventually have to reckon with Williams, whose notorious career and reputation for never backing down made him the most popular man on the force, a role model for other cops. "He has been called a brutal fighter, a revengeful enemy, and a fearless defier of public opinion," Steffens wrote. "The men hear him insult newspaper men.... They hear him boast in the station houses and the halls at police headquarters. The coarseness of his language is familiar, and is the envy of most police sergeants, who imitate him." Associate counsel Jerome made it clear he intended to put Williams's entire career on trial, "to begin with his whole history and show his biography right down."

For now, Jerome and Goff offered only tantalizing hints, as two stories revealed. Henry Schuchert, a sixty-year-old German carpenter with a pronounced accent, recounted a tale from twenty years earlier. In 1874 Schuchert ran a respectable boarding house on Rose Street until the city tore it down to make way for the Brooklyn Bridge. He moved to Pearl Street, where he fitted up a new place with a bar, a small kitchen, and a few rooms to rent. Schuchert, his wife, their servant girl, and a few male friends were enjoying some beer at a housewarming party when Captain Williams, then in command of the Oak Street station, burst in with two detectives. Schuchert recalled the captain demanding, "How can you start a business like this, without you come and see me?" Williams accused Schuchert of running a whorehouse and demanded a $75 initiation fee and $75 every month. When the carpenter protested, Williams clapped him and his wife in jail. Friends bailed them out and charges were dropped. But Schuchert had to leave the house and lost his investment.

More explosive were claims that Williams had a financial interest in a company called Hollywood Whiskey and had used cops to act as liquor salesmen, strong-arming saloonkeepers and liquor stores to carry the brand. Witnesses from the Wholesale Liquor Dealers Association, founded in 1888 for mutual protection against police interference, recounted how they petitioned the state legislature, including a detailed report on "The Police as Liquor Sellers." The legislature eventually passed a law barring police from holding a commercial interest in or meddling with the sale of liquor. But fear of police retaliation made enforcement impossible.[30]

A few witnesses also touched upon the long-rumored practice of men paying for appointments to and promotions on the force. Dr. Parkhurst and his allies had argued for years that such payoffs were routine, and that they helped explain the prevalence of police blackmail. Men who needed to pay off their debts were obviously more likely to demand tribute. "Criminals to commence with," as Goff put it, "could they be ought but criminals in their official life?" The committee had heard scattered testimony to the effect that the price of an appointment to patrolman cost between $300 and $400. But what about promotion, especially to captain? Leroy Lyon, a downtown fruit merchant, had for twelve years gladly paid an annual assessment of $60 to local wardmen, to avoid fines for blocking the sidewalk. Recently a new wardman had visited the merchants on Worth Street, busily writing down their names and inspecting the use of sidewalks. Lyon recounted their conversation: "I said, 'I have been paying for ten years, and I don't propose to be bothered now; what do you mean by it?' and he said, 'We have got a new captain and I have got to find out how much I can raise,' and he said he had to raise $15,000 very soon, for the captain had to pay that much for his appointment; that was the words he used . . . he said that the captain had to pay $15,000, because that is what the office costs them." As it turned out, Lyon's assessment remained at $60 per year. His testimony made page one headlines—but digging deeper into the issue of payment for promotion would have to wait until the fall.[31]

Indeed a great number of lingering questions would have to be put off, including what the captains, inspectors, and superintendent might have to say. The *Morning Journal* pithily summarized the revelations about what it called the "Wolf Police": "Tribute from harlots, tribute from dive-keepers, tribute from saloonkeepers, tribute from gamblers, tribute from bunco men, tribute from green goods men, tribute from sidewalk obstructers, tribute from steamship operators, tribute from peddlers—blackmail and licensing of crime and law-breaking everywhere. Such is the public impression from the evidence given." Yet there was no consensus on where all that tribute had gone. "Who received the sums of money, vast in the aggregate," asked the *Press*, "levied not only on tolerated vice and crime, but on lawful and respectable business.... that is the question which citizens of New York are asking, and which they mean to have answered." The issue promised to define the fall mayoral campaign, and for Republicans, non-Tammany Democrats, labor activists, socialists, and most newspapers the answer appeared obvious: "there is no moral doubt that the lion's share of the blackmail went to Tammany bosses and Tammany officials." What about the actual amount involved? All sorts of enormous numbers got thrown around, though with little hard evidence to support them. The *Morning Advertiser* estimated police collected $600,000 every month in blackmail, more than $7 million a year, or an astounding $196 million in today's dollars. Figures like these were surely exaggerated, but their regular appearance in the press gave them credence. Former mayor Abram S. Hewitt—the iron manufacturer whose election in 1886 depended upon strong Tammany support—now called for an anti-Tammany coalition across party affiliation. Hewitt stunned a meeting of Good Government Clubs by telling them he believed that "the amount of annual official blackmail in New York actually exceeds the gross sum raised by taxation." He added, "Do not imagine that the revelations of the Lexow inquiry are any novelty. I do not know of a single thing disclosed which was not going on while I was mayor."[32]

The committee might be adjourning for the summer—but the final sessions showed there would be no respite from political maneuvering. On June 27 Matthew O'Connor, a ticket agent for a steamship line, testified that he had lost his position because of his support for a local anti-Tammany candidate. Goff got into a heated exchange with Senator Jacob Cantor, the Tammany Democrat from Brooklyn, when Cantor questioned what this all had to do with the police department. Why had O'Connor not sought justice through the courts? Cantor asked. Because, Goff replied, he knew that the court system "was controlled not by responsible officers appointed or elected for the enforcement of the criminal law, but by the overshadowing power of Tammany Hall behind it. We have got to meet this question squarely." A long burst of applause followed and Chairman Lexow threatened to clear the room. As the argument intensified Goff warmed to his topic. Shouting and red faced, he served up a highly personal tirade on Tammany's sway:

I announce this today, and I take full responsibility for it, and I am not in the habit of making reckless statements, that it has become a question of bread and butter, in the city of New York, for a man to belong to Tammany Hall, as a question of necessity. I announce myself, in my own person, here today, that my professional work has been injured and clients taken from me because they felt I had no pulls in court, and influence. I have suffered myself, Mr. Chairman, and I can point to scores of lawyers today who have suffered, and I can point to scores of lawyers today who had to go into Tammany Hall to protect their practice.

No wonder many had begun calling for Goff to run for mayor come the Fall.[33]

On Friday, June 29, the committee adjourned for the summer. This was a far cry from the committee that had adjourned so abruptly in mid-April. The previous six weeks had transformed the Lexow Committee from a highly partisan look at vote fraud into an unprecedentedly detailed and frank revelation of how police managed the vice economy and extorted legitimate business. And it continued right down the wire. Rhetorical fireworks erupted just before Chairman Lexow gaveled adjournment until September 10. That afternoon, the police commission announced it would commence its own investigation, led by Superintendent Byrnes and in cooperation with the district attorney's office, and hold trials of accused officers. A furious John Goff denounced the plan as designed simply to embarrass the committee and undermine its work. He railed about all the evidence of malfeasance and corrupt practices swirling around the police commission, stretching back so many years—"for that body to constitute itself judge, jury, prosecutor and defender, is something unheard of and something inconsistent with our ideas of justice."

For his part, DeLancey Nicoll, counsel for the department's senior officers, also appealed for justice. He vigorously opposed adjournment before accused officers had the chance to take the stand, once again attacking the character of the witnesses. Adjournment meant leaving the entire NYPD "under the stain and stigma of these charges unanswered and unexplained in their own defense" for two and a half months. He warned of the consequences to "the preservation of peace and order, and the protection of life and property in this city," particularly in the summer, when crime was particularly "rampant." "Chairman Lexow mocked Nicoll's argument, and reminded him that these were matters of public notoriety for the police commissioners as well as ordinary citizens. "Do you suppose that we can take an accusation of that kind, compelling us to sit during this summer, when for 10 years you have had that opportunity and have never exercised it?" When a burst of loud applause greeted Lexow's comments, Nicoll sarcastically asked, "Are these gentlemen hired to indulge in this performance; are they employed for this purpose?" Goff retorted, "They are not employed by this committee, but they are simply a wave from the great volume of feeling of society that rises up to-day and sweeps over Manhattan Island." Lexow reiterated that the committee was only after the system, not individuals. He reserved the power to reconvene over the summer in case the police commission's investigation threatened to undermine the committee's work.[34]

Lexow gaveled the session to a close and, as the *World* put it, "The great moral Lexow show has closed for the season." That "wave from the great volume of feeling" might well wash over the city in the fall election. First would come a long, hot summer.

7

....

"REFORM NEVER SUFFERS FROM FRANKNESS"

By the end of June 1894, a worn-out John Goff looked forward to a week of fishing and loafing in the Adirondacks. Despite the clamorous ending of the Lexow Committee's second session, and the police board's announcement that it would hold departmental trials over the summer for captains suspected of blackmail, Goff felt confident that nothing could prevent the investigation from moving forward. Even with a ten-week adjournment, the sheer weight of the revelations meant there was no turning back. The city newspapers would not let go of the story, splashing detailed accounts of testimony across their front pages. "I believe the people of our city, speaking through the press, have said that the work must go on. And the work will go on. For revolutions never turn backward." The dailies now offered complete summaries of witness testimony, lists of accused policemen and politicians. They traded rumors about what the committee might do in September and speculated about far-reaching political implications in the fall elections.[1]

The committee's revelations made the investigation news across the country. In Chicago, the *Tribune* printed daily accounts from a special correspondent who offered brief, often highly exaggerated and inaccurate summaries of Lexow proceedings. From the paper's Republican perspective, the story merely confirmed "the corruption and depravity of the Tammany system in New York," the outcome of "fifty years of Tammany domination and plundering." It estimated Tammany's annual blackmail revenue from police officials at $20 million (roughly $547 million in today's dollars), a wildly overblown figure based on no discernible evidence. No matter. Democratic rule in Chicago, the *Tribune* predicted, would inevitably bring the same. "Is not this a warning to the taxpayers of Chicago? How long, as things are going now, will it be before a Tammany blackmail machine is set up here also?"

The *Los Angeles Times* ran only occasional Associated Press reports on Lexow doings, but it kept close tabs on the travels of Tammany chief Richard Croker who, it claimed wrongly, had fled the country and abandoned politics rather than face questioning by the committee. The investigation, the *Times* believed, offered a simple, soothing lesson for reformers everywhere: "There is no difficulty about reforming municipal politics, if citizens only make up their minds that they must be reformed." The expanding national circulation of New York papers also made Lexow news available far from the city. In Prescott, Arizona, a twelve-year-old Fiorello La Guardia rushed out to buy the Sunday edition of the *NY World* when it arrived a few days later at his local drugstore. Though he was born in Greenwich Village, La Guardia's family had moved to Arizona, where he grew up and attended public schools. Eager to read every word of Lexow coverage, New York's future reform mayor recalled this as his first political education: "the amazing disclosures hit me like a shock.... resentment against Tammany was created in me at that time, which I admit is to this day almost an obsession." Indeed the national press largely adopted the historical and political perspective offered by *Harper's Weekly*. The investigation revealed how Tammany, "cut down to the roots by the fall of Tweed, has grown again greater and stronger than ever, and is more corrupt, if possible."[2]

In New York, the Lexow revelations portended a political shake-up in the coming November elections—though in early July there was still no clear path forward to electing an anti-Tammany administration. The potential anti-Tammany coalition included a crazy quilt of contentious groups deeply suspicious of each other: regular Republicans, nonpartisan municipal reformers, Chamber of Commerce businessmen, disaffected Democrats of several stripes, and a loud chorus of nativists. Despite this latest groundswell against it, Tammany remained the strongest organization in city politics. Its leaders and members were deeply entrenched in New York's judiciary, its neighborhoods, and its municipal departments beyond the NYPD. The committee's fall sessions might force top police officials to testify and produce even more startling exposures, but the ultimate effect on the political landscape remained hazy.

And what of the police department itself? The sensational disclosures had provoked dissension among the leadership and within the rank and file, magnifying long-smoldering resentments. The police board's decision to pursue its own investigation and hold departmental trials over the summer came on a split vote. Tammany commissioners James J. Martin and John Sheehan outvoted the lone Republican, Charles Murray, who vehemently opposed the move as an attempt to undermine the Lexow inquiry. (The fourth commissioner, John McClave, had been on sick leave ever since his humiliating Lexow appearance in May.) DeLancey Nicoll, the former district attorney, represented the department's superior officers before the committee—captains, inspectors, superintendent, and commissioners. By the end of June ward detectives, badly tarnished by testimony placing them at the epicenter of police shakedowns, hired their own law firm to look after their interests. And patrolmen—the vast bulk of the force—now joined the newly created Patrolmen's Benevolent Association (PBA), paying dues of twenty-five cents a month and occasional assessments to hire lobbyists in Albany to push for higher pay.

Many rank-and-file cops lamented how the Lexow hearings had dried up some of their easy pickings, such as the $5 bribe for allowing "straw bail" bonds or the few bucks given by saloonkeepers looking to stay open past legal closing. "Say, why can't they leave us alone?" one beat cop asked a reporter. "We ain't doing any harm to anybody. The crooks don't get a show in New York, and what's the use of kicking because a lot of men and women want to do business in their own way?" The PBA appealed to rank-and-file cops who felt squeezed between an aggressive Tammany, Republican legislators who resisted salary and pension increases, and moral reformers like Dr. Parkhurst who pounded the department mercilessly. Most PBA members preferred a merit system of appointment and promotion to one based on political "pull."[3]

Only Superintendent Thomas Byrnes seemed to retain his reputation and stature. Despite his long-running battle with Parkhurst and the recent Lexow disclosures, Byrnes remained a commanding figure, recognized by the press, the business elite, and ordinary citizens as the best hope for a

more professional and less politicized force. Long a master at shaping favorable press coverage, Byrnes continued to receive admiring, even fawning
profiles from journalists. Reviewing Byrnes's long detective career and his
tenure as superintendent, Julian Ralph, one of the era's first celebrity correspondents, wrote, "Such complete discipline, such soft and gentle and
yet absolute mastery of a situation I have never seen paralleled in public
or private life." Nellie Bly, interviewing "the greatest detective in the
world," tried to humanize the superintendent, describing his home life
with his schoolteacher wife and their five daughters, all living in a handsome house on Fifty-Eighth Street, very close to Cornelius Vanderbilt.
Byrnes rarely took time off, and his idea of a great vacation was spending
a few days knocking around on his twenty-one-foot catboat. "Faults or
no faults," Bly concluded, "there is no man New York can spare less.
When 'the Superintendent' dies it will be a bad day for New York." No
wonder the police commissioners announced that Byrnes would lead the
department's summertime investigation into captains suspected of corruption. The Tammany commissioners might be looking to save face by
getting rid of a few captains; but they needed to harness Byrnes's professionalism to legitimate the task.[4]

Before the departmental trials could get started, however, the city and
the police had to confront the largest and most violent conflict between
labor and capital in the nation's history: the strike of Pullman Palace Car
employees and the national sympathy boycott called by the American
Railway Union (ARU). The crisis was made to order for Byrnes, who
presented himself as a national authority on "the most dangerous kind of
criminal that exists at the present time—the anarchist." Byrnes published
two essays in the 1894 *North American Review* warning of the anarchist
threat. He reduced the radical political ferment accompanying the severe
depression to just another criminal operation, one largely controlled by
recent European immigrants. Like so many crusaders against un-American
radicals then and since, Byrnes exaggerated the peril while expressing
total confidence in the police department's ability to handle any challenge
to the social order. He described the scattered, inchoate movement of
"industrial armies," groups of unemployed men marching to Washington to
lobby for job-creating public works projects, as "the most dangerous this
country has seen since the Civil War." Byrnes acknowledged that hard
times had caused unprecedented levels of unemployment and economic
desperation, as well as the spread of "socialistic doctrines." No matter that

the largest and best known of the industrial armies, Jacob Coxey's so-called Commonwealth of Christ Army, numbered perhaps 500 men when in May of 1894 it finally straggled in to Washington, DC, where capital police promptly arrested the leaders and dispersed the protesters. "The movement," Byrnes argued, "is illegal, un-American, and a disgrace, and it should have been stopped long ago." It never reached New York City. But the true "menace of Coxeyism" for Byrnes and others lay in the sympathetic crowds, public expressions of support, and donations of food and clothing that industrial armies received in towns across the Midwest and Mid-Atlantic states, all widely covered by local newspapers.[5]

The Pullman strike and railroad boycott posed a more substantial threat to the established order, and by early July it looked as if it might spread from Chicago and other western cities and engulf New York. In May 1894 workers at the Pullman Palace Car Company had gone on strike to protest wage cuts of up to 25 percent. George Pullman, owner of the business, had justified the cuts as a response to financial reverses related to the depression. But he made no corresponding reductions in rents and other charges at Pullman, the company town he had built just south of Chicago, where most of his employees lived. Roughly a third of the Pullman workers were members of the new American Railway Union, founded the previous year by Eugene V. Debs. The ARU looked to organize all (white) railway employees in a single organization, a vision of industrial unionism sharply different from the railway brotherhoods traditionally divided by craft into engineers, brakemen, switchmen, and firemen. It claimed roughly 15,000 members represented in over 400 locals. The character and scope of the Pullman strike shifted profoundly in late June when ARU delegates, meeting in Chicago for their first national convention, voted to boycott any trains carrying Pullman cars unless the company agreed to arbitration for settling the dispute.

Debs, the ARU president, was dubious of the boycott strategy, fearing that the young union might not survive a protracted national struggle. Swayed by the enthusiasm and militancy of the delegates in Chicago, Debs reluctantly went along. Pullman adamantly refused arbitration, and along with the General Managers' Association of railroad executives, he vowed to resist the proposed boycott. On June 27 about 5,000 railroad workers left their jobs, tying up fifteen railroads. By June 30, some 125,000 railroad workers on twenty-nine lines had quit work rather than handle Pullman cars. The ARU had little strength in the East or South, but the boycott proved effective in halting railroad traffic around Chicago and points west. The boycott quickly became more than simply a show of solidarity with the Pullman strikers. It attracted support from tens of thousands of workers and their families, a flashpoint not just for railroad employees but for people suffering the effects of the depression and alienated by the growing power of distant capital. Despite Debs's pleas for order and his focus on an arbitrated settlement, wildcat strikes, local demonstrations that turned into riots, and scattered violence against railroad property spread throughout the Midwest and West.

On July 2, Attorney General Richard Olney, a former railroad corporation lawyer, obtained a federal injunction against ARU leaders, citing the boycott's threat to moving the U.S. mail. The injunction prohibited ARU leaders from inducing employees to honor the boycott and from communicating with their subordinates, thus hindering Debs's efforts to prevent violence. The next day President Grover Cleveland ordered federal troops into Chicago. The show of military power squarely on the side of the railroads enraged the strikers and their supporters. On July 6, some 6,000 rioters destroyed hundreds of railcars in the South Chicago yards. By then there were about 6,000 federal and state troops, 5,000 deputy federal marshals, and over 3,000 local police trying to restore order in Chicago. Across the nation, as many as 250,000 workers in twenty-seven states had gone on strike, halted rail traffic, or rioted. The Congress and the mainstream press strongly supported Cleveland's use of troops, calling it as urgent a defense of the nation as suppression of the South's "Great Rebellion" in the Civil War.[6]

New Yorkers followed these events closely. Press coverage, full of illustrations and cartoons, cheered Cleveland's deployment of federal troops, dismissing the strikers and their supporters as anarchists and un-American. The sensational coverage given Emma Goldman and the local anarchist riots of the previous summer grew even more lurid for this national story. Newspapers hammered Debs as a dictator, a degenerate alcoholic, a madman, a mental defective. Most wondered whether the scenes of riot and violence, of troops firing into crowds, would be repeated in New York. Superintendent Byrnes seized the moment to denounce the "spirit of Anarchism" in Chicago, comparing the Pullman strike and boycott to the secession triggering the Civil War. Asked by a reporter if the NYPD would permit the spreading strike to take possession of trains in the city and attack men who kept working, Byrnes replied confidently, "Not until the New York police had been whipped, and we haven't been whipped by a mob yet."

On July 6 Byrnes gathered all the captains, warning them to look out for any labor agitators in their precincts, and to prevent any strike supporters from taking possession of railroad cars or assaulting train employees. The superintendent beefed up plainclothes surveillance of union meetings, socialist gatherings, and any other group of strike sympathizers, particularly on the East Side. He cancelled all vacations and put the entire force on duty or reserve at their precincts. And Byrnes ordered captains to inspect all the weapons of the men in their command; anyone still using a .32 caliber revolver was to immediately buy a .38 caliber replacement. "The police are fully prepared," he announced confidently, "to meet any attempt of idlers and strikers to create a disturbance in New York." Retired members of the force put themselves forward to help out. Former inspector George W. Dilks, who had helped put down every historic riot from the 1840s through the 1870s, volunteered the services of the 300-member Police Veterans Association to help maintain public order.[7]

While Byrnes tried to reassure the public, New York's labor movement struggled with how to best respond to the Pullman crisis. In meeting halls around the city trade unionists denounced the federal injunction and Cleveland's deployment of U.S. Army troops and declared heartfelt solidarity with the strikers. Yet they expressed deep frustration over how little could actually be done on their behalf. They aimed a great deal of their anger at Byrnes and the NYPD, invoking the Lexow revelations with bravado, eager for any leverage against the force's long history of anti-labor activity and Byrnes's recent public statements on the strike. On July 8 the Central Labor Union, the city's most influential coalition of organized trades, held a crowded and turbulent meeting at its East Thirteenth Street headquarters. Before it could get started one delegate rose to announce that Byrnes had detectives watching every labor organization in the city, and he moved to go into secret session. After a hot debate the delegates rejected the idea, insisting that labor had nothing to fear or conceal.

The delegates kept up a steady backbeat of animosity toward Byrnes. Harry White of the Amalgamated Association of Garment Workers called for a mass meeting in Union Square. "The police," he declared, "are now smarting under the blows of the Lexow Committee, and they want another chance to pose before the people as preservers of society." A wave of sarcastic applause greeted his remarks. Delegate John S. Steele condemned

Byrnes even more bluntly, declaring, "It is time to put a curb on the tongue of the insolent brute at police headquarters. He wants to show the capitalists, after being roasted by the Lexow Committee, what a great man he is." Delegate Jolly of the Brewery Workers, outraged by Byrnes's order to upgrade police pistols from .32 to .38 caliber, thought "workingmen would do very well to get forty-four caliber revolvers. I do not say we should attack the police, but we ought to protect ourselves, and put ourselves, if attacked, in some place where we can use a revolver." And Matthew Barr, of the Tin and Sheet Iron Workers, addressed the same point with this provocative fantasy:

Then there's Superintendent Byrnes, who called his men together to see that they had revolvers. There are about 3,300 of these revolvers, and they are to be used against organized labor. Well, when the day comes that organized labor has to take a stand against the police the police will get left. The 3,300 police will be nowhere. We can locate every one of them in their residences, and snap the handcuffs on them, and put them under their beds if they happen to be in bed; for there are only three policemen in each election district and 300 voters. Byrnes will be the first. He will be locked up in his own house. We have the means of dealing with enemies. [A voice: "Don't give it away Matt!"]

Organized labor saw a close connection between Byrnes's military posture and the unprecedented use of federal troops to break the ARU boycott. But the bluster about guns and confronting police reflected frustration more than anything else. While the delegates might have enjoyed the scene imagined by Barr, they reaffirmed their commitment to the law, insisting that any violent disturbance would be the fault of the police. And Barr himself proposed a resolution, unanimously adopted, "That while the CLU denounces the federal government and police for their actions in connection with the strike, it places itself on record against all incendiarism and anarchy, and denounces the firebugs who have brought disgrace upon a fair fight of organized labor."[8]

Byrnes refused to respond to the inflammatory rhetoric coming out of union halls, or to disclose his plans for quelling any disturbances—except to promise that anyone who broke the peace could expect a broken head. As the CLU made plans for a solidarity rally at Cooper Union, reporters noted that the vehement oratory resembled that of anarchists more than traditionally conservative trade unionists. Their language reflected a sense that labor-capital relations had taken a new and discouraging turn: the issue was no longer labor versus Pullman but labor versus the federal government. That point had been brought squarely home on July 7 when, at the height of the violence in Chicago, federal officers arrested Eugene Debs and four other ARU leaders for violating the federal court injunction, and for criminal conspiracy to interfere with the U.S. mail. (The men eventually went to jail after the Supreme Court upheld the government's use of an injunction against the strike.)

And all the resolutions and expressions of support could not mask the weak hand held by New York organized labor. The American Railway Union had little strength in the East, and virtually no presence in the city. A failed 1890 strike on the New York Central (broken with the help of city police protecting scab replacement workers) had badly diluted union presence in the railroad industry. Of the roughly 10,000 workers on New York's surface and elevated trains, fewer than 1,000 were union members—and these were in the craft defined brotherhoods rather than the new ARU. A general strike by Chicago trade unionists had fizzled; a national walkout called by the Knights of Labor never materialized. Samuel Gompers and the American Federation of Labor refused to authorize sympathy strikes. J. J. Murphy, president of the city's powerful Typographical Union, believed it "the duty of every union man to do all he can to make the strike a success." Yet he acknowledged representing a conservative body of men, many of whom were out of work. Indeed the large number of unemployed in the city, people thrown out of work by the depression, presented the biggest roadblock to a general strike or even more modest acts of solidarity.

The Cooper Union gathering on July 12 attracted a boisterous overflow crowd of some 10,000 people, forcing most of them to listen on the street while speakers condemned the use of federal troops and court injunctions. Inspector Alexander Williams, commanding a squad of fifty uniformed police, watched over the proceedings. The socialist-dominated Central Labor Federation (CLF) held a smaller rally in Union Square two days later. Just before it took place, a confident Superintendent Byrnes told reporters, "It is apparent the backbone of the strike is broken, and that it will not extend to this city." By then, Debs had offered to call off the strike in favor of arbitration. But with President Cleveland, the federal courts, U.S. Army troops, state militia, and the nation's press all on their side, George Pullman and the General Managers' Association of the railroad industry had no incentive to negotiate. The strike dwindled and trains began moving again; the Pullman strike ended without ever reaching New York.

The railroad crisis demonstrated—and enhanced—the power of the national state to intervene decisively on the side of industrial capital. The city's labor movement was unable to muster more than symbolic support for the Pullman strike and boycott. Yet the crisis also revealed and intensified working-class resentment toward Byrnes and a police department perceived as an eager enforcer for business interests. As the investigation into the NYPD deepened, that bitterness would contribute to a broader popular opinion demanding new approaches to policing the city.[9]

The Pullman strike had forced a halt to the police board's plan to hold departmental trials for captains prominently cited in the Lexow hearings. And it created a lull in the intense speculation over political prospects for the November mayoral contest. By mid-July both subjects returned with a new rush of interest. From his vacation spot in Switzerland, Parkhurst addressed the political question in an open letter to the citizens of New York. He sent it to his close ally, Charles S. Smith, former president of the Chamber of Commerce, on July 2. Smith, no doubt waiting for the Pullman storm to pass, did not release the letter to the press for two weeks. Parkhurst excoriated Tammany in language that had become his trademark and emphasized the national stakes of the coming election. The Hall was less a political organization than a "cabal of thieves, murderers, and bunco-steerers…shaping the destiny of this controlling city of the greatest nation on earth in the midst of the era of nineteenth century civilization." Defeating Tammany in November required a rejection of politics as usual; only a nonpartisan fusion of anti-Tammany forces could succeed. He believed rank-and-file voters would embrace such a campaign. "We may be Jews, we may be Catholics, or we may be Protestants," he made a point of noting, "but we believe together in the things that are right."

Parkhurst was too savvy to suggest any specific candidates at this stage. What was crucial was finding a man who appreciated an exceptional opportunity for making good government the central issue. This political vision mirrored the work of the City Club, which in early 1893 had begun establishing Good Government Clubs in every assembly district. The idea was to counter Tammany on the neighborhood level by bringing together all citizens "who desire businesslike and nonpartisan government, and who are not subservient in city matters to any of the political machines." By the summer of 1894 it claimed to have fourteen clubs up and running, with some 3,000 members.[10]

Sharp criticism greeted Parkhurst's broadside, reminding everyone that creating an effective anti-Tammany coalition would be as difficult as ever. Thomas Platt, leader of the state Republican Party, dismissed Parkhurst's fusion idea out of hand unless the ticket was headed by "a Republican candidate for mayor, a Republican who thoroughly represents his party." Platt reiterated his support for a bipartisan police board, noting again the implications of the city vote for the state and nation. During the fall 1893 election, he claimed, the Republican ticket had lost as many as 20,000 votes because of police intimidation. Neither the Lexow committee nor the district attorney's investigation had produced any evidence for these wildly overstated numbers. Platt was surely more interested in firing up his party base, declaring "no matter what our friends in the country were able to do, the majorities they gave us were liable and almost certain to be overcome so long as the police board remained the partisan instrument of Tammany Hall." Republicans, Platt insisted, had defeated themselves too often in the past by taking the advice of Mugwumps and anti-Tammany Democrats. His long-standing suspicion of Parkhurst and other voices for nonpartisanship had only deepened. "I don't much care to be friends with a man," he declared, "when I can see the blade of a knife sticking out from under his shirt." The staunchly Republican *Tribune* acknowledged Parkhurst's honesty and good intentions but it supported a straight Republican ticket and traditional partisan identity. It rejected his call as "too sweeping in his condemnation of partisans and parties, and far too confident of the strength of some new political combination as yet unorganized and unshared."[11]

Aside from the objections of professional pols like Platt, the strong undercurrents of nativism threatened any fusion boat that might be launched. These tides had swirled throughout New York politics since the famine Irish migration a half-century earlier. By 1894 the combination of increased immigration, economic hard times, and industrial conflicts like Pullman brought them to the surface once again, most notably via the growing influence of the recently organized American Protective Association. A vigorous anti-Catholicism drove the APA, which demanded immigration restriction and had become politically influential in the Northeast and Midwest. Parkhurst, in his calls for anti-Tammany unity, had tried to rise above these appeals—but plenty of uptown Protestant ministers rou-tinely voiced nativist appeals from the pulpit. In an era when newspapers regularly reported on sermons as news, New Yorkers could find multiple nativist pleas on any given Sunday. The APA's strongest clerical supporter in New York City, the Reverend Madison Peters of the Bloomingdale Reformed Church on West Sixty-Eighth Street, denounced Tammany Hall as "a religio-political conspiracy for public plunder." He blamed "the neglect and indifference of our American people ... for the shocking scan-dals in our municipal government." Rev. Robert S. MacArthur, pastor of the Calvary Baptist Church on West Fifty-Seventh Street, denounced "Romanism" as the religion of prize fighters and urged his parishioners to "go to the polls this fall and vote for America, for our flag, for our historic and sublime past." Rev. Dr. James Chambers, of Calvary Presbyterian on Fifth Avenue, appealed to the best people to "bring about the election of a good American for mayor, for whom the Stars and Stripes are good enough."[12]

The 1894 election season was still a way off. And with the Pullman crisis over by mid-July, the police commission finally returned its atten-tion to departmental trials prompted by the Lexow revelations. These departmental trials would stretch out through July and August, a surreal, half serious and half mocking interlude before the Lexow Committee resumed its work in September. Partisan politics was there from the start, as the two Tammany commissioners, James J. Martin and John Sheehan, had outvoted their Republican colleague, Charles Murray, insisting that the board try officers prominently named as receiving blackmail or ne-glecting their duty. Everyone understood their political motives. The police trials, as the *Tribune* succinctly put it, were merely an attempt "to embarrass the committee's investigation and at the same time to make a counterfeit show of virtue and rigor."

The police were nonetheless determined to out-Lexow Lexow. The gravity and unprecedented nature of the Lexow disclosures—more dam-aging than any in New York history—brought calls for immediate prose-cution from even the most hardened partisans. Tammany mayor Gilroy favored the department trials: If charges of misconduct proved false, no officer should be forced to labor under that cloud. But, the mayor added, any policemen found guilty "should be thrown out of office bodily, as being unfit to hold any position in the public service." The list of men implicated in Lexow testimony included two inspectors and fifteen cap-tains, along with the Steamboat Squad, and a large group of wardmen and patrolmen. Which of them would be called—and what of the commissioners themselves, accused of taking bribes for appointments and promotions? While Commissioner Martin talked expansively of going through the Lexow Committee transcripts, the legal landscape was unmapped. The police commission could compel witnesses to appear at actual trials of cops, but it had no power to subpoena witnesses for examination before trials. Indeed Frank Moss, associate counsel for the Lexow Committee, began advising Lexow witnesses that they were under the committee's protection and could not be prosecuted for refusing to testify at police trials. And what did conviction by the police commission even mean? John Goff noted the long history of men convicted at police trials having their verdicts overturned by the courts via a *writ of certiorari*.[13]

An arrangement hammered out in the mayor's office finally allowed the board to proceed. (Along with Mayor Gilroy and the police commissioners, the meeting included Moss, District Attorney John Fellows, and City Corporation Counsel William Clark.) Superintendent Byrnes would present the cases before the police board, aided by Assistant District Attorney Francis Wellman, who had won high praise for his handling of the election fraud cases the previous winter. The DA's office would pursue criminal prosecutions against policemen the board found guilty of blackmail, extortion, or related crimes. The final piece of this very political puzzle fell into place on July 17, when Police Commissioner John McClave, on sick leave for "nervous exhaustion" since his humiliating Lexow appearance in May, announced his resignation. Mayor Gilroy immediately appointed General Michael Kerwin, a steadfast Republican ally of Thomas Platt, to replace him.

As a young boy Kerwin had emigrated from Ireland with his family in 1847. He fought with distinction in the Civil War, earning promotion to Colonel, and he later served time in a British prison for his activism in the Irish nationalist group Clan-na-Gael. (Critics charged that Kerwin had the blood of secret assassinations on his hands.) One of the most prominent Irish-Americans active in Republican circles, Kerwin was appointed by President Harrison in 1889 as Collector of Internal Revenue for the city. As rumors swirled of a deal between the Tammany Mayor Gilroy and the Republican leader Platt, one fact was indisputable: For the first time in five years, the police commission included two Republicans and two Democrats. In the wake of Parkhurst's campaign and the Lexow investigation, and with gloomy prospects for the fall elections, Tammany leaders evidently regretted overplaying their hand in putting the police board under Democratic control. Kerwin credited Mayor Gilroy for returning the board to its traditional political balance, telling reporters, "I think the bipartisan character of the board of police commissioners will redound to the good of the city." This was precisely the sort of coziness between the two party organizations that infuriated Parkhurst and other reformers: bipartisanship was no substitute for nonpartisanship in city affairs.[14]

The police board trials began the same day Kerwin took office, continuing through August at department headquarters on Mulberry Street. They played out as a kind of summer replacement for the Lexow show, complete with return appearances from several star witnesses and endless speculation about what might happen in September when the committee would reconvene. Superintendent Byrnes, who sought to discipline subordinates regardless of their political affiliations, brought the formal charges before the board. Assistant DA Wellman, determined to show that police were not immune to criminal charges, acted as prosecutor. Wary of the department's insular job culture, he employed private Pinkerton detectives to investigate city cops. (Wellman later wrote the classic legal text *The Art of Cross-Examination*). And the four commissioners looked to repair the police board's badly damaged reputation. The first trial set the tone and pattern for all that followed. Byrnes charged East Fifth Street station Captain Michael Doherty, and two of his wardmen, with neglect of duty, accepting "straw bonds" to release arrested prostitutes, and black-mailing brothel keepers. These included Mrs. Augusta Thurow, the dress-maker and boarding house keeper whose Lexow testimony had created such a stir. Mrs. Thurow once again proved an effective witness, unshaken by the aggressive cross-examination of Doherty's lawyers. Doherty denied all the charges. But in trying to explain his personal wealth, he claimed to have made $22,000 in stock speculation on a $200 investment—yet he could produce no accounts to prove it.

Doherty's own testimony revealed the limits of political "pull," the internal dissension now wracking Tammany Hall, and the blurred lines of authority within the NYPD. Doherty himself was a Tammany stalwart, promoted to captain in 1890 at the personal request of Tammany's boss Richard Croker. He testified that he had spoken confidentially to Commissioner Martin, his fellow Tammanyite, about the "straw bonds" abuses, asking him to transfer the sergeants responsible. When asked on the stand why he had not reported this instead to Superintendent Byrnes,

Doherty exclaimed, "I was a fool that I didn't. If I had something would have been done."

On July 27 the board found Doherty and his wardmen guilty and dismissed them from the department, ordering the men to hand over any police property to Superintendent Byrnes. In a dramatic moment, Doherty instead walked deliberately over to Martin and flung his gold badge on his desk. He was the first captain in twenty years to be discharged from the force, and he now faced criminal indictment by the grand jury. Doherty expressed his bitterness freely after the trial. Why had he gone to Martin instead of Byrnes? "The reason simply was that Martin was the boss and Byrnes had nothing to say. It would have offended Martin had I gone to Byrnes, and Byrnes knew it and didn't expect the complaints to be made to him." Doherty painted himself as a victim and political scapegoat. "I was an out-and-out Tammany man, and Martin had to offer me up to scatter the clouds which were gathering above his head and those of his political associates."[15]

By summer's end, the police board had tried and dismissed fifteen officers, all of whom had been prominently named in Lexow testimony, including four high-profile captains. Captain William S. Devery, another Tammany insider and a conspicuous figure in the prosecution of Parkhurst's erstwhile detective, Charles Gardner, had been acquitted of criminal charges of neglect of duty in a jury trial the previous April. Now Devery refused to attend his police board trial, pleading illness. When he declined to be examined by any doctor not connected to the force, the commissioners tried him in absentia, with no attorney present. Devery preferred getting sacked, he told friends, and then pursuing reinstatement through the courts. Captain Adam Cross (nicknamed "Adonis" as he was widely considered the handsomest man on the force) had been a practicing attorney before joining the police in 1878. He was also an active Republican, suggesting the board was finally ready to sacrifice partisan considerations to save what was left of its tattered reputation. The key witnesses against both men, Katie Schubert and Rhoda Sanford, had testified unwillingly before the Lexow Committee—they now admitted to lying then to protect police who had blackmailed them. Captain John Stephenson was found guilty of levying tribute on downtown fruit and produce dealers, selling them the privilege of blocking the sidewalks. For some, Stephenson's case was the most troubling of all because he received tribute not from keepers of illegal and disreputable resorts, like those blackmailed by

Doherty, Devery, and Cross, but from men engaged in legitimate business. "The absence of public spirit and respect for law that they showed," the *Times* observed, "is quite as bad as the greed he showed, and much more discouraging to people who hope to see a reform in the local government." All the discharged captains, citing perjured witnesses and violations of their legal rights, announced plans to appeal to the New York State Supreme Court for *writs of certiorari* to overturn their dismissal.

As the Lexow Committee prepared to resume hearings on September 10, its principals scorned the summer police trials. John Goff, back from an Adirondack vacation, underscored how the "contradictions and absurdities" in the police system cried out for radical reform. "What sort of discipline can you expect," he asked reporters, "when the results of a trial by the supreme authority of the force may be overturned like that, on some technicality?" Goff channeled the anti-authoritarian streak he had developed as an Irish nationalist. After decades of growth and special laws, he argued, "the police force of New York considers itself above the law." Clarence Lexow criticized the trials and dismissals for the chilling effect they would have, particularly on rank-and-file cops. The police board's summer actions gave "an incentive of the strongest kind to every man whose conscience is agitated to get dangerous witnesses out of the way, and it may have the effect of depriving us of valuable aid."

Others disagreed. The *Tribune* praised the "energy and thoroughness" of the board trials, and judged them important "for the absolute confirmation by a separate process and tribunal of the damning evidence elicited by the [Lexow] Committee." The *Herald* applauded the trials as a good-faith effort to purify the police department "whether it suits the convenience of the Lexow Committee or not." Assistant DA Wellman, lead prosecutor in the summer trials, defended the dismissals and potential criminal prosecutions as crucial to any reform effort. While praising Goff and the Lexow Committee for putting "the brand of disgrace upon the men who deserve it," he emphasized that "they have no power to punish, and cannot possibly right an injustice to a citizen." He feared much of the Lexow testimony, shot through with perjury and immune from cross-examination, would prove worthless in court. Police intimidation was also a serious problem. Wellman estimated that 90 percent of the nearly 1,000 witnesses interviewed by his office over the summer had faced harassment from police detectives, patrolmen, and ex-cops, including "shadowing" to their homes, physical threats, and offers of money to leave the city. Within the police department, he had trusted only Superintendent Byrnes to aid his work. That's why he had to hire Pinkerton's for investigative work, along with detectives from other cities to watch the Pinkertons—shadows shadowing shadows all over the city.[16]

Meanwhile, the police board suspended any further trials as the Lexow Committee prepared to reconvene. Just before it did, Thomas Byrnes released a report outlining his own proposals for overhauling the NYPD, one the police board had directed him to make in June. Whatever his critics might think, Byrnes had always presented himself as the lonely voice of professionalism in the department, a stance combining equal parts self-promotion and administrative truth. Byrnes's sharp attack upon the demoralizing effects of political influences corresponded with Parkhurst's, though the minister would never admit it. Byrnes wanted to bar policemen from belonging to political clubs, where captains and patrolmen met commissioners and district leaders on equal footing. Social in name but political in reality, these clubs elevated political "pull" and personal influence above official authority, subverting discipline, honest ambition, and promotion based upon merit. (Byrnes held up his own reorganization of the Central Detective Bureau in the early 1880s as a model.) He acknowledged that the excise laws were routinely flouted—his own investigation had uncovered over 60,000 excise violations in just the past three months. But how could it be otherwise given the widespread popular opposition to Sunday blue laws, the political strength of the saloonkeepers, the refusal of the municipal courts to prosecute, and the police board's own rule forbidding cops to enter saloons in citizens' clothes to obtain evidence of illegal liquor sales?

As for other aspects of the vice economy, Byrnes's report indicated that he had found no public gambling save for a few isolated cases where it was carried on behind bolted and barred doors. Disorderly houses and prostitution presented a more difficult problem. Even when the police closed brothels, prostitutes could ply their trade in tenements and fancier apartment flats. Like most policemen, Byrnes advocated a European-style licensing approach to prostitution; but after years of tangling with Parkhurst and his allies, he called only for the state legislature to consider the subject. Byrnes recommended abolition of the inspection districts established in 1875; they had become semi-independent fiefdoms run for the benefit of the inspectors rather than the public, further diluting the superintendent's authority. In short, as the *Times* put it, "the main trouble is that the commander of the police force is not permitted to command it." Byrnes's report received much praise everywhere except from the police board that commissioned it. The only recommendation it accepted was to abolish the position of wardman, the precinct detectives whom so much testimony had shown put loyalty to their captain above the law.[17]

Parkhurst arrived back from his annual mountain climbing vacation two weeks earlier than usual to attend the Lexow hearings set to resume September 10. He began working the press while waiting to clear quarantine on the *Germania*. He was especially gratified, he told a crowd of reporters, to hear of the dismissal of his old nemesis Devery. But Parkhurst waved off the breaking of a few police captains as a minor matter compared to the political task at hand. When reporters pressed him on his own political ambitions, Parkhurst denied having any. "Under no circumstances will I run for mayor. No one is more anxious than I to see the city redeem her honor, but my work lies in other directions." The Lexow Committee must continue to show the connection of Tammany Hall with fraud, vice, and crime. Parkhurst bluntly expressed what the entire city—even the entire nation—understood: It would be impossible to separate the Lexow investigation from the mayoral election.

Lexow Committee members felt more confident and self-assured than they had in May, and their legal team had worked hard all summer preparing for the new sessions. Getting beyond the captains and pursuing the "higher ups" now had nearly universal support, especially within the press. Newspapers pursued aggressive coverage of various side stories, especially disturbing accounts of police interference with Lexow witnesses. The summer police board trials and dismissals, whatever the motives of the commissioners, had reinforced popular outrage over captains and wardmen acting as a law unto themselves. Yet despite all the anti-Tammany talk and the damaging revelations already made, the electoral situation was by no means clear. After all, police corruption had been shown to flourish for many years, regardless of which party held power. For his part, Parkhurst retained faith in the power of maximum disclosure. As he told a local reporter while visiting his wife's family in Northampton, Massachusetts, "Reform never suffers from frankness."[18]

A large, eager throng of spectators began lining up for seats outside the Tweed Courthouse hours before Chairman Lexow gaveled the committee back into session on September 10. The crowd in Superior Court included six police captains, decked out in gold braid and gold shields; but sullen and dejected looks now replaced their old confident air. The committee met for only three days before adjourning until October 1, allowing the senators to attend their parties' state conventions. But these few sessions suggested new directions for the inquiry: revealing corruption among central office detectives, thereby damaging Superintendent Byrnes's reputation; moving up from a focus on captains to establishing the historic pattern of bribery in Inspector Alexander S. Williams's career; demonstrating how green goods operators had compromised not only the NYPD but the U.S. Postal Service and Western Union.

John Goff, looking tanned and rested, accepted warm handshakes from the senators, Parkhurst, and other dignitaries. Cagey as always, Goff had refused to tip his hand about where the inquiry might go next. With a theatrical flourish, he quickly let everyone know. Goff casually asked his first witness, Detective Sgt. Charles Hanley, "What time is it?" Hanley pulled out a gold watch to check, and when Goff asked where he got the handsome timepiece, the detective recounted buying it for $50 from a pawn shop. Goff then launched a scathing line of questioning laying out the corrupt traffic in stolen goods between police and pawnbrokers. Stolen property frequently wound up in pawnshops—the city had over 1,000 of them—and citizens seeking recovery of their possessions first had to pay for official police postal cards, sent out to pawnbrokers with descriptions of the valuables. These postal cards included the promise, "Owner will pay all advances," referring to any money pawnbrokers had "loaned" to thieves on stolen property. Pawnbrokers routinely split these payments with police. Significantly, Hanley was no precinct wardman but a ten-year veteran of the central office, the corps that Superintendent Byrnes had founded and held up as the incorruptible alternative to precinct-based detectives.[19]

Goff delved deeper into the "green goods" business as well, and the official protection it enjoyed. William Applegate, a tall red-haired young man with a bad complexion, had worked as bookkeeper for James McNally, reputed "king of the green goods men" and currently living in Paris. Applegate offered a far more detailed account of the business than the committee had heard during George Appo's reluctant appearance the previous spring. Applegate recounted payments he had personally made to different police captains and central office detectives, bribes buying both noninterference with the scamming of out-of-towners and security against rival gangs. When one captain, William Meakim, was transferred from a downtown precinct to Harlem, the green goods operation followed him there. Even more troubling to the committee was Applegate's convincing description of how McNally penetrated the U.S. Postal Service and Western Union, buying collusion from clerks overseeing extensive mail and telegraph traffic crucial to the business.[20]

And in a preview of his determination to reach higher up, Goff explored bribes received by Inspector Williams. James H. Perkins, a retired contractor, described his former business renting scows to the city's street cleaning bureau in 1879–80, at that time a division of the police department commanded by Captain Williams. Perkins recalled that the city had run up an unpaid bill of $5,000 (about $123,000 in today's dollars). A police commissioner at the time told him he must get Captain Williams to sign off before the bill would be paid. Williams informed Perkins and his partner that his standard fee for approving any invoice was 10 percent. When the two men brought Williams a check for $500, the indignant captain told them, "if you are going to deal with me you must pay me in money; I do not take checks." They obliged by replacing the check with an envelope of cash that Williams tucked into his pocket. Their bill got paid right away.

The day after Perkins's Lexow appearance, police arrested him at the Cortlandt Street ferry on a warrant charging him with abandonment of his wife, Maria Ann Perkins. Lexow associate counsel William Travers Jerome personally appeared at the Tombs Police Court to defend Perkins. It turned out his wife had come forward on her own, after a seven-year estrangement from Perkins. His newfound celebrity, rather than police interference, might have been the real reason she pressed charges. If so, this would not be the first or last time that Lexow-related notoriety upset the lives of witnesses. After the judge released Perkins to Jerome's custody, the couple left together and patched up their differences. But even if Jerome was mistaken, the assumption of police persecution was not, and, as the *Times* put it, "his action in appearing to protect his witness was not only commendable but necessary." Inspector Williams remained silent through it all.[21]

The very last witness to testify before adjournment until October 1 presented the most astonishing story yet. Mrs. Caela Urchittel, a widow of about forty and dressed, according to the *Sun*, "like a stage gypsy" was a Russian Jew who spoke excitedly and rapidly in Yiddish. The official interpreter, Arnold Ehrlich from United Hebrew Charities, had a hard time understanding her, even with the help of Chairman Lexow, and she repeatedly burst into tears on the stand. Nonetheless the power of her story came through. She had immigrated first to Hamburg with her husband and four children. After her husband and one of the children died in Germany, Mrs. Urchittel made it to New York with the surviving children in tow. She received a loan from United Hebrew Charities, which helped her set up a boarding house catering to other Jewish emigrants. She managed to save $600 and eventually opened up a small cigar shop at the corner of Broome and Ridge Streets on the Lower East Side, living in a cramped back room with her children. Eight days after she opened the store she received a visit from a ward detective who accused her of running a disorderly house and demanded she pay him $50 to avoid arrest. Mrs. Urchittel denied any connection to prostitution—but frightened and confused, she gave the detective $25, telling him it was all she could afford. The detective came around again, this time with a patrolman, looking for another $25. When she refused, the policemen took her for a long walk around the neighborhood and forced her to take down her stockings in search of cash. On the street they ran into Max Hochstim, a concert saloon owner with strong Tammany connections and a reputation as a political "fixer" among immigrant Jews. He often provided "straw bail" (unsecured bond) for prostitutes, thieves, and others under arrest. She begged Hochstim for help and he told her she must pay the other $25, which she did reluctantly. The detective arrested Mrs. Urchittel anyway and dragged her off to the Essex Street police station, just after she watched him and Hochstim divide the $25 between them.

Mrs. Urchittel was released from jail but a few days later the same detective came around demanding another $50. This time he threatened to have her three children taken away if she refused to pay. She was arrested again, locked up in the Tombs for three days, then tried on a complaint that a man had paid her fifty cents for sex. In May 1893 she was convicted in the Court of Special Sessions of keeping and maintaining a house of prostitution in the back of her Ridge Street cigar store. Mrs. Urchittel, with a limited understanding of English, had no lawyer and the court would not allow any witnesses to testify to her honest character. The court fined her $50. Her brother had to sell her cigar store to pay the fine and get her released. But where were her three children? No one seemed to know. After her arrest, the court had turned them over to Society for the Prevention of Cruelty to Children (SPCC), which then committed them to the Hebrew Benevolent Orphan Asylum, way uptown at 136th Street and Amsterdam Avenue. Mrs. Urchittel traveled to the Asylum, begging to have her children released, but no one would hear her. Wracked with grief, she fell ill and spent six months in the hospital. After getting out she managed to open a small candy stand on lower Broadway. At the time of her Lexow appearance she had not seen her children for seventeen months.[22]

The committee could not identify the policemen in her story. Associate counsel Frank Moss had the Society for the Prevention of Crime (SPC) investigating her situation and working to reunite her with the children—so far with no success. "Here is a case," he angrily told the committee, "of a poor Russian coming to the country and preyed upon by these police detectives, and threatened if she did not give up her money." Though Chairman Lexow dutifully noted that "the committee is not here to remedy a personal wrong," Mrs. Urchittel's testimony and the loss of her children brought a new level of visceral emotion to the proceedings. "No story told before the committee," the *Sun* reported, "has so deeply affected the senators who heard it." The *Herald* called it "the most astounding story of police blackmail that has yet been heard in this city." With the committee adjourning for several weeks, reporters tried to fill in the gaps. They identified the two policemen involved, Edward Shalvey and Ambrose Hussey. The pair claimed they had arrested Mrs. Urchittel on a complaint made by the St. Mary's Roman Catholic Church on Ridge Street, and that their captain had ordered them to get evidence. The original police blotter showed the arrest of "Annie Rochetil" in May 1893. United Hebrew Charities had vouched for Mrs. Urchittel's respectability and honesty. Superintendent Jenkins of the SPCC, evincing the casual anti-Semitism of the day (particularly strong against Russian Jews), told reporters he did not believe or sympathize with Mrs. Urchittel. No matter what she said, he thought "she was glad to have her offspring cared for at the orphan asylum." There were many unanswered questions in the Urchittel case, but they would have to wait until the committee returned in early October.[23]

The committee reconvened for three weeks in October, with frequent breaks for attention to the 1894 midterm elections: for mayor, governor, state legislature, and the U.S. Congress. Indeed until November 6 the committee's work would be impossible to separate from the election season. The Lexow revelations, the worsening depression, high unemployment, and the lingering hangover from Pullman and related industrial violence portended a sharp reversal of the national and local Democratic sweep of 1892.

Defeating Tammany Hall in the city was by no means a given. On September 6 some 300 citizens, invited by a circular drafted by leading members of the Chamber of Commerce, gathered in the recital hall at Madison Square Garden, determined to plan a united anti-Tammany campaign. Most were members of the Good Government Clubs, the City Club, and the German American Reform Union; other attendees included Republican Party operatives, various anti-Tammany Democrats, and a few unaffiliated anti-Tammany figures, such as Rev. Madison C. Peters, a leading voice of the anti-immigrant, anti-Catholic American Protective Association. Chamber of Commerce men dominated the platform and the meeting. The gathering produced a statement of principles centered upon nonpartisanship in city affairs. "Municipal government," it declared, "should be entirely divorced from party politics and selfish ambition or gain. The economical, honest and businesslike management of municipal affairs has nothing to do with the questions of national or state politics." Beyond November's election, the goal was "a citizen's movement for the government of this city entirely outside of party politics."

Robert B. Roosevelt, uncle of Theodore, treasurer of the Democratic National Committee, and a longtime Tammany foe, summarized the skepticism of political veterans by posing a practical question from the floor: "You haven't an organization. Where's the machine to nominate the candidate and get your ticket to the polls?" Respondents pointed to the two dozen or so active Good Government Clubs, the 80,000 votes controlled by the German American Reform Union, and an estimated 200,000 anti-Tammany voters looking for an alternative. Still, Roosevelt's question cut to the core of the electoral task ahead. To tackle it, Good Government activists created a Committee of Seventy to run the campaign. Controlled by Chamber of Commerce members, Republicans, and corporate lawyers, the Committee included many who had contributed funds to keep the Lexow Committee going following Governor Flower's appropriations veto. The name deliberately invoked the 1871 Committee of Seventy that had toppled Boss Tweed. Back then, a potentially devastating credit crisis— would Tweed's massive frauds mean default on New York's bonded debt?— drove the city's financial and mercantile elite into the electoral arena. They found powerful allies among such anti-Tweed Democrats as Samuel Tilden, many of whom helped rebuild Tammany after Tweed's fall.[24]

In 1894 the fight, at least rhetorically, was directed not against one corrupt man and his "ring" of accomplices, but rather against Tammany Hall as a political institution. For all the talk of rising above partisanship and separating municipal affairs from national politics, the new Committee of Seventy operated on very different terrain. Through the 1880s and 90s Tammany Hall had strengthened its hold in city departments and among elected officials. Former Mayor Abram S. Hewitt predicted Tammany would nominate for mayor a respectable citizen of high character—precisely what it had done when it nominated Hewitt himself in 1886 as the best hope for defeating Henry George, the popular United Labor Party insurgent. Hewitt defeated both George and Republican Theodore Roosevelt but found himself powerless to dislodge Tammany influence once in office. Hewitt warned against a repeat, arguing no reform was possible "until Tammany influence is entirely extirpated." The always blunt Hewitt made reformers wince when he acknowledged that the Lexow investigation and the recent police trials added nothing to the knowledge of those familiar with city government. "Things were quite as bad, or even worse, when I was elected mayor," he recalled, "and although reforms were made it was not possible to secure such evidence as would convict the offenders."

And while the Committee of Seventy called for separating municipal from national politics, it never lost sight of the national implications for what happened in New York. Tammany's strong support for Cleveland in 1892 had helped elect a Democratic president and Democratic Congress for the first time since before the Civil War. No wonder the Committee of Seventy claimed the upcoming mayoral election had more consequence than either the tariff or free silver. Implied, but left unsaid, was their unease over the growing political clout of Democrats in urban America. Charles Stewart Smith, former president of the Chamber of Commerce, framed the problem as the rapid growth of large cities, soon to comprise half of America's population. He described the governance of large cities over the past twenty-five years as "a reproach to republican institutions," and warned "the character of the government of our cities will fix the character of the general government and determine the destiny of the Republic." Chaired by Joseph Larocque, president of the New York City Bar Association and a leader in the Chamber of Commerce, the Committee of Seventy began raising money and reaching out to a variety of groups, with the goal of fielding a united anti-Tammany ticket.[25]

Meanwhile a re-energized Parkhurst resumed his favorite role as a moral freelancer, hurling righteous lightning bolts at wicked pols. Throughout September he directed them at Tammany Hall and the police in appearances at City Vigilance clubs and churches all over the city. Before an overflow crowd at the Eighteenth Street Methodist Church he dismissed Superintendent

Byrnes as "nothing but a detective," ridiculing him as "the impersonation of execution in this department, which is thoroughly and intrinsically rotten." He recalled with relish Byrnes's wild and unsubstantiated claim, made in 1892, that Parkhurst's crusade somehow originated in the divorce suit of one of his parishioners. The focus must now be on achieving a viable fusion ticket for the election. "It is easy and simple for us to come together and have our hearts beat with one throb," he reminded his audience. "The question is whether they will beat in one throb at the polls." At a CVL meeting held in the Second Reformed Church on Thirty-Ninth Street, off Seventh Avenue, Parkhurst once more angrily denied any war on prostitutes, gamblers, or disorderly houses. He invoked his own rural upbringing and his "deep and tender interest in young men" to explain the roots of his movement. After coming to New York City, "I learned of temptations of which I never dreamed. Perhaps I should not have been so innocent, but I was. I set to work to diminish the temptations that beset these young men." To a storm of applause, he implored his audience: "Let each of us be the apostle of a better city government. . . . I believe tremendously in divine sovereignty, but I believe as well in individual effort to give divine sovereignty effect."[26]

Parkhurst showed his political savvy with direct appeals to the city's Jewish voters and to women. He appeared before a Lower East Side audience on Rivington Street, the throng so large that policemen had to be called in to maintain order. The man he wanted for mayor must be pure of character, sincere, and beyond the domination of Democratic or Republican "bosses." And, he told this enthusiastic crowd of tenement dwellers, "he should have a warm spot in his heart for the workingman, and for the foreign-born people who live in this city." He noticed that women comprised half of his listeners on Rivington Street. Parkhurst maintained his opposition to woman suffrage while groping for new ways to get women involved. He urged women as parents to support reform and "the idea that a pure municipal government was a necessity." Refusing to be pinned down about specifics, Parkhurst, referring to the battle over suffrage, said only, "If the women would only fight for this reform with the energy with which they fought each other last Spring, [referring to pro and anti-suffragists] I think it would be a very good thing."

Two weeks later, after meeting with Parkhurst, veteran reformer Mrs. Josephine Shaw Lowell announced creation of the Woman's Municipal Purity Auxiliary (soon changed to Woman's Municipal League) to aid

Dr. Parkhurst and the reform campaign. Several feminists criticized her, citing Parkhurst's opposition to suffrage. But Elizabeth Cady Stanton, the most venerable and respected suffrage fighter of all, thought it a great chance for women of all viewpoints to get practical political experience. And it might even force the good reverend to change his own position. "If Dr. Parkhurst does not believe in suffrage now," Mrs. Stanton observed, "he will soon. He cannot help it when he sees what a power women can exert."[27]

By October 1, when the Lexow Committee resumed its hearings, the political rumor mill was in high gear. Parkhurst made it clear he was not interested in being a candidate for anything. Several of the anti-Tammany groups loudly began "booming" John Goff for mayor. And some Republicans thought Clarence Lexow might make an excellent candidate for governor. Goff kept mum on his own political aspirations. Whatever they might be, he pushed the investigation deeper into exposing the human cost of unchecked police power, particularly the everyday oppression of the city's immigrant poor.

Goff wanted to focus on the longstanding failures of internal police discipline, emphasizing three points. First, police violence against innocent citizens nearly always went unpunished. Secondly, police found guilty of felonies and misdemeanors before the police board routinely got off with only a reprimand or small fine, and even then could appeal their convictions in the courts. And, finally, as he put it, "the air of the trial room at police headquarters is blue with perjury." With the help of NYPD's chief clerk, Major William Kipp, Goff entered into the record all the complaints and verdicts in police board trials over the last three years, nearly 12,000 in all. He had Frank Moss recount the strange circumstances by which, in 1887, the police board promoted Captain Alexander S. Williams to inspector at the very same meeting where it had tried him on seven specifications for conduct unbecoming an officer. Former police commissioner Charles MacLean, who had served for ten years, described how the right of appeal to the courts subverted the board's ability to dismiss any officer. Louis J. Grant, a politically connected attorney, estimated defending some 500 policemen before the police commission in recent years, and representing over one hundred who had appealed their dismissals in the courts.[28]

The October 2 session presented a startling sight that put human—and battered—faces on police immunity from the law. In what the *Times* described as "a spectacle without parallel, as amazing as it was unique,"

Goff summoned ninety uniformed policemen to appear, each of whom had been convicted by the police board over the past three years for brutality. Many of their victims, some of them bandaged and bloodied, were present as well. A long procession of cops told how the police board had found them guilty of clubbing, punching, kicking, or choking citizens, only to be fined a few days' pay. None had been dismissed from the force. Thomas Lucas, a truckman on the Lower West Side with no police record, appeared before the committee with his head swathed in bandages, two black eyes, and lips so swollen he could barely speak. His tale was both harrowing and too typical. A month earlier, Lucas had fallen asleep on a friend's doorstep on Hudson Street after attending a picnic. He awoke to find $4 dollars missing from his vest pocket, and when he asked three policemen standing nearby if they knew anything about it, they just laughed and told him to go home. Several weeks later he ran into one of them, Patrolman Bernard Dunn of the Macdougal Street station, in plain clothes, and asked if he had found out anything about the $4. Dunn answered by punching Lucas in the mouth, then clubbing his head and face while Lucas lay helpless in the gutter. After being dragged off to the station house, another policeman attacked him and "called me a son-of-a-bitch; there the blood was running down by the pailfuls out of my head." A sergeant intervened finally and Lucas needed twenty-seven stitches on his scalp. He was arrested for interfering with a policeman's arrest. The effect of his testimony on the room was palpable. There were sharp intakes of breath. Any city policeman, John Goff railed, "can brain a citizen with a club, and he may reasonably expect that all the penalty he will have to pay for that is about the sum of $30, while an ordinary citizen, if he commits that offense, is almost certain to go to state's prison." The entire day's testimony, Goff declared, "goes home to the very question of the rights, the liberties, and the safety of the citizens of New York." The accumulated weight of the day's display, the *Morning Advertiser* concluded, demonstrated to the world that "New York has the most brutal police force on the earth."[29]

This public exhibition on brutality—victims, perpetrators, and the impunity they enjoyed—could only scratch the surface. There were many cases deemed too shocking for open hearings, but they were surely notorious in the tenements and streets of the Lower East Side and other neighborhoods. One example involved the 1891 case of Patrolman William J. Gregory, tried by Police Commissioner Voorhis, for raping Samuel Aperwitz, a fourteen-year-old who worked in his uncle's coal business. The boy lived and slept in the office on Monroe Street. Gregory told Aperwitz he had no right to be there, arrested him, and took the boy to a hall across the street. As Aperwitz testified at Gregory's trial: "He said, 'If you won't let me do that I will lock you up [for being underage at work].' He pulled my pants off and squeezed me against the wall. He took out his instrument and pushed it in me about so long." Gregory denied everything but was found guilty of "a crime against nature." As punishment, the board fined him three days pay, a total of $8.21. Gregory resigned from the force the following year and never faced any criminal charges.[30]

The next day's session demonstrated the reality of "law-proof" police with frightening power. Goff linked police brutality and blackmail to the widespread assaults, threats, and intimidation endured by Lexow subpoena servers and witnesses. The press had reported on many of these incidents, including an attempt on the life of George Appo, whose testimony had detailed the workings of the green goods con. Goff called a number of witnesses to testify about routine police oppression of restaurant owners, soda water sellers, and other small businesses on the Lower East Side. One of them, Norbeth Pfeffer, who had done some investigative work for the committee, detailed the tight connections between police blackmail and pervasive bribery around the Essex Market Court.

Another witness was Ambrose Hussey, the former wardman identified by Mrs. Caela Urchittel as the cop who arrested her for running a disorderly house when she refused to pay him off. Right after Hussey left the stand, he approached Pfeffer and said in a voice loud enough for others to hear, "You stinken son-of-a-bitch of a loafer, I will blow your brains out, I will kill you and will shoot you down like a dog." Goff quickly summoned four witnesses to the stand who corroborated this courtroom threat. Hussey, recalled to the stand, denied it, but finally acknowledged telling Pfeffer, "You are a dirty loafer, you are not fit to live." The larger point: an officer in full uniform had threatened to murder a Lexow employee right in front of the committee.[31]

Goff's success as the Lexow Committee's chief counsel made him a hot political property. Among the Committee of Seventy, working feverishly to create a united anti-Tammany ticket, many thought Goff's growing popularity and unassailable integrity made him the ideal choice for mayor. On October 3 the German American Reform Union announced Goff as its choice. Before the Committee of Seventy could offer him the nomination, the city's Republicans declared him unacceptable. Goff might have been widely admired as Tammany's nemesis—but he was still an active Democrat, closely associated with the so-called County Democracy, the most influential anti-Tammany faction in the 1880s and early 1890s. (Goff had run for district attorney on its ticket in 1890.)

Republicans insisted that any fusion ticket must have a Republican at the top or risk losing tens of thousands of votes. They put forth William L. Strong for mayor. The sixty-seven-year-old Strong had made a fortune as a dry goods merchant and then moved into banking and insurance. He was also a Union Leaguer, former member of the Republican National Committee, and president of the Business Men's Republican Association. When the State Democracy faction, led by former Mayor William R. Grace, announced its support for Strong, the Committee of Seventy found its hand forced. After several tense meetings in the Chamber of Commerce offices on Nassau Street, the Committee of Seventy bowed to Republican wishes and formally offered Strong its nomination. A Strong mayoralty promised the sort of "business men's administration" craved by Chamber of Commerce men. Only someone like Strong, they believed, so successful in the commercial and financial world, could bring the skills and acumen needed to reform the city's public administration. Goff would have to settle for second place on the ticket, as the Committee of Seventy's candidate for recorder. Elected for a term of fourteen years, the recorder presided over the court of general sessions as the chief criminal court judge in the city.[32]

The wounded Tammany Tiger still presented a formidable foe. Never as monolithic or united as its critics claimed, the Lexow Committee and its revelations, as well as economic hard times, aggravated the factionalism and personal feuds that were always just under the surface. Since Richard Croker had resigned his leadership earlier in the year, no clear successor had yet emerged. About the only thing Tammanyites and other politicos agreed upon was the urgent need to nominate a candidate perceived as respectable, honest, and well-known. The Hall obliged, but with an unusual twist. On October 10 it named Nathan R. Straus as candidate for mayor. Straus, a German Jew born in 1848, became one of the city's merchant princes after his family's china and crockery import business took over R. H. Macy's in 1887. He later became a partner in Abraham & Straus, giving him ownership of two of the city's largest department stores.

He was even more renowned as one of New York's leading philanthropists. In 1892 Straus founded a laboratory and depot to distribute pasteurized milk among poor children; illness from drinking unprocessed milk was a huge public health problem at the time. During the harsh depression winter of 1893–4 he issued over 2 million five-cent tickets, entitling the bearer to coal or groceries at any of the distribution depots he set up around the city. He opened and maintained four lodging houses which, for five cents, gave bed and breakfast to some 65,000 of the city's unemployed, hungry, and homeless. Sounding very much like Tammany leaders such as Big Tim Sullivan, Straus scoffed at critics who advocated a more discriminating approach to relief, including home investigations: "When a poor woman comes down to take coal away in a baby carriage, she is investigated enough for me." An added bonus was Straus's high standing among national Democrats, including a personal friendship with President Grover Cleveland. Tammany, recognizing the changing ethnic face of the city, the growing appeal of Parkhurst on the Lower East Side, and the flood of Lexow stories describing police oppression against immigrants, had nominated its first ever Jewish candidate for mayor.[33]

Amidst all the political jockeying, and just a month to go before the election, the Lexow Committee pushed on. There was some criticism of Goff's new dual role as chief counsel and nominee for recorder, largely from Democrats. "Goff the reformer and Goff simultaneously the candidate make a very unfortunate combination," the *Sun* grumbled. Goff's personal popularity and the investigation's momentum deflected such disapproval. Through October the committee heard testimony expanding upon earlier disclosures and uncovering new ones. Augustin Forget, general agent for the French Cunard line, reluctantly admitted that he personally paid $500 to Captain Max Schmittberger shortly after he took over as head of the Steamboat Squad. Schmittberger kept it all for himself, ending the traditional divvy with the squad's cops. Vincent Majewski and J. Lawrence Carey calmly detailed the city's wide open policy (numbers) business, with some 600 shops taking bets of anywhere from one cent to $100. As with green goods, the business thrived under the protection of captains, central office detectives, and wardmen around the city.

The committee heard more dolorous accounts of how police and their political friends squeezed even the poorest immigrant businesses, as in demands for $5 payoffs from soda water sellers on the Lower East Side. And it learned the modern versions of some ancient city scams, unintentionally reinforcing the point that these cons, especially against out-of-towners, flourished no matter which party held power. Two African-American prostitutes, Lucy Harriot and Hattie Ledyne, laconically explained the workings of the "panel house game," a feature of the vice economy since at least the early nineteenth century. While the women turned tricks in brothels along Wooster and Bleecker Streets, thieves entered the room through fake walls, robbing the johns while they slept. Police answered any complaints with threats to expose the johns, many of them out-of-towners deathly afraid of publicity, particularly if they patronized black women. A cop might get as much as half the loot, with the madam and thief dividing the other half. And when the women walked the streets as "cruisers," a dollar per week tribute to the police made them immune to arrest. No wonder Goff described these operations as "the lowest form of oppression and corruption that possibly could be conceived by the human mind."[34]

By mid-October Clarence Lexow and other committee members, weary of the mind-numbing accumulation of testimony, urged the legal team to investigate "the fountainhead of the department." Newspapers joined the call for moving "higher up"; a mountain of evidence had already displayed "the system." A frustrated Lexow asked, "Why can you not have the police commissioners here to answer why they permit those men to still wear that uniform and use that club?" For Goff the accumulated evidence of police oppression vindicated his strategy of working up from the bottom rather than starting at the top. Most New Yorkers, he argued, especially the Lower East Side poor, small business owners, and working-class tenement dwellers, did not care much about whether a police commissioner had accepted bribes. "They have been under the iron heel of the pantata or wardman; their whole subsistence has been taken from them; and it is to arouse these people and arouse public conscience that we thought we were doing best in that line." This was good politics as well for Goff the candidate. Frank Moss, not running for any office, put a different spin on the strategy. "There are a great many people in this city," he told the senators, "who are in terror of the police, who have felt their club . . . these people began to realize that they can come here and be protected in telling their story."[35]

On October 19, in a dramatic illustration of their approach, Goff and Moss arranged for the most emotional scene yet presented before the committee. During testimony about the seedy world of panel house thievery, spectators watched a court officer restraining an excited Mrs. Caela Urchittel, the most pitiable victim of police oppression. Instead of threadbare old garments, the poor Russian widow now wore a new black dress and jacket topped by a black bonnet with white-tipped plumes. After the two black prostitutes, Lucy Harriot and Hattie Ledyne finished their testimony, Frank Moss gave a signal and Mrs. Urchittel was released. She rushed into the arms of her three children sitting in the audience. Amidst hugs and sobs of joy, after a seventeen-month separation, she finally had her children back. Sinking to her knees, Mrs. Urchittel loudly thanked and blessed the senators in Yiddish. "Tears rolled down the cheeks of many of the spectators," the *World* reported, "and several of the hardened and abandoned characters, who had been gathered together to tell the horrors of a certain stratum in New York society, cried like babies." Senator Jacob Cantor, the only Jew on the committee, had intervened with the Hebrew Sheltering Guardian Society for the children's release. "While we have had many harrowing scenes here, and listened to many harrowing stories upon this witness stand," a smiling Goff announced, "there is at least one silver lining to the black cloud."[36]

The same day a bombshell rocked the political world. Nathan Straus, named as Tammany's candidate for mayor nine days earlier, announced his resignation from the ticket. Straus's decision revealed how the prospective fusion campaign intensified Democratic discord. The reluctant Democratic nominee for governor, Senator David B. Hill, also faced an uphill fight. Hill insisted that state Democratic ballots be printed with both the State Democracy city ticket, headed by Committee of Seventy's nominee William L. Strong, and the Tammany Hall city ticket led by Straus. Straus demanded that Hill not allow his name to be on the State Democracy ticket with Strong; when Hill refused, Straus made good on his threat to withdraw. The Hall's leaders, badly divided and facing an electoral disaster, scrambled to find a replacement. They convinced former mayor Hugh J. Grant, elected in 1888 and again in 1890, once again to stand for the office. No one could recall a similar situation in the city's political history. Straus may have had other reasons to bail out. A good many loyal Tammany men viewed him as both a political and ethnic outsider and never warmed to his candidacy. And Straus had counted upon an endorsement from President Cleveland. Yet in private correspondence Cleveland, whose independence from Tammany helped make his name in New York state politics, declined to offer one. He asked Straus to honor their personal friendship "by relieving me of the embarrassment" of public support for his mayoral campaign.[37]

Less than three weeks remained until Election Day.

8

· · · ·

"A LANDSLIDE, A TIDAL WAVE,
A CYCLONE"

It was already close to 10:00 p.m. as Reverend Parkhurst, clad in his long black-caped mackintosh, walked the twisted streets of Greenwich Village, on his way to address yet another meeting. With the mayoral election only days away, Parkhurst's daily routine now kept him on the move from early morning to late at night, delivering as many as six speeches every day. He had just finished speaking at the African Methodist Episcopal Church on Bleecker and West Tenth Street, the oldest black congregation in New York State. Frederick Douglass and Sojourner Truth had both worshipped at historic "Mother Zion," long a center of abolitionist and civil rights activism among the city's black community. Invoking that history, Parkhurst told his large audience that the city was practically enslaved now by Tammany rule, and he urged them to vote for William Strong and John Goff to help make it free. Now he had one more stop to make a few blocks away, at a small ground floor flat on Waverley Place. He was late and unsure about exactly who his host was and who might be present. Resolute as always, he rang the doorbell and entered the dimly lit apartment.

This was the home of Marie Louise David, a well-known French anarchist who had invited twenty of her friends to meet with Parkhurst. After some nervous introductions and stiff handshakes, Parkhurst announced his desire to keep the meeting informal and asked what they proposed. Mrs. David and her friends were especially intrigued by the activism of the newly formed Woman's Municipal League and suggested forming an anarchist branch to help depose Tammany. Parkhurst noted that he had met with people of all shades of opinion, religious sects, and nationalities. Looking for common ground, he told the anarchists that "the government of the city of New York is not what it ought to be. No government is what it ought to be." This broke the ice and brought expressions of approval from the group. Mrs. David beamed and announced her plan to call a meeting, telling Parkhurst, "We have a speaker we can rely upon— Miss Emma Goldman." And there she was, sitting in a dark corner, the city's best-known anarchist, recently released from Blackwell's Island, where she had served time for inciting riot in the summer of 1893. "Why, is that Miss Goldman? I am very glad to meet you," Parkhurst exclaimed as he walked toward her. "And I have heard of Dr. Parkhurst," Goldman replied, rising to shake his hand amid smiles and some laughter. She sat down next to the minister, asking for his address, and that of John Goff and Frank Moss, which Parkhurst gave her while also asking for hers. When Parkhurst ascribed the origins of his movement to his New England rural roots, where he was raised on brown bread and pork and beans, Goldman replied this was the kind of food she got in the penitentiary. Parkhurst agreed to arrange a meeting between the Woman's Municipal League and women anarchists—perhaps more a polite way out of the meeting than a genuine offer. After Parkhurst left, Mrs. David and her guests excitedly talked through plans to form their new group which, they hoped, would mean new and larger audiences for their views on rapacious landlords, oppressive factory owners, and the injustices of the wage system. "He thinks he's got us," Emma Goldman exulted, "but we'll show him that we've got him." She favored the new organization as long as it did not have any laws. She even objected to any rule excluding men from the Woman's Municipal League.[1]

Parkhurst's meeting with Emma Goldman made for a strange scene, one that reflected a unique political ferment in the fall of 1894. The anarchists never did form their chapter of the Woman's Municipal League. And Parkhurst was far too shrewd to believe that a single election could somehow bring the millennium to New York. The 1894 campaign presented the first public referendum on his three-year-old crusade against Tammany rule and police corruption. With Lexow Committee sessions running concurrently into early November, it would be impossible to separate the investigation from the election. The city press now ran full blast with Lexow-related stories, including more sidebar investigations, more self-congratulation, and more illustrations. John Goff, now the Committee of Seventy official candidate for recorder, announced he would not make any stump speeches. William Strong, the reform choice for mayor, was a poor orator and, at sixty-seven, a man with limited energy. Parkhurst thus became the most in-demand speaker for the reform ticket, his presence guaranteeing large crowds all over the city. Above all, the campaign to depose Tammany demanded new strategies for challenging deeply held partisan identity in the Democratic city. The most important of these would help reshape the city's political landscape for many decades to come: the unprecedented involvement of women in electoral politics; direct appeals for reform votes in Tammany strongholds, especially among Jews and Italians; and the push for a permanent reform presence built along the lines of fusion and nonpartisanship.

The Woman's Municipal League (WML), founded by Josephine Shaw Lowell at the suggestion of Parkhurst, opened up important possibilities for female political activism. It built on the recent failed campaign to amend the New York State Constitution to grant women the vote. That movement, led by Susan B. Anthony and funded by a small group of elite, mostly Republican women, had circulated some 5,000 petitions and garnered over 330,000 signatures, along with memorials from labor organizations and the Grange. The suffragists presented their petitions to the Constitutional Convention during the spring and summer of 1894, and their public testimony there drew a great deal of attention. Their argument, reflecting the social composition of the New York State Woman Suffrage Association, emphasized how much money property-owning women paid in taxes. This was the older tradition of woman suffrage that invoked the "taxation without representation" protests of the Revolutionary era in support of citizenship rights for women. The convention rejected equal suffrage and the anti-suffrage position articulated by one of its most prominent delegates, Elihu Root, rested firmly upon the "separate spheres" view of gender relations. "In politics," Root said, "there is struggle, strife, contention, bitterness, heart-burning, excitement, agitation, everything which is adverse to the true character of woman. Woman in strife becomes hard, harsh, unlovable, repulsive...far removed from the gentle creature to whom we all owe allegiance and to whom we confess submission."[2]

Mrs. Lowell had founded the WML not as a "ladies auxiliary" but as an independent political club. For the WML activists, the nonpartisan rhetoric stressed by Parkhurst, the Committee of Seventy, and other male reformers created a new space for women that subverted traditional gender boundaries. If partisan politics was the male realm—indeed, men without partisan identity risked being labeled unmanly or unsexed—the nonpartisan movement could take advantage of women's moral superiority and harness it to the cause of reform. Regardless of whether a woman was pro- or anti-suffrage, she could take a public, visible role in the campaign as a moral duty, an expression of her conscience.

On October 19, Mrs. Lowell presided at the first large gathering of the WML at Cooper Union, possibly the largest mass meeting of women in the city's history, with no men allowed in (save for speakers and the police), and about one hundred elite women on the platform. Once the city's women were educated about the disgraceful state of municipal rule and police corruption, she told the crowd, their "moral indignation would be so strong that no man outside the criminal class would dare publicly to support Tammany Hall or to be its candidate." Parkhurst spoke along the same lines, describing his movement and the nonpartisan campaign as "a conscientious and God serving effort to put out the devil of which our city government is possessed." He made a point of recounting the pitiable story of how Mrs. Urchittel had lost her three children to police oppression, the ultimate crime against domestic life, losing his normal composure while reading at length from Lexow testimony. To be politically effective, Parkhurst insisted, the largely Protestant and economically well-off members of the WML must reach out to immigrants, the working poor, the uneducated and "show them you are in sympathy with their condition and that your heart is with them."[3]

WML activists began with old-fashioned, by-invitation-only meetings in fashionable uptown homes. They often held these jointly with Republican women groups, Good Government Clubs, and other anti-Tammany organizations. They also moved into new activist territory when they fanned out from their parlors to bring the message home in Tammany's traditional strongholds below Fourteenth Street and among the large riverfront tenement districts. Mrs. Ellen Parkhurst, in nearly as great demand as a speaker as her husband, threw herself into the work. Like her husband, she was not a supporter of women suffrage, sharing the traditional view that the "dirty" business of partisan politics was no place for a woman. Yet her work for the WML demonstrated how the nonpartisan campaign opened up new political opportunities for activist women, one where their presumed moral superiority could contribute to the reform of city problems. Significantly, the major reform organizations—the City Club, the Committee of Seventy, the City Vigilance League, the Society for the Prevention of Crime—all excluded women. The 1894 mayoral campaign thus offered the first opportunity for reform-minded women to engage directly in electoral politics, regardless of their views on suffrage.

Mrs. Parkhurst kicked off the campaign—invariably described as an "invasion" in press accounts—at a makeshift ground-floor meeting hall in a Columbia Street rear tenement. "Women must exert their home influence," she told the gathering of WML activists and downtown immigrants, emphasizing how Tammany Hall corruption polluted East Side home life. "Here we are not Hebrews, Catholics or Protestants. We are simply women fighting for that which is right." A few days later, in nearby Willet Street, she spoke to a large crowd of immigrant women, this time accompanied by a colleague who also addressed the group in German. A group of well-dressed WML activists from Murray Hill braved a driving rain to reach Thalia Hall on Broome Street, in the rear of a saloon, startling the men quietly drinking at the bar. There were no chairs, only hard benches, for the crowd of mostly young working girls. Among the speakers was Dr. Jane Robbins, head worker of the College Settlement on Rivington Street, who linked police corruption and Tammany misrule to the deplorable state of East Side tenements and garbage-strewn streets. Kate Bond, a leader in the Charity Organization Society, told a WML meeting in Harlem that "Tammany means vice, fraud, stealing, iniquity and every abomination." "The conscience of woman," she insisted, "can never be stilled if there is a reform to be made, and her work has never been needed more than at the present time." WML organizers reached out to African-American women as well, appealing to their traditional Republican allegiance in the fight to dislodge Tammany.[4]

All over town WML campaigners linked domestic housekeeping to the mess in city government, advising women on how to best influence their husbands to vote and vote well. One widely distributed leaflet, "Have I All My Rights?" offered a catechism of questions and answers like the following: "Is the street in which I live dirty and unhealthy for my children to play in? Yes. Then it is because the Tammany city government wastes the money given to make it clean." "Is there water standing in the cellar which makes my family sick and my doctor's bill big? The Health Board of New York is run by Tammany Hall." It recounted the Lexow revelation of Mrs. Urchittel getting clapped into jail, losing her children and business to police oppression. And it urged women to support the fusion ticket by influencing their husbands and neighbors.[5]

The Woman's Municipal League injected an exciting and innovative new energy into city political life. Yet plenty of New Yorkers, and not only Tammanyites, agreed with Mayor Thomas Gilroy's caustic dismissal of female activism. "I think women would be far better occupied," he told reporters, "in attending to their home duties than in attempting to manage political affairs of which they necessarily know very little." The WML initiative by no means eclipsed the long-established, ornate, male-dominated rituals that made electoral politics the most popular Gilded Age sport for spectators and participants alike. The 1894 campaign featured all of them: the nominating conventions, the more rowdy ratification meetings, the "monster" rallies with long lists of honorary vice presidents, the florid speeches, the neighborhood torchlight parades, the fierce, often highly personal fights for every office from alderman to assemblyman to Congressman. The newspapers devoted enormous space to all of it, reprinting lengthy speeches and detailed platforms, zeroing in on particularly nasty contests, covering the shifting odds offered by professional gamblers, and blurring news with self-fulfilling prophecy for favored candidates.

Still, the Lexow revelations, along with the depressed economy and the Committee of Seventy's fusion ticket, put Tammany on the defensive in ways unthinkable only two years earlier. The abrupt withdrawal of Nathan Straus further weakened an already weak hand. His last-minute replacement, former mayor Hugh Grant, was popular among Tammany's Irish base; but he offered little hope, as Straus did, for stemming the flow of Jewish voters from Tammany. Tammany's leaders, its orators, and its disciplined rank and file of election district captains tried their best to avoid discussing the Lexow Committee. They preferred pounding away at the Committee of Seventy ticket as merely a stalking horse for national Republicans. They believed that appeals to Democratic identity, heavily inflected with ethnic and class rhetoric, could still get the job done. Former Assembly Speaker and future Governor William Sulzer defined the election simply before a Tammany nominating convention: "It is Democracy versus Plutocracy. It is the masses versus the classes." There

Clarence Lexow, Republican State Senator from Nyack, who chaired the Special Committee to Investigate the New York Police Department. The phrase "to be Lexowed" became shorthand for political investigations of all kinds. (Collection of the New York Historical Society)

A formal portrait of the Lexow Committee, 1894. Its legal counsel included (standing, left to right) William Travers Jerome, John Goff, and Frank Moss. (*Harper's Weekly*, January 5, 1895)

John W. Goff,
the hard-driving lead counsel
for the Lexow Committee,
as sketched in the *NY World*,
October 14, 1894.

John W. Goff, c. 1915,
as a justice of the
New York Supreme Court.

Harry Hill, c. 1880, the famous "sporting man," dance hall owner, and vaudeville entrepreneur whose Lexow testimony detailed how the once friendly NYPD forced him out of business. (New York Public Library)

James J. Martin, Tammany District Leader and President of the Police Board of Commissioners, who clashed frequently with Superintendent Thomas Byrnes over "politicizing" the force. (*NY Herald*, December 12, 1894)

Captain Timothy J. Creeden, the highly decorated Civil War veteran who first denied then admitted to paying $15,000 for his promotion. (*NY Herald*, December 14, 1894)

Creeden's confession as depicted in the *NY Herald*, December 15, 1894.

Captain Max Schmittberger, whose Lexow testimony laid bare the inner workings of police graft. Schmittberger later became a Police Inspector, as pictured here, c. 1905. (Courtesy of the Police Museum)

Schmittberger's sensational Lexow confession depicted in *Harpers Weekly*, January 5, 1895.

Mathilde Hermann, the wealthy brothel keeper whom the police tried to prevent from telling her story to the Lexow Committee. (*NY World*, October 25, 1894)

"Higher Up!" "Capt. Schmittberger declares that Police Commissioner James J. Martin compelled a policeman to apologize to a disreputable woman for having done his duty." (*NY World*, December 22, 1894)

Cartoon satirizing the "reform" claims of Republican leader Thomas C. Platt, after the election of Fusion candidate William Strong as Mayor. (*NY World*, December 18, 1894)

"Shake!" Lexow revelations and the drawn-out battle in Albany over reorganizing the NYPD convinced many that Democratic and Republican leaders were more focused on dividing spoils than genuine reform. (*NY Herald*, May 18, 1895)

"Public Contempt" reflected the widespread suspicion of so-called "bipartisan" government. (*Harpers Weekly*, April 13, 1895)

was a great deal of talk about defending civil and religious liberty from the threat of the anti-Catholic American Protective Association.

Police Justice Thomas Grady lumped Parkhurst and reformers together with the APA, denouncing them all before a ratification crowd of 12,000 packed into Tammany Hall on Fourteenth Street. "He was the witness and procurer of the vilest of vices," Grady shouted to the cheering throng. "He told you he did it for virtue's sake, but he was simply looking for an avenue through which bigotry could assail the Democracy. Bigotry and intolerance have always been opposed to Democracy." Grady linked Tammany's historic strength to the sacred power of the vote. He told listeners at a campaign rally on the Bowery he knew they faced "a hard grind between poverty and life itself" and "a corner in the frame of some tall tenement" might be their home. "But God and our institutions give us one day in the year when the hod carrier stands equal to the millionaire and casts his vote for the candidate and principles dear to his belief."[6]

The Committee of Seventy campaign was well funded and attracted energetic support from a broad coalition, including Republicans, settlement house workers, the Woman's Municipal League, independent Democrats of many stripes, and disaffected Tammanyites with scores to settle. Its central message built on the idea Parkhurst had promoted for years: that Tammany Hall was not a political body at all, but rather "a purely personal one, existing solely for selfish and dishonest ends," its administration wringing systematic blackmail and extortion from citizens. Nor did the increasing expenses of city government bring any corresponding benefits to the city. At least 30,000 New York children—perhaps as many as 100,000—could not be accommodated in city public schools. Tammany opposed plans to expand mass transit via a new underground subway, a plan that would relieve downtown overcrowding. And Tammany seemed incapable of keeping the streets clean or building new parks. The Committee of Seventy ran daily newspaper ads and hoisted banners around the city with terse slogans like "More Schools for the Children" and "More Parks for the People."

Another banner—"No Discrimination on Account of Religion or Race"—signaled its determination to deflect Tammany's charges of anti-Catholic bigotry and to appeal to the growing Jewish vote. Ethnic appeals could be a double-edged sword. Tammany had attacked William Strong for alleged anti-Catholic views expressed years earlier, and it accused him

of joining in the infamous "blackballing" of the son of Jewish banker
Jesse Seligman, denying him membership in the exclusive Union League
Club. (Both charges were false.) Strong, a poor speaker and reluctant campaigner at best, nonetheless understood the need to challenge Tammany
in its strongholds. While touring the Lower East Side, he told a cheering
crowd of 500 Jewish clothing workers, "I have always been a working man
and worked as hard and as long hours as any one. Race prejudice is foreign to my brain." He addressed 2,000 Italians, many of them longshoremen, declaring they now represented 10 percent of the city's population.

Even if these rallies included only limited numbers of voting citizens,
the larger point had to be made: Tammany had no monopoly on celebrating the "cosmopolitan city." Parkhurst put his own spin on this sort of
appeal. He had attracted enthusiastic crowds of Jews in his forays downtown. At a joint Good Government/City Vigilance League meeting held
in a stuffy East Broadway hall packed with hundreds of Jews, the crowd
impatiently chanted "Parkhurst! Parkhurst!" as they waited for him to
speak. Nathan Straus had not yet resigned from the Tammany ticket, and
Parkhurst asked, "Why should you vote for Mr. Straus simply because he
is generous? It is the vicious organization we want to kill." When the shouting
swarm finally let him out of the hall, several hundred people from a
Socialist Labor Party rally across the street joined the throng, calling his
name, eager for a handshake or just a look. Hundreds escorted Parkhurst
to Chatham Square for his ride home on the elevated. At the end of October
the New York Board of Jewish Ministers (later the Board of Rabbis) expressed unanimous support for the Strong ticket. Parkhurst also warned
of the limits of ethnic identity. He told a meeting of Germans at the
YMCA on Second Avenue and Ninth Street, "As long as we have in our
city a Rome, a Berlin, a Belfast, a Jerusalem, there can be no community
interest among its citizens. Race prejudices and affiliations must be swept
aside if we would reform our municipal government."[7]

Tammany also looked diminished among other constituencies. The
Patrolmen's Benevolent Association (PBA), representing the vast majority
of rank-and-file cops, had unanimously endorsed the Tammany ticket in
1892. Now, at a meeting of delegates from every station house, the PBA
voted no endorsement. They resented how the Lexow Committee had
unfairly tarnished them, and they were also angry with Tammany's failure
to support a pay raise. With 3,400 votes, and control of perhaps 12,000
more from friends and family, this was an unsettling loss. It also belied

the idea of the police force as merely a compliant tool of Tammany. As much as two-thirds of the "police vote" leaned toward Strong and Goff. In one measure of the police vote's strategic importance, friends of Tammany mailed an anonymous typewritten circular, purportedly from the PBA, urging members of the force and their friends to vote against the entire fusion ticket, and John W. Goff in particular. Their victory, it warned, would mean passage of a law legislating out of office every person connected to the NYPD, with little chance for reappointment.

Revolt among large sectors of the organized working class presented an even more serious problem for Tammany. An unskilled Jewish garment worker or Italian longshoreman might have little in common with a native-born skilled carpenter or typographer. Yet the shared hatred of police brutality and historic use of the force as strikebreaking muscle for employers ran wide and deep. So, too, for Superintendent Byrnes's aggressive, nonstop spying on labor unions. During the previous summer's tension over the Pullman strike, these feelings found wide expression among even the most conservative elements in the Central Labor Union. Tammany fronts like the Democratic Workingmen's Association of New York could muster only lukewarm support for the Grant ticket. Union activists attacked Grant's labor record and suspected Tammany of embezzling large amounts from a million dollar relief fund the legislature had earmarked to hire unemployed men for work in the parks. When hundreds of these men were let go, the CLU demanded but never received an accounting from the Gilroy administration.[8]

A tumultuous strike of garment workers in October brought labor's anger against Tammany and the police to a new boil. Some 12,000 cloak makers and tailors from 300 shops joined the largest needle trades strike in the city's history to that point. Their demands included a ten-hour day, work by the week instead of "by piece," a minimum wage scale, and a union shop. Despite ferocious factional and doctrinal disputes among socialists, anarchists, and more moderate trade unionists, the strike attracted strong support among Lower East Side Jews and Italians. On October 11 the strikers held a large rally on Rutgers Square, off East Broadway, to be followed by a parade up to Union Square. The boisterous crowd of at least 5,000 got into a dispute with police over whether they had obtained a permit from Superintendent Byrnes. There were only a few police on duty and they began clubbing some of the demonstrators. Captain Donald Grant of the nearby Madison Street station arrived with a reserve force of twenty-five men who joined in the fray. Joseph Barondess, the charismatic leader of the Operators and Cloakmakers Union, was taken to the station house where police received word from Byrnes that he had indeed issued a permit. At Union Square, a furious Barondess denounced the police as allies of "the sweaters" before a crowd that had swelled to 10,000. "Here," he said, "is a specimen of the protection the police afford you. We have been clubbed and brutally used by the men you pay to protect you. One Lexow committee is not enough to investigate these men."

The incident made front-page news, and in the aftermath, Byrnes ordered Inspector Alexander Williams to investigate. Unsurprisingly, Williams, no friend of labor and a notorious anti-Semite, found no fault with Captain Grant or his men. The Cloakmakers Union produced sworn affidavits from clubbing victims, along with evidence that Byrnes had directed Detective Sgt. Charles Jacobs to secretly hire cloak makers to spy on Barondess and disrupt the strike. Jacobs, fluent in German and one of the few Jews on the police force, was the same detective Byrnes had employed to arrest and help convict Emma Goldman in August 1893. The Central Labor Union pressed the police board, already facing great pressure from the Lexow revelations on police brutality, to investigate further. The board overruled Byrnes and Williams and ordered the superintendent to bring charges for clubbing against Captain Grant; those charges were eventually dismissed.[9]

The Central Labor Union also demanded that the Lexow Committee investigate the police violence against strikers. Yet, as with other such petitions from organized labor, the committee ignored the request. The investigation never addressed the issue of antilabor violence by the police. It framed the question of police brutality purely as a byproduct of corruption, leading to the abuse of "respectable" citizens. The dramatic parade of clubbing victims staged by Goff and Moss in early October included not a single example of union or strike-related police violence. As outraged as they were by police brutality, the Lexow investigation refused to consider how routine it had become in managing New York labor relations and political protests.[10]

Amidst all the election excitement, the Lexow Committee continued to meet and generate headlines. Its broader effect on New York journalism was already evident. Back in March a healthy dose of skepticism had accompanied newspaper coverage of the committee's awkward start. By mid-October the Lexow investigation had steadily pushed the city's press to pursue far more aggressive coverage of witnesses and the overflow of sidebar stories spilling out from their testimony. Even the staidest, most conservative papers altered their journalistic practice, with reporters making themselves adjuncts, in effect, to the committee's work. For example, the *Evening Post* had never given any space to police news; its editor E. L. Godkin viewed it as sensational, indecent, and beneath the paper's dignity. Godkin, as fierce a Tammany critic as anyone in New York, finally assigned twenty-seven-year-old Lincoln Steffens to cover the NYPD from an office across the street from the Mulberry Street headquarters. By mid-October Steffens had inserted himself into a story about a tense police board meeting, producing a nasty public row with board president James J. Martin. After Martin accused Steffens of lying, the young reporter visited his office to ask where his report was inaccurate. "Advancing in a threatening manner," Steffens recounted in the *Post*, "he shouted: 'It is a damned lying report, and you get out of here. If you don't I'll kick your ------- out,' at the same time putting his hand on the reporter's arms to push him." Steffens received full support from Godkin but he relished even more the praise he received from Parkhurst. The minister, he wrote his father, had defended Steffens in public speeches "as one of the most intelligent and accurate [reporters] such as he had ever known in the newspaper business." Steffens soon became part of Parkhurst's trusted inner circle.[11]

The Lexow Committee met intermittently over the three weeks before the November 6 vote, swapping front-page space with election stories, producing new sensations and adding sordid details to old ones. Three key witnesses provided more ammunition for the Committee of Seventy's reform campaign. Goff finally went "higher up" the last week of October, putting Tammany police commissioner John C. Sheehan on the stand over five tense sessions. His appearances attracted a crush of people that filled the entire rotunda of the Tweed Courthouse and spilled out into Chambers Street and Broadway. Policemen had to help committee members, counsel, and reporters push through the crowds. A mustachioed, athletic looking man in his mid-forties, Sheehan, like his fellow Tammany commissioner J. J. Martin, was a classic machine type—a professional clerk, lawyer, and influence trader. Born and raised in Buffalo, he served as that city's controller before moving to New York City in 1886 as secretary of the Aqueduct Commission. He was close to Governor (later Senator) David B. Hill, and Sheehan's younger brother William was elected lieutenant governor in 1892. That same year Mayor Grant appointed John Sheehan to the police board, cementing Tammany's control.

Before a packed courtroom, with hundreds more pushing to get in, Goff lost no time going after Sheehan. He forced the police commissioner to admit he was unsure about the locations of police stations around the city. He had Sheehan detail the workings of the Tammany Pequod Club (he was president) and how its political influence led to appointments and promotions on the force. After exploring Sheehan's other sources of income—legal fees without ever appearing in court, a lucrative side business as a contractor—Goff zeroed in on the commissioner's laconic attitude toward rooting out the blackmail and bribery that he acknowledged existed in the department.

The fault lay with Superintendent Byrnes, Sheehan insisted, who as executive head of the department had failed to enforce the law and who, Sheehan speculated, probably received protection payoffs himself. He accused Parkhurst and the Society for the Prevention of Crime of starting up disorderly houses on the Lower East Side as part of a scheme to discredit Inspector Alexander Williams, to make him out as "an official liar." This charge drew loud laughter from spectators. Sheehan's appearances grew more tense with each day. On October 31, Sheehan became enraged when Goff demanded he make his private bank books available to the committee. Goff introduced evidence that Sheehan had stolen nearly $6,000 while serving as Buffalo's controller. When he called Sheehan "a grand larceny thief," Sheehan exploded in anger, shouting "You are a liar, Mr. Goff, and you know you are lying!" Sheehan never produced his bank books, and Goff was unable to show that the commissioner had received any bribes directly. The committee threatened Sheehan with a grand jury contempt citation and his Lexow appearance shredded whatever was left of his reputation.[12]

After finishing with Sheehan, Goff elicited a remarkable tale from Mrs. Matilda Hermann, the "French madam" known as one of the city's most successful brothel keepers. She had been a fugitive witness for a month after the grand jury indicted her for contempt in ignoring a Lexow subpoena. Following trips to Montreal and Chicago, Lexow investigators caught up with her in Jersey City, where local police had tried to prevent her from testifying against their New York City brothers. The thirty-seven-year-old Mrs. Hermann presented a striking physical appearance on the witness stand. About 5 feet, 7 inches and stout, she wore a dark blue dress with silver spangles, and a broad brimmed hat with enormous feathers. The committee had heard from many other brothel keepers already, but

Mrs. Hermann's story, told over two days, offered even clearer evidence of police corruption and the entrepreneurial possibilities open to women in the vice economy. A native of Alsace-Lorraine, she had emigrated in 1882 to New York, where she worked first as a dressmaker (like Augusta Thurow) for women who kept brothels in the French quarter around Greene and Wooster Streets. She eventually moved into the brothel business herself, employing two dozen women in five different houses operating on West Third Street. Between 1886 and 1892 she cleared from $1,000 to $1,500 each month; she bought property on West Third, paying $15,000 for one house (about $400,000 today) after putting down $5,000 in cash, and subletting houses to other madams.

Before getting into the specifics of her relations with police, Goff first had her detail a shocking family scandal. According to Mrs. Hermann, her own niece had become a prostitute in a brothel run by her mother, Mrs. Hermann's sister, after coming over from France. According to Mrs. Hermann, she had tried all she could to get her niece out of the life, threatening her sister and even appealing to a police captain for help. Even if her story of a mother pimping her own daughter could not be corroborated, Goff understood the emotional force of such testimony. No one could dispute that Mrs. Hermann was an extremely shrewd businesswoman. And the cost of doing business, she testified, included an estimated $30,000 (about $800,000 in current dollars) paid out in protection money to five police captains, various wardmen, lawyers, and courts. When served with a subpoena for criminal contempt charges, several New York police had conspired to send her out of the city with a travel fund of $1,700. Now, to quash that subpoena and the contempt charges, she named names and denounced the police who had forced her to leave New York. She lashed out against policemen and police justices in a defiant tone that startled her listeners. The *World* described her testimony as the worst outrage yet, "a new phase of police criminality, and one more shocking than any that has hitherto been laid bare." It got Mrs. Hermann out from under her legal troubles. She left New York and a few years later re-emerged as a successful brothel keeper in the thriving vice district of Johannesburg, South Africa.[13]

Had the bottom been reached for tales of police rapacity and depravity? On November 3, just after Mrs. Hermann completed her defiant testimony, the committee listened to an even uglier story, one Goff called the "climax of the horrible in this city." This was a rare Saturday afternoon sitting and the last Lexow session before the election. The main witness was Dr. J. E. Newton Whitehead, a physician who had practiced in the city for nearly thirty years. A small man of about sixty, with a close-cropped beard and a precise manner, Dr. Newton described his specialty as "diseases of females." He was one of New York's best known abortion providers. Whitehead noted he had been arrested multiple times on bench warrants for performing illegal abortions, but he had never been tried or convicted. He offered a meticulous account, backed up by cancelled checks, receipts, and corroborating witnesses, of how policemen, lawyers, and police justices colluded in regularly blackmailing him and other abortion providers. (Midwives, who also performed abortions, never seemed to get arrested, as the police did not think they had enough money to play the blackmail game.) During one six-week period in early 1894 he was arrested three times and paid out $2,825 (about $77,000 today) in police bribes and lawyer fees, half of which went to fix police justices. Tired of being squeezed by incessant police blackmail and greedy judges, Whitehead gave up the business and approached Goff and asked him to serve as his attorney.

Whitehead then exploded a real bombshell. In April, a pregnant actress, a Miss Alexander, came to his office looking for help. The doctor informed her that he could not treat her, as the blackmailing and repeated arrests had forced him to give up the business. She replied that the gentleman who had gotten her in a family way was very influential and might be able to help with Whitehead's legal troubles. He did not think so as he was now facing a grand jury indictment. As he recalled for the committee, "[s]he insisted and said: 'Doctor, who is this man that held you'; I said, 'It was Judge Koch'; she said, 'Judge Koch,' she said, 'My God, he seduced me and got me in the family way five times, and Judge Koch paid the bill.'" After hearing from Miss Alexander, Police Justice Joseph Koch of the Essex Market Court sent for Whitehead. "I went to see Judge Koch," Whitehead continued, "and he was as sweet as sugar; he told me, 'Doctor,' he says, 'I am very sorry about this affair; I did not know that my girl had ever been to you;' he said. 'I will do all I can for you, everything'; he said there would not anything come of this case; 'Don't be afraid.'" After interceding on his behalf, Miss Alexander had expected Whitehead to perform the procedure, and she became furious with him when he continued to refuse. Scheduled to appear on stage shortly, she was forced to visit another physician.

Whitehead's story not only unveiled yet another lucrative police blackmail scheme. It also displayed the shameless hypocrisy of a Tammany-appointed judge and demonstrated the extraordinary powers that a police justice—often acting as judge, prosecutor, and jury—had over a citizen's personal liberty. Koch was one of fifteen police justices, appointed by the mayor for ten-year terms, at an annual salary of $8,000 (roughly $220,000 in current dollars). These were among the most coveted patronage plums in city politics; of the fifteen police justices on the bench in 1894, fourteen had been appointed by a Tammany mayor.[14]

Following Whitehead's appearance, Goff offered a brief review of the committee's work since its return from summer recess, describing the doctor's testimony as the most "terrible exposure" yet heard of all the "horrible realities" recounted by witnesses. The committee adjourned until November 19—in fact it would not reconvene until December 3—and the courtroom audience offered a vigorous three cheers for Goff. The election was three days away. After spending a few hours in his office, Goff made his way to the climactic Committee of Seventy election rally held at Carnegie Hall. Some 5,000 people jammed in, filling every seat, the aisles, and all the standing room in the back. On the stage, hundreds of men and women sat in tiered seats, members of the Committee of Seventy, Chamber of Commerce men, Woman's Municipal League activists, settlement house workers, and Republican and independent Democrat dignitaries. For three hours they applauded a parade of anti-Tammany speakers, impatiently waiting for Goff. Finally, at about 10:00 p.m., Goff and mayoral candidate William Strong entered the hall and made their way to the platform amidst wild cheers and shouting. Strong spoke briefly, declaring that his election would mean no partisanship, no religious or sectarian discrimination, no race prejudice in City Hall. He then introduced Goff as men jumped from their seats waving hats and hands, women fluttered their handkerchiefs, and the crowd roared his name.

It was a remarkable moment for the erstwhile Irish revolutionary, now on the brink of winning election as recorder, New York's chief criminal court judge. Blushing a deep crimson, Goff finally managed to quiet the audience down so he could deliver his first formal speech of the campaign. He referred to Dr. Whitehead's story, deemed unprintable by several newspapers, as "so unutterable, so horrible, so revolting that I dare not give utterance to it at this meeting." For forty minutes he reviewed the work of the Lexow Committee as an indictment of Tammany. "I am not making a political speech," he maintained, "because I am only continuing my work." And like Parkhurst, he insisted, the city faced not a political choice but a moral one. He stood with Strong "for better government, for cleaner morals, for the suppression of the clubber, the tyrant, the oppressor, the blackmailer, and for the betterment of our government and our republican institutions."

The next day, Sunday, election sermons condemning Tammany rang out from churches all over the city. Madison Square Presbyterian overflowed with listeners eager for Reverend Parkhurst's final words. Appropriately, he took his text from Jeremiah 25:5 (KJV): "Turn ye again now every one from his evil way, and from the evil of your doings, and dwell in the land that the Lord hath given unto you and to your fathers for ever and ever." Appraising his crusade begun nearly three years earlier, he once again framed the election in unambiguously moral terms: Election Day would be nothing less than "a public vote on the Ten Commandments." And he once more stressed the national consequences, for "a successful blow struck for God and the right here on Manhattan Island will create a thousand echoes far and wide across the continent."[15]

The day before the election Superintendent Byrnes responded to the enormous pressure to ensure a fair vote. He announced that for the first time ever patrolmen would be stationed at polling places away from their regular precincts, some 2,284 men, with two assigned to each of the city's 1,142 election districts. This plan had first been proposed by Republican police commissioners Charles Murray and Michael Kerwin and adamantly opposed by their Tammany colleagues, J. J. Martin and John C. Sheehan. Byrnes, determined to defend his own reputation and secure an honest election, decided to act on his own. "The men will be sent into districts where they are strangers," he told reporters, "and there will be no opportunity for any of them to use their influence, one way or another, or commit the offenses which it has been charged some policemen were guilty of at past elections." And he had obtained over 700 arrest warrants for men who had registered illegally, in case they showed up to vote. Fraudulent voting would not be a factor in this election. The political polling of our era was unknown. Yet the meticulous head counting traditionally performed by Tammany election district captains (and now Good Government activists as well) was usually very accurate. And all signs pointed to one conclusion: defeat for Tammany Hall.[16]

Few predicted just how crushing that defeat would be, a complete reversal from the Democratic sweep of 1892. Voters elected William L. Strong as mayor, with 154,000 votes to Hugh Grant's 109,000, a huge plurality. Goff received the largest vote of any Committee of Seventy candidate, defeating the incumbent Frederick Smyth for recorder by 159,000 to 104,000. In 1892 the city sent twenty-seven Tammany Democrats and three Republicans to the Assembly in Albany; the new contingent would have seventeen Republicans and thirteen Tammany Democrats. Voters had elected Tammany men to all thirty-one board of aldermen seats in 1892; the new board would have a Republican majority for the first time in city history. In the race for governor, Republican Levi P. Morton easily beat Democratic senator David B. Hill, who shockingly carried the city by less than 3,000 votes of a quarter million cast. Morton was the first Republican to win the governorship since 1879, and the first to win majority support since 1872. Republicans would enjoy overwhelming control of both the Assembly and State Senate. All ten of the city's congressmen had been Democrats; now half would be Republicans.

From every angle the city vote showed massive erosion of Tammany strength. This was especially clear in the so-called tenement house districts below Fourteenth Street and up the East and Hudson Rivers. Strong carried twenty-four of the city's thirty assembly districts, including six of the ten traditional Tammany bastions in lower Manhattan. For example, in 1892 two assembly districts in the heart of the Lower East Side, the Sixth and Seventh, had voted overwhelmingly for Tammany's mayoral candidate Thomas Gilroy, giving him 64 percent of the roughly 17,500 votes cast. In 1894, Strong carried both districts, with Tammany candidate Hugh Grant getting only 45 percent of 14,600 votes cast. Large numbers of Jewish and German voters abandoned Tammany, and many other Democrats had simply stayed home. Yet overall the mayoral campaign brought out an unusually large number of voters for a nonpresidential year, 274,000, only 14,000 fewer than cast in 1892.[17]

The Democratic debacle was a national one, as Republicans achieved one of the greatest midterm election reversals in American history. Democrats had controlled the House of Representatives with 219 Congressmen to 126 Republicans and 11 Populists. The new Congress would seat only 107 Democrats, 9 Populists and a whopping 240 Republicans. The talk of nonpartisanship quickly faded amid Republican jubilation over the national picture and hopeful predictions of Tammany's demise. The election, the *Tribune* crowed, "proved to be a landslide, a tidal wave, a cyclone, a political revolution of the most gigantic and far reaching proportion." The people had "redeemed" the city and state from "the worst set of political robbers and scoundrels who ever fastened themselves upon a civilized community." The *Evening Post* speculated that Tammany Hall might "go to pieces and be absorbed by some other Democratic organization." Tammany men and Democrats generally tried to blame the national trend, the depressed economy, and President Cleveland's decline in popularity. "Everywhere the Democratic rout is terrible," the *Sun* gamely noted, "but Lexow didn't do it." Hard times no doubt strengthened Republicans nationally and locally, but the Lexow revelations badly hurt Democrats in the city, especially among German and Jewish voters, and with the kind of independents who had gone strongly for Cleveland in 1892.[18]

There was general agreement, at least, that the election had been a fair one. Superintendent Byrnes received widespread praise for doing all in his power to ensure an honest vote. There were perhaps two hundred arrests of people challenged for illegal voting—but most of these were dismissed as resulting from clerical errors involving wrong addresses on the registration lists. A large corps of poll watchers affiliated with the Committee of Seventy and the Good Government Clubs helped curb illegal voting as well. One of these poll watchers was Mrs. Elizabeth Grannis, the longtime suffrage campaigner and leader of the National Christian League for the Promotion of Social Purity. In another marker of how the reform campaign mustered women's activism into electoral politics, Mrs. Grannis became the first authorized woman poll watcher in the city's history. For nearly twenty years the fifty-four-year-old Mrs. Grannis had joined other suffrage militants in publicly casting her vote "by proxy" via men sympathetic to her cause. She had allied herself with Parkhurst's crusade and threw herself into the work of the Woman's Municipal League. Clad in a blue bonnet and gown, with a velvet lace-trimmed cape, Mrs. Grannis took up her position as an official Republican poll watcher at a polling place on Oliver Street, in the heart of Tammany territory. With a small notebook in hand, she carefully checked off the names of men as they voted. As she explained to reporters, she only agreed to serve if she could have a break. "I got off at 10:30 o'clock and went uptown to vote," her ballot cast for her by the well-known Presbyterian minister Dr. Joseph Wilson.[19]

Indeed for female activists like Mrs. Grannis and those associated with the Woman's Municipal League, the 1894 election marked an important beginning. The all-male world of reform, including Parkhurst's men-only City Vigilance League and Society for the Prevention of Crime, now had women allies determined to more directly shape the city's political life despite not having the vote. Although the WML disbanded practically after the election, it reorganized for the 1897 mayoral campaign. Its constitution underscored the tight bonds between the nonpartisan approach to politics and women's engagement. The WML promised active support for movements and candidates committed to the best government regardless of party affiliation. It remained a potent force in city politics. By stressing the connections between "good government" and improving health, the schools, housing, and "moral welfare," the WML attracted many reform-minded women. The settlement house pioneer Lillian Wald, the labor activist Margaret Dreier, and the future National Consumers League president Maud Nathan all cut their political teeth in its campaigns. Nathan was part of a prominent Jewish family (her rabbi great-grandfather had attended George Washington's inauguration) and a committed suffragist. Yet as she noted in her memoir, her WML activism worried family members, forcing her to be more diligent than ever in attending to household duties, afternoon teas, and dinner parties.[20]

In the election afterglow anti-Tammany forces looked for ways to make reform permanent. The Committee of Seventy, meeting in the Chamber of Commerce offices on Nassau Street, announced it would remain in business, advising mayor-elect Strong, framing good government laws, and taking further actions it deemed "conducive to the best interests of the city and its inhabitants." A jubilant Parkhurst received a blizzard of congratulatory messages from all over the country. "People in Savannah, in Chicago, in San Francisco and in Montreal," he reported, "are saying that if we can root out and overcome official corruption in New York, they can do the same in their cities." Parkhurst emphasized what he saw as the astonishing growth of the nonpartisan vote. "Corruption is what we have been fighting. The blow at that of Tammany should be followed up by attacks on corruption whenever it reappears." He immediately announced plans for enlarging local chapters of the City Vigilance League, aimed at creating a more permanent challenge to Tammany's influence on the neighborhood level and party affiliation more broadly.[21]

The city's electoral earthquake received enormous attention around the country, where the story emphasized the total reversal of the Democratic sweep just two years earlier. Rock-solid Republican newspapers, many of which had closely covered the Lexow proceedings and police corruption, now focused on what it all meant for national politics. Most interpreted the results as a rejection of Democratic free-trade policy and an endorsement of Republican high tariff "protectionist" principles (touted as a way to bring back prosperity), combined with the repudiation of Tammany. "Tiger Is Stone Dead. New York City Snatched at Last from Tammany's Clutches," blared a typical headline in the *Chicago Tribune*. The election, it predicted confidently, meant the beginning of the end for Tammany control, and the establishment of a business, nonpartisan government in municipal affairs. The *Los Angeles Times* likewise argued that exposure of the "monstrous crimes of Tammany" meant the waning of machine rule and would further the movement to divorce municipal government from partisan control. Yet it also boasted that the GOP landslide in New York would enable Republicans "to remodel the whole fabric of the government, state and municipal." Similarly, the *Kansas City Star* translated Tammany's defeat as a cause for rejoicing wherever "there is the slightest respect and reverence for party principle and party honor." Nonpartisan victory was sweetest when it led to defeat of the partisan enemy.[22]

Parkhurst's relentless celebration of the nonpartisan spirit inflamed the simmering tensions between Republican Party politicians and moral reformers, threatening to rupture the anti-Tammany coalition at its very moment of victory. The Lexow Committee would not reconvene until December 3, leaving a month for rumor, speculation, and sniping over just how police reform should proceed. The Committee of Seventy, along with Parkhurst and his close ally Frank Moss, lost no time in pushing their solution: legislate the current department out of existence. Get rid of the current police commissioners, superintendent, inspectors, and captains, and create a new force organized along military lines, centralizing authority in a single chief, responsible only to the mayor. Parkhurst scoffed at any suggestions that Superintendent Byrnes might be kept on to help any reorganization. Frank Moss predicted the new legislature would indeed make these changes as soon as the investigation ended. (For good measure Moss also attacked the pending raise for patrolmen to $1,400, declaring, "Good men can be had for a maximum salary of $1,000 a year.") Moss's comments drew an angry reply from Senator Lexow, who noted the committee had neither finished hearing testimony nor begun considering legislation. An even more irritated Thomas Platt, Republican leader in Albany, maintained his opposition to a single-headed department, favoring instead a new law guaranteeing bipartisan balance on the police board. As long as the NYPD had full charge of the electoral machinery, "In no other way can there be a guarantee of fair elections." Platt turned the rhetorical tables on Parkhurst's continued criticism of "bossism." "Any attempts on the part of self-constituted committees, or ambitious busy bodies, to fore-stall their work and 'boss' the Legislature," he warned, "will be resented by Mr. Lexow and his associates and by the people generally."[23]

At a City Vigilance League banquet held in his honor, Parkhurst threw more fuel on the fire by insisting there was not much difference between Thomas Platt and Tammany's Richard Croker, calling any boss "unmiti-gatedly, unquestionably and thoroughly destructive," a threat to American institutions. Warming to the topic, he made many in the largely Republican audience squirm with his spirited defense of nonpartisanship. "The boss," he continued, "is the most cunningly devised scheme that has yet been invented for the purpose of crushing and drying up individual manly personality, and you and I, to our dying gasp, will fight the boss, no matter what may be his pretensions to respectability—the more respectable he is the more damnably dangerous he is." No wonder so many of the state's top Republicans—including governor-elect Levi Morton, lieutenant gov-ernor–elect Charles Saxton, mayor-elect William Strong, and State Senator Lexow—declined invitations to attend. As one New York Republican Congressman observed, "The best way for Dr. Parkhurst and his friends to crush any contemplated municipal reform legislation for New York City is to continue to abuse Mr. Platt." Parkhurst's views also incensed many of his erstwhile clerical allies, especially those identified with na-tivist and anti-Catholic attacks on Tammany Hall. Reverend Thomas Dixon, pastor of the Twenty-Third Street Baptist Church, described Parkhurst himself as "one of the most beautiful of autocratic bosses this city has ever produced."[24]

Indeed, almost as soon as the votes had been counted, the anti-Tammany forces had begun sniping at each other. Tammany was soundly defeated—but what significance did that have, who was most responsible for its overthrow, and what principles should guide Mayor-elect Strong as he prepared to take office? Two books published shortly after the election laid out very different perspectives on these questions. E. L. Godkin edited a "souvenir volume" with the grandiloquent title, *The Triumph of Reform: A History of the Great Political Revolution, November Sixth, Eighteen Hundred and Ninety Four*. What made this uprising against Tammany worthy of commemoration, Godkin argued, and different from the ear-lier removal of Tweed, was the popular support expressed for nonparti-sanship in city government. Nonpartisanship "has passed from the stage of pious opinion and obtained a foothold in practical politics." Yet Godkin had to admit that the triumph of nonpartisanship was incomplete because rural and small town voters did not yet accept it. While tens of thousands of New York City voters had abandoned their party in the election, upstate voters and officeholders balked at the novelty of nonpartisanship, reluctant to "unlearn some of the lessons of a lifetime." Still, he was confident that New York would prove a harbinger of change for all American cities and would wipe out what Godkin saw as the greatest stain on democratic government, "the gross corruption of our municipalities."

The nonpartisan ideal had been strengthened by a new feature in electoral politics, namely the various clubs and organizations that had united to defeat Tammany and replace government by party with government by sound business practices. The Committee of Seventy, the City Vigilance League, the Society for the Prevention of Crime, the German American Reform Union, the City Reform Club, the Good Government Clubs—these were the means by which reform could be made permanent. Each was the subject of a celebratory chapter in Godkin's book, as was the work of the Lexow Committee. Yet most of the book consisted of full-page photographic portraits of the leaders of these groups and the Chamber of Commerce. There could be no clearer statement that reform really meant businessmen replacing politicians in municipal government. The Woman's Municipal League received no mention at all. Nor did Parkhurst rate more than a glancing reference.

Parkhurst had begun writing his own, very different account shortly after the election, and he leaked portions to the press almost as soon as he finished them. *Our Fight with Tammany* offered a review of Parkhurst's crusade, including his famous sermons, the SPC's fight with Byrnes, the war on the captains, Gardner's trial, and the genesis of the Lexow Committee. Like Godkin, Parkhurst believed that the anti-Tammany victory in the city would "create a thousand echoes far and wide across the continent." Yet the final chapter—"Victory—Its Perils and Opportunities"—revealed Parkhurst in full Jeremiad mode. He was far more troubled about the perils than the opportunities. And the biggest threat of all was "the damnable dangerousness of a professional politician …the people's natural enemy." If Mayor Strong proved unable to maintain his independence, "the *victory itself* proves a failure." The reform movement was first of all a moral movement, one responsible for creating the popular enthusiasm that defeated Tammany. Only by continuous appeal to citizens' conscience, as in the work of the City Vigilance League, could professional politicians be overcome and the reform movement made permanent.[25]

Still, the election of Mayor William Strong demonstrated that Tammany could be defeated by the fusion of groups who opposed it. Voters in 1894 also approved a revised New York state constitution, hammered out over the summer in a convention dominated by Republicans. A reapportionment of the state senate and assembly protected and strengthened the Republican upstate rural base, ensuring GOP political control via the legislature. The anti-urban prejudice also found voice in new rules governing voter registration. Personal registration would be mandatory only in cities and villages of over 5,000 population, reflecting the deeply held assumption that rural voters were inherently more moral than city dwellers. The new constitution also inscribed one electoral reform long sought by anti-Tammany forces: separation of municipal elections from state and federal contests. Mayoral elections, starting in 1897, would take place in odd numbered years, with the mayoral term extended from two years to four. Yet the new provision applied only to cities with populations over 50,000, a clear swipe at the urban vote in New York, Brooklyn, Buffalo, and Albany. Thus what looked like an electoral "reform" to some was also a clear partisan victory for state Republicans.[26]

As the Lexow Committee resumed its work on December 3, the electoral sweep of the anti-Tammany coalition only deepened the strains between nonpartisans and partisans. These played out while the committee met, amidst unanswered questions over where the investigation might go next, how long it might continue, and how best to reform the NYPD. The election was over, but the Lexow Committee was not yet finished.

9
· · · ·

ENDGAMES

The electoral defeat of Tammany magnified the national import of the committee's work. The hearings now received regular coverage in daily newspapers across the United States that ran Associated Press reports and, in the case of some larger papers like the *Chicago Tribune*, assigned special correspondents. Dignitaries of all sorts attended the hearings, their presence carefully chronicled in press accounts. Reform politicians from Buffalo, Chicago, Newark, and other cities dropped in and talked expansively with reporters about plans "to Lexow" their own communities. At the first session on December 3, Samuel Gompers, president of the American Federation of Labor, introduced committee members and counsel to John Burns, a member of Parliament and influential trade union leader visiting the U.S. from London. Large crowds lined up for nearly every session, eager to squeeze into the Superior Court in the Tweed Courthouse, hoping to witness some new sensational revelation. When would the committee move "higher up" and call top police officials to the stand? Would John Goff, now recorder-elect, be able to continue as chief counsel after he took office January 1? Could the committee keep meeting through 1895? What about calls for an expanded charge to investigate other city departments beyond the police? The committee stuck to its policy of keeping its next moves secret, stoking endless speculation by newspapers eager to grab credit for new exposures and by politicians jock-eying for advantage.

At first, Goff continued his strategy of calling multiple witnesses each day and piling up more evidence of Tammany misrule and police black-mail. Goff roasted Commissioner of Street Cleaning William S. Andrews for his cozy business relations with employees of his department and pri-vate contractors. One of the latter was ex–state senator George Washington Plunkitt, who later became famous for his distinction between "honest" and "dishonest" graft. Frank Sanger, manager of Madison Square Garden, and William Brady, manager of the heavyweight boxing champion James J. Corbett, described how police officials had demanded and received 25 percent of the gate receipts to sanction prize fights. Other witnesses noted that, in spite of the committee's work, police continued to collect black-mail from saloonkeepers and disorderly houses in several precincts.[1]

Goff and his associate counsel Frank Moss wanted to revisit the explo-sive issue of police brutality, one they believed transcended all political and ethnic divisions and spoke to the fundamental question of personal liberty. On December 5 they called a witness whose shocking story re-vealed just how far police would go in using violence against perceived enemies. Augustine E. Costello, forty-six years old, with graying hair and ruddy cheeks, appeared unwillingly under subpoena. A deputy revenue collector, Costello had previously, worked as a police reporter for the *Herald* and had come to know the department intimately. In 1885 he pro-posed writing an authorized history of the police department, with Costello receiving 20 percent of the proceeds and the rest going to the police pen-sion fund, which was very low at the time. The police commissioners officially endorsed the project, and the celebratory history Costello pub-lished, *Our Police Protectors*, remains one of the most valuable accounts of the evolution of New York's police. However, when Inspector Thomas Byrnes's book *Professional Criminals of America* appeared in 1886, the commissioners withdrew their official endorsement, and sales of Costello's book dried up. He then decided to write a history of the city's fire depart-ment, making a similar arrangement with the trustees of the Firemen's Pension Fund. After sinking thousands of dollars into printing 2,500 copies of the fire department history, Costello suddenly found that, once again, official endorsement had been cancelled. A rival history of the fire department, put together by a politically connected writer, undermined support for Costello's book. He now had to recall copies of the official letter of authorization that his canvassers used in selling subscriptions and ads for the book. Costello learned that two of those canvassers had been arrested at the Old Slip station; a fire captain had complained that the men held the official letters illegally.

On November 7, 1888, Costello went to police headquarters to try to free the salesmen and to explain his efforts to retrieve the official letters. Inspector Alexander Williams had a long memory and was having none of it. As a police reporter Costello was the first to use the term "Tenderloin" in print to describe the Nineteenth Precinct commanded by Captain Williams. And Williams had long resented the reporter's write-ups of tolerated vice in the district. Now the inspector kept Costello in his office for five hours without arresting him. Finally, at around midnight, he declared Costello under arrest and ordered two detectives to take him on the elevated down to the Old Slip station, First Precinct, located in one of the most deserted parts of the city. As soon as they arrived, Captain William McLaughlin and two other policemen attacked Costello, beating him to a bloody pulp with brass knuckles. They dragged him from the gutter into the station house where the beating continued. Badly injured, he fainted in his cell. Costello was so sure he would die that he tore a leaf from his notebook and scribbled a message that he hid in his stocking: "If I am found dead here to-morrow, I want it known I am murdered by Captain McLaughlin and his crowd." The next day Costello was brought to the Tombs Police Court and charged with trying to destroy evidence (the canvassers' letters), but the charges were quickly dropped. The physical injuries were so severe and the humiliation so great that Costello shared the affair only with a few intimate friends until his Lexow appearance. He was ruined financially as well. When asked why he had never taken any legal action, he replied simply, "no use to go to law with the devil and court in hell."[2]

Costello's testimony made front-page news in every paper simply because, as the *Tribune* put it, his charges "revealed a species of persecution and cold-blooded brutality on part of the police department hitherto almost unknown." McLaughlin denied it all, as did Williams, who merely smiled and told reporters, "If I should tell all I know Costello would wish that he never had been born." Follow-up testimony by the doctor who treated him, his attorneys, and other acquaintances corroborated Costello's story. Frank Moss also brought out Costello's experiences in the Irish Revolutionary Brotherhood. In 1867 the nineteen-year-old Costello, a naturalized American citizen, had crossed the Atlantic on the *Erin's Hope*, a ship running supplies in support of a failed Fenian uprising against British rule. He was captured and sentenced to twelve years' hard labor before high-level diplomatic negotiation brought his release in 1869. To underscore the extreme cruelty of the New York police, Moss forced Costello to compare his treatment at their hands to what he received in British prisons. Very reluctant to say a good word about the hated British, Costello nonetheless answered the question, "Were you ever pounded or assaulted?" by telling Moss, "I never was; they treated me within the rules with a great deal of rigor, but they never assaulted me." Costello's case had contributed to passage of the Expatriation Act in 1868, recognizing the right to renounce one's citizenship and pledging U.S. support for naturalized citizenship rights against claims made by other nations. (The equivalent legislation in Great Britain was known as the Warren and Costello Act.) One of the very few people Costello had confided in after his beating was John W. Goff, his fellow Irish revolutionary. Goff knew the story and subpoenaed his friend reluctantly to testify, but he let Frank Moss handle Costello's appearance.[3]

Politics kept intruding, creating real friction within the committee itself. Moss, the counsel closest to Dr. Parkhurst, continued to argue for abolishing the current force and starting all over. On December 11 he got into a nasty spat with Chairman Lexow, who thought the idea impractical and resented Moss's effort to write legislation for the committee. "How in the world," Lexow demanded angrily of Moss, "are you going to legislate the police out of existence? What could you suggest that would legislate out of existence 4,000 men substantially by legislation, without producing conditions of anarchy in this city?" Goff interrupted the discussion, rebuking them both for debating the issue in public. Meanwhile Republican leader Thomas Platt, Lexow's political patron, kept up a steady drumbeat of support for maintaining a bipartisan police board through new legislation or even a constitutional amendment. The November election, he insisted, produced not a triumph for fusion but rather "a Republican victory, made possible by Republican effort and by Republican agencies.... This Republican triumph in New York City is mainly to be credited to the bipartisan police board." At the same time Platt sent out a circular to small-town newspapers around the state ridiculing reformers and urging editors to toe the party line. Republicans "will not take dictation from the hands of the Committee of Seventy or of the good Dr. Parkhurst or any other unauthorized person."

Clarence Lexow, for his part, reiterated the deeply anti-urban sensibility shared by Platt and so many Republicans. Speaking at a testimonial dinner in his honor, Lexow mirrored Platt's view that Democrats owed any victories in the city or state to massive, organized vote fraud. "We who live in the rural districts," he told a well-heeled audience at the Waldorf Hotel, "looked with ever increasing concern toward the great municipalities of the state as the danger spots of our liberties.... We saw corruption, immorality, and crime triumphant over purity, virtue, and justice." For Lexow, the vast concentrations of people within cities had produced new conditions never contemplated by the Founders, threatening a republic built upon the rock of individualism.

Goff recognized the political pressures that kept threatening to derail the inquiry. As recorder-elect he was exasperated by the horde of office seekers looking for jobs. (As recorder he would have six clerk positions to fill, each paying $1,000 per year.) "They come by the mail, by messenger, and in person," he complained. "I wade into the hall of my house through an ocean of letters. I stumble over them on the sidewalk. They haunt me in my dreams." Digging deeper into police abuses provided his only real respite. Time was now short. Under terms of its creation, the Lexow Committee could theoretically keep meeting through 1895. Senator Lexow kept hinting that the committee would keep meeting at least into January. Goff, scheduled to assume the recorder's office on January, declined to say whether he might continue as chief counsel. It looked to most observers that the investigation would have to end by New Year's. With only a couple of weeks to go, Goff was determined to confront two of the worst abuses entrenched in department routine: payment for promotion and regular blackmail collection. Both had long been rumored, and the committee had heard plenty of related testimony from criminals—but it still had no hard evidence from police themselves.[4]

On December 13 Goff began a two-day examination into the practice of buying a captaincy. He zeroed in on Capt. Timothy J. Creeden, fifty-five, currently commander of a precinct in the Annexed District (the Bronx). Common rumor had it that Creeden put up $15,000 to buy his promotion to captain in 1891, and Goff had worked on the case for three months. Before asking Creeden on the stand about the money, Goff made sure to review the details of his admirable career. As a thirteen-year-old boy, Creeden had emigrated to New York from Ireland in 1852 with his family. He worked at unskilled jobs and as a volunteer fireman before enlisting in the Union army three days after the Confederate attack on Fort Sumter. His military record was exemplary. He saw action in twenty-three different campaigns, including Bull Run, Antietam, Fredericksburg, and Gettysburg. He suffered serious wounds to his shoulder and back, earning a promotion to sergeant for bravery before mustering out in 1864. He then joined the NYPD in 1864, and his record over thirty years on the force was virtually spotless. The easy-going, gray-haired Creeden spoke with a lilting brogue and was a very popular figure. He emphatically denied knowing anything about a fund allegedly raised by some friends to move him up from sergeant to captain. Even after reassurances of im-munity—that his testimony could not be used against him in court or before the police commissioners—Creeden refused to budge. A frustrated Goff had expected a different answer, telling the committee and his wit-ness, "I am surprised, intensely surprised, and disappointed at Captain Creeden's attitude." After the captain stepped down, Goff called a proces-sion of East Side politicians and saloonkeepers who acknowledged con-tributing anywhere from $250 to $1,000 to a fund raised on Creeden's behalf. One of them, the theater owner and congressman-elect Henry C. Miner, testified that Creeden had repaid it all over two years.

The next day Goff recalled Creeden to the stand before a crowd listening in a dead hush. Clearly under great mental strain, twisting and pulling at a crumpled handkerchief, the captain announced that upon reflection and after consulting with his family, he now wanted to amend his testimony. Goff first asked him why he had hesitated to tell the truth the first time around; Creeden said he did not want to implicate any friends. The Irish nationalist connection, once again, surfaced in his exchange with Goff:

Q. In other words you were determined to sacrifice yourself sooner than be called an informer—that is true? A. That is true.

Q That is your nature, captain? A. Yes sir.

Q. And a distinguishing feature of your race? A. With my family particularly so.

Q. For what reasons particularly? A. Being revolutionists.

Q. Revolutionists in Ireland? A. Yes, sir.

Q. So that the word informer carries with it a terrible significance there? A. It does, sir.

Q. More than it does even in our own country; hence you have hereditary dread of having that name applied to you? A. Yes, sir.

Q. And it was that dread and terror that caused you to hesitate yesterday in giving your testimony? A. Yes, sir.[5]

Creeden swore that he had paid $15,000 (roughly $400,000 today) for his appointment, with the understanding that the money would go to then–police commissioner John Voorhis. For many years Creeden had been frustrated by failure to gain promotion despite his stellar record. He'd made the captain-eligible list in 1887 with a very high score on the required civil service exam—but men with inferior records kept winning promotions over him. He had twice refused propositions from friends to raise a fund on his behalf. In debt, and with eight children to support, Creeden finally agreed when several friends offered to raise the fund, as other sergeants looking for promotion had done. The plan called for John Voorhis to receive $10,000 for promoting Creeden, with the rest going to a couple of the police commissioner's political associates. Creeden described his negotiations with several go-betweens. When Voorhis finally summoned Creeden to his office to discuss a possible promotion, the police commissioner asked if he had any knowledge of rumors about a fund being put together on his behalf. Creeden "naturally denied it," believing Voorhis asked the question merely "to provide a kind of retreat for himself"—plausible deniability.

Goff excused Creeden from the stand, expressing the committee's strong sympathy for his position and its view that he ought not suffer any punishment or reprisals for his testimony. As Creeden stood up to leave and shake hands with the committee members and staff, the crowd applauded wildly, slapping his back as he made his way out—except for the other captains and policemen in the room who turned their faces aside as Creeden walked passed. When word of Creeden's confession reached police headquarters, Superintendent Byrnes asked the police commissioners to suspend the captain for perjuring himself. This news caused another uproar at the committee hearing. Chairman Lexow called the decision "abominable" and immediately subpoenaed Byrnes and Board President Martin to explain their action. Both men apologized on grounds of ignorance—they had not realized the committee felt so strongly about protecting Creeden—and they rescinded Creeden's suspension.[6]

This brought another exultant round of applause, what the *Herald* described as "the most remarkable outburst of emotion that has been witnessed at any of the sessions." Creeden's admission was, as the *Tribune* put it, "by far the most sensational and dramatic scene" yet produced by the Lexow investigation. There was a great deal of praise for his "frank and manly confession," and for the committee's quick action forcing a reversal of his suspension by the police board. And Creeden won enormous sympathy, in the *Times*'s estimation, as "a decent man absolutely forced to enter into a corrupt bargain, or else to abandon the prospect of a promotion he has earned in a service which he has made the business of his life."[7]

Where had the money actually landed? John Voorhis, the former police commissioner in question and now a police justice, vehemently denied receiving anything. Voorhis insisted he promoted Creeden based on his seniority and superior war record. Creeden "was bunkoed out of $15,000. Had not one dollar been collected he would have been promoted to the captaincy by me." Voorhis made his bank books and checkbooks available to Lexow counsel and repeatedly asked to testify to clear his name—but he was never called.

The Creeden case revealed much about the seamier side of city politics, not all of which could be laid at the feet of Tammany Hall. John Voorhis was the leader of the New York State Democracy, one of several anti-Tammany factions active in the 1880s and 90s. The two men most prominently named as go-betweens in the case, John Martin and John Reppenhagen, were both East Side saloonkeepers active in the same organization. Reppenhagen admitted pocketing $5,000 from the fund and giving the remaining $10,000 to Martin, who was known as the dispenser of patronage for the New York State Democracy. A third confederate, the saloonkeeper Barney Rourke, notoriously shifted his loyalty between the Republican Party and Tammany. Voorhis himself would later join Tammany Hall and win elevation to Grand Sachem. The prospect of patronage trumped all loyalty and principles, encouraging chameleon-like behavior among local pols. And the claim of representing or speaking for someone with control over appointments was itself a common practice for asserting political power or making money.

John Reppenhagen embodied all this. Only five feet tall, hunchbacked and suffering from dwarfism, with beady green eyes and a deep voice. Reppenhagen personified the professional politician. Amoral, corrupt, grasping, devious, he was a serial failed candidate for local offices—assemblyman, alderman, coroner. Asked what he had done with the $15,000 entrusted to him on Creeden's behalf, he replied firmly, "I spent them . . . in pleasure and in business," evoking roars of laughter from the crowd. Goff expressed his disgust with Reppenhagen, reflecting the prevalent view of politicians driven only by the pursuit of patronage: "I consider it really a disgrace to our civilization and our institutions that this creature should sit on a chair under the sanctity of an oath, in a proceeding, and testify in the way he is doing."[8]

Just a day before Creeden's appearance, a jury found ex-captain John Stephenson guilty of bribery, the first policeman tried and convicted as a result of Lexow exposures. While commanding the Leonard Street station, Stephenson had allowed a Duane Street fruit seller to obstruct sidewalks partially in return for four baskets of peaches, worth $6, sent to his home in Tremont. Back in June, testimony about police blackmail of legitimate merchants had aroused great resentment, much of it aimed at businessmen who paid off cops to skirt the law. Stephenson had been dismissed from the force during the summer trials before the police commission. Few expected a criminal conviction for a bribe so paltry. "Who in the world thought a police captain would ever get convicted because he took peaches?" wondered one surprised courtroom observer. Parkhurst ascribed the guilty verdict to Lexow disclosures altering the atmosphere around the courts and in the district attorney's office. Victory in such a weak case augured well for many more future convictions. Stephenson received a stiff sentence of three years and nine months in Sing Sing and a $1,000 fine, the first New York police captain sentenced to state prison. And a day after Creeden's confession, Stephenson's former wardman, August Thorne, under indictment for bribery and perjury, made a detailed statement to the district attorney implicating eight more captains under whom he had served. Although Thorne's statement remained secret, news stories leaked out details.[9]

Creeden's confession and Stephenson's conviction sent shock waves through police headquarters and every station house in the city. Lincoln Steffens reported that many police officers expressed bitterness toward Creeden's admission; and the stiff sentence meted out to Stephenson signaled that even captains and perhaps higher police officials might face jail time. There was frustration as well that the Tammany commissioners—Martin and Sheehan—had thus far escaped direct implication. As one high officer complained, "It really looks as though the worst sources of corruption, the representatives of the vilest system in the department, might escape." Rumors swirled about that Captain Max F. Schmittberger, currently commander of the Tenderloin precinct, might be the next to "squeal" in exchange for a deal. Schmittberger was under felony indictment for having accepted a $500 bribe from the French Cunard line while he ran the Steamboat Squad. Immediately before Creeden confessed, Schmittberger had made a brief Lexow appearance. Under the advice of his attorney William F. Howe, New York's most prominent criminal defense lawyer, Schmittberger had refused to answer any questions on the grounds of self-incrimination. Howe laughingly dismissed stories that the captain might disclose what he knew about police corruption in exchange for quashing the indictment. "I don't think there's a word of truth in the report," Howe told reporters. "Schmittberger is not that kind of man."[10]

On December 21 Captain Schmittberger showed himself to be exactly that kind of man. Behind the scenes, Goff and Jerome had summoned Schmittberger to a private dinner, confronting him with French Cunard books that recorded years of his bribe taking. They promised not to prosecute him and to protect his position in the department if he confessed to what he knew. Word had spread quickly that he now intended to tell all. Some 700 people, standing in every available space, somehow jammed into the Superior Court room that had a capacity of 200. The crowd gathered outside the room was the biggest yet seen at any Lexow session. Schmittberger, a burly man with huge hands, dressed this time in a fashionable suit rather than his captain's uniform, looked pale and sleep-deprived. His calm testimony promised to give the committee what Lexow and Goff most wanted: an account of "not only individual or specific cases of fraud or corruption, but the general system."

Schmittberger had joined the force in 1874 after leaving the confectionery business. He spent his first sixteen years working in the Tenderloin district, a protégé of then Captain Alexander S. Williams. Although Schmittberger denied ever paying to get on the force or for any promotion, he detailed the "custom" of routine payments made to captains, mostly from liquor dealers, saloonkeepers, and night clubs breaking the excise laws. He emphasized the national draw of the Tenderloin in its 1880s heyday when, as he put it, "These dives were resorts for the criminals of the whole country, who came there to meet women, prostitutes; and that portion of New York was the center for the criminal classes." After his promotion to captain in 1890 Schmittberger received 20 percent of money collected from liquor dealers, disorderly houses, and policy shops running in the various precincts he commanded. In one midtown precinct he estimated receiving $500 to $600 monthly (between $13,000 and $16,000 today).

And as a captain, Schmittberger had to take care of his immediate superiors as well. The crowd buzzed with excitement when he described how he personally gave up to $200 every month to Inspector Williams and later Inspector Thomas McAvoy, as insurance that illegal resorts would run undisturbed. He delivered cash in an envelope monthly to Williams, either at police headquarters or in the precinct house. Asked if there were any conversations on these occasions, Schmittberger replied, "No; I would simply say, 'Here is something for you,' and he would take it; there would be no talk made about it." No words were needed, as the "custom" of captains receiving and making payments was so universally understood. So, too, was the "common understanding" that captains "were to take advantage of any opportunity that presented itself to make money out of their respective precincts."

Even more explosive were the accusations Schmittberger made against Tammany police commissioners Martin and Sheehan. He told how Martin had personally intervened on behalf of a brothel owner on Fifty-First Street, forcing Schmittberger as captain to send an officer to apologize to the madam after a raid. And Sheehan intervened in a similar way to protect a gambling house run by a political friend. Schmittberger made a point of defending Superintendent Byrnes as "an honest and fair man," intending to do right but hampered by politicians outside the force. Like Byrnes, he joined the chorus damning political influence, and Tammany clubs in particular, for demoralizing the rank and file—"it is either politics or money," not merit, that determined careers. He believed the men appointed in the 1870s and early 1880s to be far superior to the men who joined the force in the past decade. Asked why he decided to make a clean break now, Schmittberger replied, "I feel that the pillars of the church are falling and have fallen, and I feel in justice to my wife and children that I should do this."[11]

By laying out the inner workings of "the system" and directly implicating two police inspectors and two police commissioners, Schmittberger, as the *Herald* put it, "told the most astounding and complete story of police corruption that has yet been heard in the committee rooms." His revelations, the *Tribune* said, were the talk of the entire city, "in all the hotel corridors, the social clubs, the political organizations, the theaters, the fine cafes, in the fashionable streets and avenues and the rumshops and 'dives' of the East and West Side." Some questioned Schmittberger's motives after it became known that Goff had obtained a promise from

District Attorney John Fellows to drop the bribery indictment against Schmittberger. (The captain had insisted that the $500 he received from Cunard was simply a New Year's present, not a bribe, since "there was no police duty rendered or violated for it.") Others saw the hand of Superintendent Byrnes behind the change of heart; why else would the captain praise Byrnes so highly while turning on his former mentor and Byrnes's longtime rival, Inspector Williams?

Mrs. Schmittberger declared it a victory for her own influence. "I am the mother of eight children," she told a reporter calling at their East Sixty-First Street house, "and I have been able to see only state prison staring my husband in the face unless he confessed to the whole story." The morning of his Lexow appearance, "I confronted him in the dining room with the eight little ones and said, 'Max, are you going to prison and leave your wife and children to starve or go on the street?' He broke down then and told me he that he would tell all. I shall sleep tonight as I have not slept for many weeks, for the worst is over now." Immediately following his Lexow testimony, her husband took to bed at home with an attack of "nervous prostration."[12]

Schmittberger's testimony revealed even more clearly than Creeden's organized police grafting so deeply rooted that it required no words. Chairman Lexow concluded that the committee had no need to call any more "outside" (non-NYPD) witnesses; it had enough evidence to make its report and recommendations to the state senate. The committee broke for the Christmas holiday, with a last week of hearings set to begin December 26. The end was near but still unclear, as rumors, denials, and demands to move "higher up" flowed freely. Many predicted, like the *Times*, that a stampede of police "may be expected to vie with each other in their eagerness to turn state's evidence." Police Commissioners Martin and Sheehan both issued halting defenses of their actions protecting political friends, weak explanations that essentially corroborated Schmittberger's charges. Everyone wanted to hear from Inspector Williams. But there was friction between Goff and Frank Moss over how to handle Superintendent Byrnes. Goff was unable to find anything against Byrnes that would bear the legal test in court, so he and the committee decided to call him to testify not as a suspect but as an authority on how best to reorganize the force.

Parkhurst denounced the "deal" he saw: In exchange for convincing Schmittberger to confess, Byrnes would be treated as an expert witness. "An expert!" he exclaimed to one reporter. "He has been superintendent for years of the most corrupt police force in the whole world." He told Lincoln Steffens, "A gentleman said to me recently that he would as soon think of asking Satan's advice on the reorganization of hell as Byrnes's on the reorganization of the police. That expresses my opinion exactly." Parkhurst was right at least about the deal. On Christmas Day, at Goff's request, Byrnes summoned three inspectors and nine captains to head-quarters and personally served them with subpoenas to appear before the committee.[13]

The scheduled appearance of Inspector Williams stirred enormous ex-pectations. Newspapers exhausted every combat metaphor available in anticipation of Goff's questioning of "Big Aleck": it would be a duel, a heavyweight boxing match, a bullfight, a military campaign. For nearly thirty years Williams had personified the tough, gruff, take-no-prisoners ideal of the New York cop, a model of masculinity and authority for younger policemen, and a man known for his aggressive pursuit of criminals and unapologetic use of the club. Many New Yorkers viewed him as the most outrageous ruffian on the force. Yet his Republican political connections, his role in helping suppress riots and violent strikes, and his popularity among businessmen had protected him throughout his controversial career. He reassured friends, promising ominously, "It's all right, only I won't go to jail without Byrnes."

In the late afternoon of December 26 Williams began his highly an-ticipated appearance before the committee, one that stretched out over three days. The biggest Lexow crowd yet showed up to see him. There was no ventilation, and the gas jets turned on to provide light seemed to suck out the remaining air. Williams took the witness stand in full dress uni-form. Still an imposing figure at fifty-five, his hair and big iron gray mus-tache carefully brushed, he was decked out in brass buttons, gold stripes, and the velvet cuffs denoting the rank of inspector. Both Goff and Williams were nervous and ill-at-ease at first. It quickly became clear that the in-spector would not be offering anything like the confessions heard from Captains Creeden and Schmittberger. Instead, he had evidently made up his mind to deny under oath every charge that had been made against him by other witnesses. His answers were by turn evasive, defiant, flip-pant, sarcastic, and peppered with coarse jokes.

Williams played to his many friends in the audience, confident that he could "bluff" his way through it all. He acknowledged being worth some $20,000 (around $325,000 today) when he first joined the force in 1866.

He had earned it, he said, through real estate speculation in Japan and China, where he had worked for a time at his trade of ship carpenter. Williams curtly dismissed Schmittberger's testimony as that of a liar under indictment and desperate to stay out of prison. Goff tried to pin him down about contractor James Perkins's claim that he had to bribe Williams $500 to get bills paid by the Street Cleaning Bureau back in 1876. He denied ever meeting him. Perkins might have sworn he saw him, Williams noted, but he was mistaken. "I am so well known here in New York," Williams joked, "that car horses nod at me in the morning." This last drew a sharp rebuke from Goff "to refrain from making these side remarks.... You are not here to provoke laughter or crack jokes." Yet the jokes and bluster continued.

On the second day Goff concentrated on reviewing Williams's long career, including the eighteen trials he had faced before the police board. Goff emphasized that the official records of many of those trials seemed to have disappeared. These included the controversial 1887 trial where Williams, captain of the Tenderloin district, faced charges for neglect of duty in failing to suppress brothels and gambling houses. The board vote split two for conviction, two against, meaning an acquittal. Immediately afterward, the board voted to promote Williams to inspector in the sort of political horse trade that infuriated department critics. Goff used newspaper and other accounts, but gaps in the official records made it easier for Williams to evade direct answers and cite his faulty memory.

Goff tried baiting Williams about his reputation as "a champion clubber," reviewing several notorious cases where he had been charged with gross violation of citizens' rights. As in the following exchange, however, he succeeded only in baring a usually unspoken police code: any clubbing by police was by definition legal and appropriate:

Q. Did you ever club any man? A. Yes, certainly I did.
Q. And a great many, Inspector Williams? A. Never one respectable man in my life.
Q. I don't care about a respectable man; it is not for you to determine who is respectable? A. I know who I am dealing with.
Q. You are only a common policeman, paid by the people of the city of New York? A. Yes, sir.
Q. What right have you to determine who is respectable? A. Those people go around looking for a fight, and they are pretty liable to get it...

Q. You have been charged with more clubbing than any man on
  the police force? A. Presumably so; yes; but not in fact.
Q. But, in fact, you have been charged with more clubbing than
  any policeman? A. Yes.
Q. And you rather glory in it? A. No, I do not.

They had long disputations about various charges he had faced, from stealing stockings and cigars from a madame to neglect of duty for allowing brothels to run in his precincts. Questioned about why he had not closed disorderly houses while commanding the Eighth Precinct (modern day SoHo), he replied, "Because they were kind of fashionable at the time." This prompted a stunned Senator Lexow to ask, "Don't you apprehend that that is rather an extraordinary answer to the question?" Williams countered, "Well, I don't know how to put it any other way, Mr. Chairman; the houses had been there for years; they were closed up and raided when there was complaint made . . . you could not wipe them out; they seemed to exist." Even more audaciously, he acknowledged refusing during the same period to cooperate with a board of education inquiry into brothels operating right next to public schools. Williams defended his view that "Houses of ill fame do not interfere with the children when they go to school in the morning, neither do they when they come out." He instead ordered the houses to close their shutters.[14]

On the third day Goff tried focusing on Williams's personal wealth—property in the city and in Cos Cob, Connecticut, where he had a summer home and a steam yacht—but the inspector admitted to a net worth of only $30,000 to $40,000. His East Tenth Street house was in his wife's name. As for the Tenderloin district he had commanded for a decade, the inspector would admit only to giving it its name. Upon his transfer there he told a reporter, "I have been living on rump steak in the Fourth Precinct, I will have some tenderloin now; he picked it up and it has been named that ever since." He said he meant it only in the sense of better living—better saloons, better hotels. Asked, "Are you prepared to swear you never received a dollar outside of your salary while you were captain of the Tenderloin?" Williams replied, "I received money, but not from the Tenderloin, as you call it." He would only acknowledge receiving $6,000 over several years from his friend William Fleiss. Nonetheless, that was not for promoting Fleiss's Hollywood Whiskey, as had been charged. "He said he would take chances on stocks," Williams recalled, "and if successful would give me the returns."

Goff appeared exasperated and tired out. "You have become rich upon police corruption," Goff blurted out at one point. "If I was rich, Mr. Goff," Williams shot back, "I wouldn't be here answering questions." Toward the end Goff asked, "You mean to say, that in the face of this mountain of evidence against you both as a neglectful man and as a corrupt man that you are yet in a position to say everyone has lied about you?" Williams replied, "Yes, sir." When Williams finished testifying on December 28, he bounded from the stand into a crowd of about forty friends and supporters shaking his hand and congratulating him on what they saw as his complete vindication. His critics saw it differently. Goff, the *Times* believed, "has succeeded in inducing Williams to give an unconscious exhibition on the stand of his own temper and character. In that respect the examination has been highly successful." How had Williams managed to maintain his place on the force, win promotions, and even gain enough influence to have the reports of his trials removed from police headquarters? As a disappointed *Evening Post* editorial put it, Goff had not forced Williams "to confess to anything worse than habitual neglect of duty, disregard of truth, and brazen defiance of public opinion, and what chance is there of sending him to Sing Sing for that?" At best, "the magnificent audacity with which he lied and forgot in his testimony . . . is his sufficient condemnation."[15]

Following Williams, the Lexow Committee met for one more session, Saturday, December 30, with Superintendent Thomas Byrnes scheduled as its last witness. The committee first heard from several captains and Inspector William McLaughlin. No new ground was broken, as McLaughlin vehemently denied laying a hand upon journalist Augustine Costello or that he was even beaten. He spent most of his time on the stand fending off Goff's probes into his personal wealth: It came from his wife, his in-laws, stock speculation, vague patent royalties, every place but from the collection of police blackmail. Not nearly as blustery or controversial as Williams, McLaughlin's testimony had an element of farce to it, canned answers to familiar questions.[16]

Finally, at 5:30 p.m. Superintendent Byrnes took his turn. Dressed in formal civilian clothes, a dark cutaway coat and grey trousers, New York's most famous policeman and the nation's best known detective looked grayer and fleshier than he once did. Three years as superintendent had taken their toll on the fifty-two-year-old Byrnes. His four hours on the stand, often rambling and defensive at times, made clear the committee's decision to treat Byrnes more as an expert witness than a suspect. Previous witnesses evaded questions about personal wealth—or, as in the cases of police commissioners McClave and Sheehan, expressed outrage over requests for bank books and confidential records. By contrast, Byrnes testified candidly and without hesitation when Goff began by inquiring into the sources of his wealth. Indeed Byrnes's estimated fortune of $350,000 (about $9.6 million in current dollars) dwarfed that of any previous witness. Yet it had nothing to do with collecting blackmail from madams or saloonkeepers or gamblers or counterfeiters or other cops. "I defy any man in the police department that wears a uniform today," Byrnes declared firmly, "or any man outside of the police department, to point his finger at me and ever say he gave me a dollar in his life in a dishonest way." Instead, as Byrnes recounted with the pride of a poor immigrant who had risen to influential heights, he owed his pile to favors given by two of the richest men in the nation, Cornelius Vanderbilt and Jay Gould.

The realities of Gilded Age policing were never so transparent. In 1872, while he served as captain of the Mercer Street precinct, Byrnes's men had a wild altercation on the street with a brother-in-law of Vanderbilt, Robert Crawford. After shooting a detective, Crawford hid in Vanderbilt's Washington Place mansion until Byrnes and his men forced their way in, without a warrant, over Vanderbilt's loud protests. After his lawyer assured him the police had a perfect right to be there, Vanderbilt calmed down. "The Commodore [as Vanderbilt was known] sent for me," Byrnes recalled, "and in his abrupt way asked me if I had any money." Byrnes brought him $2,000 (about $40,000 today) to invest on his behalf. A few months later, the seventy-eight-year-old Vanderbilt suffered life-threatening injuries in a carriage accident. Fearing loss of his capital if the Commodore died (they had no agreement on paper), Byrnes quickly arranged to get paid back. His $2,000 had turned into $6,000.[17]

Even more lucrative possibilities opened up when Byrnes took over the detective bureau in 1881. Late that year financier Jay Gould showed Byrnes a series of anonymous letters he had received, threatening him with blackmail and murder. Using personal ads in the *Herald* and an elaborate system of surveillance on mailboxes, Byrnes soon captured Gould's tormentor. From the police board Byrnes received a medal and a commendation for his "zealous and skillful efforts." From Gould Byrnes received a more material reward. He gave Gould $10,000 to invest in stocks, eventually netting $185,000 from companies Gould controlled, including

Union Pacific and Western Union. After Gould died his son George made an additional $40,000 for Byrnes, a total return of $225,000 (nearly $6.2 million in current dollars). Byrnes had been called in on many other Wall Street blackmail cases "where the ends of justice have been better served where they would refuse to make a complaint... and they have from time to time advised and bought me stocks which I have made money out of."

Such men as the Goulds craved privacy and counted upon Byrnes's discretion. He was glad to have their friendship and gratitude but insisted there was never any *quid quo pro*. Here was a more private, intimate, and entrepreneurial version of the "dead line" he had announced with great fanfare in 1881, a promise to arrest any known criminal found in the Wall Street neighborhood. "My official position," as he saw it, "was placed at their disposal for the purpose of protecting their property and their business." Byrnes's "official position" included the routine deployment of police to break strikes, spy on union meetings, and suppress all manner of radical activism in the city.[18]

Byrnes offered many men protection from blackmail—and he evidently engaged in the practice himself. When Goff asked if any of his wealthy friends "had the benefit of your aid or services in getting rid of unpleasant persons, and particularly females," Byrnes could not recall a case of that kind. Yet just a few weeks earlier George H. Richardson, a wealthy fruit importer, dreading exposure by the Lexow Committee, had slit his own throat. News accounts of his suicide did not include the unsavory details of why. For years Richardson led a double life, one devoted to his wife and his Greenwich Street business, the other as "John Holmes," living with a prostitute mistress and running the "Chelsea," a Tenderloin saloon. Mrs. Richardson learned the truth unexpectedly, while questioning a process server who had come to their house to serve papers relating to a litigation over the Chelsea. Byrnes had known about the arrangement for years and he protected Richardson from legal action by threatening anyone who proposed to reveal it. He summoned the process server, Frederick Ladd, to his office, where a furious Byrnes accused him of an extortion scheme against Mrs. Richardson. "You are a God damn liar and blackmailer," an enraged Byrnes shouted. "What right have you to find these things out about the man, and write to his wife? I have known this case for three years, but I have never said anything about it." In fact, this was only one of numerous cases where Byrnes provided protection. As Mrs. Richardson's brother, Wall Street attorney C. Amory Stevens, wrote to

Mayor Strong the following year, "Byrnes prostituted his office and received liberal compensation from the malefactor to help him deceive his wife." It is impossible to know how many such cases involved Byrnes; the Lexow Committee never dug into this side of his career and the story never became public.[19]

Yet the power, the mystery, and the reputation Byrnes had so carefully cultivated over his career could not help him as superintendent. When asked about the systemic corruption and blackmail throughout the department, Byrnes emphasized his weak position. The superintendent lacked the power to transfer men, root out corruption, or discipline the force; he might be the NYPD's executive head, but the police commission held the real statutory authority. Any reorganization of the department would have to beef up the superintendent's power. He told with relish his confrontation with James J. Martin during the 1892 election, during which Byrnes vowed to honor the authority of U.S. marshals over polling places. Politics was "a curse to this department," elevating "pull" and money above merit, and thus badly demoralizing the rank and file. He denied knowing anything of the systematic payoffs laid out by Schmittberger and others; his twelve years running the detective bureau had shielded him from any knowledge of "the system." As for police managing and profiting from the city's vice economy, Byrnes claimed to know only what the captains and inspectors reported to him.

The superintendent's job had transformed the world's greatest, most fearless detective into something of a modern bureaucrat, a skilled administrator astute enough to claim the successes and blame the failures on others. Thief-taking had always been his strength. As head of the detective bureau, "I obtained more years of convictions against criminals than the detective force of Scotland Yard, Paris, and Jersey all put together, nearly 10,000 years; there is no such detective system in the world." Byrnes grudgingly praised Parkhurst for creating public sentiment for reform— "I want to give [him] all the credit I can, although he is just pounding me every time he gets a chance." Yet when Goff read out various newspaper quotes of Byrnes lashing out at Parkhurst and the Society for the Prevention of Crime, he conveniently claimed not to recall making them. He had tried his best to further reform by transferring captains regularly and investigating corruption on his own. Byrnes presented himself as a man trapped in the superintendent's job: "I do not think I was in accord with the commissioners; I had them on one side; had Dr. Parkhurst on the other side with the two edged sword coming along and taking a smash at me once in a while, and between them both I thought I had better get out."

With that, Byrnes ended his testimony by dramatically handing Goff a letter he had written to mayor-elect Strong. Goff read it out loud to a stunned audience. Byrnes had given Strong "my request to be retired from the post of superintendent, to be used by you or not at any time after the 1st of January as you see fit." A burst of loud applause followed, as Byrnes told the committee he put reorganization of the department above retaining his position. Yet, as many quickly noted, Byrnes cannily had not resigned but instead put his fate in the hands of the incoming mayor, preserving the possibility of continuing on and perhaps having a large hand in whatever reorganization might occur. The superintendent stepped down from the stand to another round of applause and handshakes from the committee. Unlike Williams, who had brashly burned his bridges before the committee, Byrnes won a great deal of sympathy and public support. He had again proven himself the ultimate survivor through a remarkable blending of bureaucratic skill, political shrewdness, stroking of the press, favors for the wealthy, and the claim of police professionalism. Hovering above it all was Byrnes's genuine power, both real and reputed, an inscrutable force on the New York scene since the early 1880s.[20]

On December 30, after holding 78 sessions and hearing from 678 witnesses, the Lexow Committee adjourned for good. There was still a report to write and serious disagreements over how best to reorganize the NYPD. Yet committee members and counsel all agreed that their work had produced something new and extraordinary. And the city's press had demonstrated a remarkable ability to make it known all over the world. John Goff lauded "that great and mighty fountain of intelligence, the New York newspapers." He thought it unique in the history of civilization, "for, throughout this broad land, go to the smallest village, and you have found the New York papers, or extracts from them, disclosing the testimony taken before this investigation." The committee voted to present Dr. Parkhurst with the high-backed witness chair, a gift recognizing his unflagging work. But Parkhurst freely expressed his disgust with how the committee's work concluded. On New Year's Eve he released a long, caustic statement attacking how, in the end, the committee "flinched at the crisis" and treated Byrnes with kid gloves rather than "being as criminal as any other member of the force." Sullenly, he told reporters, "I am only a poor little Presbyterian clergyman, and what has taken me two years to do, Superintendent Byrnes, with ample power at his command, would be able to do in a week if he were so minded." Asked his opinion of what might follow from the Lexow investigation, Parkhurst kept his powder dry regarding that and his own future plans.[21]

As New Yorkers rang in 1895 the prospects for police reform looked simultaneously promising and complicated. The inner workings of the NYPD had been laid bare for all to see. The newly inaugurated Mayor Strong, still basking in the glow of Tammany's defeat, made all the right noises about running a nonpartisan administration. Yet in Albany, where any new police legislation would have to be approved, Republicans enjoyed their largest majority in a generation and held the governorship for the first time since 1882. New York Republicans, their eyes already fixed upon retaking the White House in 1896, now exploited reform rhetoric and the defeat of Tammany to press their partisan advantage in the nation's largest and most politically important state. The political center of gravity shifted from the open proceedings and revelations of the Lexow Committee to the compromises and secret deals of lawmaking.

The committee released its official report, drafted by Clarence Lexow himself, on January 18. That same day newspapers reported the death from cancer of Mrs. Caela Urchittel, the Russian Jewish widow whose tale of oppression by East Side cops had provided perhaps the most emotionally charged moment of the entire investigation. Over the next few months echoes of the committee's work continued ricocheting in the press and the courts: human interest profiles of Lexow figures, stories about prominent witnesses leaving the country, policemen's trials and retirements, legal appeals. After nearly a year of work, six months of unprecedented press coverage, and an historic election, small wonder that the official report proved anticlimactic.

The bulk of it provided a vivid summary of the investigation's second phase: the informal but systematic licensing of "protected" vice; the blackmailing of legitimate business; the routine oppression and brutality directed against the city's poorest classes; the purchase of appointments; the regular interference of politicians; and the overall demoralization of the force. The briefer first section emphasized how, in a very large number of election districts, "almost every conceivable crime against the elective franchise was either committed or permitted by the police" on behalf of Tammany Hall. At the same time the report acknowledged it was "not able to furnish accurate figures showing the effect of police crime and police interference" in voting while asserting "the practices of the police exerted an important and decisive influence upon results."

Lexow member Sen. Jacob Cantor, a Tammany man representing the Lower East Side and New York City's only representative on the committee, refused to sign on and issued a dissenting account as a protest against what he called "the grossly partisan character of the report of the majority." As Cantor noted, testimony showed voting irregularities in fewer than fifteen election districts out of more than 1,100; nor did the committee acknowledge the indictments and prosecutions for vote fraud that followed the 1893 elections. As for laying all police mismanagement at the feet of Tammany, Cantor reminded his colleagues that testimony about crimes and abuses clearly showed "they were committed under a bipartisan police board which seemed to be powerless to either prevent, prove or punish them." Cantor acknowledged and criticized police oppression, especially of the immigrant poor; but blaming the department's problems on one party simply ignored the NYPD's history since the Civil War.[22]

The real controversy was now over legislation: What was the best path forward for reform? The breach between regular Republicans, led by Thomas Platt and his Albany point man Clarence Lexow, and the reform forces of Parkhurst and the Committee of Seventy, opened immediately. Lexow introduced a series of police bills reflecting Republican strength and goals. His legislation would inscribe a bipartisan police board into law and leave the board of elections under the control of the NYPD. Parkhurst and the Committee of Seventy called for a single police commissioner to oversee finances, appointments and pensions, and a chief of police, with expanded disciplinary powers, to manage the force. Both would be responsible to the mayor. And in line with their call for separating municipal politics from national and state matters, they wanted the board of elections removed from police control. Reformers also supported a police reorganization bill that called for an independent commission, with members appointed by the governor or the mayor, to revamp the department. The recently expanded powers of the mayor's office also confounded matters. Under the new 1894 constitution, any law reorganizing a New York City department had to be supported by the mayor; only a two-thirds vote in the legislature could override his veto. Thus, whatever police legislation made it through Albany would need Mayor Strong's approval.

The intricate political dance over police reform played out through the winter and spring of 1895. Parkhurst, eager to expand his municipal crusade into a national one, took to the road and escalated his attack on the Republican establishment. In late January he attracted a crowd of 3,500 in Chicago at a meeting sponsored by the Marquette Club, a Republican social organization, and the city's recently formed Civic Federation. Municipal reform—government administered on business principles—was now the center of public attention across the nation, Parkhurst declared, but reformers had to avoid professional politicians and prepare for a long fight. New Yorkers might have defeated Richard Croker and Tammany, but the fight against Republicans would be much harder: "Platt has streaks of respectability as a hog has streaks of lean, but fat predominates." Back in New York Parkhurst appeared as the final speaker before an overflow mass rally at Cooper Union organized by the Committee of Seventy and allied reform groups. The crowd, including hundreds of women, came to protest the Lexow police bills and to support the spirit of nonpartisanship they believed responsible for electing Mayor Strong. After several minutes of a standing, handkerchief-waving ovation, Parkhurst again attacked Platt and "bossism." Referring to the state legislature, he roused the audience to cheers by announcing, "We are not asking them to do anything, we are not requesting them to do anything; we are insisting upon and demanding that they should do a lot." And asserting "We are one, we and the mayor," he reminded the assembled that only the nonpartisan strategy had defeated Tammany three months earlier.[23]

A follow-up lobbying trip to Albany only deepened the split. Parkhurst and a delegation from the Committee of Seventy met with Lexow's committee and other senators in the State Capitol building, stressing their main demands: A single commissioner and single chief would fix responsibility where none had existed before; divorcing the bureau of elections from the police would eliminate the need for a bipartisan police board. Right after they left town, Edward Lauterbach, chair of the New York County Republican Committee and Thomas Platt's personal attorney, ridiculed the reformers as "a lot of amateur clubs who represent nobody." The insane asylums, he told reporters, were full of people who believed in nonpartisanship in public affairs, and he likened a single-headed police force to the czar of Russia. Platt, for his part, denounced nonpartisan reformers for their "vicious spirit of intolerance" and he called the idea of a single police commissioner a scheme to cheat and oppress Republican voters and menace free elections. "If this is bossism," Platt said defiantly, "those who think so can make the most of it. I think it is good citizenship." Platt also organized a personal attack on Parkhurst by printing copies of the official court minutes from the Hattie Adams trial in May 1892. Designed to embarrass Parkhurst by publicizing the lurid details of his testimony and the case, he circulated these pamphlets to every member of the legislature and to scores of newspapers around the state.[24]

The legislative session in Albany dragged on. Amidst intense lobbying from police and various reformers and a growing welter of new bills and amendments in both the senate and assembly, Platt and Lexow held fast, determined to push through legislation that would reflect their top priorities: a bipartisan police board (with no separation of the bureau of elections from the NYPD) and a police reorganization bill whose key provision empowered the police board to weed out corrupt policemen with no court appeals permitted. Representatives of the NYPD simultaneously lobbied hard to ensure that any policeman dismissed from the force by the police board would have the right to appeal his case in the courts. In mid-March, a Lexow-related case underscored both the urgency of new legislation and the power of the courts to undo it. On March 15 Captain Adam Cross, dismissed from the force the previous August after the police board found him guilty of bribery and neglect of duty, won reinstatement in a unanimous decision by the Superior Court. This was the first time a court passed judgment on the testimony of Lexow Committee witnesses, in this case the brothel keepers Katie Schubert and Rhoda Sanford. The court found the evidence against Cross to be insufficient, doubtful, and contradictory, and it noted that Cross's defense counsel had been denied the right to cross-examine witnesses. Their claims to now be leading respectable and creditable lives thus went unchallenged. The jubilant Cross also won back pay and court costs.

The implications were clear: The evidence produced by the Lexow Committee could not sustain criminal convictions, and many cases against captains and wardmen would now be reversed. A disgusted Dr. Parkhurst declared, "It is evident that the courts are not going to reform our police department." Still angered by what he saw as the committee's kid-glove treatment of Thomas Byrnes, Parkhurst now denounced the committee's work as worthless, its failure to produce reform legislation practically making it "the ally of the very rascals that they came down here to investigate."[25]

Just three days later, however, an extraordinary grand jury investigating Lexow-related charges handed down a clutch of new indictments that gave Parkhurst and his allies renewed hope. Eleven officers, including

Inspector William McLaughlin, head of the detective bureau, four captains, three former captains, and three former wardmen faced criminal charges for bribery, extortion, and corruption. The active officers were all suspended pending trial. In addition, the grand jury's presentment made a scathing critique of the force's leadership, singling out Thomas Byrnes's personal fortune, accumulated through personal favors from wealthy citizens, as contributing to the general demoralization of the force. "The distinction between the receipt of such favors and the taking of direct gratuities for official service," it dryly concluded, "is not one that his subordinates are likely to appreciate." Byrnes dismissed this criticism, repeating his claim that he had never in truth been head of the department. As for his fortune, "I told the truth about it to the Lexow Committee. If anyone chooses to put a construction upon it to my disadvantage, I cannot help it. I concealed nothing, as I had nothing to conceal."

Byrnes still had plenty of defenders. The *Times* acknowledged that Byrnes's taking money from rich men "lacks delicacy; but it is no more morally than it is legally on the same footing with taking money for protecting instead of suppressing vice and crime." Parkhurst had no truck with such distinctions. He saw no moral contrast between "receiving hundreds of thousands of dollars for police services rendered and being the recipient of a basket of peaches for police services not rendered." The grand jury indictments further weakened a dispirited and crippled force. The detective bureau was headless; a total of twenty-five officers were now under indictment; a third of the precincts were now run by sergeants replacing captains dismissed or suspended pending trial; there were some 300 vacancies in the ranks; and hundreds more had made applications for retirement.[26]

Reorganization of the force was a given, but the political wrangling in Albany and among Republicans made the way forward anything but sure. Relations between Platt and Mayor Strong continued to deteriorate. Parkhurst was fond of saying that the city had elected a Republican to be mayor but it did not elect a Republican mayor. For Platt and the regular Republicans this was a distinction without a difference. Platt believed Republican votes had elected Strong, and he thought he had a clear commitment from the mayor to consult on key appointments. Reformers supported the so-called power of removal bill, passed in early February, giving Mayor Strong six months to replace twenty-seven department heads and the four police commissioners. They believed "home rule" a prerequisite for any meaningful improvement in municipal administration. Platt supported the power of removal in expectation of patronage plums for regular Republicans. The new mayor angered him by spreading his appointments among the various factions that had supported his fusion campaign, including Democrats. He replaced Tammany police commissioner John Sheehan with Avery D. Andrews, a West Point graduate, lawyer, and independent Democrat. Even more infuriating was Strong's choice of William Brookfield as Commissioner of Public Works, the most patronage-rich position in city government. Brookfield was a leader of the anti-Platt forces within the city's Republican Party, a group that included many men prominent in the Union League Club and Chamber of Commerce— the political "amateurs" so disdained by Platt and his allies. These eminent Republicans—such as Seth Low and Elihu Root—tried to steer a middle ground between their lifelong devotion to the GOP and their growing commitment to greater "home rule" for the city under a nonpartisan administration. Platt loyalist Edward Lauterbach dismissed them as "the plutocratic faction" and warned they would "place in jeopardy the deserved supremacy of the Republicans in the State and in the Nation."[27]

The reform coalition that elected Strong believed—or wanted to believe—that the mayor would veto any new police legislation from Albany that did not embody the nonpartisan principle. By early April Mayor Strong, impatient with the legislature's lack of progress and exasperated by the continued attacks from Platt and his allies, decided to act on his own. Invoking the new Power of Removal Law, he announced plans to replace the three holdover commissioners. The term of James J. Martin, the Tammany stalwart, would expire in May. Strong also demanded the resignations of the Republicans Charles Murray and Michael Kerwin appointed by Mayor Gilroy with Platt's support. Both men had resisted reform proposals put forward by fellow commissioner Avery Andrews. They both noisily refused to resign, aggravating even further relations between the mayor and those Republicans who thought Strong insufficiently loyal to his party. By late April Strong identified the three men he proposed to appoint: Frederick Grant, a Republican, eldest son of Ulysses Grant, and former U.S. minister to Austria-Hungary; Andrew Parker, a member of the anti-Tammany County Democrats and a former assistant district attorney; and Theodore Roosevelt, former state assemblyman, Republican candidate for mayor in 1886, naturalist and historian, and for the last six years a U.S. civil service commissioner in Washington, DC.[28]

Strong viewed Roosevelt as the key figure all along. He had originally proposed making him commissioner of street cleaning, a department badly in need of an overhaul. Roosevelt, uninterested in supervising the daily cleanup required by the city's 60,000 horses, declined the offer but let it be known he was interested in the police commission. Senator Henry Cabot Lodge of Massachusetts, a leading national Republican and Roosevelt's mentor, helped convince him that a police commissionership could help aid his political climb and raise Roosevelt's national profile. Roosevelt wanted assurances that he would have "decent colleagues" on the board and once Strong reassured him, and expressed his desire that Roosevelt serve as board president, he accepted. Strong's election rekindled Roosevelt's desire to return to the city and play a role in a reform administration. Still, along with the political opportunity Roosevelt understood the risks of diving back into New York's political scene. The new job, he wrote prophetically to his sister Anna, is one "in which it is absolutely impossible to do what will be expected of me; the conditions will not admit it. I must make up my mind to much criticism and disappointment." Roosevelt reassured Lodge that, "you need not have the slightest fear about my losing interest in national politics," and he expected to stay in the new job for no more than two years.[29]

Mayor Strong now had his new police commissioners, but he delayed swearing them in pending news from Albany as the legislative session wound down. The two key measures, the bipartisan police and police reorganization bills, were both authored by Clarence Lexow and they had both been subject to fierce debate and multiple revisions as they made their way through the legislature. Strong wanted authority to appoint an independent commission to oversee police reorganization, but that bill never made it through, done in by opponents insisting on the right of dismissed policemen to appeal decisions in court. The bipartisan police bill finally passed both houses on April 24. The decisive votes came from "country Republicans," rural and small town legislators, because, as the *Tribune* observed, "it seemed to offer the only possible guarantee of protection to the voters of the rest of the State from frauds in state and national elections." In accordance with the new constitution, it now landed on Mayor Strong's desk for his approval or veto. Strong announced he would hold a public hearing on May 1 in City Hall before making his decision.[30]

The City Hall hearing, held in the Governor's Room to accommodate the large crowd, was raucous, punctuated by laughter, hissing, and frequent outbursts of applause. All the arguments had been heard before but Strong, seated behind a writing desk once owned by George Washington and calmly chewing tobacco, listened to speakers for over three hours. Opponents, most of them from the Committee of Seventy, invoked the mass meetings at Cooper Union, the votes of the 154,000 citizens who had elected Strong, and they decried the failure of the bill to separate the bureau of elections from the police department. Parkhurst, introduced to a cheering welcome, read from a prepared statement and at times seemed to be lecturing the mayor. He spoke for the Society for the Prevention of Crime, "which inaugurated the movement that placed you in the Mayor's chair," and the City Vigilance League, "whose one ambition is to make that movement a permanency through the assembly districts of the city." He reminded the mayor of his campaign pledge to pursue a nonpartisan course if elected. Bipartisanship simply meant partisan twice over, Parkhurst argued, and the principle had been rejected by all the citizens—native-born American, Germans, Bohemians, Jews, Italians, and Poles—who had filled halls during the election campaign. Looking directly at the mayor, Parkhurst said, "We have taken you, Sir, as our champion for a long, hard, and uncompromising fight against boss interference and boss manipulation." Parkhurst cast the mayor as the leader of a growing movement of progressive citizens around the nation, a revolt against partisan politics and for municipal emancipation, a determination to have cities governed for their own requirements and interests. Acceptance of the bill would mean surrender, a betrayal of principle, and demoralization for the reform movement.

Only one speaker advocated acceptance. Edward Lauterbach, Platt's right-hand man, ignoring catcalls and derisive laughter, defended the bill, arguing "You cannot have nonpartisanship without bipartisanship." He declared himself a spokesman for Republicans across the state calling for the mayor, as a Republican, to sign the bill. He invoked the specter of urban vote fraud with an image that Lexow and Platt had used many times: upright Republican majorities north of the Harlem River cheated out of victory by dishonest counts at the city polls. And separating the bureau of elections made no sense, since "it would not be possible to guarantee the safe conduct of elections without the assistance of the police."[31]

A week later Mayor Strong announced his decision: he would approve the bill. The pressure from prominent Republicans, like Governor Levi Morton, had been intense. Close advisers urging him to sign, like Elihu

Root and Cornelius Bliss, in the end chose the hard reality of party affiliation over the campaign promise of nonpartisanship. Strong's acceptance
message to the state senate reiterated the main argument offered by Lauterbach.
Only a bipartisan board could "prevent the votes of the people in all parts
of the state for president and governor from being nullified by fraud and
intimidation here." State policy had to balance out the needs of municipal administration, Strong argued, and "I am bound to respect the wishes
of the people of the whole state regarding it." And he rejected the idea
that he must veto the measure because it did not reflect what the people
of the city demanded. The new law, he thought, would offer some improvements, including expanding civil service provisions for police recruitment and promotion. If representatives of the people refused to pass
laws that people demand, "their constituents must settle with them for
that at the polls."

Parkhurst was deeply disappointed even if not surprised. He understood the forces bearing down on Strong and weeks before the hearing,
speaking in Boston, he anticipated the mayor would cave. His biggest
regret was that Strong did not seem to appreciate "the full significance of
the crisis" and how his decision betrayed the principle—"to drive national
issues out of municipal administration"—that elected him. "We elected
him to be mayor of the City of New York not of the State of New York."
Once again, the city's needs were reduced to merely the tail on the state
kite. The city of the future, Parkhurst predicted, would be governed either
by nonpartisanship or by Tammany. Denunciations of Strong and Platt
poured in from all over, especially from Republicans who had supported
fusion at some risk. *Harper's Weekly* agreed that the new law, making the
formal recognition of partisanship a legal requirement in constituting the
police department, paved the way for Tammany's return to power. Strong
had yielded to secret partisan pressure and Platt was no more than "a spoils
huckster." The Republican Party, including the so-called "better element,"
had lost any standing it might have had as a reform organization.[32]

The day before approving the new Bipartisan Police Law Strong swore
in his three new commissioners, with Roosevelt immediately elected president at the mayor's request. The legislature adjourned on May 16 without
passing any police reorganization bill, which meant the overhaul would
have to be carried out by the four men Strong appointed. Roosevelt, by
force of his personality and instinct for publicity, quickly emerged as the
dominant figure. He saw no contradiction between promoting efficiency

and honesty and proudly wearing his political colors. "I am, as always, a strong Republican," he told the press when he accepted the position, "but as police commissioner I shall pay no heed whatever to any party consideration, either in shaping the policy of the commission or in appointing or removing men." For Strong, Roosevelt's appointment promised a way to please both regular Republicans and reformers. As the new board organized itself in early May—divvying up assignments, forming committees—two personnel decisions hung over all others: what to do about Alexander Williams and Thomas Byrnes.[33]

On May 24 Inspector Alexander Williams retired from the police force at his own request. The fifty-six-year-old inspector had just returned from a two-week vacation during which he concluded that it was time to go, but on his own terms. The police board had discussed his case privately and Roosevelt in particular wanted him out. The law required the board to accept application for retirement, with an annual pension of half pay, from any policeman with twenty-five years of service and no outstanding charges pending. After Williams had a long conference with Roosevelt at headquarters, the commissioners met briefly and voted unanimously to retire him with an annual pension of $1,750 (about $50,000 in current-day dollars). The most controversial policeman of the Gilded Age, perhaps in the city's entire history, was audacious and confident to the end. He told reporters he had been ready to retire, but only if his name was clear. The recent grand jury that had indicted Inspector McLaughlin and others brought no charges against him. "Not a thing was found against me," he gloated, "and I can now leave the force when I am not under fire."

Despite all the charges made against him over two decades—for bribery, blackmailing, and physical brutality against innocent citizens—and all the testimony given before the Lexow Committee, Williams now walked away from the force he had served since 1866. He could not resist a final taunt directed at his enemies, none worse than a fellow cop who had "squealed." "There was a man who threw mud at me while he was before the Lexow Committee," he told reporters, referring to his protégé Max Schmittberger's sensational account implicating Williams in systematic bribe-taking. "He is thinking now of going to Carlsbad to take mud baths for his health. He ought to." The bipartisan system had served Williams well. As the highest ranking and most influential Republican in the department, he not only had escaped serious punishment but had risen to the number two position of authority in the NYPD.[34]

No newspaper or public figure expressed any regrets as Williams bowed out. Byrnes's situation was more complex. He was still chief of police (the change in title came with the new law) and he enjoyed a large reservoir of good will among portions of the business community and among many elected officials. Some advisers who had Mayor Strong's ear urged him to keep Byrnes to help with reorganization of the police. Byrnes himself wanted to stay on. He had at least one ally, Frederick Grant, on the police board but Theodore Roosevelt and Avery Andrews wanted him gone. Byrnes had influential friends in Albany and actively pushed for new legislation that might save his job. The so-called supplemental police bill, passed at the very end of the legislative session, would have made the chief virtually independent of the police board, expanding his power to conduct police trials and discipline members of the force. Mayor Strong, however, responding to the strong objections raised by his new commissioners, vetoed the legislation. At the mayor's public hearing all four commissioners denounced the bill for giving the chief all the power and none of the responsibility. Roosevelt declared it a step that would prevent the board from enforcing discipline, one "calculated to perpetuate the abuses that have permeated the department." Grateful for the mayor's veto and a strong believer in unified executive authority, Roosevelt acted quickly to force a change at the top. "I think I shall move against Byrnes at once," he wrote to Henry Cabot Lodge. "I thoroughly distrust him, and cannot do any thorough work while he remains."[35]

On May 27, 1895, after private conversations with Commissioner Parker, Byrnes took the same route as Williams. The board immediately granted his request for retirement with a pension of $3,000 (about $82,000 today), and it named Inspector Peter Conlin as acting chief. Unlike Williams, Byrnes, a New York cop since 1863, went quietly. "What is there to say? It is the fortune of war, I suppose. There is nothing for me to say." Dressed in a business suit he spent a few hours packing up his office and saying goodbye to old friends in the detective bureau. The press agreed that despite all his knowledge and experience he could not lead reform of the department. Yet despite all the troubles of the last few years, the Parkhurst crusade, the Lexow revelations, and the current state of the department, he had been the city's greatest champion of law and order and protector of property. Unlike Williams, Byrnes received profuse praise for what he had accomplished, as the *Times* put it, "in the ordinary service of preserving public order and keeping the criminal classes in subjection." Over three decades, the *Tribune* noted, Byrnes had been "a grim and resolute foe of the malignant and turbulent element in society." For the *Sun,* he was perhaps the only policeman of genius ever produced by America and "a distinguished figure in the history of the metropolis." The city would be fortunate to find a successor equally equipped "to strike terror into the hearts of the wicked, and to make New York a safe place for honest people to live in and do business in." Roosevelt would have preferred compelling Byrnes and Williams to retire or trying them on charges, either of which would have been the clearest, most forceful message proclaiming a new regime. He had to settle for accepting their "voluntary" retirement and staying mum about the whole business in public. "I am getting the police department under control," Roosevelt wrote his sister Anna in early June. "I forced Byrnes and Williams out, and now hold undisputed sway."[36]

Roosevelt was now the commanding figure for police reform, and Parkhurst could not be more pleased. The two men had a great deal in common. Both were scholars and outdoorsmen, proponents of muscular Christianity, and contemptuous of those respectable and well-off citizens who thought politics beneath them. Both welcomed ambition and polit-ical activism among new immigrants as long as they embraced assimila-tion and rejected hyphenated identity. And both expressed righteous belief in the rule of law, moral and secular, and the fundamental impor-tance of enforcing it. Though they lived in overlapping circles, the two men had never met before Roosevelt's appointment to the police com-mission. While still serving as civil service commissioner in Washington Roosevelt had initiated a correspondence that no doubt made Parkhurst smile. He asked the minister's support for a man Roosevelt wanted Mayor Strong to appoint to the city's excise commission. He was already thinking about the need to revamp and enforce laws governing the sale of alcohol. "What I want," Roosevelt had concluded, "is to see the law executed, and all wrongdoers, no matter who, punished.... don't know exactly what ought to be done, but I wish to see it done in the right way!" He pledged to serve the cause of decent government and flattered Parkhurst, telling him "you have a peculiar right to be heard on any question of civic mo-rality in New York."[37]

Reformers now looked to Roosevelt to uphold nonpartisan principles. Every week the board issued new directives embodying these: No political or religious considerations in making appointments and promotions, stricter physical and mental requirements for recruits, tougher rules for certifying election officials, public recognition for men receiving bravery commendations, and more frequent and swifter department trials for accused officers. To check whether patrolmen and roundsmen actually walked their beats, Roosevelt began late-night rambles, often in the company of his friend Jacob Riis, making sure to notify the newspapers, which reported them in minute detail. The new police board president appeared regularly before Good Government Clubs and other groups, taking all questions, debating his critics, stoutly maintaining his commitment to administer the department with no regard for politics.

Parkhurst became Roosevelt's staunchest ally. He was a frequent visitor to Roosevelt's office at police headquarters, discussing policy and even getting his first tour of Byrnes's old office and his famous museum of crime. The City Vigilance League, now incorporated under a state charter, had with great fanfare opened a new permanent office at the United Charities Building. It was flush with a $29,000 endowment (about $825,000 today) given it by Parkhurst himself, the money originally raised as a testimonial fund in his honor. Some 350 CVL volunteers would help police enforce the excise laws and, like Roosevelt himself, persistently watch police work. The contrast with the old regime could not have been more striking, Parkhurst noted. "We are now in hearty cooperation and constant communication with the board of police." On June 5, he appeared with Roosevelt at a Good Government Club dinner held on Madison Avenue. Roosevelt described at length how he was putting reform principles into action. Again threading the needle of nonpartisanship, he declared, "I shall act in my official position wholly without regard to party affiliations, although I am a strong party man." The same day brought news that Parkhurst's old nemesis Captain William Devery had been reinstated, with back pay, by a court decision overturning his dismissal the previous summer. Nonetheless Parkhurst was upbeat about what he saw as the tremendous progress made since November. Hearing Roosevelt talk, he could scarcely believe he was listening to the president of the police board or that the city now had four commissioners "that have no earthly ambition but to do their duty."[38]

Just before leaving for his annual three-month stay in Europe, Parkhurst sketched plans for a new kind of progressive campaign in the fall. After nearly four years of war against the NYPD Parkhurst now shifted his sights to developing what he called "municipal conscience": the rights and prerogatives of the city. "The idea of municipal rule," he declared, "untainted and undebilitated by political interference, has come, and it has come to stay." Yet the legislature had betrayed the nonpartisan defeat of Tammany. It had failed to pass meaningful police reform; and Clarence Lexow himself had ignored the truths revealed by his own committee. Parkhurst now promised to "set back fires in Westchester and Nyack and other places," stumping around the state, monitoring candidates for senate and assembly, developing the spirit of nonpartisan municipal reform among rural and small-town voters. As his crusade had taught him, "every step we have taken has revealed a broader battleground upon which the conflict must be carried on."[39]

The irony could not have been lost on him. Home rule meant getting state and national issues out of municipal politics—but that goal required a deeper engagement in state politics and the looming presidential election of 1896. For now, Parkhurst looked forward to his long mountain-climbing vacation. Theodore Roosevelt had already planned a summer of strict excise enforcement, including fully dry Sundays. Compared to that goal, or to spreading the nonpartisan gospel across New York State, the highest Alpine peaks offered little challenge.

EPILOGUE: THE LEXOW EFFECT

What, in the end, had the Lexow Committee accomplished? Some forty police officers, including an inspector and fourteen captains (nearly half of the department's total) faced indictments on Lexow-related charges of bribery, extortion, and neglect of duty. Yet structural change remained elusive. The committee's final report and the 1895 legislative session rejected both major goals of reformers: replacing the four-man police board with a single head and separating the police department from election machinery. Bipartisanship had soundly defeated the nonpartisan ideal. In the immediate aftermath, Dr. Parkhurst and his allies pinned their hopes on the newly reformed police board, led by Theodore Roosevelt. They admired Roosevelt's repeated insistence that he would uphold his oath of office by enforcing the laws as they existed, regardless of political fallout. Throughout the summer of 1895, between mountain-climbing expeditions, Parkhurst sent a stream of open letters to the newspapers extolling Roosevelt's tough new excise policy that banned Sunday drinking. By the end of July Roosevelt proudly proclaimed that New York City now had the driest Sunday in its history.

Roosevelt served two turbulent years as president of the police board. His achievements as a police commissioner, though often overstated by his friends and biographers, were real enough. In particular, Roosevelt deserved credit for improving the quality of the rank-and-file force, largely through tighter executive control and by strengthening civil service requirements for appointment and promotion. Physical and mental attributes would now count more than political affiliation. Under Roosevelt's watch the department added 1,700 new men, half of them native-born Americans from outside the city. Police officers recognized for extraordinary service received medals and citations in public ceremonies. Roosevelt's famous late-night prowls, meant to surprise cops who had abandoned their posts or were drinking in saloons, embodied his hands-on approach to supervision and discipline. So, too, Roosevelt's more impartial, less partisan demeanor in presiding over police board trials. The Roosevelt board increased the numbers of detectives in each precinct, inaugurated a bicycle squad, improved communications by installing telephone call boxes on the streets, and standardized the firearms policemen carried. He used plainclothes cops in a controversial attempt to ramp up investigation and prosecution of prostitutes and brothel keepers. Through it all, Roosevelt made sure the newspapers knew about and publicized all of his initiatives.

Yet when he resigned in 1897, returning to Washington as assistant secretary of the Navy, Roosevelt's legacy was mixed at best. His imperious manner and domineering personality badly alienated two of his fellow commissioners, leaving the board increasingly deadlocked over even the most routine business. And along with the reforms he had pushed through, Roosevelt's aggressive enforcement of Sunday blue laws quickly estranged large numbers of New Yorkers. For hundreds of thousands of working men and women, a dry Sunday meant no beer, wine, or spirits on their only day off. German Americans, with their long tradition of Sunday family outings to beer gardens and outdoor picnics, expressed particular outrage. Roosevelt's repeated claims that he wished to remove politics from policing rang hollow for people deprived of enjoying their day off as they pleased. Democrats, the German American Reform Union (prominent supporters of Mayor Strong's fusion campaign), and some liberal Republicans denounced his war on "personal liberty" as bigoted and puritanical. A mass movement of United Societies for Liberal Sunday, including some 350 groups with over 150,000 members, soon took root, holding mass meetings and organizing parades around the city. Roosevelt would not back down, and indeed could not resist confronting his critics. During one large demonstration in September 1895, featuring 30,000 protesters marching up Lexington Avenue, Roosevelt defiantly took his place on the reviewing stand. When one German protester mockingly cried out, "Wo ist den der Roosevelt?" the commissioner flashed his white teeth, smiled, and promptly shouted back, "Hier bin ich!"

Whatever his accomplishments and missteps, Roosevelt could not be blamed for the total collapse of criminal cases related to the Lexow investigation. That, however, is what happened. By the time Roosevelt left office in the spring of 1897, not a single New York police official was in jail and all the men dismissed from the force had won reinstatement with back pay. Captain Adam Cross had won restoration of his position in March 1895 when the Superior Court reversed his dismissal by the police board. His case provided the key precedent for all the legal reversals that followed. The courts consistently held that evidence supplied by persons of "disorderly character" was insufficient for conviction of bribery or extortion. Without corroborating evidence to support the testimony of brothel keepers, prostitutes, green goods men, gamblers or other law breakers, indictments and convictions must be overturned. Many of these cases had dragged on for years. In 1898 the Appellate Court ordered reinstatement, with over three years of back pay, for Captain John Stephenson, dismissed from the force in 1894 for accepting baskets of peaches from a merchant grateful for the captain's turning a blind eye toward violations of sidewalk encumbrance laws. From the strictly legal perspective of punishing police officers found guilty of criminal behavior, the Lexow Committee's impact was, in the short term, nil.

Nonetheless, the long-term Lexow Effect was profound on police affairs and beyond. Lexow inaugurated a cycle of investigations into police scandals, roughly one every twenty years over the next century. These included the 1912 inquiry into police involvement with the sensational murder of gambler Herman Rosenthal; the 1931–32 Seabury investigation by a joint legislative committee, forcing the resignation of Tammany mayor Jimmy Walker; the 1950 judicial probe into police collusion with syndicate crime, compelling Mayor William O'Dwyer, a former beat cop, to leave office; the 1971 Knapp Commission, investigating police graft from narcotics and gambling; and the 1992 Mollen Commission, focusing on police brutality, theft, and abuse of power. As in 1894, all of these investigations were highly publicized and politically charged; and they all reinforced the sense that whatever limited reforms might be achieved, pockets of corruption, often deep and protected, endured within the NYPD.

The persistence of the "bipartisan" administration of the police force badly hindered movement toward a more professional, civil service–oriented model for policing. In the decade following Lexow, disgraced police officials often found themselves back in office depending upon which way the political winds blew. Thus when Tammany came back into power in 1897, William S. Devery re-emerged to become chief of police. Others, like Captains Max Schmittberger, John Stephenson, and Adam Cross resumed their careers after successful appeals through the courts. Police brutality against individual citizens, organized labor, and political radicals continued for decades. Thomas Byrnes's regular use of police as spies and informants, keeping tabs on unions and strikes lived on in the "red squads" and "Bomb Squads" of the department, especially active during the World War I era, the 1930s, and the 1960s. A depoliticized approach to police recruitment and police leadership would take many decades to achieve.

For rank-and-file cops, the most enduring Lexow Effect was the creation of the Patrolmen's Benevolent Association. Squeezed on all sides—by Parkhurst's crusade, by the demands of Tammany leaders, by relentless newspaper criticism, by unfriendly Republicans in Albany—the PBA emerged in 1894 as the prototype for urban police associations. Its emphasis on improving pay and working conditions, enlarging pension benefits, and expanding legal protections, made it a pioneer for municipal unionism that relied more on flexing political muscle than on job actions. Ironically, the police, for so long a blunt and effective instrument used to crush strikes and weaken organized labor, built the PBA over the next century into the city's strongest municipal union.

The PBA gave beat cops a new voice and in effect institutionalized the insular job culture that put loyalty to fellow cops above all else. In August 1900 the uglier side of that job culture exploded in one of the worst race riots in city history. On a corner in the Tenderloin an African-American man challenged a plainclothes cop over the arrest of his girlfriend for "soliciting." A fight resulted in the stabbing and death of the policeman, triggering a wild night of rioting, as thousands of whites poured onto Eighth Avenue, chasing and beating blacks wherever they found them. Scores of policemen joined the street mobs, clubbing blacks and refusing to go after their attackers. It was a long way from the Draft Riots of 1863, when police stations offered refuge for the victims of racist violence. The city's black population had more than doubled during the 1890s (to roughly 60,000), with the largest concentration of Southern and Caribbean migrants settling in the Tenderloin and nearby West Side neighborhoods. Prominent African Americans organized a Citizens' Protective League (with Frank Moss as its counsel) to gather evidence and press claims against the NYPD. Yet despite a massive amount of eyewitness testimony, an official investigation by Chief Devery and the police board whitewashed the entire affair. Not a single policeman faced any riot-related charges.

The 1900 police riot represented a newly racialized police brutality that would only intensify across the twentieth century. Police brutality and routine harassment against minority citizens remains a continuing disgrace in too many American cities, from New York to Baltimore to Cleveland to Chicago to Ferguson. The racial dynamic of today is of course different from the 1890s—although the Lexow inquiry revealed an ethnic/racial component in the regular police abuse of Jews, Italians, and other poor immigrants. Yet one underlying dynamic connects Lexow-era police abuses to those of the present: the extreme reluctance of prosecutors and grand juries to punish cops found guilty of abusing their authority.

As the first modern political investigation, Lexow demonstrated the expanding influence of modern media, making sensational, publicity-driven investigations valuable new tools for both reform movements and partisan advocates. Beyond police scandals, deeper political and cultural legacies stretched forward through the twentieth century and beyond. If Parkhurst's crusade and the investigation it triggered marked a turning point in the emergence of a "Progressive" movement, they did so with all the messiness, inconsistency, and internal tensions that have forced historians to stop looking for any single, unified, authentic "Progressivism." Parkhurst's approach embodied a sensibility and belief system admired by and familiar to many Progressive activists: rooted in evangelical Protestantism, proudly moralistic, emphasizing the power of informed individuals, and committed to awakening public conscience through dramatic publicity. Determined to reform the cosmopolitan city, Parkhurst looked backward for his model, to the well-ordered, quiet, and socially homogeneous world of the New England towns that produced him. The Lexow investigation pointed to a newer model for reform. While it also maximized the exposure of corruption through the press, it stressed the legislative and legal possibilities available to reformers, as well as putting a premium upon carefully gathered evidence.

Like Parkhurst's moral crusade and the investigation itself, the Lexow Effect reflected the tangled world of New York politics and the mounting anti-urban and anti-immigrant sentiments that accompanied metropolitan growth. Parkhurst's ideal of political nonpartisanship became one principle defining urban Progressives all over the country. The "good government" movement, led by the National Municipal League (founded in 1894, and later renamed the National Civic League) fought to make city management a nonpartisan, even nonpolitical, process by bringing the administrative techniques of large corporations to cities. Reformers revised city charters in favor of stronger mayoral power and expanded use of appointed administrators and career civil servants. They drew up blueprints for model charters, ordinances, and zoning plans designed by experts trained in public administration. Business and professional elites became the biggest boosters of structural reforms in urban government. Under one example, the so-called city commission plan, cities appointed commissioners who combined both administrative and legislative functions to improve services. Voters could more easily identify and hold accountable those responsible for city services. The city commission model proved very effective, for example, in rebuilding Galveston, Texas, after the disastrous flood of 1900. By 1917, nearly 500 cities, including Houston, Oakland, Kansas City, Denver, and Buffalo, had adopted the city commission form of government. Another approach, the "city manager plan," gained popularity in small and midsized cities. In this system, a city council appointed a professional, nonpartisan city manager to handle the day-to-day operations of the community.

Yet in New York, the Lexow investigation intensified rather than eroded partisan differences, especially as these played out against the urban-rural split in New York State. The breakthrough mayoral victory of William Strong proved, among other things, just how fragile fusion campaigns could be. By the fall of 1895 the anti-Tammany fusion coalition had collapsed. While city Republicans, independent Democrats, and the Chamber of Commerce combined their forces, the Good Government Clubs mounted their own candidates, splitting the anti-Tammany forces and resulting in a Tammany sweep of local offices. Across the state, Republicans increased their majorities in the state legislature. On the mayoral front, the "triumph of reform" lasted only two years. By 1896 the movement to "consolidate" New York City, with one central municipal government replacing forty local jurisdictions, had received the requisite support from popular referendums and the Albany legislature. Supporters of consolidation believed it would make government more efficient, allow the city to develop more effectively its harbor, roads, and overall infrastructure, and expand the tax base. Republicans also hoped it would cut into Tammany's influence. Yet in 1897 Tammany roared back into power, electing an obscure judge, Robert Van Wyck, as the first mayor of Greater New York. Seth Low, president of Columbia University and former mayor of Brooklyn, ran as the candidate of the Citizens Union; but Republican Benjamin Tracy split the anti-Tammany vote, putting Van Wyck in office. A united fusion campaign (with no Republican candidate) managed to elect Low mayor in 1901, emphasizing nonpartisan municipal administration. Low failed to win re-election and Tammany would control the mayoralty for another thirty years, with the exception of fusion mayor John Purroy Mitchell (1917).

Theodore Roosevelt's crackdown on Sunday drinking, his in-your-face approach to enforcing all excise laws (regulating the alcohol trade) made drinking the most divisive issue in city politics and one that underscored upstate/downstate divisions as well. Parkhurst and other fusion advocates grasped the political threat posed by strict alcohol law enforcement in the city. It made it much more difficult to attract traditional swing voters, especially German Americans, to the fusion banner, driving many back into Tammany's arms. The state Republican Party, meanwhile, had its own reasons for loudly supporting excise enforcement in the city and banning Sunday drinking. Upstate Republicans feared that taking a more liberal stance would only swell defections to the Prohibition Party, which in the 1890s regularly polled 40,000 votes across the state. Democrats and the well-organized German community advocated a "local option" approach, which would have allowed New York and other cities to set their own excise regulations independent of the state legislature. Parkhurst and most advocates of nonpartisan fusion, including many city Republicans, supported local option as crucial for challenging Tammany. But the inconsistency, even absurdity, of their position was evident to all. Parkhurst and the nonpartisans had struggled for years to keep state (and national) issues out of municipal politics. Yet the only path to local option—more liberal excise laws—went through Albany.

Instead of structural reform of the police department and municipal governance, Lexow inaugurated a cycle of state investigations into New York City affairs, essentially partisan inquiries made by Albany Republicans to create political capital out of alleged Tammany depredations. Thus, in 1899 the assembly created the so-called Mazet Committee to investigate police collusion with crime, the growth of prostitution, lax law enforcement, and the tightening grip of Tammany under the Van Wyck administration. This was a weak Lexow sequel, even more driven by purely partisan motives. Although his old ally Frank Moss served in the John Goff role as chief attorney, generating over 10,000 pages of testimony, Parkhurst dismissed the Mazet Committee as motivated purely by Republican desire to make political capital by attacking Tammany. Reform had very little to do with it.

Parkhurst had begun his crusade with harsh rhetorical attacks upon Tammany and police collusion with crime. The Lexow revelations and attendant publicity had demonized Tammany Hall far more successfully than even the Tweed scandals of the early 1870s. Through the 1890s and into the early twentieth century, Republicans and nonpartisans consistently made fear of Tammany corruption and its "dictator," Richard Croker, the centerpiece of election strategy. Tammany was responsible, they claimed, for the expansion of the city's vice economy, especially streetwalking and tenement-house prostitution, gambling houses, pool halls (off-track betting), and the saloon trade, all of it greased by payoffs to cops, district leaders, and even the mayor. The phrase "wide open New York" became the code for this perspective. It was first popularized by a *Harper's Weekly* journalist in 1898 as an argument for supporting Roosevelt's successful gubernatorial campaign. The message was simple: only a righteous Republican in Albany could prevent the "Tammany-ization" of the entire state. The condemnation of "protected vice," led by Episcopal Bishop Henry Potter, played a big part in electing Seth Low mayor on a fusion ticket in 1901. By then, Richard Croker and other Tammany leaders had begun to sense the need to deflect such charges more aggressively than they had in 1894, especially among the working poor and recent immigrants.

Tammany appointed its own Committee of Five in 1900 to investigate vice conditions. And while critics denounced it as a ridiculous sham, the very creation of the committee reflected Tammany's concern over political fallout from the attacks. Still, it was not enough to fend off Low's successful challenge. Throughout the first half of the twentieth century Tammany's opponents would routinely depict the machine as solely responsible for prostitution, illegal gambling, and excise violations, lining its coffers with millions every year as the price for protection. A corollary held that the police force would always be corrupt as a result of Tammany domination. Clearly there were Tammany district leaders and others with ties to the vice economy, often hidden by complex real estate partnerships and dummy corporations. Was there any real evidence that the vice economy expanded under Tammany administrations like Van Wyck's? The growing numbers of new immigrants, as well as the businessmen, seamen, tourists, and slummers attracted by the Tenderloin or the Bowery, many of them looking for commercial sex, gambling, and other pleasures unavailable at home, paid little attention to which party held office. Or was it just that under Tammany administrations the underground economy appeared to be more open to public view? Abram S. Hewitt, who as mayor in the 1880s had vigorously tried cracking down on dives, illegal concert saloons, and brothels, acknowledged the impossibility of eliminating them altogether. Yet in 1900, still spry at seventy-eight and an active supporter of Low's fusion challenge to Tammany, he proudly took credit for compelling these places to at least put on the garb of respectability. The problem was less vice than the flaunting of it.

Escalating rhetorical attacks on Tammany could be effective politically. Yet the Lexow Committee had yielded no evidence for their more exaggerated claims. Did a big chunk of the money collected by corrupt cops make its way to Tammany coffers, fueling a perfectly centralized party government previously unknown in America? There was no proof at all for this. Rather, Lexow had revealed a much more decentralized system of bribery and extortion, run by police captains and inspectors, many of whom were solid Republicans. Nor did Tammany have a monopoly on putting together the financing needed to promote a man to captain. As Timothy Creeden's startling testimony had shown, the $15,000 he needed to make captain came not from Tammany men but from activists in the rival State Democracy faction. Tammany district leaders, like police officials, took advantage of entrepreneurial prospects available in the underground economy. The notion of Tammany as a kind of perfectly structured corporate organization, with flow charts and all, was more a product of partisan oratory than a reflection of reality.

Rather than becoming rich from vice, Tammany's real money came from land deals, construction companies, inside information on city expansion, and emerging opportunities presented by commercial mass culture. Richard Croker, the Hall's leader from 1886 to 1901, owned half of a lucrative real estate business specializing in judicial land sales controlled by judges and their appointed referees. He was also part owner of U.S. Fidelity and Casualty, an insurance business that bonded city officials and contractors. (It was often in co-surety with Fidelity and Deposit Company, run by Republican leader Thomas Platt.) Big Tim Sullivan made a fortune not from "white slavery" or illegal gambling joints, as his critics charged, but from his investments in a national chain of vaudeville theaters and the early motion picture industry. The point is not to apologize for or justify Tammany, but rather to insist that the relentless attacks upon it came in the context of a highly partisan and closely contested political system that featured regular, often coded, appeals to ethnic, religious, and regional identities.

Inflated claims of vote fraud became part of the enduring criticism of Tammany as well, though the Lexow investigation found little evidence for it. Tarring Tammany with this brush became a regular part of Republican strategy, especially with rural and small-town upstate voters. This was the basis of their opposition to a supposedly nonpartisan police administration. Again, while individual Tammany district leaders and activists (and Republicans as well) might have engaged in vote-rigging, especially in heated intra-party primaries, the organization as a whole relied more upon enrolling new voters, getting them to the polls, and distributing patronage to its most loyal and effective workers. There was no point in padding the vote when the city's steady growth and demographic shifts provided Democrats with a natural advantage. The association of vote fraud with urban Democrats continued for decades, from Al Smith's historic run for president in 1928 to the present day. Around the nation, state efforts to make voting more difficult—requiring government issued photo IDs, complicating registration, restricting early voting option—are squarely aimed at reducing the overwhelmingly Democratic votes of racial minorities, the elderly, students, and the poor. There is a direct line between these contemporary actions and the work of John Davenport and the federal election regime. As in the 1890s, the cry of vote fraud is closely associated with the reality of vote suppression.

After Lexow, Thomas Platt and the state Republican Party pressed their partisan advantage to remake the police force and increase the authority of the state over Democratic big cities. The failure to reform the department along the lines that Parkhurst and his allies had demanded left police business as highly politicized as ever. Thus in 1898 Chief of Police John H. McCullagh, formerly captain and inspector, and a steadfast Republican, found himself at odds with the new police board appointed by Mayor Van Wyck. The mayor soon removed McCullagh and replaced him with none other than Parkhurst's old nemesis and Tammany loyalist, Captain William S. Devery. The state legislature, concerned over how

Devery might conduct elections, quickly passed the Metropolitan District Elections Law, establishing a state superintendent of elections, with seven hundred deputies and the power to arrest without warrant alleged election law violators. Governor Roosevelt named McCullagh state superintendent, while Tammany denounced the "Metropolitan Force Bill" as designed to intimidate Democratic voters. Platt also pushed for a new approach to police reorganization: creation of a state constabulary for large cities, with a state commissioner appointed by the governor. The bill never passed, but in 1901 the legislature finally enacted a law that created a single commissioner for the NYPD and a separate board of elections.

Platt and state Republicans tried to remove the divisive alcohol issue from politics entirely, while simultaneously punishing big cities. In 1896 they pushed through new liquor tax legislation, the so-called Raines Law, named for its chief sponsor, upstate Republican Sen. John Raines. It established a state department of excise, shifting the regulation of alcohol from local communities to Albany, and it sharply increased the license fees for saloons. The law prohibited the sale of alcohol on Sunday, with an exception made for hotels serving guests in their rooms. It defined a hotel as having ten rooms and serving food with its liquor. Scores of saloon-keepers hastily added furnished rooms to their business and applied for hotel licenses. Critics noted that "Raines Law hotels," often run as brothels, had made the prostitution situation worse. Yet from Platt's perspective, the Raines Law was a political boon: it neutralized the Democratic push for local option in liquor regulation, increased tax revenue in the state's coffers, and made possible a decrease in property taxes.

Platt himself, though, would ultimately fall victim to the Lexow Effect. He returned to the U.S. Senate in 1897 for two terms; after 1902 he was no longer the state Republican leader, though he remained an influential force in state and national politics. In fall of 1905, responding to a developing scandal in the state's insurance industry, the legislature appointed a special committee to investigate mismanagement of company funds, exorbitant executive salaries, falsified profit and loss statements, tax evasion, and the bilking of small policy holders. The committee named Charles Evans Hughes, a prominent Republican attorney in private practice, to lead the insurance investigation. For three months Hughes conducted a masterful inquiry into the largely secret dealings of big firms like Equitable, Mutual, and New York Life, laying bare a world that few citizens knew about. The most startling revelations concerned political bribery and graft, albeit on a grander scale and scope than wringing payoffs from a neighborhood brothel or saloon. Hughes's probe exposed a systematic pattern of insurance executives spreading large amounts of cash among state senators and assemblymen to oppose insurance regulation and to reduce taxes on the industry.

When Hughes called the seventy-two-year-old Platt to the stand, he forced him to admit that during election campaigns he received tens of thousands of dollars from the largest companies eager to buy protection for their interests. Other prominent state Republicans, such as U.S. Senator Chauncey Depew and Governor Benjamin Odell were likewise tarnished. Platt's testimony provided the clearest picture to date of how big business routinely corrupted the political process. The investigation made Hughes's reputation as a fearless prosecutor. These events catapulted Hughes to the governor's chair in 1906, and he went on to be the Republican presidential nominee in 1916, and later secretary of state and chief justice of the Supreme Court. Conducting highly publicized investigations of corruption had become one of the most effective ways to build a political reputation. The Lexow Effect boosted the reputations of men like Hughes and Theodore Roosevelt, progressive Republicans enjoying a growing national influence defined by their independence from party machinery.

Parkhurst's crusade and the Lexow investigation prefigured much of what was later called Progressivism. In the decade before World War I, Progressivism had become a national movement, yet it originated in the cities, with attacks on political corruption and the appeal to a nonpartisan approach to governance and reform. Parkhurst's campaign and the Lexow exposures also revealed the limits and contradictions that would vex Progressive reform as it wrestled with the problems of cities struggling to provide decent existence amid the excesses of industrial capitalism and unprecedented mass immigration. Progressives attacked the power of machine politics for contributing to and aggravating the dismal material conditions endured by big city populations. City governments, especially in the Northeast and industrial Midwest, were simply not capable of providing the basic services—clean water, sewer connections, adequate housing, waste removal, public school spaces for all—needed to sustain large populations. Yet hundreds of thousands of working-class New Yorkers, especially those of non-Protestant immigrant stock, saw Parkhurst's movement and groups like the City Vigilance League as blind to the realities and rituals of their everyday working lives and leisure preferences.

But other Progressives, especially women such as Jane Addams, Florence Kelley, and Lillian Wald, pioneered the settlement movement, so-called because adherents lived in poor communities and worked for immediate improvements in the health and welfare of the immigrant poor and working class. Settlement workers found they could not transform their neighborhoods without confronting a host of larger social questions: chronic poverty, overcrowded tenement houses, child labor, industrial accidents, public health. They soon saw that confronting the grim realities of an urban and industrial society required national and even global strategies for pursuing reform. The Woman's Municipal League expanded after its work supporting fusion 1894, attracting more female activists into electoral politics, though they lacked the vote. New female-dominated occupations, such as social work, public health nursing, and home economics, allowed women to combine professional aspirations with the older traditions of moral reform, especially those centered on child welfare. The new professionalism, in turn, sustained reform commitments and a female dominion that simultaneously expanded the social welfare function of the state and increased women's public authority and influence.

Progressivism was no unified movement with a single set of principles. It is perhaps best understood as a varied collection of reform communities, often fleeting, uniting citizens in a host of political, professional, and religious organizations, some of which were national in scope. As with so many Progressive campaigns, Parkhurst's began with a sense of personal outrage that impelled him to organize others angry over police and government collusion with crime. Parkhurst and the Lexow investigation, along with early muckrakers such as Jacob Riis and Lincoln Steffens, demonstrated the potential for mobilizing citizen opinion through seizing the headlines in newspapers. New mass circulation magazines, such as *McClure's* and *Munsey's*, also discovered that muckraking, a combination of factual reporting and moral exhortation, paid off handsomely in terms of increased circulation. The middle-class public responded to articles exposing insurance scandals, patent medicine frauds, urban graft, stock market swindles, and ruthless business practices. Yet the term "muckraking" was originally a pejorative one, coined by President Theodore Roosevelt. Angered by an article examining corruption in the U.S. Senate, including several of his friends and supporters, Roosevelt denounced the "muckrakers" who "raked the mud of society and never looked up."

Progressives believed in using the democratic institutions available to them—the vote, the courts, the legislature—to address social problems. They emphasized social solidarity and common bonds, largely rejecting the ideal of individualism and laissez faire capitalism that had dominated nineteenth-century economic and political thought. They pressed for state and federal intervention to ease the hardships imposed by laissez faire capitalism: protection from dangerous machinery and other occupational hazards, the abolition of child labor, widows' pensions, unemployment relief, limits on working hours, and a minimum wage. Like Parkhurst, many Progressive activists had roots in the "Social Gospel" wing of American Protestantism, adapting its old emphasis on individual salvation into a new social politics focused on finding the common good. Others looked to natural and social scientists, and experts trained in statistical analysis and engineering, for making government more efficient and responsive to human needs. The social scientific approach, emphasizing careful observation and collection of data, would become a hallmark of the Progressive movement, embodied in such institutions as the New York Bureau of Municipal Research, founded in 1907. The New York City Board of Health expanded its work by applying cutting edge scientific research to solving such public health problems as tuberculosis, diphtheria, adulterated milk, and high infant mortality rates.

Progressivism thus offered an uneasy combination of social justice and social control, a tension that would mark American reform for the rest of the twentieth century. Little wonder that so much of the urge to "reform" American cities was often indistinguishable from the deep currents of anti-urban prejudice that had long flowed—and still flow—through the nation's political and cultural life. The drive for a more open and democratic political process, in particular, had the effect of excluding some people from voting while including others. For African Americans, progressivism largely meant disenfranchisement from voting altogether. Stricter election laws—another echo of the Lexow Effect—made it more difficult for third parties, such as Socialists and Populists, to get on the ballot, reinforcing the bipartisan duopoly in American politics. Voting itself steadily declined after 1916. Overall, party voting became a less important form of political participation. Interest-group activity, congressional and statehouse lobbying, and direct appeals to public opinion gained currency as ways of influencing government. Business groups and individual trade associations were among the most active groups pressing their demands on government. Political action often shifted from legislatures to the new administrative agencies and commissions created to deal with social and economic problems.

The Lexow Effect forced Tammany, the *bête noire* of Progressives everywhere, to evolve as well. Fusion campaigns continued to attack Tammany around the "protected vice" problem—which Lexow had made a national issue—, most successfully in the 1901 campaign electing Seth Low as mayor. Machine politicians could no longer ignore the political fallout from this criticism. And they faced growing competition for votes and local influence from organized labor, socialists, and progressive Republicans. In 1902, after Richard Croker retired to Ireland to breed horses, the new Tammany boss, former docks commissioner Charles Murphy, turned the organization in a progressive direction. Tammany shifted its politics from one defined by personal, service-based appeals and negative government toward one more centered on legislative achievements in social welfare. After the disastrous Triangle Shirtwaist fire of 1911, killing 147 mostly young, immigrant, female garment workers who were trapped by locked fire exits, Tammany Democrats made alliances with reformers. Thus in Albany, Big Tim Sullivan, in the twilight of his career, teamed up with Frances Perkins, a lobbyist for the National Consumer League, to push through landmark legislation limiting the hours of labor (to fifty-four hours a week) for some 400,000 women toiling in the state's textile shops, canneries, candy factories, and other industrial workplaces. Sullivan's outspoken support for woman suffrage anticipated a key Democratic shift on this issue. Perkins served as secretary for the Factory Inspection Commission, which exposed the deplorable work conditions around the state and led to tougher laws improving workplace safety, fire regulations, and building codes. It was co-chaired by young Tammany men Assemblyman Al Smith and State Senator Robert F. Wagner. A crucial transformation of the Democratic Party was underway. By the 1920s, under Smith's governorship, and through the New Deal era, "machine politics" helped define and provide the social base for an urban liberalism that looked to the state and federal government for improving conditions of everyday life.

In the cultural realm, the commercial potential for exploiting the Lexow Effect, especially for audiences outside New York, was apparent from the beginning. Both Parkhurst's crusade and the Lexow investigation built upon and expanded the public fascination with the city's underside. The "secrets of the great city" were no longer so secret. From the vaudeville stages and concert saloons of the 1890s through today's digital media, the Lexow Effect would make it more difficult to separate the intertwined strands of reform and spectacle, analysis and sensationalism, empathy and tourism in representing New York and its place in American life.

In December 1894, weeks before the Lexow Committee's adjournment, a new play titled *In the Tenderloin* opened at one of the city's largest stages, the People's Theater on the Bowery. Its cast included George Appo, the green goods swindler whose Lexow testimony had shocked the city, and Tom Gould, longtime proprietor of the notorious Sans Souci concert saloon. Appo and Gould played themselves, distinguishing this show from typical Bowery melodramas of the day by putting real criminals on the stage, introducing a new kind of sensational realism. Unlike traditional melodrama, where criminals were purely evil and always received their just due, *In the Tenderloin* represented men like Appo with some sympathy, products and even victims of the modern city's complexities. The show ran only two weeks in New York and received mixed reviews. Significantly, it enjoyed much greater success on the road, in cities like Syracuse, Youngstown, and Cincinnati, where it pulled in large audiences and won praise for its realistic portrayal of urban lowlife.

Perhaps most fundamentally, the Lexow Effect created the prevailing twentieth-century understanding of "the system"—the moment at which the public learned the extent to which it was rigged. No wonder that Parkhurst's crusade and the Lexow investigation seem, a century and a quarter later, quaint and comical. A corrupt and politicized police force? Tainted election results? Weren't imperious and crooked cops always a part of the New York landscape, along with venal politicians and protected vice? Didn't everyone know that all Lexow revealed was the more or less permanent reality of New York—and urban—life? Cynicism and resignation was in part a Lexow Effect, and it was one that inspired reformers to redouble their efforts. In 1903 Lincoln Steffens's groundbreaking *The Shame of the Cities* applied his experiences covering Lexow to a damning indictment of municipal government around the country. The title and method of this muckraking classic reflected the moralism and optimism of Parkhurst and so many Progressives: One had a duty to expose deplorable conditions, arouse the conscience of citizens, and thereby create the conditions for reform. By the 1920s this sensibility defined tabloid journalism as well, from streetwise columnists, to headline writers, to political reporters. From Damon Runyon through Jimmy Breslin and Pete Hamill, the Lexow Effect shaped the world-weary skepticism of generations of urban reporters and columnists writing stories detailing how corrupt municipal politics continually thwarted the human needs of city dwellers.

The further one gets from the 1890s, the more comic and derisive overtones creep into historical chronicles and the echo chamber of commercial culture. William Riordan's 1904 faux memoir *Plunkitt of Tammany Hall*, still among the most widely cited sources on machine politics, presented its purported author, George Washington Plunkitt, as an Irish comic actor (even though he was a native-born Protestant). Prohibition marked a crucial cultural turning point that intensified cynicism, especially in cities, where the law was openly flouted and corrupted from the beginning. Before 1920, entrepreneurs engaged in the saloon trade, prostitution, gambling, and other aspects of the underground economy depended upon political protection. After 1920 there was so much money to be made from supplying liquor that criminal syndicates could buy and sell political influence with unprecedented ease. By the 1920s most New Yorkers viewed Parkhurst, who was still living, as a faintly amusing figure himself, his moral campaign against vice and corruption an archaic vestige of the Gay Nineties. Parkhurst had first used the term "organized crime" in the 1890s to describe the corruption of city government. Since the 1920s that term has been reserved for syndicate crime historically rooted in the Prohibition era.

This perspective pervades Herbert Asbury's 1927 pulp-history classic *The Gangs of New York*, which has remained arguably the most widely read and quoted source for New York City's history. An entertaining tour through selected aspects of the city's underworld, Asbury's book recycled the "secrets of the great city" tradition of New York guidebooks, a genre that played to the intense anti-urban tides flowing through American culture. Yet with its invented dialogue, sensational tone, uncritical stance toward sources, and slew of factual errors, it is preposterous as history. Reading it, one would assume that every inhabitant of lower Manhattan was a thief, murderer, gangster, prostitute, drunk, or some combination of these. While lamenting the passing of the city's old-time gangs, Asbury made the astonishing claim that no real New York gangsters existed any longer. Wistful, even nostalgic, for the nineteenth-century gang world, he was blind to how Prohibition had created newer, more powerful structures of criminal enterprise.

The Lexow Effect could be felt in film. D. W. Griffith's *The Musketeers of Pig Alley* (1912) was the first gangster film and set on the Lower East Side. It ends with a scene depicting a political payoff and the reminder that "one hand washes the other." Mack Sennett's Keystone Cops (1912–1917), with their anarchic burlesque of police inefficiency and dishonesty, echoed Lexow as well. By the 1930s, dozens of Hollywood films set in big cities reflected the Lexow view of how cities worked, especially in popular gangster movies like *The Public Enemy* (1931) and *Scarface* (1932). By then, the widespread cynicism about Prohibition and the rise of syndicate criminals made many nostalgic for an earlier era. Mae West, the most popular Hollywood star of the early sound era, set her smash hit *She Done Him Wrong* (1931) in a sepia-tinged, golden-age Bowery of the 1890s, complete with a political boss modeled on Big Tim Sullivan and Cary Grant as an undercover federal agent posing as a temperance reformer. The 2002 Martin Scorsese film version of *Gangs of New York* spared no expense in its breathtaking recreation of how the Five Points looked in the mid-nineteenth century. Yet in other ways the movie was as wildly inaccurate as Asbury's book, internalizing Asbury's prejudices and distortions while cluttering the story with numerous fictions masquerading as historical fact.

In 1955 M. R. Werner, a veteran journalist and early historian of Tammany Hall, published a multi-part *New Yorker* profile, "Dr. Parkhurst's Crusade," the first narrative account of Parkhurst's campaign and its political impact. Werner was surprised that his series stirred more interest than anything he had ever done. He received an avalanche of mail. In 1957 the *New Yorker* pieces were included in Werner's collection of popular history, *It Happened in New York*. Werner tells a vivid tale—but without attention to larger historical issues or any critical consideration of sources. Like Asbury, he relied solely upon old newspaper morgues, and, like Asbury, he included chunks of invented dialogue.

Even Broadway took its shot. The 1960 musical comedy *Tenderloin*, adapted from the popular novel by Samuel Hopkins Adams, featured book and lyrics by Jerry Bock and Sheldon Harnick (their next show would be *Fiddler on the Roof*). It starred the English Shakespearean actor Maurice Evans as Reverend Brock, an 1890s Parkhurst-like anti-vice crusader. But lukewarm reviewers complained there was too much rectitude in the Reverend Brock character and not enough sizzle on stage. The show closed on Broadway after a short run and then found a new home at the Dunes in Las Vegas, where it presumably played less righteous and more Rat Pack.

From a twenty-first-century perspective, the Lexow Effect in our culture may seem too distant to trace directly. Yet with every new highly publicized political investigation, with every promise of upright reformers taking on government corruption, with every fresh attempt to cash in on the seamy side of urban life, with every promise to substitute nonpartisan efficiency for partisan gridlock, or with every claim that New Yorkers and other big city inhabitants are somehow more prone to graft and corruption, one hears the Lexow Effect echoing to the present day.

The fates of the original players of this drama were as varied and unpredictable as the city itself; some figures gained in prominence, others faded into obscurity. John W. Goff served as recorder until 1906 when the legislature abolished the position. He then won election to the New York Supreme Court, where he remained until he reached the constitutional age limit of seventy in 1918, earning a reputation for unrelenting toughness toward defendants. His most controversial case once again revolved around police collusion with criminals. Goff presided in 1912 at the first murder trial of police lieutenant Charles Becker, who had been indicted for killing a Tammany-connected gambler named Herman Rosenthal. The jury found Becker guilty, but Goff had rushed the proceedings along and his rulings showed clear bias in favor of the prosecution. The Court of Appeals reversed the decision and reprimanded Goff for his prejudice. He retired to a farm in upstate New York; he remained active in Irish nationalist politics until his death in 1924.

Goff's associate counsel William Travers Jerome remained a vigorous anti-Tammany Democrat as well. Mayor Strong appointed him as judge in the new Court of Special Sessions (replacing the old police courts), and he then won election as New York's district attorney as part of Seth Low's 1901 fusion ticket. Taking a page from Parkhurst, Jerome personally led highly publicized raids on gambling houses and brothels during his eight years as DA. Good government and honesty in office were his watchwords, yet he disdained the label "reformer"—and freely acknowledged his fondness for drinking, smoking, and a friendly game of poker. Jerome maintained his residence on the Lower East Side and remained popular with New Yorkers until his death in 1934.

The more austere and remote Frank Moss replaced Theodore Roosevelt as president of the board of police commissioners in 1897, later serving as first assistant district attorney under Charles Whitman, Jerome's successor. A lifelong Republican and Union League member, Moss persisted as one of the city's most determined anti-Tammany and anti-vice activists before his death in 1920.

Clarence Lexow won a national reputation for the work of his committee, yet he never really escaped from the shadow of his mentor, Thomas Platt. The ultimate machine Republican, he resisted efforts to draft him for governor but remained active in national party circles, supporting the presidential campaigns of William McKinley and Theodore Roosevelt. He left the state senate voluntarily in 1898, returning to Nyack for private law practice. In 1910 he died of pneumonia at only fifty-eight. Newspapers all over the country ran obituaries, explaining how the phrase "to be Lexowed" had become a popular synonym for any investigation into government mismanagement or corruption.

Thomas Byrnes considered starting his own private detective agency after he left the NYPD, but the plan never materialized. Instead, he enjoyed a mostly quiet retirement, consulting on security matters for insurance companies and advising mayors and legislative committees on how to improve policing. His fortune grew through real estate and stock investments. Just before Byrnes died in 1910 at sixty-eight from stomach cancer, he transferred to his wife ownership of a building on Fifth Avenue and Forty-Sixth Street worth $55,000 (nearly $1.4 million today).

Alexander Williams tried his hand at electoral politics just a few months after leaving the force in 1895. He ran as a Republican for state senate from the East Side but was defeated, partly due to vigorous opposition from the Central Labor Union, which sent speakers and organizers all over the district promising "a labor club for the clubber." Williams gave up on his political career and worked in the insurance business before his death in 1917 at age seventy-seven. He never amassed the kind of fortune enjoyed by his lifelong rival Byrnes.

William S. Devery's post-Lexow career revealed him to be the most politically connected cop in the city's history. He had been targeted by Parkhurst, dismissed by the police board, reinstated by the courts, and then appointed chief of police by Mayor Van Wyck. When the state legislature reacted by abolishing his position, he was appointed as deputy police commissioner. Devery's long police career finally ended with the election of Seth Low. He made a fortune in real estate and he eventually became co-owner of the New York Highlanders baseball team, later renamed the Yankees. Devery's real estate deals included at least one intriguing reverberation from the distant Lexow days. In 1902 Devery and an associate acquired twelve valuable parcels of midtown property at an estate sale. His friend then transferred two houses in the West Forties, each valued at $45,000 (roughly $1.2 million in current dollars) for a consideration of $1. The recipient was Lillie Clifton, who ten years earlier had helped Devery entrap Parkhurst's detective, Charles Gardner. Devery died in 1917.

The two police captains whose testimony provided the most damning evidence of bribery and the "system," Max Schmittberger and Timothy Creeden, escaped prosecution and remained on the force. Both men endured the "squealer" label and social ostracism from rank-and-file cops, but reform elements protected and even promoted their careers. Schmittberger in particular became something of a folk hero outside the department. Where some saw real courage behind his sensational testimony, others wondered if the threat of felony indictment had more to do with it. Lincoln Steffens drafted a novel with Schmittberger as its hero, but it never saw print. When he died in 1917 at sixty-seven, Schmittberger had risen to chief inspector, the highest rank a policeman could attain. Creeden remained a captain until his retirement in 1902, a thirty-eight-year veteran of the force. He died in 1936, age ninety-six, the oldest Civil War veteran in New York City. By then the obituaries were much less interested in his stunning Lexow testimony than in recounting his battlefield exploits from seventy years earlier.

The Reverend Doctor Parkhurst continued to lead the Society for the Prevention of Crime, speak out on the city's political and ethical failings, criticize the police force, and attack Tammany candidates for mayor. Yet he never again achieved the kind of influence—local or national—that his crusade attained in the early 1890s. The City Vigilance League contributed to several fusion campaigns, but it fizzled as a permanent alternative to Tammany. Parkhurst himself proved to be the last Protestant clergymen to lead a New York City reform movement. By the early 1900s most New Yorkers were uncomfortable with the kind of moral surveillance associated with the CVL or with Parkhurst's "civic Christianity," appropriate perhaps in a small Berkshire town but not for the nation's most cosmopolitan city.

Parkhurst outlived them all. He remained at Madison Square Presbyterian until he resigned his pastorate in 1918 at age seventy-six. Ellen, his wife of fifty years, died in 1921; six years later Parkhurst married Eleanor Marx, sixty-seven, his former secretary, who died in 1931. In 1933 he was still giving interviews, supporting Fiorello La Guardia's fusion campaign for mayor and insisting that Tammany corruption was no different than it had been forty years ago. He died in September 1933, age ninety-one, after falling off the porch on his Atlantic City home. He had been sleepwalking, a restless dreamer to the end.

ACKNOWLEDGMENTS

....

Writing history is a solitary pursuit, but it is never done alone. I could not have completed this book without the support and thoughtful criticism I received from fellow historians and friends. For their encouragement and perceptive comments on individual chapters, I am grateful to Joshua Brown, John Mack Faragher, Jane Gerhard, Jack Gilhooley, Richard Kilberg, Daniel T. Rodgers, Joshua Ruff, Robert W. Snyder, Andie Tucher, and Mike Wallace.

Bruce Laurie read several chapters and offered insightful and sympathetic editorial suggestions for each of them. More importantly, Bruce has engaged me in a long-running conversation as this project evolved, sharing his deep knowledge of American political and social history, and sharpening my own understanding in the process.

Timothy J. Gilfoyle graciously read an early version of the entire manuscript. His keen editorial eye, along with his matchless knowledge of the social history of New York's underworld, were invaluable for improving the final product.

I received vital fellowship support for this project from the National Endowment for the Humanities and Mount Holyoke College. And I am grateful for the valuable research assistance of my former MHC students Jennifer Cote, Amy Richardson and Maura Young.

Over the years Mount Holyoke's librarians have been crucial in helping me identify and track down sources from all over the world. In particular, my thanks to Marilyn Dunn, Bryan Goodwin, and Kathleen Norton for their dedication, diligence, and professionalism. I am indebted as well to James Gehrt, the Library's Digitization Center Coordinator, for his superb work in digitizing many of the images in the book.

Other librarians and archivists offered me support and aid along the way. Kenneth Cobb, currently assistant commissioner at the New York City Department of Records, and for many years director of the Municipal Archives, has somehow always found the time to answer my questions and offer informed advice on the whereabouts of various sources. Anyone who has tried to navigate the vast, often uncharted sea of the city's history knows just how indispensable Ken has long been for historians of New York City. Joshua Ruff, formerly director of the New York City Police Museum, also generously shared his knowledge of police history and access to historical images before Hurricane Sandy shut down the museum in late 2012. I am also grateful for the help I received at other libraries, including the Archives and Manuscripts Division, New York Public Library; Manuscripts and Special Collections at the New York State Library in Albany; Rare Book and Manuscript Library, Columbia University; the Library of the New York Historical Society; and the Historical Society of Rockland County, in New City, New York.

Early on in this project I was fortunate to get very sage advice from two excellent editors who helped teach me how to translate an idea for a book into something that might interest publishers. Carole DeSanti encouraged me at every step, and she also connected me with Michael Denneny, a gifted and accomplished freelance editor who taught me the nuts and bolts of crafting a successful book proposal.

I am deeply grateful to my agent, Wendy Strothman, who expressed confidence and belief in this book from the beginning. She pushed me to clarify the book's story and argument, reshaping it into a work that could appeal to a general audience beyond academic specialists. Her patience and wise guidance were essential.

During the production phase, Alyssa O'Connell, editorial assistant for trade history at Oxford University Press, was always generous with her time, expertise, and sense of humor. I received superb editing assistance from Joellyn Ausanka, Elizabeth Borka, and Keith Faivre.

Timothy Bent, my editor at Oxford, has made this book better in ways too numerous to mention. I could always count on Tim's editorial eye for improving the narrative flow, sharpening key characters, and cutting repetition and florid language. Whenever I became too engrossed in specific details or textures, Tim steered me back to the larger historical questions at stake. Whatever strengths the book may have owe a great deal to his excellent editing. Any mistakes or factual errors are, of course, my responsibility alone.

NOTE ON SOURCES

. . . .

Some years ago, while poking around a long-gone used bookstore on Fourth Avenue, I came across a yellowing set of five volumes with a suggestive title: *Investigation of the Police Department of the City of New York, 1894*. This was the official transcript, nearly 6,000 pages, of the so-called Lexow Committee. I was familiar with the broad outlines of the Lexow investigation, and also suspicious about the few existing historical accounts. I snapped up the set and lugged it home. I was not at all sure what I might do with it, but there was something about this long, dry, and utterly bureaucratic document that attracted me. Could it offer an alternative way into understanding Gilded Age New York?

An official transcript is not the same, of course, as a flesh-and-blood history. But those six volumes of Lexow testimony certainly made the familiar strange, and they forced me to dig deeper. To understand the lives and motives of the key players, and to get a handle on such major city institutions as the NYPD, Tammany Hall, the Republican Party, and the metropolitan press, I needed to read between the lines of the stenography. I saw my main challenge as writing a vivid narrative with the strongest possible foundation in primary sources—an antidote to the long tradition, dating back to the early nineteenth century, of popular accounts that have endlessly caricatured and distorted the city's history, particularly the history of New York's underside.

None of the major characters in this book—Charles H. Parkhurst, John Goff, Clarence Lexow, Thomas Byrnes, Alexander Williams, John I. Davenport to name a few—left behind any substantial collections of papers or correspondence. The NYPD destroyed its papers in 1915, although some bits remain sprinkled throughout the Mayors' Papers at the Municipal Archives and Research Center. In 2012 Hurricane Sandy devastated much of the manuscript and photographs collections in the New York City Police Museum at Old Slip (now closed and with no reopening in sight). Archives related to Tammany Hall, such as the Edwin P. Kilroe Papers at Columbia and the Tammany Society Manuscript Record Books at the New York State Library in Albany, are very thin, reflecting a political culture centered more around handshakes and face-to-face meetings than written correspondence. Whatever materials related to the Lexow investigation that might have been tucked away in Albany archives were destroyed by a ruinous 1911 fire at the New York State Capitol, which at the time housed the state library. Other manuscript collections, such as the records of the Society for the Prevention of Crime at Columbia, were disappointingly silent for the 1890s.

Thus I had to rely a great deal upon newspapers to put flesh on the bones of the investigation. The city had sixteen daily English language newspapers in the early 1890s, and only by deep immersion in them could I hope to make sense of the political issues, personal rivalries, popular responses—in short, the complex and messy world that I wanted to present. Aside from the acres of daily newspaper microfilm that I read, the New York district attorney's scrapbooks (NYDAS) were an invaluable aid for understanding events, personalities, and organizations, and the full range of public opinion. The scrapbooks, begun in 1882, concentrate on press coverage of criminal cases, police investigations, prominent trials, court decisions, and attendant political fallout. The scrapbook clippings do not provide page numbers, and sometimes not even the dates for an article. Any citation in the notes followed by (clipping, NYDAS) refers to a newspaper story found in the NYDAS between 1882 and 1895. All other newspaper citations include story title, the paper's name, date, and page number.

At times, I felt more like an archeologist than an historian, amassing small shards of information that might only become meaningful when placed aside other fragments. Newspapers, like any other historical source, must be used critically and carefully. I have tried wherever possible to use at least several newspaper accounts as sources for specific events and for checking quotations. The latter present especially thorny issues for historians. Did someone actually utter the words being quoted? We cannot really know, and it was not uncommon for reporters to edit or even invent quotations. Yet inaccurate newspaper reports created another kind of social fact by their very publication, thickening and complicating the broader discourse of public opinion.

Historians of New York may indeed face special challenges in their efforts to research, comprehend, write (and re-write) the city's past. Like New York itself, that past can seem daunting, mysterious, too complicated, even unknowable. And it is always competing with the pulp history that remains a favorite subject of so many novels, films, and television shows. But in the end, like learning the subway system or how to drive a taxi, one must get lost before one is found.

MANUSCRIPT AND ARCHIVE COLLECTIONS

Amherst College Archives, Amherst, Massachusetts:
  Charles H. Parkhurst Papers
Columbia University, Rare Book and Manuscript Library, New York, New York:
  Edwin P. Kilroe Papers
  Joseph Pulitzer Collection
  Lincoln Steffens Papers
  New York Chamber of Commerce Archives
  New York *World* Collection
  Society for the Prevention of Crime Records, 1878–1973
Edison Archives, Edison National Historic Site, West Orange, New Jersey
First Presbyterian Church, New York, New York:
  Madison Square Presbyterian Church Archive, Charles H. Parkhurst
    Correspondence
Historical Society of Rockland County, New City, New York:
  Clarence Lexow Papers
Library of Congress, Washington, DC:
  Jacob A. Riis Papers (microfilm)
  Papers of the Pinkerton National Detective Agency, 1861–1883 (microfilm)
Municipal Archives and Research Center, New York, New York:
  Mayor's Papers to 1898 for William H. Wickham (1875–6); Edward Cooper
    (1879–80); William R. Grace (1885–6); Abram S. Hewitt (1887–8); Hugh J.
    Grant (1889–92); Thomas Gilroy (1893–4); William Strong (1895–7)
  New York District Attorney Files, *Catherine Amos v. Charles W. Gardner*,
    December 5, 1892
  New York District Attorney Scrapbooks, 1882-1895 (microfilm)
National Archives and Records Administration, Washington, DC:
  Letters sent by the Department of Justice: Instructions to U.S. attorneys and
    marshals, 1867–1904 (microfilm)
  Letters sent by the Department of Justice to executive officers and members
    of Congress, 1871–1904 (microfilm)
New York Historical Society Library, New York, New York:
  The City Vigilant, 1894–5
  Charles S. Fairchild Papers
  Clarence Lexow Scrapbooks
  Collection of printed material issued by the Society for the Prevention of
    Crime, 1877–91
  Examination of trials by the police board from January 1, 1891 to May 1, 1894,
    typescript, 1894
New York State Library, Albany, New York, Manuscripts and Special Collections:
  Tammany Society, Manuscript Record Books

Queens College, Queens, New York, Historical Documents Collection:
   Records of the Supreme Court, City and County of New York
United Church of Christ, Lenox, Massachusetts:
   Records of the Church on the Hill
Yale University, Beinecke Library, New Haven, Connecticut:
   Thomas C. Platt Papers
Newspapers (Microfilm)
Irish American
National Labor Tribune
New York Evening Post
New York Herald
New York Sun
New York Times
New York Tribune
New York World

NOTES

· · · ·

1: PARKHURST'S CHALLENGE

1. Rev. Charles Henry Parkhurst, *Our Fight With Tammany* (New York, 1895), pp. 9, 10, 23–24, 14. None of the newspaper accounts printed the full text of the sermon, and there were considerable differences among them as to the phrasing Parkhurst used. I have relied upon this published version of his sermon for all direct quotes; but it no doubt includes some changes from the sermon he preached in church. For background on Billy McGlory, see Timothy J. Gilfoyle, *City of Eros: New York City, Prostitution, and the Commercialization of Sex, 1790–1920* (New York, 1992), pp. 229–31, and George Chauncey, *Gay New York: Gender, Urban Culture, and the Making of the Gay Male World, 1890–1940* (New York, 1994), pp. 37–39.

2. "Mr. Nicoll and Dr. Parkhurst," *NY Times*, February 16, 1892, p. 8 (Nicoll); "Vice Not Rampant Here," *NY World*, February 16, 1892, p. 7 (Murray, Gilroy, Voorhis).

3. "City Officials Scored," *NY Tribune* editorial, February 15, 1892, p. 4; *NY World* editorial n.t., February 15, 1892, p. 15; "Bring Him To Account," *NY Sun* editorial, February 17, 1892, p. 6.

4. Parkhurst, *Our Fight*, pp. 18, 24.

5. For more on these changes, see the excellent overview in Edwin G. Burrows and Mike Wallace, *Gotham: A History of New York City to 1898* (New York, 1999), pp. 1041–70.

6. "Sketch of Rev. Dr. Talmage," *NY Times*, April 13, 1902, p. 7 ("Young man"); "The Fanciful Elephant," *NY Times*, November 4, 1878, p. 8 ("can only be"; "the deliberate plan"); "Talmage's Experiences," *NY Times*, October 21, 1878,

p. 5 ("I could call names"); T. DeWitt Talmage, *The Masque Torn Off* (Chicago, 1882), p. 518 ("honest Christian").

7. Charles H. Parkhurst, *My Forty Years in New York* (New York, 1923), p. 13; Charles H. Parkhurst to Rev. B. W. Wyman, September 23, 1919, Records of the Church on the Hill (now the United Church of Christ), Lenox, MA. My thanks to Rev. Natalie C. Shiras, pastor, and Emily Wilson, church historian, for making this correspondence available to me. The original Church on the Hill, built in 1805, still stands today. The sketch of Parkhurst's early life is based upon Winthrop Parkhurst, "Memorial Sketch of Charles Henry Parkhurst," in Charles H. Parkhurst Papers, Amherst College Archives, and his account in *My Forty Years in New York*, pp. 3–58. See also "Installing a Pastor," *NY Times*, March 10, 1880, p. 8.

8. Mission statement quoted in Dorothy Ganfield Fowler, *A City Church: The First Presbyterian Church in the City of New York, 1716–1976* (New York, 1981), p. 130; Charles H. Parkhurst, *Opportunities and Resources for Christian Work*, Sermon preached Dec. 9, 1888 (New York, 1888) p. 9. New York Historical Society has a published copy of this sermon. Fowler offers a detailed picture of Madison Square's activities in the post–Civil War years;

9. "Constitution, By-laws, and Charter," in *Second Annual Report of the Society for the Prevention of Crime* (1878), p. 5; Howard Crosby, "Crime and Punishment in New York," *North American Review* 133 (August 1881), pp. 175, 174. See also Howard Crosby, "A Letter to the People of New York," *Forum* 2 (December 1886): 420–28, and "The Dangerous Classes," *North American Review* 136 (March 1883): 345–52.

10. For background on the new preventive societies created in the 1870s and 1880s, see Timothy Gilfoyle, "The Moral Origins of Political Surveillance: The Preventive Society in New York City, 1867–1918," *American Quarterly* 38 (Fall 1986): 637–52, and Gilfoyle, *City of Eros*, pp. 186–91. For detailed accounts of SPC legal activity, see for example the summaries in *Third Annual Report* (1879), pp. 5–19, and *Fifth Annual Report* (1881), pp. 10–18.

11. For a summary of the 1891 Annual Report, see "Crime Slowly Decreasing," *NY Times*, March 14, 1891. See also SPC, *Twelfth Annual Report* (1888), p. 3. For estimating the current (2015) worth of historical dollar figures throughout this book, I have used the calculator of the Consumer Price Index (Estimate), 1800–Present, Federal Reserve Bank of Minneapolis, https://www .minneapolisfed.org/community/teaching-aids/cpi-calculator-information/ consumer-price-index-1800.

12. Parkhurst, *Our Fight With Tammany* (February 14, 1892 sermon), pp. 21, 10. To get a sense of Parkhurst's work and influence in NYC evangelical circles, see his closing remarks at a Protestant ministers' conference devoted to addressing the religious needs of the city's increasingly foreign born and non-Protestant population, in Rev. J. M. King, et al., *The Religious Condition*

of *New York City* (New York, 1888), pp. 189–195. He discussed the dangers of sexuality outside marriage more obliquely in some of his published sermons. See, for example, "The Pharisee's Prayer," in *The Pattern in the Mount* (New York, 1885), pp. 167–79, and *Talks to Young Men* (New York, 1897), pp. 93–125.

13. "Dr. Parkhurst Is Rebuked," *NY Times*, March 2, 1892, p. 8 (Grand Jury presentment, Nicoll); Parkhurst, *My Forty Years in New York*, p. 119, 121. For grand jury coverage see also "Mr. Nicoll Whitewashed," *NY Tribune*, March 2, 1892, p. 3; "Parkhurst Rebuked by the Grand Jury," *NY Herald*, March 2, 1892, p. 3; "Dr. Parkhurst and the Grand Jury," *NY Times*, March 2, 1892, editorial, p. 4. On Parkhurst's finding the origins of his crusade in Nicoll's "personal pique," see Parkhurst, *Our Fight With Tammany*, pp. 47–48.

14. Parkhurst, *My Forty Years in New York*, p. 123–24; Edward Crapsey, "Private Detectives," in *The Nether Side of New York; Or the Vice, Crime, and Poverty of the Great Metropolis* (New York, 1872), pp. 54–55, 62; James A. Scrymser, *Personal Reminiscences In Times of Peace and War* (privately published, 1915), p. 112. Crapsey's thoughtful and detailed account of the private detective business reflected his experience as a police reporter for the *New York Times*); Background on Charles W. Gardner and other SPC detectives can be found in *People of the State of New York vs. Charles W. Gardner*, Stenographer's Minutes, General Session, Before Recorder Smyth, 2 vols. (New York, 1893), in New York Public Library Annex.

15. Charles W. Gardner, *The Doctor and The Devil, Or Midnight Adventures of Dr. Parkhurst* (New York, 1894; reprint ed. Vanguard Press, 1931). I have supplemented Gardner's report with details that emerged in the press from interviews with some of the madams and prostitutes who were visited, and from press coverage of the subsequent trials of brothel keepers Hattie Adams and Marie Andrea. See "How Parkhurst Saw Vice," *NY World*, March 19, 1892, p. 1; "What Dr. Parkhurst Saw," *NY Sun*, April 7, 1892, p. 1; "Dr. Parkhurst in Court," *NY World*, April 7, 1892, p. 3; "Dr. Parkhurst a Witness," *NY Times*, April 7, 1892, p. 3; "Parkhurst's Sightseeing," *NY Sun*, May 6, 1892, p. 7; Hattie Adams Convicted," *NY Sun*, May 7, 1892, p. 2; "Marie Andrea Found Guilty," *NY Times*, May 11, 1892, p. 3; "Erving's Testifying Ended," *NY Sun*, May 11, 1892, p. 5. On earlier sensational vice exposes of the old Fourth Ward waterfront neighborhood during the 1860s, see Daniel Czitrom, "The Wickedest Ward in New York," *Seaport Magazine* 20 (Winter 1986–7): 20–26.

The first detailed account of Parkhurst's crusade was M. R. Werner, "Dr. Parkhurst's Crusade," in *It Happened in New York* (NY, 1957), pp. 36–116. Werner's piece originally appeared in 1955 as a two-part series in *The New Yorker*, and he relied heavily upon Gardner's book for details of the underworld tour. The rest of his work seems to have been drawn almost exclusively from newspaper sources—and since Werner included no bibliography or source notes, it is impossible to check many of his claims and "facts." On the "sunshine and shadow" guidebook tradition, see Daniel Czitrom, "The Secrets of the Great City," in Ric Burns and James Sanders, eds., *New York: An Illustrated History* (New York, 1999), pp. 210–15.

16. "After the Police Now," *NY Sun*, March 14, 1892, p. 1 ("eager for"); quotes from Parkhurst's sermon from *Our Fight With Tammany*, pp. 74, 60, 65, 73–74, 75, 77, 78. See also "Dr. Parkhurst Speaks Out," *NY Times*, March 14, 1892, p. 1; "Hot Shot For Tammany," *NY Tribune*, March 14, 1892, p. 1.

17. "Vices of the City," *NY World*, March 14, 1892, p. 8 (Nicoll); "An Attack On Parkhurst," *NY World*, March 28, 1892, p. 10 (De Costa); "Dr. Parkhurst's 'Particulars," *NY Times*, March 14, 1892, editorial, p. 4; "Parkhurst and His Work," *NY Tribune*, March 20, 1892, p. 22 ("preacher of righteousness"); Dr. Parkhurst's Crusade," NY World, March 15, 1892, editorial, p. 4 ("opposed by public sentiment"); "Dr. Parkhurst's Function," *NY Sun*, March 15, 1892, editorial, p. 6 ("if he had hunted"; "thousands of respectable").

18. "Illegal and Bad Motives," *NY Times*, April 2, 1892, p. 1 (includes complete text of the presentment); Parkhurst, *Our Fight With Tammany*, pp. 88–89 ("out of the region"). See also "Backing Up Parkhurst," *NY World*, April 2, 1892, p. 1; "Police Poke Fun at Taber," *NY World*, April 6, 1892, p. 1 (Taber's charge of $7–$10 million collected by police each year).

19. "Hot Shot For the Police," *NY Tribune*, April 2, 1892, p. 3 ("I say again"); "Police Poke Fun At Taber," *NY World*, April 6, 1892, p. 1 ("clearly indicate").

20. "The Morality of New York," NY World, March 16, 1892, p. 10 ("It is a fact"; "Never in their history"); "Angry at the Grand Jury," *NY Times*, April 3, 1892, p. 16 ("the members").

21. "The Police and the Law," *NY Times*, April 3, 1892, editorial, p. 4 ("is more than"). On crime statistics: *Annual Report of the Board of Commissioners of the Metropolitan Police, 1865*, NY State Assembly Documents (1865), 88th Session, vol. 3, no. 36, p. 9; *Report of the Select Committee Appointed by the Assembly of 1875 to Investigate the Causes of the Increase in the City of New York*, NY State Assembly Documents (1876), vol. 6, no. 106, p. 7; James F. Richardson, *The New York Police: Colonial Times to 1901* (New York, 1970), p. 157 (crime statistics of the 1860s); Christopher P. Thale, "Civilizing New York City: Police Patrol, 1880–1935," PhD diss., University of Chicago, 1995, p. 975 (robbery statistics, 1885–93); Eric H. Monkkonen, *Murder in New York City* (Berkeley, CA, 2001), Figure 1.4, p. 16 (homicide rates).

22. "How Parkhurst Saw Vice," *NY World*, March 19, 1892, p. 1 ("impossible to say"); "What Dr. Parkhurst Saw," *NY Sun*, April 7, 1892, p. 1 ("Do you not think"); "The Jury Did Not Agree," *NY Times*, April 8, 1892, p. 8 ("I hadn't the heart"); *NY Times*, April 8, 1892, editorial, p. 4 ("bald perjury," "no right thinking"); see also, "Dr. Parkhurst a Witness," *NY Times*, April 7, 1892, p. 3; "Dr. Parkhurst in Court," *NY World*, April 7, 1892, p. 3; "Two to One for Mrs. Adams," *NY Sun*, April 8, 1892, p. 1.

23. Once More Before Jurors," *NY Times*, May 6, 1892, p. 8 (Erving testimony); "Hattie Adams Convicted," *NY Sun*, May 7, 1892, p. 2 (Howe); "A Hard Problem to Solve," *NY Times*, May 8, 1892, p. 9 (Adams). For further coverage of the trial, see also "Hattie Adams in Court," *NY Times*, May 5, 1892, p. 9; "Hattie Adams on Trial," *NY World*, May 6, 1892, p. 2; "Parkhurst's Sightseeing," *NY Sun*, May 6, 1892, p. 7; "Hattie Adams Convicted," *NY Times*, May 7, 1892, p. 8; "Triumph for Parkhurst," *NY World*, May 7, 1892, p. 8; "Hattie Adams Sentenced," *NY Sun*, May 13, 1892, p. 5.

24. "Parkhurst Wins Again," *NY World*, May 11, 1892, p. 8; Parkhurst, *Our Fight With Tammany*, p. 102; "The Facts of the Case," *NY Sun*, May 12, 1892, p. 6. On the Andrea trial see also "The Case Against Marie Andrea," *NY Times*, May 10, 1892, p. 8; "Maria Andrea Found Guilty," *NY Times*, May 11, 1892, p. ?; "Erving's Testifying Ended," *NY Sun*, May 11, 1892, p. 5; quote from Rylance, *NY Tribune* (undated clipping), New York District Attorney Scrapbooks, Microfilm Rolls 1-19, 1882-1896, Municipal Archives and Research Center. Hereafter, any newspaper citation with (clipping, NYDAS) is taken from these scrapbooks. See also the profile, "Young Erving at Home," *NY Press*, May 15, 1892 (clipping, NYDAS).

25. Lloyd quoted in "Will Fight for Purity," *NY World*, May 23, 1892, p. 4; on the White Cross Society study, see "Dr. De Costa's Plan for Fighting Vice," *NY Press*, (undated clipping, NYDAS); On the CLU debate, see also "Dr. Parkhurst's Methods, *NY Times*, May 23, 1892, p. 4; "Slumming with Dr. Parkhurst," *NY Sun*, May 23, 1892, p. 6.

26. "Leagued with Criminals," *NY Times*, May 13, 1892, p. 1 (Parkhurst); "Who is the Devil?," *NY Sun*, May 14, editorial, p. 6. See also "Parkhurst's New Attack," *NY World*, May 13, 1892, p. 1; "Dr. Parkhurst's Methods," *NY Sun*, May 13, 1892, p. 1; "To Aid Parkhurst," *Morning Advertiser*, May 13, 1892 (clipping, NYDAS). On the City Vigilance League, see William H. Tolman, *Municipal Reform Movements in the United States* (New York, 1895).

27. "Praise for Dr. Parkhurst," *NY Times*, May 27, 1892, p. 1 (Arnoux, Parkhurst); "Dr. Parkhurst Indorsed," *NY Tribune*, May 27, 1892, p. 1 (Smith). See also "Cheering Dr. Parkhurst," *NY World*, May 27, 1892, p. 1; "Crusading Against Crime," *NY Sun*, May 27, 1892, p. 1; *NY Morning Journal*, May 27, 1892 (clipping, NYDAS).

2: THE BUTTONS

1. "Brave Showing of Police," *NY Times* June 1, 1892, p. 8.

2. "New York's New Police Chieftains," *Harper's Weekly* 36 (April 23, 1892): 404; "The New Police Superintendent," *NY Tribune*, April 13, 1892, p. 6; "Mr. Byrnes's Opportunity," *NY Times*, April 15, 1892, p. 4. See also "Byrnes Succeeds Murray," *NY World*, April 13, 1892, p. 8, 7.

3. Byrnes and Parkhurst quoted in "Parkhurst Talks Back," *NY World*, April 14, 1892, p. 8.

4. For background on the evolution of the city's police force the best sources are Wilbur R. Miller, *Cops and Bobbies: Police Authority in New York and London, 1830–1870* (Chicago, 1977), esp. pp. 140–66; James F. Richardson, *The New York Police: Colonial Times to 1901* (New York, 1970), pp. 51–81; Raymond B. Fosdick, *American Police Systems* (New York, 1920), pp. 63–107.

5. Richard Wheatley, "The New York Police Department," *Harper's New Monthly* 74 (March 1887): 502; Wheatley also includes figures on ethnicity, and an 1890 survey produced essentially the same picture: "This Will Be News," *NY Times*, May 10, 1890, p. 5. See also Ernest Ingersoll, "The Police of New York," *Scribner's* 16 (July 1878): 342–56; Richardson, *New York Police*, pp. 170–74; John Crank, *Understanding Police Culture* (New York, 2004). For a detailed schedule of the fees paid to constables and city marshals in the early nineteenth century, see Augustine E. Costello, *Our Police Protectors: A History of the New York Police* (New York, 1885), pp. 58–9. On the entrepreneurial nature of nineteenth-century urban policing more generally, see Allan E. Levett, "Centralization of City Police in the Nineteenth Century United States," PhD diss., University of Michigan, 1975, especially pp. 38–59. See also Selden D. Bacon, "The Early Development of American Municipal Police," PhD diss., Yale University, 1939, especially pp. 273–322, and Richardson, *New York Police*, pp. 45–67. For comprehensive treatment of the police and the Draft Riots, see Iver Bernstein, *The New York City Draft Riots* (New York, 1990) and Adrian Cook, *The Armies of the Streets: The New York City Draft Riots of 1863* (Lexington, KY, 1974). The best full study of the Orange riots is Michael A. Gordon, *The Orange Riots: Irish Political Violence in New York City, 1870 and 1871* (Ithaca, NY, 1993).

6. For a good description of conditions in station houses and how new cops learned the job, see Cornelius W. Willemse, *A Cop Remembers* (New York, 1933), pp. 71–92. Willemse, an activist in the Patrolmen's Benevolent Association (PBA) and later a captain, joined the force in 1899. See also James Lardner and Thomas Reppetto, *NYPD: A City and Its Police* (New York, 2000), pp. 60–71.

7. On the Byrnes brothers service, see Frederick Phisterer, comp., *New York in the War of the Rebellion, 1861 to 1865* (Albany, 1912, 3rd ed.), "Registers and Sketches of Organizations." On Ellsworth and the Zouaves see also, Ruth Painter Randall, *Colonel Elmer Ellsworth* (Boston, 1960), pp. 241–76; Charles A. Ingraham, *Elmer E. Ellsworth and the Zouaves of '61* (Chicago, 1925), pp. 59–155; Henry Miller, "Ellsworth's Zouaves," in *Reminiscences of Chicago During the Civil War*, Mabel McIlvaine, ed. (New York, 1967), pp. 15–40; *NY Times*, April 30, 1861, p. 1. For a first-hand account of the New York Fire Zouaves at Bull Run, see "With the Fire Zouaves at First Bull Run: The Narrative of Private

Arthur O. Alcock, 11th New York Volunteer Infantry," ed. Brian C. Pohanka, *Civil War Regiments* 5 (1996): 80–104. For an example of the contemporary press coverage, see *Frank Leslie's Illustrated*, June 28, 1860; May 11, 1861.

8. "Enemies of Crime," *NY World*, April 17, 1892, p. 13 ("I became"); "The Manhattan Bank Burglars," *NY Times*, June 6, 1879, p. 2 ("The present case"). On Byrnes's early career: See his Testimony, May 12, 1884, in *Hearings, NY State Special Committee Appointed to Investigate the Local Government of the City and County of New York, 2 vols.* (Albany, 1884), II: pp. 2216–38; "Byrnes in His New Office," *NY Times*, April 14, 1892, p. 9; *NY Times*, May 10, 1910, p. 1 (obituary); *NY Tribune*, May 8, 1910, p. 1 (obituary). On the Manhattan Savings Bank robbery: "The Manhattan Savings Bank," *NY Times*, January 26, 1879, p. 12; "A Night Watchman's Tale," *NY Times*, June 2, 1879, p. 5. Lardner and Reppetto, *NYPD*, pp. 72–79 offers a more detailed analysis of the case—but this work includes no source notes.

9. "The Ward Detectives," *NY Times*, July 9, 1882, p. 7 ("simply pliant"); Thomas Byrnes testimony, *Hearings, NY State Special Committee*, II (1884): p. 2211. See also "Captain Byrnes in His New Place," *NY Times*, March 14, 1880, p. 5; "Police Department Matters," *NY Times*, April 24, 1880, p. 3; "The New Detective Bureau," *NY Times*, May 26, 1882, p. 8.

10. Thomas Byrnes testimony, *Hearings, NY State Special Committee*, II: p. 2237. See also "Inspector Byrnes's Men," *NY Tribune*, January 10, 1892; Jurgen Thorwald, *The Century of the Detective* (New York, 1965), pp. 95–98.

11. Thomas F. Byrnes, *Professional Criminals of America* (New York, 1886; reprint edition, 1969), pp. 2, 1; "All Men Detectives," *NY Times*, October 1, 1886, p. 8 ("There will be nothing"); "Inspector Byrnes's Book," *NY Tribune*, October 3, 1886, p. 11 ("the work of"). On Byrnes's place in the broader historical context of detective work and writing, see David Ray Papke, *Framing the Criminal: Crime, Cultural Work, and the Loss of Critical Perspective, 1830–1900* (Hamden, CT, 1987), pp. 140–64, and Larry K. Hartsfield, *The American Response to Professional Crime, 1870–1917* (Westport, CT, 1985), pp. 54–59.

12. "Testimony of Thomas Byrnes, February 10, 1905, Chamber of Commerce of the State of New York, in *Papers and Proceedings of Committee on the Police Problem* (New York, 1905; reprint edition, Arno Press, 1971), p. 191 ("All this fancied idea"). Thomas Byrnes to Ernest A. Young, May [?], 1886; Thomas F. Adams to Ernest A. Young, August 24, 1886; Thomas F. Adams to Ernest A. Young, November 2, 1886, in Ernest A. Young Papers, in private possession of Victor A. Berch, Archivist of Special Collections (retired), Brandeis University. My thanks to Victor for making these letters available to me.

13. Julian Hawthorne, *Another's Crime: From the Diary of Inspector Byrnes* (New York, 1888), p. 2. For other examples of the Hawthorne-Byrnes collaboration, see Julian Hawthorne, *The Great Bank Robbery: From the Diary of Inspector*

Byrnes (New York, 1887) and Julian Hawthorne, *An American Penman* (New York, 1887). On the popular success of these dime novels, see Gary Scharnhorst, *Julian Hawthorne: The Life of a Prodigal Son* (Urbana, 2014), pp. 123–24; see also Maurice Bassan, *Hawthorne's Son: The Life and Literary Career of Julian Hawthorne* (Columbus, 1970), pp. 183–84; *NY Times*, May 10, 1910 (obituary), p. 6.

14. Wheatley, "New York Police Department," pp. 512–13; Augustine Costello, *Our Police Protectors: History of the New York Police From the earliest Period to the Present Time* (New York, 1885), p. 410; Charles Williams, "The New York Police," Contemporary *Review* 53 (February 1888), p. 221 ("more of a terror"); Jacob Riis, "1,400 Years in Jail," *NY Morning Journal*, April 15, 1883 ("The source"), in "Newspaper Articles by Jacob Riis, 1881–1892," Scrapbook, reel 6, container 12 (microfilm), Jacob A. Riis Papers, Library of Congress; Steffens, *Autobiography*, p. 226.

15. Harold C. Syrett, ed., *The Gentleman and the Tiger: The Autobiography of George B. McClellan, Jr.* (Philadelphia, 1956), pp. 298–99. For corroborating discussions of the brutal side of Byrnes's methods, see Jacob A. Riis, *The Making of An American* (New York, 1903), pp. 340–44; Steffens, *Autobiography*, pp. 201, 210.

16. "Hanier's Murderer Found," *NY Times*, February 2, 1882, p. 8 ("Did I turn white"); "Traced by His Pistol," *NY Tribune*, February 2, 1882, p. 8 ("Were you there?"); Riis, *Making of an American*, p. 342 ("'come over to the wake'"). For other sources for this case, see "Aid for Hanier's Family," *NY Times*, February 7, 1882, p. 3; "The Murder of Louis Hanier," *NY Times*, March 2, 1882, p. 8; "M'Gloin's Trial," *NY Times*, March 3, 1882, p. 3; "M'Gloin Convicted," *NY Times*, March 4, 1882, p. 8; "The Murderer Sentenced," *NY Tribune*, March 7, 1882, p. 2; "To Die For Murder," NY Telegram, January 31, 1883 (clipping, NYDAS). "Their Last Night On Earth," *NY Times*, March 9, 1883, p. 2; "Hanged Side By Side," *NY Tribune*, March 10, 1883, p. 2; "A Hangman's Work Done," *NY Times*, March 10, 1883, p. 3; "M'Gloin Carried to His Grave," *NY Times*, March 12, 1883, p. 8.

17. Costello, *Our Police Protectors*, p. 414; "Enemies of Crime," *NY World*, April 17, 1892, p. 14 ("I got a woman"); Riis, *Making of an American*, p. 342; Herbert Asbury, *The Gangs of New York: An Informal History of the Underworld* (New York, 1928), p. 227; Luc Sante, *Low Life: Lures and Snares of Old New York* (New York, 1991), p. 215; James Lardner and Thomas Reppetto, *NYPD: A City and Its People* (New York, 2000), p. 85.

18. Alexander S. Williams's testimony, New York State Senate, Report and Proceedings of the Senate Committee Appointed to Investigate the Police Department of the City of New York (Albany, NY, 1895), vol. V: p. 5448 (Hereafter cited as LC [Lexow Committee]); Ingersoll, "The Police of New York," p. 354 ("the steady nerve"); Wheatley, "The New York Police Department,"

p. 500 ("enjoys the reputation"); "Our Captains of Police," *NY Times*, September 23, 1878, p. 3 "the most conspicuously efficient"). These and other sources for Williams's early life and career are scanty and often unreliable; see also Costello, *Our Police Protectors*, pp. 364–69; Richardson, *New York Police*, pp. 204–206; Williams's Testimony, April 13, 1884, in *Hearings, NY State Special Committee Appointed to Investigate the Local Government of the City and County of New York* (Albany, 1884), vol. 2, pp. 1922–61.

19. "Mainstays of Civic Life," *NY Times*, June 29, 1889, p. 5 (Cockran). On the Police Athletic Club, including descriptions of its public competitions, see for example "Police Athletic Club," *NY Times*, April 21, 1877, p. 10 and "Police Athletic Club," *NY Times*, June 24, 1877, p. 12. "See also "Dining with the Police, *NY Times*, January 18, 1887, p. 2; "Cheers for Capt. Williams," *NY Times*, June 2, 1886, p. 8.

20. A. E. Costello, *Our Police Protectors*, pp. 367–68. On the evolution of Madison Square neighborhood, see Miriam Berman, *Madison Square: The Park and Its Celebrated Landmarks* (New York, 2001) and Dorothy Ganfield Fowler, *A City Church: The First Presbyterian Church in the City of New York, 1716–1976* (New York, 1981).

21. "The Giant Knocked Silly," *NY Times*, August 7, 1883, p. 1 ("at whose glance"). For Williams's role at other fights, see also for example "Sullivan's Heavy Blows," *NY Times*, May 15, 1883, p. 5; "Mr. Sullivan Has a Picnic," *NY Times*, November 11, 1884, p. 1. In one fight Williams, following the orders of higher ups, jumped into the ring and arrested Sullivan and his opponent for engaging in an illegal prize fight. But at the trial Williams defended the fighters, comparing their bout to Police Athletic Club events, testifying that "I've seen hundreds of sparring matches where the blows struck were harder." "Only a Sparring Match," *NY Times*, December 18, 1884, p. 8; and "Both Pugilists Arrested," *NY Times*, November 19, 1884, p. 1. On John L. Sullivan's career, see Michael T. Isenberg, *John L. Sullivan and His America* (Urbana, IL, 1988) and Elliott J. Gorn, *The Manly Art: Bare-Knuckle Prize Fighting in America* (Ithaca, NY, 1986), pp. 207–47.

22. Williams testimony, LC, vol. 5: pp. 5569–70; H. L. Mencken, *The American Language: An Inquiry into the Development of English in the United States* (New York, 1919; rev. ed., 1921), p. 191; Augustine Costello testimony, LC, vol. 4: p. 4524; Costello, *Our Police Protectors*, pp. 367–68; A. H. Hummel, "Origin of 'Tenderloin,'" *NY Herald*, December 29, 1894, p. 5. For the best overview of the term's contested history, concluding that its etymology would always remain murky, see H.M.L., "Tenderloin," *American Notes & Queries* 5 (August 1945):72-4. For an excellent brief overview of the Tenderloin's evolution as a neighborhood, see Timothy J. Gilfoyle, *City of Eros: New York City, Prostitution, and the Commercialization of Sex, 1790-1820* (New York, 1994), pp. 203–8.

23. "A Six Day Tramp Begun," *NY Times*, March 10, 1879, p. 5 ("the terrible blows"); "Capt. Williams Exonerated," *NY Times*, April 23, 1879, p. 8 (Erhardt); "Editorial," *NY Tribune*, April 23, 1879, p. 4. For further coverage of this trial see for example: "Capt. Williams on Trial," *NY Times*, April 4, 1879, p. 8; "Trials of the Police," *NY Tribune*, April 4, 1879, p. 5; "Capt. Williams's Trial," *NY Times*, April 13, 1879, p. 5; "Defence of Captain Williams," *NY Tribune*, April 14, 1879, p. 8; "Capt. Williams on Trial," *NY Times*, April 18, 1879, p. 8; "Trial of Capt. Williams," *NY Times*, April 22, 1879, p. 2. For another example of brutality charges against Williams during a Police Athletic Club exhibition (for which he was actually arrested), see "Capt. Williams Arrested," *NY Times* January 12, 1878, p. 8 and "Capt. Williams' Accuser," *NY Times*, January 16, 1878, p. 8. Figures on Williams's record from Richardson, *New York Police*, p. 205 and "New Police Inspectors," *NY Tribune*, August 10, 1887, p. 2.
24. "The Police," *NY Times*, March 22, 1874, p. 4. See also "Local Miscellany," *NY Times*, March 20, 1874, p. 8; "Metropolitan Police Rule," *NY Tribune*, March 20, 1874, p. 8; On the commercial sex trade in this neighborhood during these years see Gilfoyle, *City of Eros*, pp. 213–15. He estimates that this area housed 20 percent of the city's brothels.
25. "Police Trials," *NY Tribune*, August 12, 1875, p. 8 (Brown, Williams); "Williams On Trial," *NY Times*, August 13, 1875, p. 2 (Brown); "Police Captains Punished," *NY Times*, November 24, 1875, p. 2. See also "Trials of Police Officers," *NY Tribune*, August 6, 1875, p. 8; "Capt. Williams on Trial," *NY Times*, August 12, 1875, p. 8; "Capt. Williams' Trials," *NY Times*, August 22, 1875, p. 2; Richardson, *New York Police*, pp. 217–19.
26. For an excellent description of how the police administered the nuts and bolts of elections in New York, see "A Perfect Election Law," *NY Times*, December 26, 1886, p. 5. On the political affiliations of captains, see "Our Captains of Police," *NY Times*, September 23, 1878, p. 8.
27. "Police Captains Blamed," *NY Times*, May 4, 1883, p. 3 (grand jury presentment); "Police Captains Accused," *NY Tribune*, May 5, 1883, p. 2 ("This presentment"); *NY Truth*, May 5, 1883 (clipping, NYDAS, "gambling will always").
28. "Capt. Williams's Defense," *NY Times*, February 15, 1885, p. 3 (Root); *NY Tribune*, February 28, 1885, editorial, p. 4; "Favoring Capt. Williams," *NY Times*, February 20, 1885, p. 3 (any action"); "The Charges Dismissed," *NY Times*, February 28, 1885, p. 3 (French). See also, "Capt. Williams on Trial," *NY Times*, February 14, 1885, p. 8; "Witnesses for Williams," *NY Tribune*, February 20, 1885, p. 8 "Capt. Williams Acquitted," *NY Tribune*, February 28, 1885, p. 8; "Capt. Williams Honored," *NY Times*, May 27, 1885, p. 5; "The Police in New Hands," NY Times, June 10, 1885, p. 8.
29. See "Against Captain Williams," *NY Tribune*, May 25, 1887, p. 5; "The Charges Against Capt. Williams," *NY Tribune*, May 26, 1887, p. 5; "Not

Fearing His Accuser," *NY Times*, July 7, 1887, p. 1; "Capt. Williams on Trial," *NY Tribune*, July 7, 1887, p. 2.

30. Prosecution Brief, "In the Matter of the Charges Against Alexander S. Williams," June 28, 1887, Mayor's Papers, 87-HAS-28, Municipal Archives and Research Center; "New Police Inspectors," *NY Tribune*, August 10, 1887, p. 2 (Voorhis). See also, "Capt. Williams Promoted," *NY Times*, August 10, 1887, p. 1.

31. "Communistic and law defying," *NY Tribune*, quoted in Burrows and Wallace, *Gotham*, p. 1036; "A Communist Failure," NY Tribune, July 26, 1877, p. 1 ("the resolutions"); "The Communists' Meeting," *NY Times*, July 26, 1877, p. 8 ("the officers"); "The Right of Public Assemblage," *NY Times*, July 27, 1877, editorial, p. 4 ("white livered"); Erhardt, 1884, quoted in Richardson, *New York Police*, p. 199. See also Robert V. Bruce, *1877: Year of Violence* (Indianapolis, 1959), pp. 279–81; Philip S. Foner, *The Great Labor Uprising of 1877* (New York, 1977), pp. 118–24.

32. "Stopping All Cars," *NY Times*, March 5, 1886, p. 1 ("I know my duty"; "zealously fought off"); "The Victory of the Strikers," *NY Tribune*, March 6, 1886, editorial, p. 5 ("a pitched battle"); "Superintendent Murray's Incompetence," *NY Times*, March 6, 1886, editorial, p. 4 ("It was his duty"). See also "A Car Run With Trouble," *NY Tribune*, March 5, 1886, p. 1; "Ten Hours Without Cars," *NY Times*, March 6, 1886, p. 1; "Not One Car For Ten Hours," *NY Tribune*, March 6, 1886, p. 1; "The New York Car Strike," *Harper's Weekly* 30 (March 13, 1886), p. 172 (illustration on pp. 168–69); Burrows and Wallace, *Gotham*, pp. 1095–96.

33. "More Street Cars Run," *NY Tribune*, January 31, 1889, p. 1 (Murray); "Many Street Cars Idle," *NY Times*, January 30, 1889, p. 2 ("It was necessary"); "Clubs Quell the Rioters," *NY Times*, January 31, 1889, p. 2 (Williams); "Breaking the Tie-Up," *NY Tribune*, February 1, 1889, p. 2 (Williams).

34. "Opening More Car Lines," *NY Tribune*, February 3, 1889, p. 2. See also "The Lawless Spirit Awed," *NY Times*, February 3, 1889, p. 3.

35. "The Strikers Yield," *NY Tribune*, February 6, 1889, p. 1 ("greatest fight"); p. 2; Murray quoted in "How the Police Handle a Strike," *Harper's Weekly* 33 (February 9, 1889): 107; "The Work of the Police," *NY Times*, February 13, 1889, p. 9 (Murray's report). On the CLU's angry protest of police brutality against strikers, see "Workingmen Call on the Mayor," *NY Tribune*, February 3, 1889, p. 2. On the use of immigrant strikebreakers see, for example, "Immigrants to Care for Horses," *NY Tribune*, January 31, 1889, p. 2, and "Little Disturbance in Second Ave.," *NY Tribune*, February 1, 1889, p. 2.

36. "New York's New Police Chieftains," *Harper's Weekly* 36 (April 23, 1892): 404 ("more men"); "New York's Home Guard," *NY Tribune*, January 26, 1892, p. 7 (Depew). See also "Six Hundred Bottles Vanish," *NY Times*, January 22, 1884, p. 2; "The Police Captains' Dinner," *NY Times*, January 27, 1885, p. 5.

3: DEMOCRATIC CITY, REPUBLICAN NATION

1. "Praise for Dr. Parkhurst," *NY Times*, May 27, 1892, p. 2 ("There is no"); "Dr. Parkhurst Home Again," *NY Tribune*, September 24, 1892, p. 4 ("My fight"). See also "Dr. Parkhurst's Plans," *NY Press*, September 24, 1892 (clipping, NYDAS).

2. For an analysis of pre–Civil War machine politics that emphasizes the confluence of Irish emigration, universal white male suffrage, and early industrialization, see Amy Bridges, *A City in the Republic: Antebellum New York and the Origins of Machine Politics* (Ithaca, NY, 1984). See also Martin Shefter, "The Emergence of the Political Machine: An Alternative View," in *Theoretical Perspectives on Urban Politics*, Willis D. Hawley, et al., eds. (Englewood Cliffs, NJ, 1976), pp. 14–44. For an excellent critical overview of national urban machines dominated by Irish-Americans see Steven P. Erie, *Rainbow's End: Irish Americans and the Dilemmas of Urban Machine Politics, 1840–1985* (Berkeley, CA, 1988). Erie emphasizes the dominance of Irish-Americans to the exclusion of other ethnic groups, as well as the severe economic and political constraints faced by urban machines.

3. For the best recent account of the transnational impact of famine Irish migration on New York, see Tyler Anbinder, "From Famine to Five Points: Lord Landsdowne's Irish Tenants Encounter North America's Most Brutal Slum," *American Historical Review* 107 (April 2002): 351–87. See also Edward Spann, *The New Metropolis: New York City, 1840–1857* (New York, 1981), pp. 313–61.

4. On the deep and evolving factionalism within the Democratic Party in these years, see Jerome Mushkat, *Tammany: The Evolution of a Political Machine, 1789–1865* (Syracuse, 1971), pp. 300–63, and his *Fernando Wood: A Political Biography* (Kent, OH, 1981); Spann, *New Metropolis*, pp. 364–400.

5. Even before the Civil War, when mass emigration from Ireland and Germany radically reshaped the city's demographics, New York City had been ground zero for the bruising political battles over who could vote. New York state's first voter registry law in 1859, born of an alliance between the nativist American Party and the emergent Republican Party, represented the first of many efforts to accomplish what its supporters called "purification of the ballot box." But the only thing pure about the fight over this and the endlessly amended state registry laws was partisan politics itself, and the many amended versions in later years were decidedly mixed. Partisan goals—the desire to suppress the Democratic vote in the city and check the growing political influence of immigrants—led to very narrow, usually self-interested notions of what constituted vote fraud. The law required voter registration only in New York City and county, while ignoring the realities of rural corruption and electoral abuses by employers. In 1866 the law

declared that no voter could be registered unless he personally appeared before election inspectors of his district—but this rule applied only in New York City and Brooklyn. Reflecting the bitter partisan divisions of the era, the state registry laws were long, detailed, complex statutes, endlessly amended and resulting in nonstop legal challenges and appeals. The best overview of early registry laws in New York state, and how they reflected complex relations between the Republican and American parties, is Joel Silbey, " 'The Undisguised Connection': Know Nothings into Republicans: New York as a Test Case," in *The Partisan Imperative: The Dynamics of American Politics Before the Civil War* (New York, 1985), pp. 127–65. See also the discussion in Alexander Keyssar, *The Right to Vote: The Contested History of Democracy in the United States*, rev. ed. (New York, 2009), pp. 118–31.

6. U.S. Congress, House of Representatives, Select Committee on Alleged New York Election Frauds, *New York Election Frauds*, Report No. 31, 40th Cong., 3rd Sess., 1869, pp. 2, 4. Hereafter cited as Lawrence Committee.

7. *Minority Report*, Lawrence Committee, pp. 107–8. See also Albie Burke, "Federal Regulation of Congressional Elections in Northern Cities, 1871–1894," *American Journal of Legal History* 14 (1970): 17–34; Robert Anderson Horn, "National Control of Congressional Elections," PhD diss., Princeton University, 1941, pp. 137–45.

8. See Burke, "Federal Regulation of Congressional Elections"; David Quigley, "Constitutional Revision and the City: The Enforcement Acts and Urban America, 1870–1894," *Journal of Political History* 20 (2008): 64–75. The best overview of this topic remains Albie Burke, "Federal Regulation of Congressional Elections in Northern Cities," PhD diss., University of Chicago, 1968. For a detailed, but often hard to follow, account of these laws in the context of the struggle for African-American voting rights, see Xi Wang, *The Trial of Democracy: Black Suffrage and Northern Republicans, 1860–1910* (Athens, GA, 1997), pp. 57–92. Wang includes the full texts of the five Enforcement Acts in appendices, pp. 267–93. See also Richard M. Valelly, *The Two Reconstructions: The Struggle for Black Enfranchisement* (Chicago, 2004), pp. 99–120; Everette Swinney, "Enforcing the Fifteenth Amendment, 1870–1877," *Journal of Southern History* 28 (May 1962): 202–18; Scott C. James and Brian L. Lawson, "The Political Economy of Voting Rights Enforcement in America's Gilded Age: Electoral College Competition, Partisan Commitment, and the Federal Election Law," *American Political Science Review* 93 (March 1999): 115–32.

9. Grant quoted in Benjamin F. Butler, *Butler's Book: Autobiography and Personal Reminiscences* (Boston, 1892), p. 900. For Davenport's biographical information, I have relied upon *Congressional Record*, Senate, 53rd Cong., 2nd Sess., pp. 1928–37, and U.S. Congress, Committee on the Expenditures in the Department of Justice, *Expenditures in the Department of Justice: The*

Secret Service Fund, Report No. 800, 44th Cong., 1st Sess., August 5, 1876, pp. 42–62.

10. John I. Davenport, *The Election and Naturalization Frauds in New York City, 1860–1870*, 2nd ed. (New York, 1894), p. 47; Burke, *Federal Regulation of Congressional Elections*, pp. 167–203. All of the many congressional investigations into Davenport's accounts and the administration of the Federal Election Law were highly colored by partisan motives (as when the Democrats won control of the house in 1878). But they include much detailed and revealing testimony about Davenport's careful strategies for creating and amending a federal voter registry, and his sophisticated methods of voter intimidation. See especially, U.S. Congress, Committee on the Expenditures in the Department of Justice, *Expenditures in the Department of Justice: The Secret Service Fund*, Report No. 800, 44th Cong., 1st Sess., August 5, 1876, pp. 135–55; U.S. Congress, House of Representatives, Committee on the Judiciary, *Investigation of John I. Davenport*, Misc. Doc. No. 23, 45th Cong, 3rd Sess., February 13, 1879, pp. 53–89; 240–386; U.S. Congress, Select Committee to Inquire into Alleged Frauds in the Late Elections, *Alleged Frauds in the Late Elections*, Report No. 916, 46th Cong., 3rd Sess., February 25, 1881, pp. 1–31; 609–777.

11. Nathan Glazer and Daniel Patrick Moynihan, *Beyond the Melting Pot: The Negroes, Puerto Ricans, Jews, Italians, and Irish of New York City* (Cambridge, MA, 1963), p. 228. On the enduring yet complex relations between Tammany and the "Swallowtail" Democrats, see David C. Hammack, *Power and Society: Greater New York at the Turn of the Century* (New York, 1982), pp. 109–39. On Kelly's inability to create effective discipline, particularly in state and national contests, see Mark Wahlgren Summers, *Rum, Romanism, & Rebellion: The Making of a President 1884* (Chapel Hill, 2000), pp. 149–55.

12. Croker quoted in "Mr. Richard Croker and Greater New York" (1894), reprinted in W. T. Stead, *Satan's Invisible World Displayed, or Despairing Democracy* (New York, 1897), pp. 268–69. See also Shefter, "The Emergence of the Political Machine, 14–44, and Martin Shefter, "The Electoral Foundations of the Political Machine: New York City, 1884–1897," in *American Electoral History: Quantitative Studies in Popular Voting Behavior*, Joel Silbey, et al., eds. (Princeton, 1978), pp. 263–98. There is no reliable biography of Croker—he surely deserves one, but it would be a very difficult book to write.

13. Richard Croker, "Tammany Hall and the Democracy," *North American Review* 154 (January 1892): 229.

14. For a fuller account of Sullivan's life and career, see Daniel Czitrom, "Underworlds and Underdogs: Big Tim Sullivan and Metropolitan Politics in New York, 1889–1913," *Journal of American History* 78 (September 1991): 536–58. See also Richard F. Welch, *King of the Bowery: Big Tim Sullivan,*

Tammany Hall, and New York City from the Gilded Age to the Progressive Era (Albany, 2008).

15. Sullivan quoted in *NY Herald*, May 19, 1907, Magazine section, pt. 1, p. 2.

16. "Big Tim" Sullivan quoted in "Big Tim Sullivan, the Rain Maker," *Current Literature* 47 (December 1909): 623–24; "Little Tim" Sullivan quoted in "Tammany as 'Little Tim' Sullivan Sees It," *NY World*, March 29, 1908, clipping in Edwin P. Kilroe Papers/Ephemera, Columbia University.

17. See Jacob Riis, *How the Other Half Lives: Studies Among the Tenements of New York* (New York, 1890).

18. For the best overview and analysis of this campaign to restrict suffrage, see Sven Beckert, "Democracy and Its Discontents: Contesting Suffrage Rights in Gilded Age New York," *Past & Present* 174 (February 2002): 116–57.

19. Henry W. Bellows, *Historical Sketch of the Union League Club of New York, Its Origin, Organization, and Work, 1863–1879* (New York, 1879), pp. 161–62.

20. E. L. Godkin, "Criminal Politics," *North American Review* 150 (June 1890): 706, 713, 714; "A Journalist Before a Police Court," *NY Sun*, April 17, 1890, p. 6 "(has more than once"); *NY Tribune*, April 20, 1890, p. 6 ("performed a valuable"). See also William M. Armstrong, ed., *The Gilded Age Letters of E. L. Godkin* (Albany, 1974), pp. 403–14; Rollo Ogden, ed., *Life and Letters of Edwin Lawrence Godkin* (NY, 1907), pp. 169–74.

21. William M. Ivins, *Machine Politics and Money in Elections in New York City* (NY, 1887), pp. 35, 38, 64. See also William M. Ivins, "Address on Electoral reform, in *Proceedings of the 29th Annual Meeting of the New York State Bar Association* (Albany, 1906), pp. 227–53; William M. Ivins obituary, *NY Times*, July 24, 1915, p. 15. For a similar structural analysis of machine politics by a Tammany critic, see Daniel Greenleaf Thompson, *Politics in A Democracy* (NY, 1893), pp. 63–130. For a pioneering examination of party finance at both the local and national levels, see C. K. Yearley, *The Money Machines: The Breakdown and Reform of Governmental and Party Finance in the North, 1860-1920* (Albany, 1970), especially pp. 97–134

22. "Byrnes Makes a Report," *NY Tribune*, May 25, 1892, p. 4 (Byrnes quotes). See also "Without Fear or Favor, *NY Times*, May 25, 1892, p. 9; "Byrnes Makes a Report," *NY World*, May 25, 1892, p. 10.

23. "What Will the 'Shake Up' Do?," *NY Times*, April 24, 1892, p. 4. For coverage of Byrnes's first moves, see for example, "The Big Police Shake Up," *NY World*, April 20, 1892, p. 1; "A Police Earthquake Here," *NY Sun*, April 20, 1892, p. 7; "A Cyclone Hit the Police," *NY Times*, April 20, 1892, p. 9.

24. "What Will Tammany Do," *NY World*, April 30, 1892, p. 1 ("You can get"); "The Same Old Story," *NY Sun*, April 26, 1892, p. 6 ("Even the members"); "Thirsty Souls Welcomed," *NY Sun*, May 23, 1892, p. 1 ("and one of those"). See also the following coverage: "Even Delmonico's Dry," *NY World*, April 19, 1892, p. 3 (semi-weekly edition); "It Was a Very Dry Sunday," *NY Sun*,

April 25, 1892, p. 2; "Not Very Dry After All," *NY Times*, April 25, 1892, p. 1; "Was Not a Thirsty Day," *NY World*, May 2, 1892, p. 1.

25. On James J. Martin's background and career: "Seven Appointments," *NY Tribune*, May 23, 1889, p. 1; "The Mayor's Labor Over," *NY Times*, May 23, 1889, p. 1; "Mr. Martin Will Resign," *NY Times*, January 1, 1895; Obituary, *NY Times*, May 18, 1918, p. 20; Hammack, *Power and Society,* pp. 162–65; James J. Martin, Testimony, *LC*, v.1, pp. 417–21.

26. Text of September 1891 resolution in "It Wasn't Byrnes's Fault," *NY Times*, May 5, 1892, p. 1; "Going to Enforce the Law," *NY Sun*, May 3, 1892, p. 2 (a great hindrance"); "A Crisis at Police Headquarters," *NY Tribune*, editorial, May 3, 1892, p. 6. See also "Police Called Off," *NY Tribune*, May 2, 1892, p. 1; "Mr. Byrnes Says Little," *NY Times*, May 3, 1892, p. 8; "Mr. Byrnes and 'Jimmy,'" *NY Times*, editorial, May 4, 1892, p. 4.

27. "Friend of Law-Breakers," *NY Tribune*, May 3, 1892, p. 1; "Tammany's Swift Revenge," *NY Tribune*, May 6, 1892, p. 1. See also "Martin Tries to 'Crawl,'" *NY Times*, May 4, 1892, p. 1; "Martin Smoothes It Over," *NY Tribune*, May 4, 1892, p. 1.

28. "Dr. Parkhurst's Plans," *NY Press*, September 24 1892 ("complete overthrow," clipping, NYDAS); Dr. Charles H. Parkhurst, "Our City Vigilance League," *North American Review* 156 (January 1893): 103 ("civic responsibility").

29. "New York for Cleveland," *NY World*, October 28, 1892, p. 10 (Croker); "New York City Vote," *NY World*, October 30, 1892, p. 1. On Cleveland's difficult relations with Tammany, see Summers, *Rum, Romanism, & Rebellion*, especially pp. 148–61. For useful overviews of the 1892 campaign, see H. Wayne Morgan, "Election of 1892," in Arthur M. Schlesinger, Jr. and Fred L. Israel, eds., *History of American Presidential Elections, 1789–1968, Vol. II* (New York, 1971), pp. 1703–84, and George Harmon Knoles, *The Presidential Campaign and Election of 1892* (Stanford University, 1942).

30. All of the many congressional investigations into Davenport's accounts and the administration of the federal election law were highly colored by partisan motives (as when the Democrats won control of the House in 1878). But they include much detailed and revealing testimony about Davenport's careful strategies for creating and amending a federal voter registry, and his sophisticated methods of voter intimidation. See especially, U.S. Congress, Committee on the Expenditures in the Department of Justice, *Expenditures in the Department of Justice: The Secret Service Fund*, Report No. 800, 44th Cong., 1st Sess., August 5, 1876, pp. 135–55; U.S. Congress, House of Representatives, Committee on the Judiciary, *Investigation of John I. Davenport*, Misc. Doc. No. 23, 45th Cong, 3rd Sess., February 13, 1879, pp. 53–89; 240–386; U.S. Congress, Select Committee to Inquire into Alleged Frauds in the Late Elections, *Alleged Frauds in the Late Elections*, Report No. 916, 46th Cong., 3rd Sess., February 25, 1881, pp. 1–31; 609–777.

31. On the politics, debates and defeat of the "force bill," see the still valuable treatment in Stanley Hirshson, *Farewell to the Bloody Shirt: Northern Republicans and the Southern Negro, 1877–1893* (Bloomington, IN, 1962), pp. 200–235, and on its role in the 1892 election, pp. 238–46. See also Burke, *Federal Regulation of Congressional Elections*, pp. 241–47; Wang, *Trial of Democracy*, pp. 234–51. On the evolution of the federal elections bill and the waning idealism of his party viz. protecting African-American suffrage, see George Frisbie Hoar, *Autobiography of Seventy Years* (New York, 1903), pp. 150–65.

32. Democratic and Republican 1892 party platforms in Schlesinger, ed., *History of American Presidential Elections, 1789–1968*, pp. 1733, 1739. Dana and *NY Sun* quotes in Janet E. Steele, *The Sun Shines for All: Journalism and Ideology in the Life of Charles A. Dana* (Syracuse, NY, 1993), p. 148.

33. "Tammany Colonization," *NY Tribune*, October 7, 1892, p. 5; "In Defense of Dave," *NY World*, October 7, p. 1 (Foley). For a revealing look at how both parties tried to mobilize "floaters," see " 'Floaters' To Vote" and "Found a Place Among the Army of Colonizers," both *NY Herald*, October 30, 1892, p. 29. See also, for example, "Gathering in Colonizers," *NY Sun*, October 30, 1892, p. 2; "Registration Arrests," *NY World*, October 30, 1892, p. 12.

34. A good recent summary of the Fitch investigation can be found in David F. Remington, *Ashbel P. Fitch: Champion of Old New York* (Syracuse, 2011), pp. 120–48. For contemporary coverage of the Fitch Committee during the election see for example, "Davenport's Roll of Bills," *NY World*, October 26, 1892, p. 8; "Humbug John Davenport," *NY Sun*, October 25, 1892, p. 8; "Davenport's Queer Ways," *NY Times*, October 26, 1892, p. 9. See also Burke, *Federal Regulation of Congressional Elections*, pp. 248–51.

35. Davenport letter and Tammany response quoted in "No Bulldozing This Year," *NY Times*, November 4, 1892, p. 1; "Davenport's Drag Net," *NY World*, November 4, 1892, p. 7 (Sheehy); see also "A Heavy Blow for Tammany," *NY Tribune*, November 4, 1892, p. 1.

36. "Big Torchlight Parade," *NY Times*, November 3, 1892, p. 8 (Warner); "Broken Heads and Prison Cells," *NY Times*, November 3, 1892, p. 5 (Carter). See also, "State Rights May Clash with Federal Power," *NY Herald*, November 4, 1892, p. 5; "W. F. Sheehan, Read This!," *NY Tribune*, November 4, 1892, p. 1; "Davenport's Drag Net," *NY World*, November 4, 1892, p. 7; "No Occasion for Conflict" (editorial), *NY Times*, November 5, 1892, p. 4.

37. Martin quoted in his testimony, LC Vol. I, p. 52; "The Duty of Superintendent Byrnes," *NY Tribune*, November 8, 1892. Final figures on federal presence at the NYC polls from Burke, *Federal Regulation of Congressional Elections*, Table 6a, p. 185. On Byrnes and the Columbus celebrations, see "No Police Clubbing," *NY Times*, October 7, 1892; "The Real New York," *NY Sun*, October 14, 1892, p. 6; "The Climax of the Week," *NY Times*, October 13, 1892, p. 9.

"Gardner Found Guilty," *NY Sun*, February 9, 1893, p. 1; "Goff and Jerome Accused," *NY Times*, February 15, 1893, p. 8; "Lawyer Goff Fined $200," *NY Times*, February 21, 1893, p. 9.

12. See "Watching the Saloons," *NY Press*, May 16, 1893 (clipping, NYDAS); "Parkhurst on Byrnes," *NY World*, May 25, 1893 (clipping, NYDAS); "War on Wicked Flats," *Morning Journal*, July 4, 1893 (clipping, NYDAS); "Some of Dr. Parkhurst's Methods," *NY World*, August 13, 1893 (clipping, NYDAS).

13. "It is a Devil's Seminary," *NY Times*, August 11, 1893, p. 9 ("His precinct"); "Devery's Reply to Parkhurst," *NY Times*, August 24, 1893, p. 8. For the SPC's letter to police officials and the catalogue of charges made against Devery, see correspondence from Charles H. Parkhurst, Thaddeus D. Kenneson, Frank Moss (for the SPC) to Mayor Thomas Gilroy, Superintendent Thomas Byrnes, and James J. Martin, president of the board of police commissioners, June 1893 and October 12, 1893, in 89-GTF-14 (Thomas F. Gilroy), Mayor's Papers, MARC. See also Charles H. Parkhurst, *Our Fight With Tammany* (New York, 1895), pp. 177–88, for background on the campaign targeting Devery.

14. Seth Low to Thomas F. Gilroy, February 6, 1894, "Police Census of the Unemployed," in 89-GTF-12 (Thomas F. Gilroy), Mayors' Papers, MARC; White, *The U.S. and the Problem of Recovery*, pp. 26–7. See also the brief but very good overview of the depression in the city in Edwin G. Burrows and Mike Wallace, *Gotham: A History of New York City to 1898* (New York, 1999), pp. 1185–90.

15. First two cases quoted in Josephine Shaw, "Five Months' Work for the Unemployed in New York City," *Charities Review* 3 (May 1894): 341, 339; third case described in *Semi-centennial Report of the New York Association for the Improvement of the Condition of the Poor* (1894), p. 62.

16. Charles D. Kellogg, "The Situation in New York City During the Winter of 1893–94," in Isabel C. Barrows, ed., *Proceedings of the National Conference of Charities and Correction, Twenty-First Annual Session* (Boston, 1894), pp. 21–30; Leah H. Feder, *Unemployment Relief in Periods of Depression* (New York, 1936), pp. 151–57; White, *U.S. and the Problem of Recovery*, pp. 26–29; Sullivan quoted in "Big Tim Sullivan, the Rain Maker," *Current Literature* 47 (December 1909): 625.

17. Lowell, "Five Months' Work for the Unemployed in New York City," p. 323, 337. See also Josephine Shaw Lowell, "The Unemployed in New York City, 1893–94," in Barrows, *Proceedings of the National Conference of Charities and Correction*, pp. 19–28; Joan Waugh, *Unsentimental Reformer: The Life of Josephine Shaw Lowell* (Cambridge, MA, 1997), pp. 202–209.

18. On Jewish immigration in this era, see Richard Wheatley, "The Jews in New York," *Century Magazine* 43 (January 1892): 323–42; Ira Rosenwaike, *Population History of New York City* (Syracuse, NY, 1972), pp. 87–89.

19. See "Wrecked Walhalla Hall," *NY Times*, August 18, 1893, p. 2; "Unemployed Fight the Police," *NY World*, August 18, 1893, p. 1. See also "Hebrew Riot," *Daily News*, August 17, 1893 (clipping, NYDAS); "Riot in Walhalla," *Commercial Advertiser*, August 17, 1893 (clipping, NYDAS); "Idle Workers Riot," *NY Tribune*, August 18, 1893 (clipping, NYDAS).

20. "Anarchy's Dingy Stronghold," *NY Times*, August 22, 1893, p. 1. See also "Anarchists Were to Blame," *NY Times*, August 19, 1893, p. 9. Jacobs's account of what Goldman had said, hotly contested during her trial, is from *The People vs. Emma Goldman*, abridged trial transcript, in Candace Falk, editor, *Emma Goldman: A Documentary History of the American Years, Vol. 1: Made For America, 1890–1901* (Berkeley, 2003), p. 162. See also the recent brilliant short biography by Vivian Gornick, *Emma Goldman: Revolution as a Way of Life* (New Haven, CT, 2011).

21. "Where Do Anarchists Riot," *NY Times*, August 24, 1893, p. 1; "Cleared in a Jiffy," *Commercial Advertiser*, August 25, 1893 (Williams, clipping, NYDAS); "Disorder to End," *NY World*, August 25, 1893, p. 1 (Gilroy, Gompers). On Gompers and the controversy surrounding calls for city sponsored public works, see Stuart B. Kaufman and Peter J. Albert, eds., *The Samuel Gompers Papers* (Urbana, IL, 1989), vol. 3, pp. 363–85. I have also used the following clippings found in NYDAS: "Reds Locked Out," *NY Daily News*, August 22, 1893; "Clubs Used on East Side Malcontents," *NY Telegram*, August 22, 1893; "No Halls for Reds," *NY World*, August 23, 1893; "Police Clubs on Anarchist Heads, *NY Herald*, August 24, 1893; "Driven Out by the Police," *NY Sun*, August 24, 1893; "Police Prod Anarchists," *NY World*, August 24, 1893; "Italians Fled for Their Lives," *NY Herald*, August 25, 1893; "Violence Along the Piers," *NY Press*, August 24, 1893.

22. "Cleared in a Jiffy," *Commercial Advertiser*, August 25, 1893 (clipping, NYDAS). See also "Devery's Reply to Parkhurst," *NY Times*, August 24, 1893, p. 8; "Dr. Parkhurst's Charges Unrefuted," *NY Tribune*, August 24, 1893 (clipping, NYDAS)

23. "Byrnes Will Shut Anarchy's Mouth," *NY Herald*, August 25, 1893 ("this business"); "Detective Most," *Morning Journal*, September 3, 1893 ("You can say"); Thomas Byrnes, "The Menace of 'Coxeyism,'" *North American Review* 158 (June 1894): 700; "Byrnes Is Back," *NY Recorder*, August 25, 1893. See also Thomas Byrnes, "How to Protect a City from Crime," *North American Review* 159 (July 1894): 100–107. Both of the *North American Review* articles were likely ghostwritten under Byrnes's name.

24. "Emma Goldman on Trial," *NY Sun*, October 5, 1893 ("are thick," clipping, NYDAS); "A Blow to Anarchy," *Morning Advertiser*, October 10, 1893 ("they acted," McIntyre, clipping, NYDAS); "Emma Denies It," *Daily News*, October 10, 1893 (Byrnes, clipping, NYDAS). For coverage of Goldman's trial, I have relied upon the following clippings in NYDAS:: "The Trial of

Emma Goldman," *NY Tribune*, October 5, 1893; "Queen Emma's Trial," *Morning Advertiser*, October 5, 1893; "Hall is Aggressive," *NY Recorder*, October 9, 1893; "Her Words Quoted," *NY Recorder*, October 10, 1893; "Emma Goldman Convicted," *NY Sun*, October 10, 1893; "One Year for Emma Goldman," *NY Times*, October 17, 1893; "To Be Imprisoned One Year," *NY Tribune*, October 17, 1893. For Goldman's own account of the Union Square rally, her arrest, and trial, including her claim that Byrnes offered to set her free and pay her if she agreed to spy on New York radicals, see Emma Goldman, *Living My Life* (New York, 1931), vol. 1, pp. 121–32.

25. "Girds on His Sword," *Morning Journal*, September 21, 1893 ("Our society," clipping, NYDAS); "Return of Dr. Parkhurst," *NY Tribune*, September 21, 1893 ("is an organization," clipping, NYDAS).

26. "Charles H. Parkhurst, Thaddeus D. Kenneson, Frank Moss (SPC Executive Committee) to Mayor Thomas F. Gilroy, October 12, 1893, in Mayor's Papers, 89-GTF-14, MARC ("in a manner"); "Police Reply To Parkhurst," *NY Times*, October 21, 1893, p. 5 (Williams); "Blow at Parkhurst," *NY World*, October 21, 1893 (Sheehan, clipping, NYDAS,). For further coverage, see these clippings in NYDAS: "Captain Devery Called Down by Dr. Parkhurst," *NY Tribune*, October 13, 1893; "Sheehan's Say on Parkhurst," *NY Herald*, October 21, 1893; "Police Reply to Parkhurst," *NY Times*, October 21, 1893; "Dr. Parkhurst and the Police Board," *NY Tribune*, October 22, 1893. See also Parkhurst, *Our Fight With Tammany*, pp. 189–201.

27. "Parkhurst's Bomb," *Morning Journal*, October 26, 1893 (Lemmon, clipping, NYDAS); "Against Parkhurst Agents," *NY Times*, November 4, 1893, p. 8 (Williams). See also these clippings in NYDAS: "Parkhurst's Men Stoned," *NY Herald*, October 28, 1893; "Mobbed by Thugs," *NY World*, October 28, 1893; "Byrnes on Deck," *NY World*, October 29, 1893; "Byrnes's Side of It," *NY World*, November 4, 1893. For Byrnes' official report, including sworn affidavits, see Thomas Byrnes to Board of Police, November 3, 1893, in Mayors' Papers, 89-GTF-14, MARC.

28. Stanton Coit, "Vice in Capt. Devery's Precinct" (letter), *NY Times*, October 31, 1893, p. 12. For background on Coit, see Mina Carson, *Settlement Folk: Social Thought and the American Settlement Movement, 1885–1930* (Chicago, 1990), pp. 33–37, and Domenica M. Barbuto, *American Settlement Houses and Progressive Social Reform: An Encyclopedia of the American Settlement Movement* (Phoenix, 1999).

29. "Parkhurst's Bomb," *Morning Advertiser*, November 30, 1893 (Parkhurst, clipping, NYDAS); "His Wrath Aroused," *NY Tribune*, December 3, 1893 (Williams, clipping, NYDAS). See also these clippings in NYDAS:"Five Women Fined," *NY World*, November 13, 1893; "Gardner to Be Released," *NY Sun*, November 18, 1893; "Gardner Guiltless," *Morning Advertiser*,

November 18, 1893; "Police Captain Devery Indicted," *NY Herald*, November 30, 1893; "Now Devery Is on the Rack," *NY Times*, November 30, 1893.

30. "He Rules Through Fear," *NY Times*, December 10, 1893, p. 13 ("master work"); "Devery Gives Bail," *NY World*, December 1, 1863 (McClave, clipping, NYDAS); "Williams Doesn't Fear Parkhurst," *NY Herald*, December 1, 1893 (Byrnes, NYDAS).

31. "Women the Victims," *Commercial Advertiser*, December 7, 1893 ("It is a pretty late day," clipping, NYDAS); "In the Police Net," *Commercial Advertiser*, December 8(?), 1893 ("wretched pawns," Mosconus, clipping, NYDAS); "Obeyed Parkhurst," NY Recorder, December 5, 1893 ("The police,"clipping, NYDAS). See also "Capt. Schmittberger Busy," *NY Times*, December 10, 1893, p. 8

32. "Women the Victims," *Commercial Advertiser*, December 7, 1893 ("these poor women," clipping, NYDAS); "Let Them Starve Or Freeze," *NY Times*, December 19, 1893, p. 1 ("I do not care"); "Dr. Parkhurst's Utterance," *NY Times*, December 9, 1893, p. 8 ("misrepresentation"); "Decry the Cruelty of It," *NY Times*, December 9, 1893, p. 8 (Gage, Blake).

33. "Editorial," *NY Times*, December 9, 1893, p. 4. On death threats against Parkhurst, see for example "Has No Sin Money," *NY Recorder*, December 9, 1893 (clipping, NYDAS); "To Slay Parkhurst," *NY World*, December 10, 1893 (clipping, NYDAS). For a summary of the continuing "war on captains," see Parkhurst, *Our Fight With Tammany*, pp. 216–30.

34. "'Organically Rotten,'" *NY Times*, December 19, 1893, p. 3 (Parkhurst quotes). See also, "Will Give Them Aid," *NY World*, December 10, 1893 (clipping, NYDAS).

35. "Has No Sin Money," *NY Recorder*, December 9, 1893 ("We have the German," clipping, NYDAS); "A Non-Partisan Police Board," *NY Tribune*, December 12, 1893 ("thus compelling," clipping, NYDAS). See also "Parkhurst's Plan," *Morning Journal*, December 12(?), 1893 (clipping, NYDAS); "Byrnes Least to Blame," *Mail and Express*, December 14, 1893 (clipping, NYDAS). For coverage of alleged vote fraud that fall, see for example, "Wholesale Fraud at the Polls," *NY Herald*, October 22, 1893 (clipping, NYDAS) and "Freedom Stifled! Ballot's Foe Alert," *NY Press*, November 5, 1893 (clipping, NYDAS).

36 Alexander Williams to Thomas Byrnes, December 29, 1893, 89-GTF-14, Mayors' Papers, MARC. See also, "Williams Was Not Indicted," *NY Times*, December 30, 1893, p. 9.

37. "Nicoll Answers Parkhurst," *NY Times*, January 6, 1894, p. 8 (Nicoll). "Dr. Parkhurst's Side of It," *NY Times*, January 5, 1894, p. 1 ("caricature of justice").

38. "Parkhurst in Mind," *NY World*, January 23, 1894 (Gilroy, clipping, NYDAS). See also Nicoll's interview, "Did Not Instruct," *NY Recorder*, January 7, 1893 (clipping, NYDAS).

5: A ROCKY START

1. "Dr. Parkhurst Undaunted," *NY Tribune*, January 1, 1894, p. 8.

2. "Parkhurst to the Senators," *NY Times*, February 3, 1894, p. 1 (Parkhurst, Lexow quotes); "Begin with Commissioners," *NY Times*, February 4, 1894, p. 2 ("was that"). For other accounts of this first meeting, see also "Parkhurst Wants Secret Sessions," *NY Herald*, February 3, 1894, p. 3; "Witnesses Are HY," *NY Recorder*, February 3, 1894 (clipping, NYDAS). There is no published biography of Clarence Lexow. For his background, see John Dalmas, "Biography of Clarence Lexow," unpublished mss., in Clarence Lexow Papers, envelope 7, Rockland County Historical Society, New City, NY. Hereafter cited as Lexow Papers.

3. "Nellie Bly and Thomas C. Platt," *NY World*, December 9, 1894, in Scrapbook 1, Thomas C. Platt Papers, Beinecke Library, Yale University. On Platt's early life and career, see Harold F. Gosnell, *Boss Platt and His New York Machine* (Chicago, 1924), pp. 12–33. Platt's own autobiography is highly selective and should be used with care. See Louis J. Lang, compiler and editor, *The Autobiography of Thomas Collier Platt* (New York, 1910). See also Richard McCormick, "Prelude to Progressivism: The Transformation of New York State Politics, 1890–1910," in *The Party Period and Public Policy: American Politics From the Age of Jackson to the Progressive Era* (New York, 1986), pp. 289–310.

4. Thomas C. Platt to Clarence Lexow, March 2, 1894, ("constant delays") Box: Savell/Lexow Papers, envelope 2, "Tammany Investigation," Lexow Papers; "The Close of a Chapter," *NY Times*, February 9, 1894, p. 4. "the close"); Clarence Lexow, undated 1894 handwritten speech supporting the bipartisan police bill ("We are not willing"), Correspondence, 1894, Lexow Papers; "A neutral in politics," George William Curtis, quoted in Mark Wahlgren Summers, *Rum, Romanism, & Rebellion: The Making of a President 1884* (Chapel Hill, NC, 2000), p. 199. Summers has an excellent discussion of the Mugwumps and the harsh language used to describe them. For background on the repeal of the Federal Elections Law, and an evaluation of the law's significance, see Albie Burke, "Federal Regulation of Congressional Elections in Northern Cities, 1871–1894," PhD diss., University of Chicago, 1968, pp. 248–71; Xi Wang, *The Trial of Democracy: Black Suffrage and Northern Republicans, 1860–1910* (Athens, GA, 1997), pp. 254–66.

5. "Investigators Join Hands," *NY Times*, February 10, 1894, p. 1 ("the testimony"). Platt's pressure on Lexow is clearly evident in their correspondence. See for example, Thomas Platt to Clarence Lexow, February 18, March 2 1894, Box: Savell/Lexow Papers Box, envelope 2, Tammany Investigation, envelope 5, "Thomas C. Platt," Lexow Papers.

6. "Parkhurst Against Plattism," *NY Times*, February 18, 1894, p. 5.

7. New York (State) Legislature, Assembly Docs, 1876, vol. 6, no. 106, February 17, 1876, *Report of the Select Committee Appointed by the Assembly of 1875 to Investigate the Causes of the Increase of Crime in the City of New York*, pp. 5, 7, 34. For a useful contemporary summary of the committee's findings, see "Crime in This City," *NY Times*, February 18, 1876, p. 5. see also James F. Richardson, *The New York Police: Colonial Times to 1901* (New York, 1970), pp. 216–20. On 1884, see New York (State) Legislature, Special Committee Appointed to Investigate the Local Government of the City and County of New York, *Hearings,* 2 vols. (Albany, NY, 1884); Edmund Morris, *The Rise of Theodore Roosevelt* (New York, 1979), pp. 232–50. For a primary source on the incident with the upstate assemblyman, see "A Citizen" to Clarence Lexow, February 7, 1894: The writer, possibly a member of the SPC, described the incident this way: "An indiscretion of a country member of the Roosevelt investigation committee of 1884 put an end to their work. The police knew that they were to investigate that department, and Police Captain McDonald [McDonnel] 'laid' for this country member and caught him in a disorderly house." Correspondence, Clarence Lexow Papers, Rockland County Historical Society. James Lardner and Thomas Reppetto, *NYPD: A City and Its Police* (New York, 2000), p. 92, repeat the story about the upstate assemblyman's scandal, but offer no source.

8. *Testimony Taken Before the Senate Committee on Cities,* Pursuant to Resolution Adopted January 20, 1890, 5 vols. (Albany, NY, 1891), especially vol. 1, pp. 4–75 (Hugh J. Grant), and vol. 2, pp. 1690–1771 (Richard Croker). See also "Fassett's Report at Last," *NY Times*, April 16, 1891, p. 9; "The Report on City Government," *NY Times*, April 16, 1891, p. 4; "The New Collector Talks," *NY Times*, July 31, 1891, p. 8.

9. "Investigation," *NY Sun*, February 22, 1894, p. 6 ("these bucolic statesmen"); "Judge Barrett and Mr. Wellman," *NY Press*, March 11, 1894 (Wellman, clipping, NYDAS). For coverage of the election fraud cases, see "Votes Counted All One Way," *NY Times*, February 28, 1894, p. 6; "Dooley Also Convicted," *NY Sun*, February 28, 1894 (clipping, NYDAS); "No Pulls to Save Them," *NY World*, March 3, 1894 (clipping, NYDAS). For a complete list of the indictments and disposition of cases, see "How New York Has Dealt with Its Election Offenders," *NY World*, March 6, 1894 (clipping, NYDAS).

10. On the infighting over choice of counsel, see Thomas Platt to Clarence Lexow, February 16 (?) and 18, 1894, Savelle/Lexow Papers Box, envelope 5, "Thomas C. Platt"; Chamber of Commerce to Clarence Lexow, January 31, 1894, February 7, 1894; Charles H. Parkhurst to Clarence Lexow, February 12, 1894; Charles S. Smith et al. to Clarence Lexow, February 12 and March 12, 1894, all in Clarence Lexow Correspondence, 1894, Lexow Papers. This collection also contains numerous unsolicited appeals to Lexow from

attorneys and others, recommending names for the job of committee counsel. See also, "Mr. Goff Stands at Bay," *NY Times*, March 13, 1894, p. 1; Rev. Charles H. Parkhurst, *Our Fight With Tammany* (New York, 1895), pp. 244–50.

11. "Investigation in a Tangle," *NY Times*, March 9, 1894 (Lexow); "Mr. Goff Stands at Bay," *NY Times*, March 13, 1894, p. 1. On Goff's Irish nationalism, see Peter F. Stevens, *The Voyage of the Catalpa: A Perilous Journey and Six Irish Rebels' Flight To Freedom* (New York, 2002); "Goff's Part in the Rescue," *NY Times*, November 2, 1890, p. 9.

12. "Investigation in a Tangle," *NY Times*, March 9, 1894, p. 1 (Parkhurst).

13. "Supt. Byrnes's Sharp Retort," *NY Times*, March 7, 1894, p. 9 (Byrnes quotes). See also, "Policemen at Bar," *NY World*, January 15, 1894 (clipping, NYDAS); "Vile Dens Were Raided," *Morning Advertiser*, January 22, 1894 (clipping, NYDAS); "M'Gurk Held for Trial," *NY Tribune*, January 22, 1894 (clipping, NYDAS); "Byrnes Will Lay Bare the Abuses," *NY Herald*, February 1, 1894 (clipping, NYDAS); "Give Byrnes More Power," *NY World*, February 22, 1894 (clipping, NYDAS)

14. Bennett quoted in Thomas C. Leonard, *The Power of the Press: The Birth of American Political Reporting* (New York, 1986), p. 151. See also James L. Crouthamel, *Bennett's New York Herald and the Rise of the Popular Press* (Syracuse, 1989), pp. 19–43; James Stanford Bradshaw, "George W. Wisner and the New York Sun," *Journalism History* 6 (Winter 1979–80): 112, 117–20. For broader overviews of the rise of the penny press, see Michael Schudson, *Discovering the News: A Social History of American Newspapers* (New York, 1978), pp. 12–60; James W. Carey, "The Dark Continent of American Journalism," in *Reading the News*, Robert Karl Manoff and Michael Schudson, eds. (New York, 1986), pp. 146–96; Dan Schiller, *Objectivity and the News* (Philadelphia, 1981), pp. 12–75; Frank Luther Mott, *American Journalism: A History 1690–1960* (New York, 1962), pp. 418–48. (Although old, Mott remains an invaluable source on New York journalism history.) For a lively, detailed, and useful contemporary overview of the city's press in the early 1890s, see Moses King, ed., *King's Handbook of New York City*, 2nd ed. (Boston, 1893), "Journalism and Publishing," pp. 609–38.

15. Pulitzer quoted in George Juergens, *Joseph Pulitzer and the New York World* (Princeton, NJ, 1966), p. 73; "To Oust Byrnes," *NY World*, December 19, 1893, p. 1 ("As The World"). Juergens's book remains the best account of Pulitzer's journalistic innovations in the early years. For a recent full biography, see James McGrath Morris, *Pulitzer: A Life in Politics, Print, and Power* (New York, 2010).

16. *Tammany Biographies: The New York Evening Post*, 3rd rev. ed. (New York, 1894), p. 3; J. Lincoln Steffens to Joseph Steffens, November 3, 1893, in *The Letters of Lincoln Steffens, Vol. I, 1889–1919*, Ella Winter and Granville Hicks,

eds. (New York, 1938), p. 98. See also unpublished letters from Steffens to his father in Lincoln Steffens Papers, Columbia University, Original Outgoing Letters, 1866–1936 (microfilm), especially October 22 and November 19, 1893.

17. Sutherland quoted in *Report and Proceedings of the Senate Committee Appointed to Investigate the Police Department of the City of New York, 5 vols.* (NY, 1895), Vol. 1, p. 80. Hereafter cited as LC

18. Harry Cunningham testimony, LC, vol. 1, p. 192; Jacob Subin testimony, LC, vol. 1, p. 305. Otto Kempner testimony, LC, vol. 1, pp. 180ff; Robert Strahl testimony, LC, vol. 1, pp. 237ff; Ralph Nathan testimony, pp. 289ff.

19. "Senator Lexow's Mill at Work," *NY Herald*, March 31, 1894, p. 3 ("The Spectacular"); "Merrily the Play Proceeds," *NY Times*, March 11, 1894, p. 2 ("Merrily the Play"); "Where Fraud Flourished," *NY Tribune*, March 25, 1894 ("the court jester," clipping, NYDAS). See also "Parkhurst Did Not Stay Long," *NY Herald*, March 17, p. 3; "Will Be Aided by Mr. Goff," *NY Times*, March 18, 1894, p. 9.

20. "The Boss Will Have His Way," *NY Times*, March 16, 1894, p. 1 (Smith, Parkhurst, Lauterbach). See also "Bi-Partisan Police Bill," *NY Sun*, March 16, 1894, p. 2. For background on anti-Semitism in the Union League Club and among the social elite, see "Mr. Seligman Blackballed," *NY Times*, April 15, 1893, p. 1, and Edwin G. Burrows and Mike Wallace, *Gotham: A History of New York City to 1898* (New York, 1999), pp. 1087–88.

21. "Without One Word of Platt," *NY Times*, March 29, 1894, p. 5 (Choate). See also "Union League Attacks Platt," *NY Herald*, March 29, 1894, p. 5; "Rally of the Regulars," *NY Sun*, March 29, 1894, p. 1; "The Thirty at Cooper Union," *NY Times*, editorial, March 31, 1894, p. 4.

22. "Mr. Martin on the Rack," *NY Times*, April 1, 1894, p. 9 ("The Senators"); James J. Martin testimony, LC, vol. 1, pp. 534–35 (Lexow); 563 (Nicoll).

23. "A Significant Confession," editorial, *NY Herald*, April 8, 1894, p. 8 ("long been"); "Purpose of the Investigation," *NY Times*, April 16, p. 4 ("the department"); "A Question of Politics," *NY Tribune*, April 7, p. 1 ("picking up"). For further coverage of Martin's testimony see also: "Mr. Martin's Interference," *NY Times*, April 7, 1894, p. 1; "Mr. Martin and His Duty," *NY Times*, April 8, 1894, p. 9; "Martin Testifies to Queer Things," *NY Herald*, April 1, 1894, III, p. 5; "Sat in the Torture Chair," *NY Herald*, April 7, 1894, 4; "James J. Martin A Witness," *NY Tribune*, April 1, 1894, p. 1.

24. "Captain Devery's Accusers," *NY Times*, April 6, 1894, p. 9 ("bringing out"); "Devery's Suspense," *NY World*, April 9, 1894, p. 1; "Devery Not Guilty," *NY Recorder*, April 10, 1894 ("lower in the grade," clipping, NYDAS); "Dr. Parkhurst Testifies," *NY Sun*, April 6, 1894 ("directed against," clipping, NYDAS); "Devery Not Guilty, So the Jury Says," NY Press, April 10, 1894 ("vagabond detectives," clipping, NYDAS); "Parkhurst a Witness," *NY World*, April 6, 1894; "Devery Not Guilty, So the Jury Says," *NY Press*,

April 10, 1894; "Capt. Devery Acquitted," *NY Sun*, April 10, 1894, p. 1 ("A great cheer") "As Aggressive as Ever" (Williams), *NY Tribune*, April 11, 1894, p. 1 ("No jury in the land"). See also, "Police Captain Devery Acquitted," *NY Times*, April 10, 1894, p. 1; "Charles W. Gardner Drunk Again," *NY Tribune*, March 26, 1894 (clipping, NYDAS); "Parkhurst Sunbeam No. 2," *NY Sun*, April 7, 1894 (clipping, NYDAS).

25. "He Expected an Acquittal," *NY World*, April 10, 1894, p. 1 ("I am not"); Dr. Parkhurst Full of Fight," *NY Herald*, April 11, 1894, p. 6 ("Are we the sons and daughters"); "Bang! Goes Dr. Parkhurst," *NY Sun*, April 11, 1894, p. 1 ("I claim") Parkhurst, *Our Fight With Tammany*, p. 217 ("was a boon"). For further coverage of his Harlem speech, including a wide range of reactions to it, see also "As Aggressive as Ever," *NY Tribune*, April 11, 1894, p. 1; "Parkhurst on Devery," *NY World*, April 11, 1894, p. 2; "Parkhurst Fumes," *Morning Journal*, April 11, 1894 (clipping, NYDAS).

26. "Sutherland Steps Down and Out," *NY Herald*, April 15, 1894, p. 6 ("I received nothing"); "The Municipal Investigation," editorial, *NY Tribune*, April 15, p. 6 ("to dignify"). See also "Adjourned Sine Die," *NY World*, April 14, p. 1; "Committee to Take a Rest," *NY Times*, April 15, p. 1. For the transcript of the final two brief public sessions, see LC, vol. 1, pp. 579–91.

6: MANAGING VICE, EXTORTING BUSINESS

1. "A Crowd to Hear Dr. Parkhurst," *NY Tribune*, January 31, 1894, p. 3 ("We want"); "The People Making Ready to Strike," *NY Tribune*, May 11, 1894, p. 2 ("we shall pull ourselves"); "Tammany Sins Recounted," *NY Tribune*, May 4, 1894, p. 7 ("There is no"; Saxton; Peckham).

2. "Dinner to Dr. Parkhurst," *NY Sun*, May 1, 1894, p. 5 ("We are trodden"); "Dinner to Dr. Parkhurst," *NY Times*, May 1, 1894, p. 2 ("broad enough"); "Is Not for Woman Suffrage," *NY Times*, April 21, 1894, p. 3 ("to exert an influence"); "Women Score Parkhurst," *NY Sun*, May 15, 1894, p. 2 (Blake). For more on Parkhurst's opposition to woman suffrage and defense of separate spheres, see "Clergymen of Woman Suffrage," *NY Times*, May 14, 1894, p. 5.

3. The full text of Flower's veto message can be found in "Stops Police Investigation," *NY Times*, May 19, 1894, p. 8.

4. "Legislators Insulted," *NY Tribune*, May 20, 1894, p. 3; "Smith To Raise That $25,000," NY Herald, May 20, 1894, I, p. 5. The "List of Subscribers to the Lexow Investigating Committee" can be found in "Investigation of the Police Department," Box 21, New York Chamber of Commerce Archives, Columbia University Rare Book and Manuscript Library. These materials also include an 1894 bank book, "Charles S. Smith Treasurer of Fund for

Police Investigation"; Alexander E. Orr's 1894 circular letter to members requesting contributions; Orr's October 15, 1895, circular letter accompanying checks for reimbursement; and John W. Goff's invoices for payment, endorsed by Clarence Lexow. I am grateful to Karl Kusserow for his help in locating these materials.

5. "Police Bill Vetoed," *NY Herald*, May 21, 1894, p. 3 (Flower); "Gov. Flower Kills Them," *NY Sun*, May 21, 1894, p. 2 (Parkhurst); "Lexow Police Bill Vetoed," *NY Tribune*, May 21, 1894, p. 1 (Lexow); *NY Tribune*, editorial, "Police Board Reorganization," May 22, 1894, p. 6 ("Tammany systematically"). The *Herald* has the most comprehensive summary of the bipartisan bill's tangled legislative history.

6. For a good profile of Murray, see "Commissioner C. H. Murray," *NY Sun*, May 22, 1894, p. 7. See also "Bi-Partisan Again," *NY Times*, editorial, May 22, 1894, p. 4; "Police Board Reorganization," editorial, *NY Tribune*, May 22, 1894, p. 6. On the 1890 census controversy, see "The Census Figures Stand," *NY Times*, November 7, 1890, p. 8, and "A Striking Contrast," editorial, *NY Times*, March 9, 1891, p. 4.

7. "The Record of the Police Investigation," *NY World*, July 2, 1894, p. 9.

8. John Goff quoted in "The Lexow Committee," in *The Triumph of Reform: A History of the Great Political Revolution, November Sixth, Eighteen Hundred and Ninety Four* (New York, 1895), p. 124; LC Vol. I, p. 614 (Goff); LC Vol. I, p. 656 (McClave).

9. "'That Is a Lie,' Cried McClave," *NY Herald*, May 22, 1894, p. 5 ("the liveliest"); "McClave and Bribery," *NY World*, May 22, 1894, p. 1 ("dramatic"); "The Investigation," *NY Tribune*, editorial, May 23, 1894, p. 6 ("so abrupt"); Goff, "The Lexow Committee," p. 124 ("While there was"). See also the excellent coverage in the *NY Times*, especially, "Charges Against McClave," May 22, 1894, p. 1; "Granger Failed to Appear," May 23, 1894, p. 1; "Mr. M'Clave's Bank Books," May 24, 1894, p. 1; "Mr. McClave's Ordeal Over," May 25, 1894, p. 1. Gideon Granger finally reappeared for cross-examination on June 5. Unwilling to deny that he had forged over a dozen checks, he lost his credibility as a witness. But the damage to John McClave could not be undone.

10. "Priem's Charges Denied," *NY Herald*, June 3, 1894, II, p. 5 ("The Senate committee"). For details on how Goff and his office worked, see "Mr. Goff's Ammunition," *NY Herald*, June 12, 1893, p. 3; "Goff's Rack for Police," *NY Sun*, June 17, 1894, p. 3.

11. "The Finest Marched Well," *NY World*, June 1, 1894, p. 9 ("It is a good idea"; "Someone"); "Bluecoats on Parade," *NY Tribune*, June 1, 1894, p. 4 ("New Yorkers"). See also, "Policemen on Exhibition," *NY Herald*, June 1, 1894, p. 5; "Fresh Laurels for Police," *NY Times*, June 1, 1894, p. 9; "Parade of the Finest," *NY Sun*, June 1, 1894, p. 9.

12. Katie Schubert testimony, LC, vol. 1, p. 1124; Lena Cohen testimony, LC, vol. 2, pp. 1248, 1251–52; "The Police and Crime," *NY Times*, editorial, June 8, 1894, p. 4 ("she could procure"). See also Testimony of Charles Priem, LC, vol. 1, pp. 953ff and Rhoda Sanford, LC, vol. 1, pp. 1011ff.

13. Augusta Thurow testimony, LC, vol. 1, pp. 1044, 1113, 1051; "Blackmail to Captains," *NY World*, June 5, 1894, p. 1 ("was astonishing"). See also "Protection Was in Vain," *NY Herald*, June 5, 1894, p. 3; "Four Captains Under Fire," *NY Times*, June 5, 1894, p. 1. I have benefitted from the pioneering analysis of Luise White, who has urged historians to pay less attention to reform rhetoric and categories and more to the actual work done by prostitutes in the expanding wage labor economy of the late nineteenth century. See Luise White, "Prostitutes, Reformers, and Historians," *Criminal Justice History: An International Annual* 6 (1985), pp. 201–27. For a good discussion of the unstable world of women boarding house keepers of this era in New York, including Augusta Thurow, see Rachel Amelia Bernstein, "Boarding House Keepers and Brothel Keepers in New York City, 1880–1910," PhD diss., Rutgers University, 1984, especially pp. 119–60. See also Timothy Gilfoyle, *City of Eros: New York City, Prostitution, and the Commercialization of Sex, 1790–1920* (New York, 1992), pp. 251–59.

14. "The Tithes of Vice," *NY Sun*, editorial, June 6, 1894, p. 6 ("reveals a condition"); "Blackmail and the Police," *NY Times*, editorial, June 14, 1894, p. 4 ("to establish"); Goff, "The Lexow Committee," p. 125 ("when the keepers").

15. Parkhurst quotes from "Four Captains Under Fire," *NY Times*, June 5, 1894, p. 1 ("an absolute"); "Dr. Parkhurst Pleased," *NY Herald*, June 6, 1894, p. 2 ("that woman Thurow") ; "Dr. Parkhurst Sails Away Happy," *NY World*, June 6, 1894, p. 7 ("merely the expression").

16. "Flatly Deny the Charges" (Byrnes), *NY Times*, June 3, 1894, p. 9; "They All Make Denials," (Cross), *NY Herald*, June 5, 1894, p. 4.

17. Joseph Pospisil testimony, LC, vol. 2, pp. 1679–702; Joseph Vopelak testimony, LC, vol. 2, pp. 1702–14; Antone Sykora testimony, LC, vol. 2, pp. 1743–62. See also "Bribery for the Pantata," *NY Sun*, June 16, 1894, p. 1; "Bought Protection in Bulk," *NY Times*, June 16, 1894, p. 1; "Money For 'The Pantata,'" *NY Herald*, June 16, 1894, p. 3.

18. "Green Goods Men Now," *NY World*, June 15, 1894, p. 1; "Green Goods Paid Tribute," *NY Herald*, June 15, 1894, p. 3; George Appo testimony, LC vol. 2, pp. 1645, 1634–35; Frank Clarke testimony, LC vol. 2, p. 1810. See also Thomas Byrnes, *Professional Criminals of America* (New York, 1886), especially pp. 40–43, 47–49.

For a full biography of George Appo, see Timothy J. Gilfoyle, *A Pickpocket's Tale: The Underworld of Nineteenth Century New York* (New York, 2006). Gilfoyle's book traces Appo's life and career to give us the most deeply researched and thoughtful social history we have of the city's underworld. It is a brilliant book from which I have learned a great deal. Gilfoyle is especially insightful on Appo's post-Lexow theatrical career, pp. 260–70. See also, Timothy J. Gilfoyle, "Staging the Criminal: In the Tenderloin, Freak Drama, and the Criminal Celebrity," *Prospects: An Annual of American Cultural Studies* 30 (2005): 285–307.

19. "A New Light on Green Goods," *NY Herald*, editorial, June 15, 1894, p. 8 "No one"); "Worse and Worse," editorial, *NY Times*, June 15, 1894, p. 4 ("the most startling"); "Green Goods Secrets," *NY Sun*, June 15, 1894, p. 1 ("a story"); "Green Goods Men Now," *NY World*, June 15, 1894, p. 1 ("is shared by").

20. For biographical material on Hill's life—scanty and sometimes contradictory— see Harry Hill testimony, LC, vol. 2, pp. 1926–50; "Harry Hill's Experiences," interview, *NY Times*, July 17, 1895, p. 8; and obituaries, "Harry Hill Is Dead," *NY Times*, August 28, 1896, p. 1; *NY Herald*, August 28, 1896, p. 1.

21. On Hill's involvement with the 1857 police riot, see Hill testimony, LC, vol. 2, p. 1929. On Hill's relations with the Pinkertons and Matsell, see George H. Bangs, *New York Office Daily Journal*, December 8, 1865, reel 2, container 3, Papers of the Pinkerton National Detective Agency, 1861–1883, Library of Congress (Microfilm). A few years later Allan Pinkerton himself privately campaigned to be appointed as superintendent of the Metropolitan Police. See George H. Bangs to Allan Pinkerton, February 2, February 14, February 28, 1869, all in Letter Book February 2, 1869–January 5, 1870, reel 2, container 4. For good accounts of the Heenan-Sayers fight and its impact, see Elliott J. Gorn, *The Manly Art: Bare Knuckle Prize Fighting in America* (Ithaca, NY, 1986), pp. 148–59 and Melvin Adelman, *A Sporting Time: New York City and the Rise of Modern Athletics, 1820–1870* (Urbana, IL, 1986), pp. 233–40. On Harry Hill as the preeminent matchmaker of his day, see Michael T. Isenberg, *John L. Sullivan and His America* (Urbana, IL, 1988), pp. 3–5.

22. Rev. Matthew Hale Smith, *Sunshine and Shadow in New York* (Hartford, CT, 1868), pp. 436, 439; Edward W. Martin [James D. McCabe], *The Secrets of the Great City* (Philadelphia, 1868), p. 419 ("visits from curiosity"); Edward Crapsey, *The Nether Side of New York* (New York, 1872), pp. 161–62; Directions found in *New York Supreme Court, City and County of New York, the Mayor, Aldermen, etc. Plaintiff against Harry Hill & Others*, Affidavits in Opposition to Motion, April 11, 1887, in *Records of the Supreme Court, City and County of New York*, Historical Documents Collection, Queens College, City University of New York (hereafter HDC); Samuel Clemens, *Mark Twain's Travels with Mr. Brown* (New York, 1940), Letter #26, June 6, 1867, pp. 270, 274. See also "Total Depravity in New York," *NY Times*, February 5, 1871 (probably written by Crapsey). On Hill's place as a regular stop for

slumming parties, see "Slumming in This Town," *NY Times*, September 14, 1884, p. 4.

23. "Midnight Pictures: Harry Hill's," *National Police Gazette*, November 22, 1879, p. 1; "The Giant Knocked Silly," *NY Times*, August 7, 1883, p. 1. The reporter who wrote this front-page story framed the entire account around his conversations with Hill. On Hill's expert testimony in court battles involving Sullivan and others charged with illegal prizefighting, see for example, "The Stakes Returned," *NY Times*, August 13, 1882, p. 5; "Knocked Out in Court," *NY Times*, November 16, 1884, p. 14; Inspector George Dilks to Superintendent George W. Walling, May 5, 1879, Mayor's Papers to 1898, 83-CE-26, MARC. On Hill's connection with Edison and electric light, see the printed invitation, with Hill's personal note to one of Edison's friends, in "Electric Light—General," Document File 84-020, Edison Archives, Edison National Historic Site, West Orange, New Jersey.

24. "Harry Hill's Day," *NY World*, June 21, 1894, p. 1 ("came back like a ghost"); Harry Hill testimony, LC, vol. 2, pp. 1928, 1932, 1933. The official LC transcript does not include laughter or other interruptions, so I have relied upon several newspaper descriptions to piece together this moment. See "Harry Hill on the Stand," *NY Sun*, June 21, 1894, p. 1; "Harry Hill Tells Tales," *NY Herald*, June 21, 1894, p. 3; "Police Blood Suckers," *NY Tribune*, June 21, 1894, p. 1.

25. Harry Hill testimony, LC, vol. 2, pp. 1942, 1937–8; Captain William Meakim to Inspector Henry Steers, November 27, 1886; Harry Hill to Mayor William R. Grace (no date), both in MP-86-GWR-26, MARC; Injunction order, Summons, Complaint Affidavits, *The . . . v. Harry Hill*, April 11, 1887, HDC; Harry Hill obituary, *NY World*, August 28, 1896, p. 8. Press coverage of Hill's problems with Captain Murphy and Detective Moran no doubt further soured his relations with the police. See for example "Forced to Pay Tribute," *NY Times*, February 3, 1886, p. 1; "Resigning Before Trial," *NY Times*, February 17, 1886, p. 8. Former police commissioner Stephen French, who had been in office during Hill's troubles with Captain Murphy, publicly supported Hill's story and denounced Murphy. See the interview with him, "French Lashes Murphy," *NY World*, June 24, 1894, p. 5.

26. "Harry Hill Gets Even," *NY World*, June 21, 1894, p. 1 ("it is only"); *NY Times*, editorial, June 21, 1894, p. 4 ("related to").

27. "Why Adjourn, Senators," *NY Sun*, June 22, 1894, p. 1 ("Is it proposed"); "Fair Play for the Police," *NY Recorder*, June 16, 1894 ("mainly and extremely," clipping, NYDAS).

28. John H. Sweester testimony, LC, vol. 2, p. 2173; Thomas J. Roberts testimony, LC, vol. 2, p. 2182. See also, for examples, LC testimony of James D'Olier, vol. 2, pp. 1963ff; William Mayston, vol. 2, pp. 2007ff; Francisco Scholastico, vol. 2, pp. 2154ff.

29. "The Investigation," *NY Tribune*, editorial, June 24, 1894, p. 6 ("It was generally"); "O'Connor's Not a Goff Man," *NY Sun*, June 29, 1894, p. 2 (O'Connor); "Bad Citizenship," *NY Times*, editorial, June 23, 1894, p. 4 ("precisely what"); "Senators Take a Rest," *NY World*, June 30, 1894, p. 1 ("Every man of them"). For further press coverage of the last week's testimony, see for example: "Had to Pay the Police," *NY Herald*, June 23, 1894, p. 4; "From Merchant to Bootblack," *NY Herald*, June 27, 1894, p. 5; "Merchants as Victims," *NY Tribune*, June 27, 1894, p. 1; "He Would Not Submit" and "Police and Builders" (on Edward Kilpatrick), *NY Tribune*, editorial June 29, 1894, p. 1, 6; "Blackmailing of Merchants," *NY Times*, June 23, 1894, p. 1; "All Paid Police Tribute; Merchants and Bootblacks Were Alike Assessed," *NY Times*, June 27, 1894, p. 1.

30. [Lincoln Steffens] "The Police Inquiry," *NY Evening Post*, June 23, 1894, p. 1; Charles Beeck testimony, LC, vol. 2, pp. 1984–89; "The Lines Are Broken," *NY World*, June 22, 1894, p. 1, emphasized Beeck's revelations; Jerome quoted, LC, vol. 2, p. 2081; Henry Schuchert testimony, LC, vol. 2, p. 2082; John Keresey testimony, LC, vol. 2, pp. 2422–36; James Lonchein testimony, LC, vol. 2, pp. 2436–38; "Exit Lexow, Enter Police," *NY Herald*, June 30, 1894, p. 5; "Check to Pay Police," *NY Sun*, June 30, 1894, p. 1. A copy of the report "The Police as Liquor Sellers" was read into the record; see LC, vol. 2, pp. 2428–31.

    For a story similar to Schuchert's, see Lewis Niemo testimony, LC, vol. 2, pp. 1906–20. Niemo ran a restaurant on East Fourth Street and complained to Inspector Williams about rough treatment from a wardman. Williams asked him if he kept women. "Yes sir, I said I had some women," "What are they, whores?" "No; my wife, mother and grandmother…he asked me whether I sell any beer or liquor, and I says, 'No'; he says, 'How, in hell, do you make a living?' That was his exact words." (1909).

31. Goff, "The Lexow Committee," p. 127 ("Criminals to"); Leroy Lyon testimony, LC, vol. 2, p. 2165, 2170; "Captain Needs $15,000," *NY Sun*, June 27, 1894, p. 1; "All Paid Police Tribute," *NY Times*, June 27, 1894, p. 1. On men paying for appointments as patrolmen, see for example Charles W. Miller testimony, LC, vol. 2, pp. 2298–3011, and Arthur Dennett testimony, LC, vol. 1, pp. 943–50. Dennett, the SPC detective, had posed as a man looking to buy his way onto the force.

32. "The Journal and the 'Wolf Police,'" editorial, *Morning Journal*, June 6, 1895 (clipping, NYDAS); "Who Got the Blackmail?," editorial, *NY Press*, June 24, 1894 (clipping, NYDAS); "Favor Seth Low for Mayor" *NY Times*, June 29, 1894, p. 1 (Hewitt).

33. Goff quoted in LC, vol. 2, pp. 2236, 2237. See also "Mr. Goff Talks Politics," *NY Sun*, June 28, 1894, p. 1; "From Police to Tammany," *NY Times*, June 28, 1894, p. 8.

34. Quotes from LC, vol. 3, p. 2469 (Goff), 2474 (Nicoll), 2473 (Lexow); "Senators Take a Rest," *NY World*, June 30, 1894, p. 1. See also,; "Lexow Committee Adjourns," *NY Times*, June 30, 1894, p. 1; "Adjourned til Fall," *NY Tribune*, June 30, 1894, p. 1; "Exit Lexow, Enter Police," *NY Herald*, June 30, 1894, p. 5.

7: "REFORM NEVER SUFFERS FROM FRANKNESS"

1. "Goff Reviews His Labors," *NY World*, July 1, 1894, p. 1. For press summaries of the investigation's findings to June 30, see for example: "The Record of the Police Investigation," *NY World*, July 2, 1894, p. 9; "Labors of the Senators," *NY Sun*, July 1, 1894, Sec. 2, p. 1; "List of Those Accused," *NY Herald*, July 1, 1894.

2. "The Lexow Tammany Investigation," *Chicago Tribune*, June 11, 1894, p. 6 ("the corruption"); "More Criminal Operations of Tammany," *Chicago Tribune*, June 22, 1894, p. 6 ("Is this not"); "The Citizen and Pure Politics," *Los Angeles Times*, May 11, 1894, p. 4 ("There is no"); Fiorello La Guardia, *The Making of an Insurgent: An Autobiography: 1882–1919* (New York, 1948), p. 30; Sydney Reid, "General Results of the Lexow Committee's Work," *Harper's Weekly* 38 (July 14, 1894): 663 ("cut down"). For other examples of out-of-town coverage, see *Chicago Tribune*: "More Evidence of Police Bribery," June 8, 1894, p. 2; "Has a Bribery Fund," June 16, p. 5; "Vicious Influence of Tammany," June 28, p. 7, and *Los Angeles Times*: "An Artful Dodger," June 24, 1894, p. 1.

3. "Police Blackmail," *Morning Advertiser*, June 17, 1894 ("Say, why can't"). The PBA seems to have emerged out of the older Mutual Benevolent Association in early 1894, but its exact origins are unclear. See Emma Schweppe, *The Firemen's and Patrolmen's Unions in the City of New York* (New York, 1948), pp. 41–53; "Patrolmen Not Engage Counsel," *NY Tribune*, June 29, 1894, p. 2; Patrolman Peter Prial testimony, LC, vol. 2, pp. 2311–20.

4. Julian Ralph, "Our Detective System," *NY Sun*, May 13, 1894, p. 8; Nellie Bly, "Byrnes and Nellie Bly," *NY World*, August 1, 1894, p. 5.

5. Thomas Byrnes, "How to Protect a City from Crime," *North American Review* 154 (July 1894): 101 ("the most dangerous kind"); Thomas Byrnes, "The Menace of 'Coxeyism': Character and Methods of the Men," *North American Review* 158 (June 1894): 700 ("the most dangerous"). See also Carlos A. Schwantes, *Coxey's Army: An American Odyssey* (Lincoln, NE, 1985).

6. On the Pullman strike, I have relied upon David Ray Papke, *The Pullman Case: The Clash of Labor and Capital in Industrial America* (Lawrence, KS, 1999), and Richard Schneirov, Shelton Stromquist, and Nick Salvatore, eds.,

The Pullman Strike and the Crisis of the 1890s: Essays on Labor and Politics (Urbana, IL, 1999).

7. Byrnes quotes: "The Spirit of Anarchism," *NY Tribune*, July 6, 1894, p. 3 ("Not until"); "It Pleases Socialists," NY World, July 10, 1894, p. 1 ("The police are"). See also, "Police Veterans Volunteer," *NY Sun*, July 13, 1894, p. 1; "No Riots in This City," *NY World*, July 6, 1894, p. 2; "Police Vacations to Be Stopped," *NY Tribune*, July 7, 1894, p. 3; "Police in Readiness," *NY Herald*, July 9, 1894, p. 8.

8. "Labor Up in Arms," *NY Herald*, July 9, 1894, p. 3 (White); "Debs and Altgeld Lauded," *NY Tribune*, July 9, 1894, p. 3 (Steele); "Labor Leaders Threaten," *NY Times*, July 9, 1894, p. 1 (Jolly, Barr, CLU resolution). Barr's speech was reported in slightly different form in "Debs and Altgeld Lauded." See also, "They Approve the Strike," *NY World*, July 9, 1894, p. 5; "To Uphold the Strikers," *NY Times*, July 10, 1894, p. 1, for remarks mocking Byrnes by Alexander Jonas of the Socialist Labor Party.

9. "Strong Guard for New York," *NY Times*, July 10, 1894, p. 2 (Byrnes); "How Local Labor Men Feel," *NY Tribune*, July 10, p. 3 (Murphy); "Agitators Are Silent Now," *NY Tribune*, July 14, p. 2 (Byrnes). See also "Probably No Strike Here," *NY World*, July 8, 1894, p. 3; "Strike Talk Dying Out," *NY Tribune*, July 12, 1894, p. 3. For coverage of the Cooper Union and Union Square rallies, see for example, "Speeches That Sizzled," *NY Tribune*, July 13, 1894, p. 1; "Orations About Chicago," *NY Sun*, July 13, 1894, p. 1; "Standing by Debs," *NY Herald*, July 13, 1894, p. 3; "Socialism's Remedy," *NY Herald*, July 15, 1894, p. 4; "Captured by Socialists," *NY Tribune*, July 15, 1894, p. 3. On the weakness of railroad unions in the city, see Robert E. Weir, "Dress Rehearsal for Pullman: The Knights of Labor and the 1890 New York Central Strike," in Schneirov, et al., eds, *The Pullman Strike*, pp. 21–42.

10. "Dr. Parkhurst Speaks Out," *NY Times*, July 14, 1894, p. 9 (Parkhurst statement). On City Club organizing, see "For Good Government," *NY Tribune*, July 1, 1894, p. 3.

11. "Official; From T. C. Platt," *NY Sun*, July 23, 1894, p. 1 (Platt) ; "Dr. Parkhurst's Appeal," *NY Tribune*, editorial, July 16, 1894, p. 6. For good overviews of how the various anti-Tammany forces shaped up that summer, see "Tammany and Her Foes," *NY Sun*, July 29, 1894, p. 5, and "For Low and Union," *NY Herald*, July 7, 1894, p. 6.

12. All three of these examples are from one Sunday: "Let Honest Men Unite," *NY Herald*, July 2, 1894, p. 8 (Peters); "Clergymen Bled Also," *NY Herald*, July 2, 1894, p. 8 (MacArthur); "Elect a Good American," *NY Herald*, July 2, 1894, p. 8 (Chambers). On the APA's growing political influence, as well as opposition to it, see for example, "Degrading Warfare of APA," *NY Times*, June 1, 1894, p. 1; "The Results of Immigration," *NY Times*, July 16, 1894,

p. 2. See also David H. Bennett, *The Party of Fear: From Nativist Movements to the New Right in American History* (Durham, NC, 1988).

13. "Mr. Wellman and the Police Board," *NY Tribune*, editorial, July 4, 1894, p. 6 ("to embarrass"); "Police Board Investigation," *NY Times*, July 3, 1894, p. 1 (Gilroy).

14. "McClave Out, Kerwin In," *NY Times*, July 17, 1894, p. 1. See also, "M'Clave Steps Out," *NY Herald*, July 17, 1894, p. 6. For sharp criticism of Kerwin's appointment and his Irish nationalist activism, see for example, "The Appointment of Kerwin" and "Kerwin and the Clan-Na-Gael," both in *NY Times*, July 17, 1894, pp. 4, 2.

15. "A Talk with Doherty," *NY World*, August 3, 1894, p. 8 ("I was a fool"); "Declares He Is Martin's Victim," *NY Herald*, July 30, 1894 ("I was an out and out," clipping, NYDAS). See also "Doherty No Longer Captain," *NY Times*, July 27, 1894, p. 1; "Capt. Doherty to the Bar," *NY Sun*, July 17, 1894 (clipping, NYDAS); "Doherty Is Found Guilty," *NY Herald*, July 27, 1894 (clipping, NYDAS); "Doherty Found Guilty," *NY Tribune*, July 27, 1894 (clipping, NYDAS).

16. "Editorial," *NY Times*, September 7, 1894, p. 4 ("The absence"); untitled clipping, *NY Recorder*, August 28, 1894 (Goff); "Chairman Lexow Talks," *Morning Advertiser*, August 23, 1894 (Lexow); "The Police Trials," *NY Tribune*, September 7, 1894, p. 6 ("for the absolute"); "Well Done, Police Commissioners!," *NY Herald*, September 1, 1894, p. 6 ("whether it suits"); "Wellman Talks Back," *NY Recorder*, September 11, 1894 (Wellman). For extensive coverage of the summer police trials, see for example: "The Money for Devery," *NY Tribune*, August 17 1894, p. 4; "She Paid Them All," *NY Herald* August 17, 1894, p. 4; "She Had Kept Much Back," *NY Tribune*, August 18, 1894, p. 4; "Captain Doherty Appeals," *NY Sun*, August 28, 1894, p. 8; "Fruit as Well As Boodle," *NY Tribune*, August 31, 1894, p. 7; "Kate Schubert Steals Away," *NY Times*, August 31, p. 1; "Devery and Cross Dismissed," *NY Times*, September 1, 1894, p. 1; "Cross and Devery Fired," *NY Sun*, September 1, 1894, p. 1; "Stephenson Testifies," *NY Sun*, September 5, 1894, p. 7; "Stephenson Dismissed," *NY Sun*, September 7, 1894, p. 2; "Capt. Stephenson Dismissed," *NY Times*, September 7, 1894, p. 9.

17. "Police Discipline," *NY Times*, editorial, September 7, 1894, p. 4 ("the main trouble"). For the full text of Byrnes's report, see "Supt. Byrnes Speaks Out," *NY Sun*, September 7, 1894, p. 1. For other examples of supportive editorial response see "The Byrnes Report," *NY Tribune*, September 8, 1894, p. 8; "A Significant Report from Superintendent Byrnes," *NY Herald*, September 7, 1894, p. 8.

18. "Dr. Parkhurst Returns," *NY Sun*, September 7, 1894, p. 1 ("Under no circumstances"); "A Talk with Dr. Parkhurst," *Springfield Republican*, September 17, 1894, p. 4 ("Reform never suffers"). Like many papers around

the country, the *Republican* now carried regular Lexow news summaries and editorial comments. See also "Dr. Parkhurst at Home Again," *NY Times*, September 7, 1894, p. 1; "Parkhurst Is Ready," *NY Herald*, September 8, 1894, p. 3.

19. Testimony of Charles A. Hanley, LC, vol. 3, pp. 2483–25; "Pawnshops Also Get Protection," *NY Herald*, September 11, 1894, p. 3; "Police and the Pawnshops," *NY Times*, September 11, 1894, p. 8.

20. Testimony of William Applegate, LC, vol. 3, pp. 2539–67; "Paid to Captain Meakim," *NY Tribune*, September 11, 1894, p. 1 "Bribes Paid to Police Captains," *NY Herald*, September 12, 1894, p. 3; "Green Goods Sharps Again," *NY Sun*, September 11, 1894, p. 1; "Now It Is Williams Accused," *NY Times*, September 12, 1894, p. 8.

21. Testimony of James H. Perkins, LC, vol. 3, p. 2660; *NY Times*, editorial, September 14, 1894, p. 4 ("his action"). On Perkins, see also "Gloom at Headquarters," *NY Herald*, September 14, 1894, p. 6; "Hounding the Witnesses," *NY Herald*, September 15, 1894, p. 5; "Now It Is Williams Accused," *NY Times*, September 12, 1894, p. 8.

22. Testimony of Mrs. Caela Urchittel, LC, vol. 3, pp. 2733–43, and her deposition given to Frank Moss and read into the LC record, vol. 3, pp. 2960–64. Both statements contain gaps, inconsistencies, and contradictions, some of which may be the result of poor translation. I have pieced together her story from these two sources. For early press coverage, see for example, "Lexow Committee Adjourns," *NY Times*, September 13, 1894, p. 8; "Persecuted by a Ward Man," *NY Herald*, September 13, 1894; "Buncoed by the Police," *NY Sun*, September 13, 1894, p. 1. On Max Hochstim, see "Look at This, Mr. Lexow," *NY Herald*, September 23, 1894, V, p. 2.

23. LC, vol. 3, p. 2737 (Moss); p. 2738 (Lexow); "Buncoed by the Police," *NY Sun*, September 13, 1894, p. 1 ("No story"); "Mrs Urchittel's Story," *NY Herald*, editorial, September 13, 1894, p. 8 ("the most astounding story"); "To Discontinue Police Trials," *NY Times*, September 15, 1894, p. 9 (Jenkins). See also "Lexow Committee Adjourns," *NY Times*, September 13, 1894, p. 8; "Gloom at Police Headquarters," *NY Herald*, September 14, 1894, p. 6.

24. Coverage of the Madison Square Garden meeting and all quotes from "Uniting for City Reform," *NY Herald*, September 7, 1894, p. 5. See also the useful discussion in George Francis Knerr, "The Mayoral Administration of William L. Strong, New York City, 1895–1897," PhD diss., New York University, 1957, pp. 26–44. On the overthrow of Tweed, see the cogent brief account in Edwin G. Burrows and Mike Wallace, *Gotham: A History of New York City to 1898* (New York, 1999), pp. 1008–12.

25. Hewitt and Smith both quoted in "Uniting for City Reform," *NY Herald*, September 7, 1894. Neither man attended the Madison Square Garden

meeting, but both sent letters of support, which were read aloud and received with much enthusiasm. Several speakers noted the cautionary tale of Hewitt's failure to win re-election in 1888. Hewitt ran as an independent Democrat, but a Republican "straight ticket" split the anti-Tammany vote, resulting in the election of Tammany candidate Hugh J. Grant.

26. "Byrnes His Target Now," *NY Sun*, September 21, 1894, p. 1 ("nothing but"); "Open War on Byrnes," *NY World*, September 25, 1894, p. 3 ("deep and tender interest"; "Let each of us").

27. "Another Captain on His List: Parkhurst Speaks for the First Time Before an East Side Audience," *NY Times*, September 28, 1894, p. 1 ("he should have"); "Parkhurst's Suggestion to Women," *NY Times*, September 28, 1894, p. 8 ("If the women"); "They Will Aid Dr. Parkhurst," *NY Times*, October 11, 1894, p. 9 (Stanton). See also, "Women Must Act," *NY Herald*, September 26, 1894, p. 7; "Mrs. Lowell's Committee," *NY Times*, October 14, 1894, p. 4.

28. Goff quoted, LC, vol. 3, p. 2826; Testimony of William H. Kipp, LC, vol. 3, pp. 2743–66; Testimony of Frank Moss, LC, vol. 3, pp. 2827–36, 2861–69; Testimony of Charles MacLean, LC, vol. 3, pp. 2796–808; Testimony of Louis J. Grant, LC, vol. 3, pp. 2790–96.

29. "Clubbing a Minor Offense," *NY Times*, October 3, 1894, p. 1; Testimony of Thomas Lucas, LC, vol. 3, p. 2876; Goff quoted, LC, vol. 3, p. 2826; "They Are Fenced in by Perjury in the Trials," *Morning Advertiser*, October 3, 1894 (clipping, NYDAS). See also "A Pillory for Clubbers," *NY Sun*, October 3, 1894, p. 1; "Clubbers Summoned," *NY World* (Evening), October 1, 1894, p. 1; "Brutal Police Before Lexow," *NY Herald*, October 3, 1894, p. 5.

30. "Convictions of Policemen by the Board of Police on Charges of Assault, Oppression, and Other Serious Offenses, Criminal in Their Nature," Extract from William J. Gregory Trial, December 22, 1891 (emphasis in original), in *Examination of Trials By the Police Board From January 1, 1891 to May 1, 1894*. Made by counsel of the committee of the Senate appointed to investigate the police department, New York, May 1, 1894, Mss, New York Historical Society. This document, prepared by John Goff and his legal team, analyzed the nearly 12,000 police board trials held over the previous three years.

31. Testimony of Norbeth Pfeffer, LC, vol. 3, p. 2981; Testimony of Ambrose Hussey, LC, vol. 3, p. 2985. See also, "Said He Would Kill Pfeffer," *NY Times*, October 4, 1894, p. 1; "Mr. Goff Tortures Hussey," *NY Sun*, October 4, 1894, p. 1; "He Threatened Murder. The Committee Astounded," *NY Tribune*, October 4, 1894, p. 1; "Hussey Says He'll Shoot," *NY Herald*, October 4, 1894, p. 5. On the harassment of George Appo, see "Appo Says He Was Attacked," *NY Times*, September 30, 1894, p. 8, and Timothy Gilfoyle, *A Pickpocket's Tale: The Underworld of Nineteenth Century New York* (New York, 2006), pp. 254–59. For a good summary of the persecution of Lexow witnesses, see "Hounding the Witnesses," *NY Herald*, September 15, p. 5.

32. Knerr, "The Mayoral Administration of William L. Strong," pp. 31–40; "Goff's Name Rejected," *NY Sun*, October 5, 1894, p. 1; "Strong and Goff Put Up," *NY Sun*, October 6, 1894, p. 1; "Colonel Strong Is Nominated," *NY Herald*, October 6, 1894, p. 3; "Strong Indorsed for Mayor," *NY Times*, October 10, 1894, p. 1. The office of recorder was later abolished in 1906.

33. Straus quoted in David de Sola Pool, "Nathan Straus," *American Jewish Year Book* (1931), p. 140. See also, "Tammany's Men Named," *NY World*, October 10, 1894, p. 1; "Tammany Names Straus," *NY Sun*, October 11, 1894, p. 1; "Straus Named By Tammany," *NY Herald*, October 11, 1894, p. 3; "Nathan Straus for Mayor," *NY Times*, October 11, 1894, p. 1.

34. John Goff quoted, LC, vol. 4, p. 3616. See Testimony of Augustin Forget, LC, vol. 3, pp. 3058–90; Testimony of Vincent Majewski, LC, vol. 3, pp. 3130–58; Testimony of J. Lawrence Carney, LC, vol. 3, pp. 3235–64; Testimony of Samuel Ebert; Samuel Cohen, Milah Levy, Charles Lighte, William Jacobs (soda water stands), LC, vol. 3, pp. 3404–28; Testimony of Lucy Harriot, LC, vol. 4, pp. 3614–24 and Hattie Ledyne, LC, vol. 4, pp. 3624–38. All this testimony received extensive coverage in the press.

35. Lexow quoted in LC, vol. 3, p. 3275; Goff quoted in LC, vol. 3, p. 3290–91; Moss quoted in LC, vol. 3, p. 3276.

36. "Joy in Lexow's Court," *NY World*, October 20, 1894, p. 8 ("Tears rolled"); John Goff quoted LC, vol. 4, p. 3640. See also "Lexow Committee Drama," *NY Sun*, October 20, 1894, p. 3; "Restored to Their Mother," *NY Times*, October 20, 1894, p. 9; "Kay Vindicated Himself," *NY Herald*, October 20, 1894, p. 5.

37. Grover Cleveland to Nathan Straus, October 18, 1894, in Allan Nevins, ed., *Letters of Grover Cleveland, 1850–1908* (Cambridge MA, 1933), p. 372. For the best press coverage of this unprecedented situation, see "Grant Replaces Straus," *NY Tribune*, October 20, 1894, p. 1, and "Grant in Place of Straus," *NY Times*, October 20, 1894, p. 1. See also "The Nomination of Grant," *NY Evening Post*, October 20, 1894, p. 1; "For Mayor, Hugh J. Grant," *NY Sun*, October 20, 1894, p. 1; "Grant Takes Straus Place," *NY Herald*, October 20, 1894, p. 3.

8: "A LANDSLIDE, A TIDAL WAVE, A CYCLONE"

1. "Parkhurst Deceived," *NY World*, October 30, 1894, p. 1. The *World's* account of this meeting was the only one I could find. Despite some extravagant language, semi-comic tone, and breathless description of what the anarchists looked like—all typical of the era's newspapers—the details and the internal evidence convince me that the meeting actually did occur and that a *World* reporter was present. On Parkhurst speaking at the nearby "Mother Zion"

church earlier that evening, see "Dr. Parkhurst Speaks Twice," *NY Herald*, October 30, 1894, p. 6.

2. Elihu Root, Address Delivered before the New York State Constitutional Convention, August 15, 1894 (New York State Association Opposed to Woman Suffrage, 1894),pp. 2–3. On the New York State suffrage campaign of 1893–94, see Susan B. Anthony and Ida Husted Harper, eds., *History of Woman Suffrage*, vol. 4, 1883–1900 (Indianapolis, IN, 1902; Ayer Reprint ed. 1985), pp. 847–52.

3. "Parkhurst to the W.M.L.," *NY Sun*, October 20, 1894, p. 2 (Lowell); "Women Fill Cooper Union," *NY Tribune*, October 20, 1894, p. 7 (Parkhurst). See also, "New York's Dishonor," *NY World*, October 20, 1894, p. 3. On the connections between nonpartisanship and women's activism, see the pioneering work by S. Sara Monoson, "The Lady and the Tiger; Women's Electoral Activism in New York City before Suffrage," *Journal of Women's History* 2 (Fall 1990): 100–135, as well as Ellen Carol DuBois, "Working Women, Class Relations, and Suffrage Militance: Harriot Stanton Blatch and the New York Woman Suffrage Movement, 1894–1909," *Journal of American History* 74 (June 1987): 34–58. See also, Val Johnson, " 'The Moral Aspects of Complex Problems': New York City Electoral Campaigns against Vice and the Incorporation of Immigrants, 1890–1901," *Journal of American Ethnic History* 26 (Winter/Spring 2006): 74–106.

4. "Mrs. Parkhurst Speaks," *NY World*, October 23, 1894, p. 9 ("Women must"; "Here we are not"); "Women Pursuing the Tiger," *NY Tribune*, October 31, 1894, p. 7 (Bond). See also, "Invading the East Side," *NY Herald*, October 23, 1894, p. 11; Women Thoroughly Roused," *NY Tribune*, October 25, 1894, p. 7; "A Barroom Crowd Amazed," *NY World*, October 25, 1894, p. 10; "Woman's Work Against Tammany," *NY Times*, October 25, 1894, p. 9; "Enthusiastic and Active Work," *NY Tribune*, October 26, 1894, p. 3; "The Women Are Winning," *NY World*, October 28, 1894, p. 7; "Women Count Up Results," *NY World*, November 2, 1894, p. 8. On meetings among African-American women, see for example, "Women Pursuing the Tiger," *NY Tribune*, October 31, 1894, p. 7; "Women Continue Their Good Work," *NY Tribune*, November 4, 1894, p. 5.

5. "Have I All My Rights?" leaflet reprinted in "Women's Work in Municipal Reform," in William Howe Tolman, *Municipal Reform Movements in the United States* (New York, 1895), pp. 178–79.

6. "Politics Not Woman's Sphere," *NY Herald*, October 23, 1894, p. 11 (Gilroy); "Nathan Straus for Mayor," *NY Times*, October 11, 1894, p. 1 (Sulzer); "Tammany Ratifies," *NY Sun*, October 24, 1894, p. 3 (Grady, "He was the witness"); "Grady's Savage Speech," *NY Herald*, October 22, 1894, p. 4 (Grady, "But God"). Mayor Gilroy and mayoral candidate Grant both offered spirited defenses of Tammany's governance of the city. See "Gilroy

Defends Tammany," *NY Times*, October 23, 1894, p. 1; "Grant's Letter Is Out," *NY Sun*, October 29, 1894, p. 1.

7. "Tammany in the Pillory," *NY Tribune*, October 29, 1894, p. 1 (Committee of Seventy); "Strong on the East Side," *NY Tribune*, October 31, 1894, p. 2 (Strong); "Cheered on the East Side," *NY Tribune*, October 17, 1894, p. 7 (Parkhurst, "Why should you"); "Dr. Parkhurst to Germans," *NY Herald*, October 31, 1894, p. 6 (Parkhurst, "As long as"); "The Rabbies [*sic*] Are for Strong," *NY Tribune*, October 28, 1894, p. 8.

8. "Police to Bolt Tammany," *NY World*, October 27, 1894, p. 9; "To Deceive Policemen," *NY Herald*, November 6, 1894, p. 3 (forged PBA letter dated October 30); "Mr. Grant's Labor Record," *NY Times*, November 2, 1894, p. 8; "Not Associated with Tammany Hall," *NY Times*, November 5, 1894, p. 9.

9. "Cloakmakers Clubbed," *NY Sun*, October 12, p. 1 (Barondess); "Riot Preceded the Parade," *NY Times*, October 12, 1894, p. 1; "Clubbed by the Police," *NY World*, October 12, 1894, p. 1. See also "Police Beat Strikers," *NY Herald*, October 12, 1894, p. 12; "Did Jacobs Offer Money?," *NY World*, October 17, 1894, p. 1; "Strikers Lose a Point," *NY World*, October 20, 1894, p. 9; "Capt. Grant to Be Tried," *NY Sun*, October 31, 1894, p. 2; "Police Board Rulings," *NY Times*, January 9, 1895, p. 9 (charges against Grant dismissed). The cloak makers' strike eventually petered out by late November, unable to overcome the organized opposition of clothing manufacturers and the depressed business climate. The cloak makers' union eventually became the Amalgamated Clothing Workers. For good background on the cloak makers and Barondess, still valuable for its research in the Yiddish and German language press, see Louis Levine, *The Women's Garment Workers* (New York, 1924), pp. 68–83.

10. "The Clubbed Cloakmakers," *NY Times*, October 15, 1894, p. 2. See also Marilyn S. Johnson, *Street Justice: A History of Police Violence in New York City* (Boston, 2003), pp. 50–56, for a longer discussion of the Lexow Committee's failure to look into anti-labor violence by the police.

11. [Lincoln Steffens], "J. J. Martin's Irritability," *NY Evening Post*, October 18, 1894, p. 12; Lincoln Steffens to Joseph Steffens, October 18, 1894, in Lincoln Steffens Papers, Original Outgoing Letters, 1866–1936, Columbia University (microfilm). See also, [Lincoln Steffens], "J. J. Martin and the City Club," *NY Evening Post*, October 17, 194, p. 12.

12. John C. Sheehan testimony, LC, vol. 4, pp. 4033. For Sheehan's full testimony, see LC vol. 4, pp. 3681–4044. For the extensive press coverage of Sheehan's appearances, see for example, "Sheehan Begins His Testimony," *NY Herald*, October 26, 1894, p. 3; "Goff Questions Sheehan," *NY Sun*, October 26, 1894, p. 5; "Examining Mr. Sheehan," *NY Evening Post*, October 26, 1894, p. 1; "Sheehan Angry and Cries 'Liar,'" *NY Herald*, October 30, 1894, p. 5; "Ask Byrnes, Says Sheehan," *NY Sun*, October 30, 1894, p. 1;

"Either a 'Lie' or a 'Mistake,'" *NY Times*, October 31, 1894, p. 1; "His Bank Book Is Wanted Now," *NY Herald*, October 31, 1894, p. 6; "Mr. Goff's Direct Charges," *NY Tribune*, November 1, 1894, p. 11; "Goff Calls Sheehan a Thief," *NY Times*, November 1, 1894, p. 8; "Sheehan Again Wildly Enraged," *NY Herald*, November 1, 1894, p. 5.

13. Matilda Hermann testimony, LC, vol. 4, pp. 4090–92; 4117–219; "The Worst Outrage Yet," *NY World*, November 3, 1894, editorial, p. 4 ("a new phase"). (Her name appeared in the press with several different spellings; I have used the one in the official LC transcript.) See also, "A Mine of Blackmail," *NY World*, November 3, 1894, p. 1; "Mrs. Herremann in a Rage," *NY Evening Post*, November 3, 1894, p. 1; "Mrs. Herremann Paid $30,000," *NY Herald*, November 3, 1894, p. 3; "Spent a Fortune in Bribery," *NY Times*, November 3, 1894, p. 9. On Mrs. Hermann's post–New York career in Johannesburg, see Charles Van Onselen, *The Fox and the Flies: The Secret Life of a Grotesque Master Criminal* (New York, 2007), pp. 152–57.

14. LC, vol. 4, p. 4273 (Goff); Newton Whitehead testimony, LC, vol. 4, pp. 4263–64. See also "Villany's Lowest Depth," *NY Tribune*, November 4, 1894, p. 1; "Sensational Wind-Up," *NY Sun*, November 4, 1894, p. 1; "Shame Piled on Shame," *NY World*, November 4, 1894, p. 6; "Blackmail from an Evil Traffic," *NY Herald*, November 4, 1894, p. 5; "Koch Is Implicated Now," *NY Times*, November 4, 1894, p. 13. See also "Police Justices' Power," *NY Times*, November 21, 1894, p. 9.

15. "Campaign Is Closed," *NY Herald*, November 4, 1894, I, p. 6 (Goff); "Tiger Scourges in the Temples," *NY Herald*, November 5, 1894, p. 3 (Parkhurst). See also, "Wild Cheering for Goff," *NY Sun*, November 5, 1894, p. 4; "Ovation to Goff and Strong," *NY Times*, November 4, 1894, p. 5; "Parkhurst's Jeremiad," *NY Sun*, November 5, 1894, p. 2; "On the Ten Commandments," *NY Times*, November 5, 1894, p. 8.

16. "An Honest Election Today," *NY Times*, November 6, 1894, p. 8 (Byrnes); "A Deadly Blow at Fraud," *NY Tribune*, November 6, 1894, p. 1; "Transfer of Police at Polls," *NY Evening Post*, November 5, 1894, p. 1.

17. For election results in the city, state, and nation: "The City's Official Vote," *NY Times*, November 24, 1894; "Vote on the City and County Ticket," *NY Herald*, November 7, 1894, p. 7; "A Landslide in New York," *NY Tribune*, November 7, 1894, p. 1; "Tammany Crushed," *NY Evening Post*, November 7, 1894, p. 1; "The General Result," *NY Evening Post*, November 8, 1894, p. 1 (All figures rounded to the nearest thousand.) For useful comparisons with earlier elections, see "Returns of Mayoral Elections in New York City, 1834–1894," in Kenneth T. Jackson, ed. *The Encyclopedia of New York City* (New Haven, 1995), pp. 735–36; "Gubernatorial Elections," in Peter Eisenstadt, ed., *The Encyclopedia of New York State* (Syracuse, 2005), pp. 672–79. For a very convenient and useful list of the difficult to find geographical boundaries

of the city's assembly and congressional districts, see "Voters' Directory," *NY Evening Post*, November 1, 1894, p. 13.

18. "A Landslide in New York," *NY Tribune*, November 7, 1894, p. 1; "Tammany Crushed," *NY Evening Post*, November 7, 1894, p. 1; "The Same Thing Everywhere," *NY Sun* editorial, November 6, 1894, p. 6. For an excellent regional and national overview of the 1894 elections, see Samuel T. McSeveney, *The Politics of Depression: Political Behavior in the Northeast, 1893–1896* (New York, 1972), pp. 87–133.

19. "Mrs. Grannis at the Polls," *NY Times*, November 7, 1894, p. 8 (Grannis); "Women as Watchers," *NY World*, November 6, 1894, p. 1; "Mrs. Grannis's Reception," *NY Times*, November 28, 1894, p. 4. For background on Mrs. Grannis, see "To Promote Social Purity," *NY Times*, October 1, 1893, p. 21; "Women Talk Purity in Politics," *NY Times*, October 28, 1894, p. 9. See also "Byrnes Deserves Credit," *NY Times*, November 8, 1894, p. 7; "Voters in the Courts," *NY World*, November 7, 1894, p. 3; "The Police Kept Busy" and "Good Work at the Polls," *NY Tribune*, November 7, 1894, p. 3.

20. Josephine Shaw Lowell, "Woman's Municipal League of the City of New York," *Municipal Affairs* 2, No. 3 (September 1898): 465. For brief accounts of their WML activity, see Lillian D. Wald, *Windows on Henry Street* (Boston, 1934). pp. 59–60; Maud Nathan, *Once Upon A Time and Today* (New York, 1933), pp. 106–14; Mary E. Dreier, *Margaret Dreier Robbins: Her Life, Letters, and Work* (New York, 1950), pp. 18–23. See also Monoson, "The Lady and the Tiger," and Jo Freeman, "'One Man, One Vote; One Woman, One Throat': Women in New York City Politics, 1890–1910," *American Nineteenth Century History* 1, No. 3 (Autumn 2001): 101–23; Rebecca Edwards, *Angels in the Machinery: Gender in American Party Politics from the Civil War to the Progressive Era* (New York, 1997), pp. 117–21.

21. "Seventy to Aid the Mayor," *NY Times*, November 10, 1894, p. 9 (Committee of Seventy); "A Far-Reaching Triumph," *NY Tribune*, November 8, 1894, p. 12 ("People in Savannah"); "Comment on the Vote," *NY Evening Post*, November 7, 1894, p. 1 ("Corruption is what").

22. "Tiger Is Stone Dead," *Chicago Tribune*, November 7, 1894, p. 4; "Machine Rule Waning," (editorial), *Los Angeles Times*, editorial, November 16, 1894, p. 4 ("monstrous crimes") ; "The Harbor Inquiry," *Los Angeles Times*, editorial, November 13, 1894, p. 4 ("to remodel"); *Kansas City Star* quoted in, "The Republican Cyclone," *Los Angeles Times*, November 14, 1894, p. 4. See also the summary of national press views in "A Republican Whirlwind," *NY Tribune*, November 8, 1894, p. 7.

23. "A New Police Force," *NY Evening Post*, November 17, 1894, p. 7 (Parkhurst); "Byrnes Out?," *Morning Journal*, November 15, 1894 (Moss, clipping, NYDAS); "Where Mr. Platt Stands," *NY Times*, November 19, 1894, p. 1 (Platt).

24. "Banquet for Dr. Parkhurst," *NY Herald,* November 28, 1894, p. 3 (Parkhurst); "Bidden Guests Absent," *NY Times,* November 29, 1894, p. 9 (Republican Congressman); "Dixon Scores Dr. Parkhurst," *NY Herald,* November 30, 1894, p. 4 (Dixon). See also, "Police Reorganization," *NY Evening Post,* November 15, p. 1; "Police with One Chief," *NY Times,* November 20, 1894, p. 9; "Platt's Fight with Reformers," *NY Herald,* November 20, 1894, p. 6; "Dr. Parkhurst Honored," *NY Times,* November 28, 1894, p. 8. "Bidden Guests Absent," *NY Times,* November 29, 1894, p. 9.

25. E. L. Godkin, "Introduction," *The Triumph of Reform: A History of the Great Political Revolution, November Sixth, Eighteen Hundred and Ninety-Four* (New York, 1895), pp. 5, 6; Charles H. Parkhurst, *Our Fight With Tammany* (New York, 1895), pp. 289, 294 (emphasis in original). See also, Charles H. Parkhurst, "Facts for the Times," introductory chapter to Tolman, *Municipal Reform Movements,* pp. 17–23.

26. For a good overview of the politics of the 1894 constitutional convention, see McSeveney, *The Politics of Depression,* pp. 63–86. See also, "Under A New Constitution," *NY Times,* November 8, 1894, p. 9.

9: ENDGAMES

1. William S. Andrews testimony, LC, vol. 4, pp. 4374–465; Frank W. Sanger testimony, LC, vol. 4, pp. 4533–39; William A. Brady testimony, LC, vol. 4, pp. 4539–68; William L. Soyer testimony, LC, vol. 4, pp. 4491–98 (Soyer was an LC employee); Marcus B. McCarthy testimony, LC, vol. 4, pp. 4498–511.

2. Augustine E. Costello testimony, LC, vol. 4, pp. 4528, 4530. For Costello's two books, see *Our Police Protectors: History of the New York Police from the Earliest Period to the Present Time* (New York, 1885) and *Our Firemen: A History of the New York Fire Departments, Volunteer and Paid* (New York, 1887), both still available in recent reprint editions.

3. "A Tale of Police Revenge," *NY Tribune,* December 6, 1894, p. 1; Williams's remark quoted by Frank Moss, LC, vol. 5, p. 4670; Augustine E. Costello testimony, LC, vol. 5, p. 4677. For other coverage of Costello's Lexow appearance, see for example "He Accuses McLaughlin," *NY Times,* December 6, 1894, p. 1; "Costello Was Nearly Killed," *NY Herald,* December 6, 1894, p. 3; "Beaten by McLaughlin," *NY Sun,* December 6, 1894, p. 1; "Policemen and Pensions," *NY Times,* December 12, 1894, p. 9. For corroboration of Costello's story, see Dr. William T. Jenkins testimony, LC, vol. 4, pp. 4531–32; Abraham S. Hummel testimony, LC, vol. 5, pp. 4654–57; Michael Stanley testimony, LC, vol. 5, pp. 4662–68. For background on Costello's experiences in the Irish Revolutionary Brotherhood and the

political and legal importance of his case, see David Sim, *A Union Forever: The Irish Question and U.S. Foreign Relations in the Victorian Age* (Ithaca, 2013), esp. pp. 124–26, and Cullen Thomas, *Brother One Cell* (New York, 2007), pp. 23–26.

4. Clarence Lexow quoted in LC, vol. 5, p. 4631; "Not Providence's Work," *NY Times*, December 11, 1894, p. 6 (Platt); T. C. Platt's Letter," *NY Tribune*, December 12, p. 11 ("will not take"); "Senator Lexow Dined," *NY Sun*, December 12, 1894, p. 2 (Lexow); "Goff's Plague of Office Seekers," *NY World*, December 23, 1894, p. 2 (Goff).

5. John Goff, LC, vol. 5, p. 4928; Goff-Creeden exchange, LC, vol. 5, p. 4967. See also John Reppenhagen testimony, LC, vol. 5, pp. 4950–60; Henry C. Miner testimony, LC, vol. 5, pp. 4960–63.

6. LC, vol. 5, p. 4973 (Creeden).

7. "Creeden Bought His Promotion," *NY Herald*, December 15, 1894, p. 3 ("the most"); "Creeden Confesses," *NY Tribune*, December 15, 1894, p. 1 ("by far"); "Capt. Creeden's Case," *NY Times*, December 15, 1894, editorial, 4. For other coverage, see also, "Creeden Had A $15,000 Fund," *NY Herald*, December 14, 1894, p. 3; "$15,000 for Voorhis," *NY World*, December 15, 1894, p. 1; "Creeden Confesses," *NY Evening Post*, December 15, 1894, p. 1; "Creeden Confesses," *NY Sun*, December 15, 1894, p. 1. Only the *Sun*, the most fiercely partisan Democratic paper, refused to join the chorus of praise. See for example its editorial, "Capt. Creeden's Manliest Act," December 18, 1894, p. 6, which it argued was his initial refusal to offer a bribe for promotion.

8. "Justice Voorhis's Statement," *NY Times*, December 15, 1895, p. 1 (Voorhis); John Reppenhagen testimony, LC, vol. 5, p. 4950–51; John Goff, LC, vol. 5, p. 4959. John Martin, the ex-assemblyman implicated with Reppenhagen, never testified due to an "attack of paralysis." On Voorhis and the NY State Democracy, see for example, "May Demand A Hearing," *NY Times*, December 17, 1894, p. 1; "The State Democracy and the Creeden Case," *NY Sun*, December 16, 1894, p. 6; "Voorhis Wants More Light," *NY Sun*, December 16, 1894, p. 1; "The Police Confessions," *NY Evening Post*, December 17, 1894, p. 7. John Voorhis moved back into the Tammany Hall orbit. When he died in 1932, age 102, he was Great Grand Sachem, an honorary title previously conferred only upon George Washington.

9. "Stephenson in a Cell," *NY Times*, December 14, 1894, p. 6 ("Who in the world"). "Stephenson Is Guilty," *NY Times*, December 13, p. 1; "Stephenson Sentenced," *NY Tribune*, December 27, 1894, p. 3; "Stripes For Stephenson," *NY Times*, December 27, p. 3; "Another Man Confesses," *NY Times*, December 16, 1894, p. 1; "Thorne Confesses," *NY Sun*, December 16, 1894, p. 1; "Thorne Follows Creeden," *NY Herald*, December 16, 1894, p. 3.

10. [Lincoln Steffens] "The Police Confessions," *NY Evening Post*, December 17, 1894, p. 7 ("It really looks"); "Laughs at the Story," *NY Herald*, December 15,

1894, p. 5 (Howe). See also, "Police Captains Angry," *NY Sun*, December 17, 1894, p. 1.

11. Clarence Lexow, LC, vol. 5, p. 5311 ("not only"); Max L. Schmittberger testimony, LC, vol. 5, pp. 5325, 5350, 5337, 5382. The story of how Goff and Jerome pressured Schmittberger was told nearly a decade later by Jerome who, as district attorney in 1903, expressed deep disgust with Schmittberger's impending promotion to inspector. He ridiculed the idea of Schmittberger as a courageous and repentant hero: "Can you see any contrition in this, or any repentant attitude? I can only see the abject fear of a man under indictment." See "Says Schmittberger Had to Squeal," *NY Times*, February 8, 1903, p. 10.

12. "This Captain Received and Paid Bribes," *NY Herald*, December 22, 1894, p. 3 ("told the most"); "The Crowning Exposures: Schmittberger's Story," *NY Tribune*, December 22, 1894, p. 1 ("in all the"); Max L. Schmittberger testimony, LC, vol. 5, p. 5376 ("there was no"); "Victory for His Wife," *NY Herald*, December 21, 1894, p. 5 (Mrs. Schmittberger). For other coverage, see "Police Secrets Out," *NY Sun*, December 22, 1894, p. 1; "Police Commissioners Implicated" and "Martin Gravely Accused," *NY Times*, December 22, 1894, p. 1; "An Awful Story of Corruption," *NY World*, December 22, 1894, p. 1; "Another Confession," *NY Evening Post*, December 21, 1894, p. 1.

13. "The Stampede Begun," *NY Times* editorial, December 23, 1894, p. 4 ("may be expected"); "Need No More Outside Help," *NY Herald*, December 24, 1894, p. 3 (Parkhurst, "An expert!"); [Lincoln Steffens], "Parkhurst To Go On," *NY Evening Post*, December 24, 1894, p. 1 (Parkhurst, "A gentleman"). See also, "Dr. Parkhurst Suggests a 'Deal,'" *NY Times*, December 26, 1894, p. 1; "Lexow Xmas Subpoenas," *NY Sun*, December 26, 1894, p. 1. For Martin and Sheehan's responses to Schmittberger's allegations, see "Halting Explanations," *NY Tribune*, December 23, 1894, p. 1; "Denials on Every Hand," *NY Herald*, December 23, 1894, p. 3.

14. "Will Williams Tell?," *NY Evening Post*, December 22, 1894, p. 1 ("It's all right"); Alexander S. Williams testimony, LC, vol. 5, pp. 5448, 5496–97, 5467 (Lexow), 5480. See also, "Williams Under Fire," *NY World*, December 27, 1894, p. 1; "Goff Takes Up Williams," *NY Tribune*, December 27, 1894, p. 1; "Williams to His Accusers," *NY Herald*, December 27, 1894, p. 3; "Williams Denies All," *NY Times*, December 27, 1894, p. 1; "Williams Faces Goff," *NY Sun*, December 27, 1894, p. 1.

15. Alexander S. Williams testimony, LC, vol. 5, pp. 5569, 5536, 5563, 5574; "Williams on the Stand," *NY Times*, editorial, December 29, 1894, p. 4 ("has succeeded"); *NY Evening Post* editorial, December 28, 1894, p. 6 ("to confess"). See also, "Hammering At Williams," *NY Herald*, December 28, 1894, p. 1; "Williams Has a Fine 'Record,'" *NY Herald*, December 28, 1894, p. 4; "Williams Tires Goff Out," *NY Sun*, December 28, 1894, p. 1; "Williams

at the Wall," *NY Times*, December 28, 1894, p. 1; "Denial Follows Denial," *NY Tribune*, December 29, 1894, p. 1; "His $6,000 Friendship," *NY Times*, December 29, 1894, p. 1; "Williams Got Money," *NY Herald*, December 29, 1894, p. 3.

16. William McLaughlin testimony, LC, vol. 5, pp. 5639–709. For coverage of his appearance, see for example, "McLaughlin and His Money," *NY Times*, December 30, 1894, p. 3; "Byrnes Says the Police Need Reform," *NY Herald*, December 30, 1894, p. 3; "Byrnes May Quit," *NY Sun*, December 30, 1894, p. 1.

17. Thomas F. Byrnes testimony, LC, vol. 5, pp. 5740, 5715. For a good contemporary account of the Crawford-Vanderbilt fray and Byrnes's role in it, see "The Last Tragedy," *NY Times*, May 26, 1872, p. 8. See also T. J. Stiles, *The First Tycoon: The Epic Life of Cornelius Vanderbilt* (New York, 2009), p. 528.

18. Thomas F. Byrnes testimony, LC, vol. 5, p. 5721, 5722. For a detailed account of Byrnes's successful capture of Gould's blackmailer, J. Howard Welles, see "Blackmailing Jay Gould," *NY Times*, November 14, 1881, p. 1. See also "The Black Mailing Case," *NY Times*, November 16, 1881, p. 8; Maury Klein, *The Life and Legend of Jay Gould* (Baltimore, 1986), pp. 217–18.

19. John Goff, LC, vol. 5, p. 5727; Deposition of Frederick E. Ladd, July 7, 1892 (Byrnes); C. Amory Stevens to Mayor William L. Strong, May 17, 1895, both in 90-SWL-44, Mayors' Papers, Municipal Archives and Research Center. In the same file, see also the letters from Lothrop Bullock and Caleb G. Collins to George H. Richardson and "John Holmes," November 17, 1893, and to Thomas Byrnes, November 18, 1893 and to George H. Richardson and "John Holmes," November 17, 1893. Bullock and Collins worked for Mrs. Richardson's brother, C. Amory Stevens. Ladd's deposition and the Bullock/Collins correspondence lay out the details of the arrangement and Byrnes's longstanding efforts to protect Richardson behind the scenes. On Richardson's suicide, see "George H. Richardson a Suicide," *NY Times*, December 8, 1894, p. 2; "His Throat Cut in the Bathroom," *NY World*, December 8, 1894, p. 3.

20. Thomas F. Byrnes testimony, LC, vol. 5, pp. 5743, 5727, 5728, 5756. See also, "Byrnes's Large Fortune," *NY Tribune*, December 30, 1894, p. 1; "Byrnes Ready to Quit," *NY World*, December 30, 1894, p. 1; "Byrnes May Quit," *NY Sun*, December 30, 1894, p. 1; "Byrnes and His Money," *NY Times*, December 30, 1894, p. 1; "Mr. Byrnes's Sensation," *NY Sun*, December 31, 1894, p. 1.

21. John Goff, LC, vol. 5, p. 5765; "Parkhurst Finds Fault," *NY Times*, January 1, 1895, p. 1 ("flinched at the crisis") ; "Dr. Parkhurst Critical," *NY Tribune*, December 31, 1894, p. 1 ("I am only").

22. *Report of the Special Committee Appointed to Investigate the Police Department of the City of New York*, pp. 16, 15, 68, in LC, vol. 1. The majority report is on

pp. 3–61, Cantor's minority report pp. 62–76. For reports of Mrs. Caela Urchittel's death, see "Mrs. Urchittel Dies in a Hospital," *NY Times*, January 18, 1895, p. 16; "Death of Mrs. Urchittel," *NY Herald*, January 18, 1895, p. 4.

23. "Dr. Parkhurst in Chicago," *NY Tribune*, January 24, 1895, p. 2 ("Platt has"); "Let Albany Hear and Bow," *NY Sun*, February 5, 1895, p. 1 ("We are not asking"). For further coverage of Parkhurst in Chicago and the February 4 Cooper Union rally, see: "Dr. Parkhurst Talks Reform in Chicago," *NY Herald*, January 24, 1895, p. 14; "He Fires Hot Shot," *Chicago Tribune*, January 24, 1895, p. 1; "Sound Advice to Chicagoans," *Chicago Tribune*, editorial, January 25, 1895, p. 1; "The People Warn Platt," *NY Times*, February 5, 1895, p. 1; "No Boss for Them," *NY Tribune*, February 5, 1895, p. 1; "Reformers Rally Against Bosses," *NY Herald*, February 5, 1895, p. 4.

24. "Ridiculed His Reform Ideas" (Lauterbach), *NY Herald*, February 7, 1895, p. 5; "Manifesto From Platt" (Platt), *NY Sun,* January 26, 1895, p. 1; "Is This Platt's Work?" (pamphlet), *NY Tribune*, March 18, 1895, p. 1. See also "Dr. Parkhurst in Albany," *NY Sun*, February 7, 1895, p. 5; "Platt's New Edict," *NY Herald*, January 26, 1895, p. 5; "Dr. Parkhurst in Albany," *NY Times*, February 7, 1895, p. 3.

25. "Cross's Reinstatement," *NY Sun*, March 17, 1895, p. 3 ("It is now evident"); "Parkhurst Is Angry," *NY Herald*, March 17, 1895, p. 3 ("the ally"). See also, "Captain Cross Is Reinstated," *NY Herald*, March 16, 1895, p. 4; "Cross to Be Reinstated," *NY Tribune*, March 16, 1895 p. 1; "Capt. Adam A. Cross Wins," *NY Times*, March 16, 1895, p. 1; "Policemen in High Glee," *NY Tribune*, March 17, 1895, p. 15.

26. Grand jury presentment, Byrnes, and Parkhurst all quoted in "Police Indictments In," *NY Times*, March 19, 1895, p. 1; "The Police Presentment," *NY Times* editorial, March 19, 1895, p. 4 ("lacks delicacy"). See also "Indictments at Last," *NY Sun*, March 19, 1895, p. 1; "Corrupt Police at the Bar," *NY Tribune*, March 20, 1895, p. 1; "M'Laughlin Leads the List," *NY Herald*, March 20, 1895, p. 1; "Cripples the Force," *NY Herald*, March 21, 1895, p. 5; "List of Indicted Policemen," *NY Herald*, April 9, 1895 (clipping, NYDAS).

27. "Platt Men Now Appeal," *NY Times*, April 4, 1895, p. 1 (Lauterbach). This article contains Lauterbach's full statement, a scathing attack upon Strong and the entire idea of fusion. See also "Lauterbach Retaliates," *NY Herald*, April 4, 1895, p. 4. On Platt's growing dispute with Strong over patronage appointments, see for example "Sheehan out of Office," *NY Times*, February 15, p. 1; "Strong's Axe Fell Again," *NY Herald*, February 15, 1895, p. 3; "Brookfield Is the Man," *NY Sun*, February 13, 1895, p. 1; "No Pledge, Says Strong," *NY Sun*, February 14, p. 1; "The Real Question," *NY Tribune* editorial, March 16, 1895, p. 8. For Platt's version of his "pact" with Strong and the Mayor's subsequent "repudiation" of his promises, see Louis J. Lang,

ed., *The Autobiography of Thomas Collier Platt* (New York, 1910), pp. 268–95. On Low and Root voicing their support for Strong, see their remarks at the March 28 Cooper Union rally, quoted in "Reform Bills Must Be Passed," *NY Herald*, March 28, 1895, p. 3.

28. On Strong's choices for the police board vacancies and Kerwin and Murray's refusal to resign, see for example, "Strong Says It's All True," *NY Sun*, April 2, 1895, p. 3; "They Will Both Have to Go," *NY Herald*, April 2, 1895, p. 3; "Roosevelt Will Accept," *NY Herald*, April 24, 1895, p. 7; "Mr. Roosevelt Accepts," *NY Herald*, May 1, 1895, p. 6; "The Coming Police Board," *NY Times*, May 1, 1895, p. 1; "Kerwin Will Not Resign," *NY Times*, May 5, 1895, p. 1; "Mr. Kerwin Refuses," *NY Herald*, May 5, 1895, II, p. 2.

29. Theodore Roosevelt to Anna Roosevelt, April 14, 1895, in Elting E. Morison, ed., *The Letters of Theodore Roosevelt*, vol. I (Cambridge, MA, 1951), p. 442; Theodore Roosevelt to Henry Cabot Lodge May 18, 1895, in *Selections from the Correspondence of Theodore Roosevelt and Henry Cabot Lodge, 1884–1914, Vol. I* (New York, 1925), p. 143. For background on Strong's choices and Roosevelt's decision, see Kathleen Dalton, *Theodore Roosevelt: A Strenuous Life* (New York, 2002), pp. 148–51; Jay Stuart Berman, *Police Administration and Progressive Reform: Theodore Roosevelt as Police Commissioner of New York* (Westport, CT, 1987), pp. 41–44; George Francis Knerr, "The Mayoral Administration of William L. Strong, New York City, 1895 to 1897," PhD thesis, New York University, 1957, pp. 63–73. Richard Zacks, *Island of Vice: Theodore Roosevelt's Doomed Quest To Clean Up Sin-Loving New York* (New York, 2012) is the most recent account of Roosevelt's term as police commissioner, but it offers nothing new on the Strong-Roosevelt relationship.

30. "It Has Triumphed at Last," *NY Tribune*, April 24, 1895, p. 1 ("it seemed"). See also "Bi-Partisan Bill Passed," *NY Sun*, April 17, 1895, p. 1; "Lexow Bill Is Passed," *NY Herald*, April 26, 1895, p. 4; "Coming to Mayor Strong," *NY Times*, April 24, 1895, p. 5; "Strangled in the Senate," *NY Times*, April 25, 1895, p. 1 (police reorganization bill).

31. "Lexow Bill Condemned," *NY Times*, May 2, 1895, p. 1 (Parkhurst, Lauterbach). The *Times* has the most comprehensive coverage of the hearing. See also "Talked to Strong," *NY Herald*, May 2, 1895, p. 3; "Parkhurst and Strong," *NY Tribune*, May 2, 1895, p. 11; "Parkhurst as Dictator," *NY Sun*, May 2, 1895, p. 2.

32. "The Mayor Gives His Reasons," *NY Times*, May 9, 1895, p. 1 (Strong, Parkhurst); "Party Politics and Good Government," *Harper's Weekly* 39 (May 18, 1895): 456 ("spoils huckster"). See also "Board to Be Bi-Partisan," *NY Sun*, May 9, 1895, p. 1; "Strong Will Approve It," *NY Tribune*, May 7, 1895, p. 1; "Bi-Partisan Bill Approved By Strong," *NY Herald*, May 9, 1895, p. 3; "Republican State Politics," *Harper's Weekly* 39 (June 1, 1895): 504; "New York's Reform Measures," *Review of Reviews* 11 (June 1895): 624–25. For

Parkhurst's prediction of Strong's betrayal, see "Dr. Parkhurst Attacks Strong," *NY Times*, April 17, 1895, p. 1.

33. "Mr. Roosevelt Accepts," *NY Herald*, May 1, 1895, p. 6 (Roosevelt). See also Roosevelt's remarks in a debate he had with Edward Lauterbach before a Good Government Club: "I am a politician but I understand politics from the ground up.... I believe city affairs cannot be properly administered unless administered apart from politics," in "Called Strong a Crazy Quilt," *NY Herald*, May 23, 1895, p. 5.

34. "Williams off the Force," *NY Sun*, May 25, p. 1 ("Not a thing"); "Williams Retires," *NY Herald*, May 25, 1895, p. 3 ("There was a man"). See also "Will Byrnes Follow?" *NY World*, May 25, 1895, p. 1; "Farewell to Williams," *NY Times*, May 25, 1895, p. 1; "Williams in Private Life," *NY Tribune*, May 25, 1895, p. 1.

35. "Vetoed by the Mayor," *NY Times*, May 11, 1895, p. 9 (Roosevelt); Theodore Roosevelt to Henry Cabot Lodge, May 18, 1895, *in Correspondence of Theodore Roosevelt and Henry Cabot Lodge*, I, p. 144. See also Berman, *Police Administration and Progressive Reform*, pp. 50–54.

36. Arthur Brisbane, "Byrnes Is Ex-Chief," *NY World*, May 28, 1895, p. 1 (Byrnes); "The Retirement of Chief Byrnes," *NY Times,* editorial, May 28, 1895, p. 4 ("in the ordinary"); "The Retirement of Byrnes," *NY Tribune*, editorial, May 28, 1895, p. 6 ("a grim and resolute"); "Byrnes," *NY Sun* editorial, May 29, 1895, p. 6 ("a distinguished figure"); Theodore Roosevelt to Anna Roosevelt, June 2, 1895, in Morison, ed., *Letters of Theodore Roosevelt I*, p. 459. See also, "Chief Byrnes Retired," *NY Times*, May 28, 1895, p. 1; "Chief Byrnes No Longer," *NY Sun*, May 28, 1895, p. 1; "Byrnes Retires with a Pension," *NY Herald*, May 28, 1895, p. 3.

37. Theodore Roosevelt to Charles Henry Parkhurst, March 8 and March 19, 1895, in Morison, ed., *Letters of Theodore Roosevelt I*, pp. 431, 435.

38. "Parkhurst Going Abroad," *NY Tribune*, June 5, 1895, p. 5 ("We are now"); "No Politics for Police," *NY Times*, June 4, 1895, p. 1 ("I shall act"; "that have no"). On the CVL, see "Parkhurst's Vigilantes," *NY Sun*, March 9, 1895, p. 2; "Vigilance the Watchword," *NY Tribune*, March 9, 1895, p. 7; "Dr. Parkhurst Trustee," *NY Times*, May 22, 1895, p. 9. For examples of the detailed coverage given to Roosevelt's late-night inspection tours, see "Roosevelt on Patrol," *NY Sun*, June 8, 1895, p. 7; "Roosevelt as Roundsman," *NY Tribune*, June 8, 1895, p. 13; "Police Caught Napping," *NY Times*, June 8, 1895, p. 16.

39. "These Words at Parting," open letter to the editor of the *NY World*, June 5, 1895, p. 1 ("The idea"); "Parkhurst's New War," *NY World*, June 4, 1895, p. 1 ("set back fires"); "Home Rule the Issue," *NY Tribune*, June 4, 1895, p. 1 ("every step"). See also "Parkhurst Going Abroad," *NY Tribune*, June 5, 1895, p. 5; "Dr. Parkhurst Pleased," *NY Times*, June 5, 1895, p. 13.

INDEX

....

Page numbers in bold indicate tables.